THE INDIC CODE

Decoding Cultural Intelligence for Management Dynamics

THE INDIC CODE

Decoding Cultural Intelligence for Management Dynamics

DR. GEETHA MOHAN

B L O O M S B U R Y

NEW DELHI • LONDON • OXFORD • NEW YORK • SYDNEY

BLOOMSBURY INDIA
Bloomsbury Publishing India Pvt. Ltd
Second Floor, LSC Building No. 4, DDA Complex,
Pocket C – 6 & 7, Vasant Kunj,
New Delhi 110070

BLOOMSBURY, BLOOMSBURY QUEST and the Diana logo are trademarks of Bloomsbury Publishing Plc

First published in India 2025
This edition published in 2025

ISBN: 978-93-69525-46-1
2 4 6 8 10 9 7 5 3 1

Printed and bound in India by Replika Press Pvt. Ltd.

Dedicated to my loving husband, Mohan

Love is such a small Word,
For something that is so Vast.
For in it lies the Future,
The Present and the Past.

CONTENTS

FOREWORD

It gives me immense pleasure to write this foreword for the book written by Dr. Geetha Mohan. In a world increasingly driven by speed, technology, and material success, the quest for meaning and ethical grounding has never been more vital. Management as a discipline, while rooted in rationality and efficiency, cannot thrive without the deeper moorings of philosophy, culture, and spirituality. This book is a timely and thoughtful exploration of the intersection of these dimensions, tracing how India's profound philosophical heritage can illuminate the modern challenges of management and leadership. Coming from a philosophical background, Dr. Mohan has brought the essence and meaning of philosophy and spirituality into today's context, keeping management studies on a broader canvas.

Indian Ethos refers to the application of timeless Indian values, wisdom, and cultural principles to modern organizational and managerial contexts. Rooted in texts like the *Bhagavad Gītā*, *Upaniṣads*, and *Arthashāstra*, Indian ethos emphasizes ethical leadership, holistic well-being, and harmony between individual, organization, and society. The focus is on *"Yogah Karmasu Kaushalam"*—excellence in action through mindfulness, detachment, and selflessness. Indian Philosophy in Management draws from the spiritual and metaphysical insights of Indian thought – Advaita (oneness), Sāṁkhya (balance of forces), Yoga (discipline), and Buddhist ethics (mindfulness and compassion). It offers an integrated view of human nature, where the manager is not merely a profit-seeker but a karma-yogā contributing to both material and spiritual progress.

Indian philosophy in Corporates, industries, and management transforms the mechanistic, profit-centred model of management into a value-centred and humanistic paradigm, where efficiency is harmonized with ethics, and material progress is balanced by spiritual well-being. It redefines management as a means for self-development, social harmony, and sustainable prosperity, rather than mere economic gain. They bridge tradition and innovation, suggesting that sustainable progress depends on a balance between technological advancement and timeless human values.

This work thus stands as an important contribution to the emerging field of Indian Management Thought — one that does not imitate the West but dialogues with it, grounded in India's own intellectual and spiritual soil. It will benefit scholars, managers, and all who seek to understand how philosophy and spirituality can enrich professional life and societal well-being. The theme of the book is very relevant today to researchers, students, and passionate readers.

May this book inspire a renewed vision of management — one that is not merely about achieving success and material gains but about realizing harmony, purpose, peace and dharma in action!

October 2025

Dr Uma M Shankar
Director Academics, and Professor of Practice in Philosophy,
SIES, Mumbai
Ex-Principal and Head, Department of Philosophy,
SIES College of Arts, Science & Commerce, Mumbai

PROLOGUE

I have known Geetha Mohan as my student since 1979, and she continues to be a learner even today. I have no hesitation in saying that she has been one of the best.

Successful people do not have the best of everything that comes their way, for they achieve not in the **absence of** but **in spite of** problems and difficulties! No one knows this better than the author of this book. Geetha is well aware that 'Stress is not final and failure is not fatal. It is the courage to continue that counts!' And continue she did! With a strong analytic mind and supported by courage, she has bounced back into the vast realms of Philosophy, after a short lull in her career, with the desired break that she had taken.

The book *The Indic Code: Decoding Cultural Intelligence for Management Dynamics* has eleven informative chapters ranging from the most important aspects of Indian Philosophy—the six systems, the Upanishads, the Buddhist and Jaina ethics—to the ethics of Swami Vivekananda and Gandhi's concept of Sarvodaya. The simple and lucid style of writing would be of great help to a newcomer to Philosophy.

An interesting chapter on the much talked about Artificial Intelligence (AI) has also been included. Arguments for and against have been flying fast and that should set us thinking. Crores have been spent in creating AIs but in the final analysis, would it be beneficial to mankind? Or is it just one more feather in the cap of man? Is man trying to play God?

At present, AI is without emotions and feelings. If in the near future it is possible to induce emotions, would it in anyway be helpful to mankind? It is supposed to generate material wealth, but true wealth lies in showing kindness to all living creatures.

An elderly gentleman recently lamented:

'We fly in the air like birds,
We swim in the water like fish,
Wouldn't it be wonderful if we could walk on earth like humans?'

In fact, a book on the ethics of AI as a sequel to Geetha's book, with philosophy and ethics interlaced with it, would be more than welcome!

Any takers?

Wishing dear Geetha a lot of success on the occasion of the launch of the book and wishing her many more such endeavours.

Prof. (Ms.) Rita Doctor
Dept. of Philosophy (for 42 years)
Former HOD, Dept. of Philosophy, Ramnarain Ruia College, Mumbai (for 28 years)
Member, Board of Studies, Dept. Of Philosophy, University of Mumbai (for 28 years)

PREFACE

Modern humans live under the illusion of having achieved supremacy over their environment. This sense of mastery often leads them down a path marked by misery and suffering—a folly that becomes increasingly evident. It is man's folly, made evident when this sense of control isolates him, leaving him confused and lost. He lives in ignorance, and the resulting desolation and loneliness render him inert—spiritually and emotionally. Man's solace, then, is found only in himself, the path to liberation beginning within him.

Society leaves every individual striving hard to fulfil his desires, and social media has bombarded him with opinions and perspectives that further make life difficult. Today's youth is caught between screens and devices, overwhelmed by an unrelenting flood of information that breeds insecurity and helplessness. They feel overwhelmed by the excess of information and knowledge and yet feel lost; and the noise around them dims their sense of understanding, and they must have clarity in life.

Then the questions arise– Where do we go? Which is the path that leads us to silence, peace, and wisdom? How do we get ourselves fully reset and charged to face our life's challenges? Do we give up our messed-up life, do we succumb to it, or do we return to the settled patterns? Where do we find peace and solace? How do we make the 're-turn' and the 'return' to our own Self?

As a student of Philosophy, I have always wanted my teacher to give the etymological meaning of any word or concept. As a teacher of Philosophy, I found it essential to begin with the origins of both Philosophy and Management—tracing each to its etymological roots and exploring their interconnection. Hence, I deemed it necessary to begin with a clarification of the concepts and their correlation.

Addressing a class of students of Philosophy, I found myself talking of Vedic and Upanishadic teachings. The students felt it was all so ancient, and irrelevant to them. I thought I needed to link it to something that appealed to their rationality and sensibility. I attempted to connect ancient teachings to contemporary society. Yet, their focus remained fixed on trade, industry, and—wealth.

It was very important for me to understand that the young mind craved for concepts and tenets more pragmatic and applicable to real life situations. Can management be, in any way determined by the life philosophy and the work philosophy of an individual or an organisation? Can it be modified and adapted as per the demands of time? This was the challenge placed before me by the young minds. Convincing them that one's philosophy led to a *weltanschauung* for the industry depended on my own conviction and confirmation.

Suddenly I found the link: the link between the four Purushārthās and the more contemporary, western concept of Self-actualization, i.e. Abraham Maslow's hierarchy of needs; the 'Reality' as a 'Whole' in Advaita and the 'Whole' of Gestalt psychology; the three ego-states of Eric Berne's Transactional Analysis and the four levels of individual personality as given in Indian Philosophy (reference to the Varnāshrama).

I thought I could give them the continuum between Traditional Wisdom and Contemporary Thought. I had to convince them that religious, or rather, spiritual culture in India did not deny man, the earthly and sensual pleasures. It did not impose or demand austerity of any kind. It merely gave us guidelines that could be followed to relate, integrate, co-ordinate and combine Pleasure and Ethics, the Material and the Spiritual. I got the impression that the generation of today (as did many of the earlier generations too) thought that philosophy was not for them.

Various misconceptions about philosophy needed to be clarified and rectified. It is a misconception that Philosophy is not pragmatic; the common misconception is that philosophy is dull and abstract—an armchair pursuit reserved for academics and intellectuals. This kind of study is also for the aged, the old and the retired- to read, to speculate and to discuss. It is a subject which spelt intellectual and literary verbose. A critic once described philosophy as 'nothing but intellectual diarrhoea.'

It is erroneously believed that Philosophy is not within the reach of the common man. It is believed that it is not for the householder, the trader, the producer, the farmer, or a student of any other faculty. It is for the elite in society, who did not have to work for their living. It is also for those who are frustrated and have renounced worldly life. The critic believed that Philosophy cannot answer questions or solve problems in life. It cannot explain or simplify any concept. It cannot guide or direct any individual who is confused or in any doubt. It cannot comfort or console a man in distress. It is believed that one starts talking about philosophy when one is totally confused and one preaches philosophically when one has nothing better to do.

The search for the key to human progress and liberation is to be found in the eternal values that lie deep-rooted in man himself. Man needs to learn to unfold the goodness and divinity that is already within him. This leads us to a philosophy that is spiritualistic and unveils certain eternal values to humanity. These values emerge from the depths of the human spirit as man evolves. These values cannot be found in the physical environment or taught by the sciences.

The seeker of wisdom and peace needs to realize his own spirit that aligns with the cosmic Spirit. The integration of science and spirituality reveals a vital distinction between natural resources and human assets—underscoring the need to honour human uniqueness and wholeness. Man must be respected for his uniqueness and his holism. No industry can survive or progress without grasping this truth. It is the need to begin a process of soul-searching that takes us back to our roots.

Indian philosophy of life gives a holistic framework for a work ethic on the part of the employee and a value-system for a systemic organizational culture for the employer. The chapters discuss the basic tenets of Indian philosophy that are relevant and related to the concept of management. The ethics of corporate entities can be traced back to the cultural foundation of India, and their foundations to the ethical principles enshrined in our scriptures and philosophical systems.

Ancient Indian wisdom aligns seamlessly with modern management practices, proving both practical and effective in corporate environments. It does lead to a holistic development of the individual and the organization. The belief that Indian philosophy and culture are against profit as the objective of industry and business is a misconception. Indian philosophy thus, takes care of all the needs of the individual and the organization.

It is my reflection on the idea that management ethics is more like Indian philosophy in practice that is evident in this book. The pragmatism of Indian philosophical tenets and teachings needs no justification. It has been observed that individuals with a deep-rooted grounding in our cultural and philosophical ethos live with a holistic approach to life and work. The spiritual orientation in every individual leads him naturally to the teleological moorings in the culture – be it with the purpose of evolving a work culture or creating his own weltanschauung.

I am aware that my attempt to convince the youth and guide them to imbibe values from our own culture is just the tip of the iceberg. This is my humble effort to interpret the philosophy of the Vedas and Shad-Darshanas, along with the teachings of our scholars, as relevant to both personal and organizational management.

The content of the book is based on secondary sources such as reference books on philosophy and management. The linkages established between philosophy and management are more reflective and the correlation between the two areas of study, philosophy and management, is more out of personal comprehension.

Can corporate management and work-culture of any institution be determined by the personal life philosophy of an individual? This was a major challenge placed before me. I am aware that my attempt to guide the youth and the corporate with this attempt is just the tip of an iceberg. The extent and the depth of our philosophies and the texts and scriptures are wide and diverse.

An attempt to synergise and collate abstract metaphysics and the pragmatism of institutions and management is truly a herculean task. I have tried my best to understand the universal subtleties of philosophy, to expound the intricacies of Truth and Reality. This work is also an unbiased, unprejudiced understanding and exposition of Indian ethos, metaphysical and socio-cultural tenets for building the edifice of corporate structures and systems.

I would also like to affirm that the ideology and philosophy propounded here in this work is solely my understanding of the schools and texts of Indian Philosophy, in its practical dimension. My sessions with the students in the classroom and the executives in the corporate sector were welcomed and appreciated, due to the simplicity in the exposition of the pragmatism of our philosophy and culture.

Any idea or concept missed out, a word or phrase misspelt, or an erroneous transliteration of Sanskrit text is purely unintentional and solely on account of oversight. I seek forgiveness for the same, in advance, and would appreciate if the reader informs me of the same for correction of the same in my subsequent work. The reader may find a few concepts, ideas, interpretations repeated in different chapters, throughout my book. This is due to the relevance of the same concepts and philosophies in different situations and contexts. The purpose is to reiterate and reinforce the application and practice of the same and its importance for management.

To substantiate this co-relation, visits to industries, interviews with CEOs and employees are conducted, and the practical experience of all is shared. This is primarily done to support the hypothesis that the work culture and work ethics of industries are an expression of the basic cultural ethnicity of India, with its roots deep into Indian philosophical thought, for an ideal corporate culture. **Philosophy is not a distant, abstract pursuit—it is a living framework that shapes our values, decisions, and work culture. By bridging ancient Indian wisdom with contemporary management, we rediscover a holistic path to personal and professional fulfilment.**

Dr. Geetha Mohan

I

PHILOSOPHY AND MANAGEMENT

Ethos, culture, traditions, rituals, and social behaviour – all are based on a philosophy, be it social philosophy, linguistic philosophy, political philosophy, moral philosophy, philosophy of religion or a philosophy of management. Various misconceptions about philosophy need to be clarified and rectified.

What is Philosophy?

Existence and Reality have always baffled man. The various mysteries in life lead man to ask in wonder, questions on the nature of Reality, the nature and content of Knowledge and the validity and value of life and existence. Philosophy is a form of enquiry, a process involving and depending on analysis, criticism, interpretation, and speculation, leading to comprehension. Etymologically, the term 'Philosophy' comes from two Greek words: '*philos*' meaning 'love of' and '*sophia*' meaning 'wisdom'.[1] Philosophy is also understood to lead one to a *Weltanschauung*, i.e., a worldview.

Philosophy is an attempt to study and understand Life, its mysteries and the concepts of existence and reality. It tries to discover the nature of truth and knowledge. It helps in finding out the essence of everything, thus giving the significance and relevance of the various dimensions of man's life. It also examines the relationship between humanity and nature, individual and society. When it is beyond Man to study the Ultimate Reality, it is termed as metaphysics. When one studies man in relation to other living beings, it is termed as social philosophy. When there is an attempt to understand man and his political activities and tendencies, it is political philosophy. A study of the religious concepts and tenets underlying man's behaviour is called the philosophy of religion. An analysis of man's value systems, duties, right and good, and principles is again a philosophical pursuit—the philosophy of ethics. Economic systems and practices also have philosophical bases when applied to man's behaviour.

Philosophy arises out of wonder, curiosity, and the desire to know and understand. 'Philosophy,' as Mortimer J. Adler says, 'is everybody's business'.[2] What he implies is that every thinking individual, whether he knows it or not, shows some incipient/ inherent talent of philosophical insight or analysis in his moment of thought and reflection. To be reflective about one's experience in life is to be philosophical about it. Many times, the common person calls it 'common sense'.

The term 'Philosophy' is interpreted to imply the acquisitive use of intelligence, as against mere knowledge, which spells a passive possession of a person. Every thinking individual is, in reflective moments, a philosopher, and everyone speculates with the intention of enriching oneself. But this does not imply that the individual is a student or teacher of the subject called Philosophy. Philosophy is thus seen as something that is as natural to an existential, reflective being as breathing is to a living organism. One now begins to realise the difference between philosophising as a natural behaviour of man and philosophy as a vocation.

For example: A man was walking down a dark alley on a lonely night. He suddenly felt the butt of a gun at his back. A gruff voice said to him, 'Your money or your life.' The man was petrified and said, 'Take away my life. What will I do without money anyway?' The man's behaviour and reply to the attacker spoke of his philosophy in life. He made his priority in life clear to the other.

In contrast is the story of Gautama Buddha who was out in the city one day with his charioteer. The sights of sickness, aging, death, and the agony and misery of man, perturbed him. His faith in happiness and life was shaken. This made him curious to know and understand the cause of misery in man's life. His philosophical inquiry dwelt on man's misery and the ways of transcending it. His findings brought to light man's bondage, due to attachment to things that are temporary and perishable. His teachings showed man the way to enlightenment and freedom from all bondages, which helped man to eliminate suffering and misery in life. Thus, philosophy arises out of one's own life, recognising and fostering eternal values.

Philosophical inquiry always begins with a doubt, so believed Rene Descartes, the French philosopher. He doubted the validity of his own sensations and perceptions. His question, 'What is the proof that I exist?' led to a dissertation on the proof of his own existence and the existence of things around him.

The philosophic attitude is one against dogmatism. There is critical analysis and an evaluation of all interpretations of thought and rationality. **Philosophy, in its acquisitive sense of intelligence, can satisfy the thinker only if he works persistently and with detachment. The search for Truth, thus, goes on.**

Since every institution or organisation has its own Weltanschauung, it follows that every institution in society is based on philosophic ideas—be it the government, the legal system, religion, industry, business, marriage, education, or family. The list is never-ending. Some individuals and groups have come together due to having similar ideologies. Some situations have brought about differences in philosophic ideas that have led to the overthrow of agencies, even governments. Ideological differences have also resulted in drastic changes in legal affairs and systems, and the transformation of economic systems. Changes have occurred primarily due to differences in the beliefs that people have held about life and things. Philosophical thinking enables us to determine and distinguish between values and beliefs that are found to be significant. Such values are found to be right, good, true, and real, thus giving direction and order to life.

Traditionally, for the purpose of study, philosophy is considered to be the following main branches, each organised around a certain distinctive question. These are:

1. Metaphysics – a study of the fundamental realities and aspects of being, becoming, nature and existence
2. Epistemology – knowledge and various aspects and types of knowledge
3. Logic – basically a study of rationality, doubt and debate, reasoning
4. Ethics – study of values and principles, right and wrong, good and bad
5. Aesthetics – study of beauty, art, creativity, all aspects of creation and the created in its expression

Metaphysics is basically the result of Thought over the real essence of things, relating to 'Being' of things. The subject matter of metaphysics includes Reality, Existence, Self, World, God and Creation itself. A metaphysician tries to answer questions such as: What is ontological reality? What is Truth? What is the nature of existence? What is Creation? Is there a God? What is the world made of? and other such questions.

The subject matter of metaphysics is further sub-divided into the following:

- **Ontology:** the study of Being. It comes from two Greek words 'ontos' meaning 'Being' and 'logos' meaning 'knowledge'. The metaphysician studies the eternal and the temporal, the creator and the created, the limited and the unlimited, the finite and the infinite and their inter-relations.

- **Cosmology:** the study of the physical universe or the Cosmos, taken as a whole. Cosmology is also the branch of science that studies the origin, nature, organisation, history and future of the universe. Cosmogony is considered a section of Cosmology which studies Nature and causes of creation/evolution.
- **Theology:** the study regarding the existence, nature and function of God.
- **Eschatology:** the study of life after death.

Epistemology aims to study all aspects related to knowledge. Etymologically, the term 'epistemology' comes from two Greek words: 'episteme' meaning 'knowledge' or 'science' and 'logos' also meaning 'information' or 'knowledge'. It includes the study that determines the nature, basis and extent of knowledge. It also explores the various ways of knowing, the nature of Truth, and the relationship between knowledge and truth, and knowledge and belief. According to philosophers, knowledge gained by man may be through reasoning and experience. The distinction between knowledge that is a priori, and a posteriori is brought out by the philosopher, where the former is arrived at without the independent appeal to experience and the latter is arrived at through observation and experience. Epistemology, thus, gives us an idea of all aspects of knowledge, its sources, needs, extent, and conditions of validity and so on.

Logic is defined as the study of the principles and methods of reasoning. Etymologically, the word 'logic' comes from 'logos', meaning thought or knowledge. The subject matter of logic includes methods of judgement, types of propositions, forms of inference and argument, hypotheses, definitions, comparisons, divisions, classifications and laws of thought and reasoning. It highlights the distinction between good/ sound reasoning and bad/ unsound reasoning. In logic, there is a study of human thought that involves rationality, and every instance of reasoning is called an argument or inference. It proves man as different from the other intelligent, living beings as the capability to rationalise, argue, justify and prove is given only to man. Indian philosophy emphasises on the need and the use of *tarka*/ argument in the process of philosophising. Logic is a branch of philosophy concerned not only with inferences and proofs, but also with the study of language, its syntax and semantics.

Ethics studies human conduct, character and values. Etymologically, the word 'ethics' comes from the Greek word 'ethikos' or 'ethos' meaning custom or usage. According to Aristotle, the term included both the ideas of 'character' and disposition'. Cicero introduced 'Moralis' into the vocabulary of philosophy, especially into the branch of ethics as equivalent to 'ethikos'.[3] It studies the nature of right and wrong and also studies human actions in respect to their being right or wrong. It brings out the distinction between good and evil. Ethics highlights the characteristics of a just society and explores the nature of justice. It emphasises the need to explore one's obligations to oneself, to others and society. Ethics asks questions such as: 'What makes actions right and wrong?'; 'What are values and what ought to be the proper values of life?' The actions of individuals and social groups supply the subject matter for ethics. Ethics distinguishes between actions that are voluntary and involuntary and studies only voluntary actions. It makes a systematic study of our moral ideals and goals, our motives and intentions, our choices and acts of volition, and our patterns of good and bad conduct. It brings out the distinction between right and good, wrong and bad.

Aesthetics deals with creation and the principles of evaluation and appreciation of art and beauty. Etymologically, the term 'aesthetics' comes from the Greek word 'aesthesis' meaning sensation. But the term was used to refer to only that part of the 'sensible' to which the term 'beauty' could be applied. This branch of philosophy also studies thoughts, feelings and attitudes in the individual that arise when he/she experiences the created world. Man has the ability and the passion to enjoy and study any natural phenomenon or even a work of art, which is a human creation. Aesthetics gives direction to man's expression of creativity and guides him in his activities such as painting, music, dance, sculpting or even simple cooking. Aesthetics involves both, the beauty found in nature and the works of art created by man. It studies the affective, intellectual and emotional responses of individuals who interact with and understand the beauty in creation. It is, thus, rightly called the Science of Beauty.

In addition, the philosophy of language, political philosophy, philosophy of religion, theology, axiology and linguistic analysis have become so important that they are almost considered branches of philosophy today.

Philosophy of language is the study of nature, use and necessity of words, thoughts and expression for communication and meaning. Familial, social, political and economic contexts are significant in understanding language, its uses and relevance. The significance of language representing and expressing Reality is the philosophy of language.

Axiology broadly discusses the concept of values, be it ethical values, aesthetic values or economic values, attributing worth to everything in the Universe. These values are classified as Intrinsic value and Instrumental value, meaning that which is valued for itself and that which is valued for its significance for others.

Philosophy of religion studies the basic concepts and ideas that religions propagate with the help of rational and critical thought. There are certain basic questions on Reality, God and Morality propagated by religion, linking ethics to theistic concepts, that are questioned and challenged rationally and critically. Theology, on the other hand, studies the same concepts, more with faith and belief as its basis. There is an acceptance of certain traditions, concepts and realities of a particular faith as true, and certain texts and studies related to a particular religion are accepted. Philosophy of religion is a critical study of religions universally practised, and is open for theists, atheists and agnostics, for debate, review, and discussion. Theology, on the other hand, is a study which is almost dogmatic at times.

Indian Philosophy: An Overview

In India, philosophy has shown two major trends, philosophy as a process of pure rational enquiry and philosophy as translating into life, both secular and spiritual. Philosophic thought in India, to a substantial extent, is intermingled with religion. The religious character and aim of our culture are seen in many philosophical thoughts. There are commentaries on religious and sacred texts that emerged as philosophy.

Man is in constant struggle with himself and the environment for his existence and survival. He uses his intellect to understand the conditions and meaning of the struggle. Man as a rational being thus needs to 'see' for satisfying the unending desire to 'know'. Indian schools of thought are called '*Darśanas*' which mean 'vision/seeing' or 'realisation'. There is no equivalent to the term philosophy as used in the derivative sense of 'love of wisdom' in Sanskrit. The term 'Darśana' comes from the root word '*Dṛśa,*' meaning 'to see' or 'one that can be seen'. 'To see' is the act of perception. The question then arises: Should one understand perception in the physical sense of perceiving matter or is it taken to mean intuitional perception? Philosophers agree that it is more than mere sense perception as understood in the physical sense.

Dṛśyate anena iti Darśanaṁ

All schools of philosophic thought in India were guides to humans to have a vision of the Ultimate Reality or Truth. 'What is the truth,' asks Umesh Misra, 'which a *darśana* helps us to realise? The only truth—the final aim of Indian thought—is the perception—the direct realisation—

of the *ātman*. All the *Darśaṇas* aim at the true knowledge of the *ātman* according to their angles of vision.'[4]

Dr S. Radhakrishnan said, '*Darśaṇa* is a word which is conveniently vague, as it stands for a dialectic defence of extreme monism as well as the intuitional truth on which it is based. Philosophically, *Darśaṇa* is putting the intuition to proof and propagating it logically... A *Darśaṇa* is a spiritual perception, a whole view revealed to the soul sense. This soul sight, which is possible only when and where philosophy is lived, is the distinguishing mark of a true philosopher.'[5] By 'putting intuition to proof' means 'its realisation in life'. Hence the word 'Darśaṇa' is said to correspond to the Greek word '*philosophia'*. Philosophy as 'Darśaṇa' never began or even ended as an intellectual activity. No system of Indian philosophy, however, allows any purely isolated treatment.

Its inter-connections and its contradictions with the other schools have largely conditioned each system of Indian philosophy, in its development. Hence, it makes it necessary for us to understand one school in the light of the others, with constant reference to the similarities and differences with them. 'The word "*Darśaṇa*",' says Dasgupta, 'in the sense of true philosophic knowledge has its earliest use in the *Vaiśeśika-sūtra* of *Kaṇāda* which I consider pre-Buddhistic.'[6] It is highly doubtful whether the word 'Darśaṇa' ever meant philosophy in the earlier schools. Jacobi conveys that the word 'Darśaṇa' was hardly mentioned in the earlier treatises like the *Arthashāstra*. The word used to refer to philosophy then was '*anvikṣikī',* which later came to be used for logic.

The intuitive perception of the spiritual reality led to liberation or *mokṣa*. Thus, *Darśaṇa* or philosophy in India simply meant a discipline that guided us to liberation. The majority of schools of philosophy were thus considered to be '*mokṣa–ṣāstra*'. All other disciplines gave us knowledge of the phenomenal world. In India, people conceived of philosophy as a way of life, not mere intellectual activity. The main aim and objective of Indian philosophy was to show man the way to liberation, which implied freedom from the bondages created by the phenomenal world and its temptations. It taught man how to relieve himself from ignorance and the consequent suffering and tensions caused by the body and the senses and their attachment to the worldly matter. In Indian philosophy, any study of human behaviour, as ethical or otherwise, has seldom been conducted in isolation from religious convictions and practices. Religion is presumed to be a major and dynamic force that affects the attitude of individuals and communities.

According to many academicians, it seems illogical to say that all Darśanas were *mokṣa–śāstras* as there were also Indian philosophies that were called so, yet mocking at the ideal of *mokṣa*, as in the *Lokāyata* or *Cārvāka* system. Moreover, the early *Mimāṁsakās* too gave us a system that was called Darśana, which however did not throw light on mokṣa.

Philosophy, when understood in its true significance and relevance, is known to be a way of life for every man. It helps to integrate the physical and the spiritual, and the material and the spiritual. It fosters man to lead his life ethically and guides him in times of confusion and dilemma. It is like a signpost when man is at the crossroads of life. Philosophy also helps man to think rationally and exercise his choices with his own volition. It gives expression to his creativity through works of art, literature, music, dance and even his daily routine activities. It integrates the different dimensions of life in everything that is in him and around him to make it all look like a part of a larger Reality. Every individual or institution behaves in a manner that reflects his/her philosophy. Societal culture depends on philosophical ideas. It determines man's culture and ethos.

As per Webster's Encyclopaedic Dictionary, the term 'Ethos' reflects the fundamental character or spirit of a culture. It refers to the underlying sentiment that informs us of the beliefs, customs and practices of a group or society, which involves the moral element. Hence, it may be termed as 'moral disposition' of a community or group. The word 'Ethos' corresponds to the German '*Sitten,*' meaning the moral habits of thought and action of people at various times and places. It is partly made by rules and regulations and partly by certain religious precepts such as the *Puruṣārthās* of Indian thought, the Ten Commandments of the Jews, the Sermon on the Mount of Sinai, the tenets of Islam, the *Aṣṭāngika Mārga* of Buddhism, and the Ethics of Jainism. It is the environment in which society manages to integrate, nurture and help individuals to grow, as it consists of ideals, habits, customs, traditions, and social and moral institutions.

When philosophy is so integral to man's life, can it now be discarded as abstract, dull, and insignificant?

Indian philosophic schools are normally classified into two: Āstika Darśaṇas, the orthodox schools, and Nāstika Darśaṇas, the heterodox schools. The classification is done based on their relation to the Vedas. Āstika Darśaṇas are those schools that accept the infallibility and supreme authority of the Vedas. The Nāstika Darśaṇas are those schools that deny, reject, or refute the authority of the Vedas. According to the lawgiver Manu, the Nāstikaḥ is simply a vilifier of the Veda—'Nāstikah Veda–nindakah.' The terms Āstika and Nāstika have nothing to do with belief or disbelief in God.

Under the category of Āstika Darśaṇas, there are six schools called the Śad-Darśaṇas. The Āstikas are:

1. Nyāya
2. Vaiśeṣika
3. Sāṁkhya
4. Yoga
5. Mimāṁsa
6. Vedānta

The Āstika schools of thought are normally studied as twin schools, thus pairing Nyāya with Vaiśeṣika, Sāṁkhya with Yoga, and Mimāṁsa with Vedanta, for in each pair, the philosophies are complementary to each other.

There are three major schools under the Nāstika Darśaṇas. The Nāstikas are:

1. Buddhism
2. Jainism
3. Cārvāka

They are schools that have developed independently of the acceptance of the Vedic inspiration and authority. They have evolved their own spiritualism and ritualism.

The texts of the Śad darśaṇās are also called Veda Upāṅgas. They are in the form of short aphorisms, and a Rishi is credited with having written each philosophy. Gautama's *Nyāya*, Kaṇāda's *Vaiśeṣika*, Kapila's *Sāṁkhya*, Patañjali's *Yogasūtras*, Jaimini's *Pūrva Mimāṁsa* and Bādarāyaṇa's *Vedānta-Sūtra*, (also called as Brahma Sūtra or Uttara Mimāṁsa) are the six doctrines. Nyāya and Vaiśeṣika literatures together are also classified under the sub heading Tarka Śāstra. While Āgama literature is theological, the Darśaṇa literature is philosophical and logical. The Itihāsa (Rāmāyaṇa and Mahābhārata) and Purāṇās are for the masses, appealing to their hearts, whereas the Darśaṇas are for the scholars, appealing to their intellects.

Darśaṇas are basically six systems of salvation. All six are equally valid ways of salvation and are divided into three groups of two each and are thought to be complimentary to each other. These are Nyāya and Vaiśeṣika, Sāṁkhya and Yoga, and Mimāṁsa and Vedanta. Some of these doctrines form the foundation for Jainism and Buddhism. The purpose of all these six philosophical systems is the removal of ignorance and aiding the learner in acquiring knowledge that will lead to attainment of perfection and bliss. The Jivātman must be united with Paramatman, and this is immortality.

Each school of the Āstika Darśaṇas has highlighted one aspect or branch of philosophy more than the others. Nyāya gives us an entire epistemological system, emphasising the rational aspect of man. Many thinkers regard Nyāya as a founder of syllogism and logic. Vaiśeṣika gives us a metaphysical system, with Substance as the Reality, with an elaborate account of its qualities. Sāṁkhya again talks of the metaphysical Reality, bringing in dualism, with Puruṣa (Spirit) and Prakṛti (Matter) as the two primordial realities.

According to Sāṁkhya, all creation is due to the evolution from these two Realities, the Uncaused First Causes. Yoga gives an ethical and practical dimension to man's life, picking up from the metaphysical basis of Sāṁkhya. Yoga comes as a guide to man's living in this created world, bringing in pragmatism to abstract metaphysics. Mimāṁsa talks about the ritualistic aspect of man's religious and spiritual life, basing itself on the Vedas. Vedānta is the philosophy of the Upaniṣads (the ending portion of the Vedas), highlighting the spirituality and essence of Vedic teachings. Mīmāṁsa is the Karma-kāṇḍa and Vedanta is the Jñāna-kāṇḍa of Indian philosophy.

As for the Nāstika schools, they show their difference in the development of thought, distinct from the orthodox systems. The variety of philosophical views that showed some allegiance to the teachings of Buddha, and that gave man an insight into his own life and sufferings, were broadly referred to as Buddhist philosophy. Jainism is a system that gives guidelines for achieving complete mastery over oneself. The name 'Jainism' comes from the term 'jina' which means 'the victor', or 'the conqueror'. Jainism is thus a philosophical school that teaches man to win control over his desires, passions, wants, greed, lust, and all those negative aspects, which make him bound to the sensory world. The third Nāstika Darśaṇa is the Chārvāka or the Lokāyata system that gives us materialistic philosophy. It denies anything that is beyond the perceptible and hence questions the validity of the tenets of the Vedic and popular Hindu religions.

Some of the common characteristics of Indian philosophy or *Darśaṇas* are:

1. **Reality of the World –** All schools of Indian philosophy recognise the reality of the world. The world is accepted as a spatio-temporal order, along with the causal order, which implies that it exists in time and space, and is governed by the laws of causality. The relation between time and space and the cause-effect relationship constitute

the cosmic order. Every finite entity is positively produced and destroyed. All schools, however, accept that atoms are indivisible and eternal. Physical causation is subordinated to moral causation. Every system must admit the reality of the world, at least as an appearance, account for its variety and multiplicity, and provide for the realisation of our practical needs. Thus, all schools of Indian philosophy are pragmatic.

2. **Spiritual Orientation** – Indian philosophy believes in the reality of the soul and seeks to realise it in its true form. Many schools accept the reality of the permanent self. All orthodox schools of Indian philosophy admit the reality of the *Ātman* or self as a permanent spiritual substance. Among the heterodox schools, the *Cārvāka* denies the reality of the self and identifies it with the body endued with consciousness. The *Cārvāka* regards consciousness as an epiphenomenon of the body. The Buddhist denies the reality of the permanent self. According to the Buddhism, the self is nothing but a series of momentary ideas. It is only the Jaina who admits the reality of the permanent self as a knowing, feeling, and thinking agent. The concept of the *Brahman* is thus, fundamental in Indian philosophy. The realisation of the real essence of oneself, thc spiritual self, is the common goal of all schools.
3. **Closeness to Life** – The stumbling block in the minds of most Indian minds is that Indian thought is either entirely abstract or is merely esoteric religion. If it is the former, then it is irrelevant to man's daily life. If it is the latter, then it is merely a conglomeration of superstitions, beliefs, rituals, and rites. Then Indian thought is like a wasteland that can never yield anything beneficial for man. But this is not true.
4. **Enlightenment for Life Situations** – Indian philosophy is not mere intellectual activity and is not an endeavour to quench intellectual thirst alone or the satisfaction of intellectual curiosity. It wants to tackle the various problems of life and is integrated with life and its various dimensions. It is regarded as a practical necessity and is cultivated to understand how individuals can best lead life. It is an endeavour to enlighten man to lead his life by foresight, insight, right attitudes, and values. Esoteric religion and religious tenets, if understood in the right perspective, can be availed of as transformational psychology. If used to influence man and his behaviour consistently, then such religion can be educative and developmental.

5. **Initial Pessimism and Ultimate Optimism and Positivism –** Indian philosophy is criticised for being pessimistic and fatalistic. The fact is that Indian philosophy owes its origin to the discontent of the spirit with mundane and routine life in the phenomenal world. It looks for something that can lead to a transformation of the individual in life, leading to his liberation. Indian philosophy, although originating with discontent from mere temporal and earthly life, made it aim for a study of the divine transformation of life with an analysis and understanding of the more permanent realities. Considering that the aim of all Indian philosophy was the removal of suffering, which was the result of *Avidya* or nescience, and the attainment of the highest happiness produced by *Vivek* or knowledge, its aim, one should call this philosophy as eudemonistic than pessimistic.
6. **Law of *Karma* –** All schools of philosophy influencing Indian thought and culture believe in the Law of *Karma*, except for the *Cārvākas*. The faith in *Karma* helped man to give himself a moral system, as *Karma* brought along with it the belief in Heaven and Hell, and reward and punishment, along with an understanding of what man called as Sin. As we sow, so shall we reap – was what man realised due to his belief in the law of *Karma*. A wrong action inevitably produces a bad consequence and a right action a good one. Thus, the concepts of *punya* and *paap*, *swarga* and *naraka* bring into the minds of the people the need to do the right and avoid the wrong. This becomes the basis for the moral law of causation in personal and social life.
7. **Faith in Rebirth and Transmigration –** Transmigration of the soul is normally understood as a corollary of the Law of *Karma*. According to Indian schools of thought, merits and demerits produced by right and wrong actions respectively in the previous birth, determine the kind of birth that one gets in the present birth. The same soul is said to continue through various births and the embodiment of the soul in a specific body is determined by the impressions of the *karmas* in its earlier births. Transmigration presupposes the permanence and continuity of the soul that merely gets embodied into different bodies in different births. The idea of transmigration is acceptable and common to all schools of Indian philosophy, except the *Cārvākas*, who do not admit the reality of the soul. The Buddhists do not accept the permanence of the soul but believe in the theory of transmigration.
8. **Saṁsāra –** *Saṁsāra* is a series of births and deaths that signifies the bondage of the embodied soul in the spatio–temporal world. It

implies the imprisonment of the pure eternal spirit in a temporary and perishable reality as the body. The recognition of entities that are eternal and permanent as distinct from those that are impermanent and transitory is alone true knowledge, according to Indian schools of thought.

9. **Liberation, the Ultimate End –** All schools of thought conceive of Knowledge as a means of divine transformation of life and liberation from worldly miseries. They unanimously hold the view (except for *Chārvāka*) that liberation enables a man to break free from the shackles of *Avidyā* and lead to *Mokṣa*. All schools talk of Liberation in diverse ways and term it differently too, such as *Mukti*, *Mokṣa*, *Nirvāna*, etc.
10. **Ignorance, the Root Cause of Bondage –** All schools of thought believe that *Avidyā* is the root cause of bondage and knowledge alone is the means to liberation. They go on to further say that *Avidyā* is not merely intellectual, but could also be psychological, moral, and spiritual.
11. ***Pramāṇas* –** Indian philosophy is not dogmatic or uncritical. Every system of thought is based on epistemology, thus expounding its own unique theory of knowledge. Most of the schools accept perception (*pratyakṣa*) and inference (*anumāna*) as the major means of knowledge. In addition to these two, *Sāṁkhya* accepts testimony (*sabda*), *Nyāya* accepts testimony and comparison (*upamāna*), *Mimāṁsā* of Prabhakara accepts testimony, comparison, and presumption as *pramāṇas*. *Mimāṁsā* of Kumārila and *Vedanta* accept, in addition to all these, *anupalabdhi* or non-apprehension as a *pramāṇa*. All schools of thought discuss nature, objects, sources, and conditions of valid knowledge, thus giving us their own unique epistemological theories.
12. **Synthesis of Philosophy and Religion –** In Indian thought, one finds the close intermingling of religion and philosophy. As all philosophical schools are closely related to the *Vedas* in some way or the other, the influence on philosophical thought by religious thought and culture is quite justified. The same is true of the reverse case too, where religious thought has evolved differently due to the influx of philosophical intervention. This has created a need to redefine Hinduism as a religion, as it is a major influence on Indian thought and culture.

The *Śad darśaṇās*, the scriptures, the epics, the *mahāvakyas*, the *ṣāstrās* and the *purāṇās* – all constitute a synthesis of philosophy (*tattva*), psychology (*manoṣāstra*), and ethics (*dharma*). The integration of the *sūkṣma* with the *sthūla* is well evident in Indian thought.

Culture and its Relevance

Culture in society refers to social, intellectual, and artistic cultivation of the minds of people. Culture may be taken to mean 'a general state or habit of the mind' or 'a general state of intellectual and moral development in a society as a whole.' The entire way of life—material, intellectual and spiritual—of a given society constitutes the individual and societal culture.

Culture is the human interpretation of meanings and values expressed in philosophy, religion, and art, of the purposes of life and society. Culture, thus, becomes a system of social management. In this sense, culture implies inevitably the material organisation of life, not discounting the non-material aspects of a society such as ideas, language, and norms. **The meaning of the term 'culture' can be interpreted as a way of life, which is necessarily inspired by fundamental values in which people live. Culture is thus the sum total of values.**

A scientific definition of 'culture' denotes that it is a complex whole which includes knowledge, belief, art, morals, law, custom and all capabilities and habits that man comes to possess as a member of a society. Culture characterises a group and it manifests human conventions through art and artifacts. It is a dynamic concept as it symbolises something that is a continuous, cumulative, and progressive process. It is the quintessence of all that is natural and good in the world, and it includes all those things that belong to man but go beyond his survival needs and basic wants. In short, culture includes all that man has acquired in his physical, mental, emotional, and intellectual sphere of his individual and social life. Culture, in addition, also includes all that man foresees and conceives through his creative thinking.

Culture connotes man's social heritage. As E.B. Tylor describes it, 'Culture is that complex whole which includes knowledge, belief, art, morals, law, customs and any other capabilities and habits acquired by man as a member of society.'[7] According to S. Radhakrishnan, culture is 'what produces the sweetness of temper, sanity of mind and strength of spirit.' As Radhakrishnan explains it, the significance of culture is highlighted to embrace not only knowledge and learning of arts and sciences, but Wisdom. It brings in an attitude of humility and servitude, of moral and intellectual integrity. It also develops a sensitivity to serve all those less fortunate than oneself, instilling a sense of solidarity with one's fellow beings. Culture thus comes as a torch to ignite the spirit of innovation and revolution to lead to social upheaval in the face of darkness and downfall. Culture as a totality expresses the varied expressions of the human spirit.

There are certain noteworthy features of culture:

- Culture is found only in human society.
- It includes all those factors and elements that man has created and in which man can improve upon by himself.
- It is transmitted from generation to generation and is a psychological aspect of the human personality.
- Culture improves and enhances with the introduction of novel and unique features that are inherently good.
- Culture is normally idealistic, and yet considered an important constituent of conduct, as it is pragmatic and existential.
- Culture possesses an order and system, and its various parts are integrated to form a cultural whole.
- Culture is important as it helps to fulfil man's needs.
- Culture helps to fulfil certain needs that are ethical and social and are ends in themselves.
- Culture is not innate but is an acquired factor in human life as it denotes traits that are learned through socialisation.

Living according to a set of values and virtues constitutes a way of cultivating (cultura) the soul, of perfecting a person's or a people's life. Culture then is the pattern of values and virtues according to which people exercise their freedom in search of self-realisation; it is the synchronic pattern of the exercise of freedom as the search for self-realisation or perfection. The exercise of life according to a set of values leads to the practice of certain ways of responding to specific challenges and opportunities. In the course of time, these set patterns develop special capacities and strengths with repetition and practice. Virtues then can be understood as special capacities to exercise freedom according to values.

A word that is very casually and normally used in today's era in corporate organisations is 'Culture', be it 'Corporate Culture', Work Culture' or 'Safety Culture.' In this context, culture needs to be defined and redefined. Culture is defined as 'the integral sum of values which individuals, groups and society at large conceive and practice.' All definitions of culture bring to focus the significance of values. If values are conceived and not practiced, they become redundant without any intrinsic merit. The culture of an individual is determined by his thoughts that are based on the values that he possesses. The knowledge and imbibing of values are the fountainhead for the individual to develop the power to discriminate. Only then is there coordination between thought, word, and action. The discipline that one develops in one's life stems from man's need to affiliate and belong to a group, be it a social group, organisation, or the nation too. This leads to an obvious declaration that management in a large way depends on cultural and moral ethos.

Management is, thus, taken to be a product of societal culture and culture is taken as the expression of a philosophy, be it individualistic or social. Philosophy is the mindset of the individual and society. Syllogistically, if $p \supset q$ and $q \supset r$, then $p \supset r$, where p stands for philosophy, q for culture and r for management.

To understand Indian Industry, it becomes necessary to understand the crucial features of Indian Culture. As India has always been inclined towards the spiritual in its cultural manifestations, the spirit of Indian culture too will reflect the same ideals. It is advisable to make references to Indian Culture rather than Hindu culture, although that was a religion and philosophy that dominated. This view stems from the fact that the ideal of our culture has always been freedom of thought and worship, extending facilities to people of all faiths. It has been glorified as a culture that respected and valued human dignity, understanding the worth of every human being.

Indian culture is not racially exclusive. Members of different races—Aryans and Dravidians, Huns and the Parthians and the various religions too—Hindus, Muslims, Christians, Sikhs, Buddhists, Jainas, Jews and the Zoroastrians—were all embraced as belonging to one faith. A great scholar, denoting a culture of assimilation, synthesis and blending called the culture that developed the 'corporate culture'.

Indian culture is manifested in all aspects and dimensions in its civilisation, and this civilisation is firmly rooted in *Vedic* and *Upaniśadic* philosophy. The organic relation of Indian culture to the *Vedic* thought and philosophy needs no reaffirmation. The *Vedic* civilisation (or the Hindu civilisation as it is more commonly recognised), with all its ideals, education, social norms, economic and political ideas and institutions, literature, religion, art, and science, exhibits strongly and deeply, its moorings with the philosophy of the scriptures. The entire socio-economic-culture complex evolved around the *Vedas*, the guiding principle being the *Purushārthās*, the main theme being *Samanvaya*, implying harmonious blending.

Philosophy provides the basic tenets that underline management principles. All principles of management aim at the objective of proving man as an asset and resource. Indian philosophy serves this purpose by recognising the holistic dimension to man's personality. Man is beheld as having a body with a Spirit that helps him be a conscious, living being. His holism is evident in his being that has physical, mental, emotional, social, and moral development. The holistic approach helps us to identify and accept man as a complete, mature, purposive, and spiritual being.

A re-reading of ancient Indian texts from the standpoint of modern management concepts would alone create instant appeal to the Indian psyche and result in concerted action. It, hence, becomes fundamental to understand that ancient values have current relevance and that they are not contradictory to modern management principles.

What is Management?

Man is a purposive being who consciously aims at achieving his goal. This is a statement of truth, an inevitable fact, which cannot be refuted. This is one statement that makes man continuously conscious of his sociological bearings and linkages right from primary to secondary, to high school, all through to the grave. No man can live as an island. Man is dependent on others as much as others are on him. This interdependence of human beings has given rise to organisations and institutions of various orders– social, economic, religious and others.

Today, we are living in a world of organisations. These organisations dominate our life. They supply us with the toothpaste and soap of daily use, the food we eat, the clothes we wear, the cars we drive and the transport we use to travel in and so many, many more. These organisations also provide us with jobs and income. The list of goods and services provided by the institutions and organisations is endless, if not eternal and infinite. If organisations are professionally managed, it means that the world will become a better place, and, of course, the converse is also true. The need for good management in every sphere of our life and activity is, therefore, of paramount importance.

Management, thus, becomes the key to success with the individual as much as at the corporate and national levels. Management, as understood by the industrial world, is a word universally used to signify an exercise of harmonising the five M's: men, money, material, machinery, and method. It is a process that aims at the fulfilling of set objectives that necessarily lead to human development. The goals are far reaching when management talks about aiming at social benefit and global welfare. Ever since people began forming groups to accomplish aims that they cannot achieve as individuals, management has become essential to ensure the co-ordination of individual efforts.

Management, as defined by Heinz Weihrich, in his book *Essentials of Management* is 'the process of designing and maintaining an environment in which individuals, working together in groups efficiently to accomplish selected aims'.[8] Peter Drucker, a scientific thinker, argued that management was not just a matter of experience, hunch or native ability. According to Drucker, the elements of management can be analysed, organised systematically, and learned by anyone with normal intelligence.

According to Drucker, every institution gives an opportunity for humans to learn, understand and practice, to achieve common goals with shared values. Drucker also claimed that the ultimate test of management was not analysis but performance. As each individual possesses knowledge and skills different from the others, there are tasks that are distributed or assigned based on his potential. Management spelt different meanings to different people, although the basis to it remained the same.

Management is an art and a science. It involves maximising the return on investment by the optimum use of resources for the sake of all stakeholders of an organisation. It is an art since human creativity, and the innovative spirit is used to motivate the stockholders. Fast responses to the changes and initiative-taking management of change in an existing situation call for initiatives and creativity. It is a challenge to the innovative nature of the individual, as he must modify decisions depending on situations that are unique or novel.

Moreover, management is a personalised activity, as every manager has his own approach to people and situations. Every activity of the manager is an expression of his capabilities, knowledge, and skills. Just as a work of art displays the innate talent and skill of the artist, every act of the manager displays his artistry in getting things done and accomplishing his work. The artist is also known for setting goals and objectives while expressing himself. In the same manner, the manager too sets objectives that he must achieve for himself and the organisation. Artistic skills are honed and developed through constant training and practice. Similarly, managerial skills can also be developed and enhanced through consistent practice and continuous training.

Management is considered a science for distinct reasons. It is a science as there are sets of rules, principles, knowledge, or theories that are enunciated to establish various relationships–namely, causal, functional dependence, and uniform and multiform diverse co–relations. Every branch of management is a discipline with its own theories evolved through experiences (trial and error, experiment, and success), all contributing to the task of performance maximisation. Just as the scientific method is universally accepted and followed in science, the process of management too is universally followed. All managers need to plan, organise, direct monitor and control activities.

The principles of management are also universally accepted such as division of work, unity of command, authority, and responsibility. The degree of application might vary from manager to manager and from organisation to organisation. As Peter Drucker highlights in his book, *Principles of Management*, management needs to be understood as a multi–purpose organ that manages a business, manages a manager, and manages workers and work. Management is a social science as it deals with human beings and their organisations. It is dynamic in nature like any other social science, as it deals with human behaviour.

Management is considered to be a profession. It has a well-defined body of knowledge that is valid universally. It is a dynamic science as it deals with humans, and, hence, it is experiencing continuous development. Acquiring management education through training is significant and necessary in today's world. Although management is not stamped as a profession yet, it has been found that managers are displaying a very professional attitude and approach to their tasks and responsibilities. Managers do not make their entry into their roles fulfilling the requirements of minimum academic qualifications, but they necessarily need to possess certain specific skills to remain there.

As a profession, management has no prescribed and written code of conduct to be followed. But it is necessary to have a sound ethical basis to one's character to be a good manager. The code of ethics is almost implied with the acceptance of the role itself, as it is a pre-requisite of every profession that deals with human beings.

Management is considered a significant activity in society as the quality of management determines the survival and progress of any organisation. The success of a group or an organisation depends on the quality of the managers. The transformation of resources into results depends on the efficient and optimum utilisation of available resources. The optimum utilisation of resources presupposes the minimisation of wastages. The work ethic and work environment depend on the quality of managers in the organisation. The level of motivation in every individual varies from time to time and from situation to situation. To keep the levels of motivation high, it becomes necessary for the manager to be dedicated and sincere himself, with an attitude of self-motivation.

Modern management is dynamic, thus encouraging innovation and initiative. Effective and motivated managers can keep introducing new methods and innovative technologies, thus keeping pace with the breakthroughs in science and technology the world over. Management is given a lot of significance as it facilitates the growth, expansion, and diversification of organisations. Management, as a specialised activity, involves getting work done by the other personnel, thus involving direction and coordination. It is the direction of the individuals in any organisation that determines the efforts of the various levels within the organisation, which in turn decides the performance of all.

Today, management is explained as being in part a social process–a process of combining techniques with men for the mutual benefit of both. The organisation today is looked at as a social system in and of itself. The informal groupings in the work situation had a dramatic and vital part to play in the organisation. No more is the individual working in an organisation viewed as a 'factor of production'. Rather, he has become a human being with 'wants, desires, attitudes and feelings' vitally affecting his productive usefulness.

The individual in an organisation needs to be looked at as a 'whole man'. No longer is he viewed solely as an economic tool but, rather, as a human being who is driven and controlled by diverse elements of society and who has fears, frustrations, expectations, and desires which affect his total makeup. It becomes necessary to discover newer and better ways of understanding man and his relation to his work. It is almost mandatory to motivate him to higher standards of performance, and to make him realise his own potential. In the changing economic, social, and technological environment, it becomes essential to study management and managerial functions in a new and dynamic perspective.

Management needs to be differentiated from Administration. Many use the two terms synonymously. Administration is concerned with the determination of policies, and the coordination of finance, production, and distribution. Management, on the other hand, is concerned with the execution of policies, and it functions within the scope set by administration. If administration is concerned with the thinking/ planning process, then management is said to be concerned with the implementation process. According to Henri Fayol, the two terms have no major differences between them. Even if they are used interchangeably, it creates no confusion, as the terms need to be understood based on usage and context.

Management is looked at as a process of utilising material and human resources to accomplish specially designated objectives in an organisation, by the organisation and for the organisation itself. It is a distinct process involving various activities such as planning, coordination, organising, direction, and evaluation to achieve the goals and objectives of the organisation. Management functions are classified based on their scope and nature. They are planning, organising, staffing, directing, and controlling. The dynamic management functions are coordinating, decision-making, innovation, representation, and administration.

Management is an integral process, and it is difficult to put its functions into separate and rigid compartments. All the various functions overlap, and they tend to merge with each other, with the sole object of meeting targets set by the organisation. Every function is effectively conducted only if the individuals involved in the various functions are healthy in all aspects of their personality. Every individual contributes to the philosophy of the organisation and the work-culture, in his own manner, as his philosophy of life determines his efficiency and effectiveness. Management is an inevitable and essential reality in all spheres of human endeavour.

Having understood the meaning and relevance of Culture and Management, we arrive at the conclusion that Managerial reality is not an absolute reality. It is purely a product of societal culture.

Philosophy and Corporate Management

All the organisations in the world are built around individuals. It is the quality of these individuals that decides the quality of the organisations and institutions. These individuals decide the conceptualising, the goals, and directions to an organisation. If these individuals who form the foundation of the organisations were brought to a level of clear thinking based on purity, peace, and self-realisation, then the result would be world prosperity. This creates a requirement of projects that are aimed at creating awareness of the importance of moral and human values. There arises a need to improve human relationships and to have a clear vision of a better world. The newly changed world creates a need for implementing a voluntary action-plan for self-transformation, self-development and, finally, self-actualisation.

Individual excellence alone leads to organisational excellence. No system or method will work, and no enactment of laws, rules and regulations can purify the society or organisation unless the individual wills it. It is impossible to always have perfect individuals, in all places and all situations. But all situations, problematic or otherwise, can and must be, ideally speaking, tackled with the individual in focus.

The Western concept of organisational management has laid **excessive emphasis on consumption, profit, improvement of technology and techniques of production, besides advertising and marketing. This**

concept of maximisation of consumption, with the simultaneous increase in production and profitability, has somehow led us to a point of zero. It implies a negative growth rate as it finally leads to a total depletion of all resources**. Indian Ethos reflects the paradigm shift. In Indian philosophy, restraint is the keyword. There is a delinking of the close relationship between happiness and growth, and growth and investment; that has always been a misconception of the West.**

Indeed, human beings cannot live without having their needs, desires, ambitions, goals, and aspirations recognised and realised. It makes it necessary for us to understand all this in the light of Maslow's hierarchy of needs. But it should also be accepted that all these cannot be done at the cost of sacrificing or delinking oneself from one's own core being, the spiritual self. An attempt to live with extroversion of self, with the objective of achieving materially, will only lead to the individual living in a self-created chaotic environment. The loss that man thus experiences, is due to the loss of the paradise within more than without. It is so true when Aurobindo defines man thus: 'Man… is a spirit veiled in the works of energy, moving to self – discovery, capable of Godhead.'

Happiness does not rest solely on earning, investment, and prosperity. Indian thought presupposes the practice of Dharma for happiness. The Indian mind stresses the absorption and practice of qualities that enables the perception of the higher things of life. The totality of the Universal environment includes the animate and the inanimate, and it aims at universal social welfare. When it comes to management of human resources, it becomes necessary for policy makers to consider the wisdom, experience and the various systems applied by the people of the past. It is mandatory to see that every system or practice should take into consideration the cultural milieu and the existing value system of every tradition and heritage.

The term 'tradition' comes from the word 'tradere' or 'to pass on'. Each generation needs to investigate its existent culture as a way of living and evaluate it. There is a pressing need to adapt to its times and pass on to the next generation only what is important for their exercise of freedom, for their way of living and seeking the good, as that which promotes life. Tradition cannot be stifling as it is seen as 'life-giving'. It needs to be differentiated from history as the latter includes all that has happened, good, bad, constructive, and destructive.

Hence, tradition is defined as 'the cumulative wisdom or practices of a people from their experience and exercise of freedom; it is their cumulative freedom. Its authority is based on the combined need to realise one's potentialities and resources of tradition to fulfil those needs. Thus, it constitutes the ultimate community of human striving.'[9]

Thus arises the need to ask whether tradition as a heritage locks us into the past or can it be a creative source for an evolving life? Tradition can be likened to the string that gets the beads of ethnic expressions together.

Value-based human qualities are clearly defined in our traditional scriptures. It is necessary to realise that sound management principles are contained in the sacred texts of India, as in the *Vedas* and more notably so, in the *Bhagwad Gitā*, the *Upaniṣads*, *Dharmaṣāstra*, *Arthaṣāstra*, *Dhammapāda, Vedanta and Upanishads.*

References

1. Reese W.L., Dictionary of Philosophy and Religion: Eastern and Western Thought, p.12.
2. Adler Mortimer J., The 4 Dimentions of Philosophy, Macmillan Publishing Co., New York, 1993, p. ix.
3. Reese W.L. Dictionary of Philosophy and Religion: Eastern and Western Thought, p. 22.
4. Misra U., Conception of Matter According to Nyāya Vaishesika, Allahabad, 1936.
5. The text is a quote from Dr. S. Radhakrishnan's classic work, Indian Philosophy, Volume I, which was then cited and discussed by Shri U. Misra in his 1936 work, Conception of Matter According to *Nyāya Vaisheshikā.*
6. Dasgupta, S.N., 'A history of Indian Philosophy' i.68.n.
7. According to S. Radhakrishnan, culture is 'what produces the sweetness of temper, sanity of mind and strength of spirit.
8. Vaz Michael & Paralikar Vinayak, 'Management and Human Resource Development', Manan Prakashan, Vile Parle, Mumbai, 1999, p. 3.
9. McLean, George F. 'Hermeneutics Faith and Relations Between Cultures', Lectures in Qom, Iran, Mofid University, Qom, Iran and The Council for Research in Values and Philosophy, 2003, p. 115.

II

SPIRITUALITY: MEANING AND PRACTICE

What is Spirituality? Is it something concerning 'the intellect' or what is often thought of as 'the better or higher part of mind'? Is it the moral aspect of life? What is the significance and relevance of spirituality in Indian ethos? Let us try and understand these aspects to relate it to corporate management.

What is Spirituality?

Spirituality is a human orientation towards meaning, a connection that involves a sense of transcendence, inner transformation, and an ethical commitment. Perhaps it may even mean a state of 'being incorporeal'. Whatever way one may define, it may be termed as an ideal that reckons all reality in essence as spiritual. When simply stated, spirituality is one's character or quality that makes one transcend the barriers of worldliness, caste, creed and sensuality and realize one's connection with the Truth.

The etymology of the word 'Spirituality' comes from the Latin 'spiritus,' and the Hebrew 'ruach'. The two words mean 'breath', pointing to an animating, incorporeal force that is energising and life-giving. Spirituality thus came to mean 'the energy or force or breath of God'. Spirituality can coincide with organised religion but also appear outside it; the two overlap where communal practices shape inner life, and they diverge when spirituality is privately oriented and non-dogmatic. A useful working definition is 'a commitment to develop one's full human potential and to help others do the same while recognising our interconnectedness.'

To define oneself as spiritual is an individual exploration of the inner world of the self, out of which compassion and wisdom ought to arise, with intuition as its strength. Spirituality and religion often overlap but are not identical. Religion provides communal structure, doctrine, and ritual that can deepen and channel spiritual experience. Spirituality can also be personal, non-dogmatic, or expressed outside formal religious institutions; when described as separate from religion it may reflect preference for individual exploration rather than rejection of communal practices.

I define a spiritual person as one 'who works to develop his full human potential and helps others to develop theirs, recognising that we are all one'. Even an atheist could be spiritual. It involves both inward transformation and outward expression through values, choices, and relationships. Examples of spiritual practice include meditation or contemplative prayer for inner cultivation and ethical service or community work for outward expression.

Spirituality is, hence, not merely an abstract idea. Inner and personal practices reflecting spirituality include meditation, contemplative prayer, reflective journaling, and mindfulness, cultivating self-awareness and inner transformation. On the other hand, there are certain external and social practices that reflect spirituality such as commitment to family and social responsibilities, acts of community service, ethical living, and artistic expression manifesting spiritual values in the world.

Spirituality has been defined in numerous ways –

- A belief in a power operating in the universe that is greater than oneself.
- A sense of interconnectedness with all living creatures.
- An awareness of the purpose and meaning of life and the development of personal, absolute values.

Although spirituality is often associated with religious life, many believe that personal spirituality can be developed outside of religion. Acts of compassion and selflessness, altruism, and the experience of inner peace are all characteristics of spirituality. Spirituality is the recognition and realisation of the Being, the reality in oneself and all others. The integration of the body, mind and spirit in a human being, which results in facilitating the realisation of a goal in life, within the ethical framework makes him a spiritual being.

In order to realise oneself, it becomes necessary to be aware of oneself. This awareness comes to us in various ways and forms and through various means, the significant ones being the scriptures, mythology and religious texts of India and the world. This learning can also be through an exposure to mystics and sages. As an innate capacity that exists in every human being, psychologically healthy spirituality is not limited to any one set of doctrines or practices. From a psychological perspective, spirituality is a universal experience, not a universal theology.

Spirituality is understood by many as an act of involvement or state of awareness or devotion to a higher being or life philosophy. It is not always related to conventional religious beliefs. A religion is considered a dogma or creed, a set of beliefs about the spiritual and a set of practices, which arise out of those beliefs, but one cannot overlook its aspects of **community, cultural heritage**, and **lived experience**, which are just as central to its definition as the intellectual framework of beliefs.

There are many religions which arise out of those beliefs. Religions are **distinct** and may be **dogmatically exclusive**, in practice or philosophy. Religion is different from spirituality where the former is normally accepted as an institution with organised doctrines, ethics, tenets and beliefs that relate everything to what is deemed as sacred. Religion is expressed with the help of socially approved and accepted rituals, practices, myths and social structures. Both, however, are based on faith and belief. The essential difference that can be emphasised is that **spirituality** is the personal, internal search for meaning, while **religion** is the external, communal, and structured framework for that search.

Spirituality: An Experiential Alignment with the Sacred

Spirituality is the lived expression of the sacred—a profound alignment with that which transcends the ordinary and imbues existence with meaning. It is the transformative experience of a deeper reality that cultivates in the individual qualities such as love, compassion, ethical integrity, and a sense of harmony and justice. A spiritual person, less constrained by social or psychological limitations, experiences a unique freedom—both personal and relational—that opens the path to wisdom and a deeper understanding of the human condition. Spirituality characterises the individual's relationship with all beings and does not necessitate formal structures, rituals, or intermediaries.

At its core, spirituality reflects the innate human impulse to seek union with a Reality beyond the transient and sensory. It fulfils the existential need for meaning and is often expressed through the pursuit of beauty, awe, and kindness—qualities that transcend conventional moral standards yet resonate deeply with human nature. Once basic needs are met, individuals often turn toward enriching their higher selves through music, art, poetry, and acts of compassion. Forgiveness, empathy, and the willingness to understand others emerge as hallmarks of the spiritually attuned. Spirituality implies the inner human urge to seek and unite with a Reality beyond the fleeting, sensory world, fulfilling the need for a meaning.

Spirituality is inclusive and participatory. It evokes a deep sense of belonging to the whole of existence. Whether consciously acknowledged or not, every human participates in the spiritual dimension. Religion, in this context, may serve as a bridge—through ritual and doctrine—to the spiritual realm. Yet, spirituality itself lies beyond religion, and religious forms may succeed or fail in facilitating this connection.

To be spiritual is to experience life subjectively—both within and beyond oneself. It is a conviction, not confined to theistic belief. Even atheists, who reject the notion of a creator, may affirm a spiritual sensibility that seeks care, meaning, and connection. This shared human impulse underscores the intrinsic value of the self and others. In simple terms, spirituality may be defined as a profound and elemental connection with something both within and beyond oneself, revealing one's essential nature.

Spirituality evokes a sense of timelessness and unity with the cosmos. The spiritual individual perceives the world as fundamentally interconnected, speaking from the heart and engaging at a level beyond rational, linear discourse. Boundaries—of time, space, class, race, and species—dissolve in the spiritual vision, replaced by a sense of universal kinship.

This realisation, that one is part of the natural world, shifts consciousness and fosters an awareness of the impermanence and transparency of all boundaries. The spiritual dimension concerns itself with meaning, truth, purpose, and ultimate reality. It manifests as a search for the Absolute and a commitment to values held as sacred. Fundamentally experiential and intuitive, spirituality resists abstraction and conceptualisation. It is grounded in direct experiences of being and insight, which elude the grasp of discursive thought and have historically challenged scientific inquiry.

In Indian philosophical traditions, the term 'spirituality' carries a distinct connotation. The 'spirit' is identified with ātman (self or soul), encompassing both jīvātman (individual self) and paramātma (Supreme Self). Divinity is thus recognised in both the cosmic and individual realms. Moreover, the Paramātma or Supreme Self is conceived as both transcendent and immanent in the phenomenal world. Hence, all creation is perceived as a manifestation of the Spirit.

Moreover, the Supreme is described through the paradigms of Sat–Cit–Ānanda (Being–Consciousness–Bliss) and Satyam–Jñānam–Anantam–Shāntam–Pūrṇam Brahman (Truth–Knowledge–Infinitude–Peace–Perfection). Spirituality, in this context, is the aspirational movement of the individual self toward realisation of the Supreme. The triad of Sat–Cit–Ānanda encapsulates the holistic nature of Indian metaphysics: Sat signifies existence (ontology), Cit denotes consciousness (epistemology), and Ānanda reflects bliss through ethical living. This synthesis represents the integrative vision of Indian thought—a consciousness of the Conscious Spirit in its fullness and the right perspective. Thus, Sat–Cit–Ānanda represents the holism of Indian thought.

Spirituality arises from within, beyond the mind's survival instincts. Each person possesses a spiritual core—a centre of consciousness and purpose aligned with cosmic intent. **Every spiritual being lives with a divine purpose, animated by an energy that transcends conditioned beliefs and values. This spiritual energy is the fountainhead of wisdom, enabling one to live passionately, purposefully, and harmoniously. Such a life is marked by humility, empathy, and love, and is oriented toward shared goals, known in Indian philosophy as the Purusarthas.**

The Puruṣārthas: Foundations of Integral Human Aspirations in Indian Philosophy

We need to understand the significance and relevance of the Puruṣārthās in Indian philosophy. The four values or goals accepted in Indian philosophy are universal and comprehensive in nature.

They are, as given in the Agni Purāna:

- Dharma – Duty/ Righteousness/ Morality
- Artha – Wealth/ Material Prosperity and Just Political Order
- Kāma – Instinctual desires and needs
- Mokṣa – Liberation, from the bondages of the soul. It could be interpreted as self–actualisation and self–realisation, as is done by many Indian thinkers, in order to give it a more pragmatic approach. Liberation is also called as Mukti, Kaivalya or Nirvāṇa in the other schools of thought as in Jainism and Buddhism.

These four aims are not mutually exclusive; rather, they represent a holistic vision of human development, integrating ethical, material, emotional, and spiritual dimensions.

The concept of Puruṣārthas is one of the most important concepts in Indian philosophy, which gives a conceptual framework of Hindu culture. The Puruṣārthas signify an integrated approach to the problems of humanity. The recognition of the integration of the body, mind and soul is clearly visible here. The harmonious development of these three aspects in man alone leads to a healthy, integrated and purposive individual. The emphasis is on the enhancement of both the personality and the social development of the individual. In any social group or organisation, if individuals have to live with co–operation and peace, with the attainment of common goals and objectives in mind, then it is necessary that every individual is aware of his real self.

'Purushartha' means and connotes the aims and purposes of life or the fundamental aspirations of man. The term 'Purushartha' not only denotes what the objectives of life should be, but it also comprehends what the objectives of life are as the result of the psychological tendencies of the individual.

The term 'Puruṣārthas' literally signifies 'what is sought by humans', so that it may be taken as equivalent to a human end or purpose. The qualifying word 'human' may give the impression that the term is not applicable to ends which man seeks in common with the other animals; but this is not really so, for we find it used with reference to seek even ends like food and rest. The qualification is hence explained in a different way. Man, like animals, acts instinctively in various situations. However, he also exercises his sense of discrimination and discretion when he makes conscious choices, using his sense of reason and values. Even choices that he makes, to satisfy his natural wants and needs, can be made with deliberation. He sets before himself ends to be achieved and then sets about fulfilling them.

It provides a Holistic Framework for human comfort and flourishing as it reflects an integrated approach to life, recognising the interplay of body, mind, and spirit. The balanced pursuit of the four goals leads to the development of a healthy, purposeful individual. This framework emphasises both personal growth and social harmony. In any collective group or situation, be it a family, community, or institution, cooperation and peace depend on individuals being aware of their true nature and living in alignment with these aims. This integrative model resonates with contemporary theories of well-being and can be compared with psychological frameworks such as Maslow's hierarchy of needs.

The theory of Puruṣārtha serves as a map of the worthwhile ends of human action. It outlines the fundamental aspirations that guide behaviour and decision-making. The term encompasses both normative ideals (what one ought to seek) and descriptive tendencies (what one naturally seeks), shaped by psychological dispositions and cultural conditioning.

While humans share basic needs with other animals—such as food, rest, and reproduction—they possess the unique capacity for deliberation. Unlike instinct-driven behaviour, human action can be guided by reason, values, and ethical reflection. Even the pursuit of natural desires (Kāma) and material needs (Artha) can be undertaken with discernment, aligning with Dharma and leading toward Mokṣa.

Mokṣa, the culminating aim, is often interpreted as liberation from the cycle of birth and death. However, contemporary Indian thinkers have rearticulated it as self-realisation or self-actualisation—a pragmatic and accessible ideal. In Jainism and Buddhism, similar concepts are expressed through terms like Mukti, Kaivalya, and Nirvāṇa. These traditions converge on the idea that true freedom lies in transcending egoistic limitations and realizing one's essential nature.

The Puruṣārthas offer more than a philosophical taxonomy—they constitute a living framework for conscious aspiration. They guide individuals toward a life of balance, integrity, and transcendence. In doing so, they shape not only personal destiny but also the ethical fabric of society. Their relevance endures, offering timeless insights into the nature of human fulfillment.

To begin with, I am discussing Artha as Puruṣārtha. It refers to the desire for wealth, economic prosperity and a just political order. It indicates that each one must engage in activities that are constructive and productive and contribute for the growth of oneself, one's family, one's community and one's own nation. This Puruṣārtha takes care of human needs and necessities, in addition to individual and national prosperity. If man decides to work effectively and rightly in a planned manner, then it even gives man his comforts and luxuries. It keeps man away from idle pursuits, inactivity and mere pleasurable, trifling indulgences. Artha is, hence, considered a goal that helps man to achieve worldly happiness. It is opposed to any defaming or mean activity that adversely affects man's esteem and principles, such as stealing, corruption, or begging. Even if ever man has to borrow in certain situations in order to meet his basic needs, he has to rightly pay back to the lender. Otherwise, it is considered an immoral act on his part. Man has to earn his livelihood in a righteous manner, not by deceiving or cheating. Man has to be self–dependent, self–reliant and should work towards nurturing his self–esteem.

As the Ṛgveda[1] says, 'Māham Rājan Nyākṛutena Bhojaṁ' which means: 'Each man should earn his livelihood by sincere efforts and should never be under anyone's obligation.' Thus, Artha as Puruṣārtha actually respects human dignity. This clearly shows us that it is necessary to achieve Artha in keeping with the guidelines of Dharma. Then only can man eat well, sleep peacefully and live his life in bliss as there is no fear or guilt regarding his richness. His wealth too can be used for good and noble causes, thus making him a philanthropist. Sharing one's wealth with others is a sign of one's magnanimity and nobility. If Artha is not within the confines of Dharma, then the individual ends up being greedy for more and jealous about all others who have more. It makes a man seek ways of making money through corruption, deceit, bribes, extortion and exploitation. Wealth gained in this manner leads to individual destruction and social degeneration, which is highly avoidable. So, it clearly teaches us that wealth should not only be earned in the right manner but should also be spent for the right purposes, thus helping man to lead a life of culture and happiness.

According to scriptures, Artha entails social security. The first treatises on economics or social functioning were written, not by economists and businesspeople, but by sages, seers and spiritualists. This clearly indicates that the great thinkers of India, in the past, did not think of renunciation of the world, but actually tried to synthesize spirituality, ethics and materialism.

Their objective was the wellbeing of man and society. As safety and security is an important need for every man, and money is a source of security, Artha needs to be recognised as an important Puruṣārthas . One needs to work in a manner that one does not run after money, but money comes to one of its own accord. For this, it is extremely necessary to specialise in a particular field, or vocation, which is most compatible with one's native endowments, aptitude and capabilities. One's job vocation or profession should be such that it is a means to serve the society. If one really loves one's work, if one is a specialist in one's field, and one has an attitude of service to the community, then money naturally comes to the worker.

The next Puruṣārthas is Kāma, the fulfillment of desires—all that stems in man as needs that are instinctual. It includes the individual's desire for food, security, safety, and sex, along with the need to create, reproduce, excrete and procreate. Kāma includes the need to fulfil the desires for acceptance, recognition, appreciation, recreation, entertainment, honour and fame too. Kāma thus takes into its fold the *Puruṣārtha* of Artha as it includes the desire to be wealthy and prosperous. Kāma refers to all those primary urges that are natural to man. In order to even enjoy what one has earned, one needs to be free from worries, hankering and egoistic problems. It becomes necessary, thus, to train one's mind to get the right disposition.

If Kāma is related to instincts, then does it not make man an animal like any other in the natural order? The justification for the recognition of kāma as *Puruṣārtha* is given in the following manner: Kāma is a value if it conforms to and operates within the framework of Dharma. When the individual deviates from the guidelines given by Dharma, then the individual becomes a mere passionate and sensual animal. Kāma needs to be guided, monitored, regulated and controlled by Dharma continuously and consistently. Otherwise, Kāma can be quite dangerous and detrimental for humans in his endeavour to gain Mokṣā. The sanction of Dharma alone gives it its sanctity. There has to be a balanced approach to Kāma. If an individual gets obsessed in life with anything that is tangible and perishable, then it leads to detrimental effects. The discriminative knowledge with regard to Kāma and Artha alone leads one to the goal of Mokṣa.

Moreover, Kāma is significant as it recognises the need for a human to procreate in order to keep the human race alive and perpetuating. It is also a means of expressing love, affection, gratitude, friendship, loyalty and all other tender emotions experienced by a human. It also provides a human with an opportunity to express and create with his innate skills and talents, whereby a human's imagination and creativity are recognised. Divergent thinking in a human is encouraged as Kāma helps a human to learn to survive under all situations. In a social context, family, social groups, religion, art, literature and architecture are resultant of activities that stem from Kāma. Kāma can be looked at as a motivator, mover and propeller in life. Thus, Kāma in tune with Dharma beautifies and simplifies a human's life, making it pleasurable and joyous.

The third Purushartha is Dharma, which is the principle of cosmic and ethical order, helping every human to live well, peacefully and with order. Dharma is an eternal goal, discussed under various aspects of Indian ethos, both as a metaphysical principle of philosophy and as a moral compass to ethical lifestyle. I will be discussing this Puruṣārtha in detail in the next chapter.

Mokṣa or Amṛta, as the earlier philosophers call it, is considered the Summum Bonum or supreme Puruṣārthas. Both Artha and Kāma have value only when they help in the attainment of perfection and harmony. Hence, the value of Dharma as the first Puruṣārthas and the goal of Mokṣa as the final Puruṣārthas keep the two Puruṣārthas, Artha and Kāma, in check. If it was not for Mokṣa as Puruṣārtha, then Artha or Kāma would have succeeded in keeping a human tied to the world of pain and suffering. Mokṣa is given a lot of importance in Hinduism and Indian culture as it leads a human to a transcendental, spiritual realm. A human has something to look forward to in life after satisfying his bodily, emotional, mental and moral needs. Mokṣa can also be interpreted as Moha-ksaya meaning the annihilation of wrong attachment and infatuation. Mokṣa means freedom from bondage, and freedom from pain and ignorance. It frees a human from the cycle of birth and death with the help of spiritual knowledge. Mokṣa is thus looked at as self–realization and God–realisation. It signifies right knowledge and right conduct that liberates a human from the fear of pain, death and saṁsāra.

The Upanishadic seers have discriminated between 'the real good' and 'the merely pleasant'. The 'really good' is called the 'Sreyas' and the 'merely pleasant' is called 'Preyas'. Sreyas refers to goals that have intrinsic value, and Preyas refers to those goals that are instrumental in bringing happiness. Sreyas is a reference to a goal that is sought for its own sake and Preyas is a reference to the goal that is sought for the sake of attaining or achieving some other end. In the Kaṭhopaniṣad, the Lord of Death has said that a thoughtful human discriminates between Sreyas and Preyas and wisely prefers Sreyas to Preyas.[2,3] In this approach, Sreyas refers to Mokṣa and Preyas refers to Kāma. The concept of Swarga (heaven), which implies abundance of happiness hereafter, is also called Preyas. The Upanishadic seers always sought the ultimate supremacy of the ideal of life and the means of its achievement.

The quest for this ideal is expressed in many prayers and shlokas, such as Om, Asato mā Sadgamaya, Tamaso mā Jyotirgamaya, Mrṛtyo mā Aṁṛtam gamaya – Br. 1-3-28. This prayer seeks to guide a person from ignorance to enlightenment, from darkness to light. The prayer is interpreted and understood in the following sense: 'Lead me from the unreal to the real.' 'Lead me from darkness to light.' 'Lead me from death to immortality.' The entire journey from mortality to immortality, from ignorance to wisdom, and from illusion to the Real is emphasised here.

The concept of Puruṣārthas leads us to the awareness that all human activities are aimed at the attainment of permanent, eternal and absolute peace and bliss. The Puruṣārthas ultimately lead a human to the state of self realisation. The acceptance of these four values as goals by our Indian thinkers, and rishis makes it clear that in our culture and tradition, a human's physical wellbeing is considered naturally necessary. Man's bodily needs have to be taken care of in a manner that leads to his mental, moral and spiritual growth. The gratification of his basic needs does not happen in the same manner as in the case of animals, as is done instinctively in the case of the latter. Man is conscious of his needs and fulfils them with a higher purpose in mind. His functioning is also within a moral framework that is value based. The four values of dharma, artha, kāma and mokṣa, thus, aim at the realization of the maximum, exhaustive and comprehensive growth and welfare of the individual and the community.

This makes it clear that it is not the end by itself that makes it a 'Puruṣārthas'. It is the conscious pursuit of the human being in order to fulfil his ends that transforms the ends into 'Puruṣārthas'. The ends that are shared by men with other animals, such as food, and rest, etc., are *Puruṣārthas* only because they are sought after knowingly and with the right means, using a human's faculties. His endeavour to fulfil his instinctual, rational, emotional, and moral needs make the ends 'Puruṣārthas'. The earlier philosophers believed that there were only three *Puruṣārthas* as initially mentioned, and they called it the 'Trivarga'. Mokṣa was included later according to them as a part of Adhyātma shāstra. Each of the Puruṣārthas is discussed separately and independently in its fullest scope by separate Shastras, such as Artha in Arthashāstra, Kāma in Kāmashāstra, and Dharma in Dharmashāstra along with Mokṣa Shastra or Adhyātma Vidya in the Upanishads or Vedānta. It is, however, now accepted as established that there are four Puruṣārthas or goals as prescribed by Indian philosophy.

The significance of the first element—puruṣa—in 'Puruṣārthas', does not imply a restriction of the scope of the ends sought, but is actually a reference to the manner in which they are sought. The significance of the second element—Artha—is seen in the implication that the end is not existent at the time when it is cognized as worth pursuing and is yet to be accomplished. It is a 'to be' which is 'not yet', and hence, it demands the efforts and endeavours of the individual desiring it. For this reason, the Puruṣārthas came to be known as 'that which is desired' or 'desirable' in the true sense of the term.

The 'Puruṣārthas' is seen as embodying a comprehensive philosophy of life. 'Puruṣārthas' is what a human seeks throughout his life, and all his efforts are directed towards achieving 'his desired goals'—Puruṣaih ārdhyate iti. It is 'what is a human's purpose in life' – Puruṣasya arthah prayojanaṁ. Hence, it is called the 'life–ideal'. *Puruṣārthas* is not any particular or specific object of desire. It is an ideal that a human seeks throughout his life. It is something that brings satisfaction to a human in both the psychological and ethical sense, which necessarily implies the fulfillment of both emotional and moral standards in a human. 'Dharmārtha Kāma Mokṣāshch Puruṣārtha Udaarihtah'—Agni Puraṇa.

The Sarva Darshana Saṁgraha conveys that the meaning of 'Puruṣārthas' etymologically suggests 'desirable goals or values desired by men', which is an indication of the desire to experience complete cessation of pain, which in turn, leads to eternal happiness. The concept of Puruṣārthas is hence, taken to imply a teleological basis that alone explains and justifies all human behaviour in all its varied manifestations. It makes all human action and behaviour purposeful. This is true of all human conduct, including morals.

It thus makes it necessary for one to have an ideal or goal, more so in the case of moral actions. Thus, the concept of 'Dharma' itself looks for an ideal, in order to reassert and reinforce the need for morality. In this sense, 'Mokṣa' becomes the highest ideal or Puruṣārthas. The desire to seek liberation alone needs no other ideal to give it its legitimacy. The concept of Puruṣārthas, with Mokṣa as the highest ideal, is said to give a human a framework for developing his purposive, right and complete philosophy of life.

Dharma holds a higher place than Artha and Kāma as it guides a human to live life well and rightly. Even artha and kāma get their beauty and significance in life with dharma as their guiding principle. As Vidura in the Mahabhārata says, 'It is by the help of Dharma that the sages have been able to cross the world. The stability of the Universe depends upon Dharma; artha and kāma too, depend for their proper management upon Dharma. Dharma is the foremost of all; artha is the middling; and kāma, it is said by the wise, is the lowest of the three. Therefore, we should conduct our lives with self–control, paying major attention to Dharma.' According to Manu, the effective and harmonious management of the Trivarga alone would lead to the essential goodness of humanity, with Mokṣa serving as the final purpose that gives the direction to a human's life.

The concept of Puruṣārthas, thus, destroys the misconception that one has about Indian philosophy and scriptures that one needs to renounce everything in this world to be a liberated soul. Indian philosophy does not advocate extremes of any kind, neither asceticism nor indulgence. It helps a human to respect himself as a biological, social, emotional and spiritual person. The Puruṣārthas merely are guidelines to the development of a human's own philosophy of life. A human needs to satisfy himself with the basic needs and also take care of his higher needs. Only then can it be said that man has had total development of himself.

What is strikingly commendable about the exposition of the Puruṣārthas in Indian thought is that the Vedantic geniuses, as we take the liberty of calling our seers, had actually foreseen the complexities of modern human life and left behind for us, as a heritage, the simpler solutions in the form of the Puruṣārthas. The theory of the Puruṣārthas clearly blends the sacred and the secular, the simple and the complex. It shows an obvious conjunction of the spiritual guidelines and the practical problems that man can envisage in his daily living. The secular goals of Artha and Kāma are blended beautifully with the ethico-spiritual goals of Dharma and Mokṣa, which deal with the spiritual and the sacred in man and in everything that man deals with in the environment.

In order to fit it into the modern context, we need to refer to Swami Vivekananda's message to all Indians that said: 'Every act is a spiritual prayer, every step is a pilgrimage.' The concept of Puruṣārthā is very significant as it is found relevant even today in designing and formulating Human Resource policies. Management gurus find its references in many of the theories that are applicable to the contemporary industrial and corporate world. An exposition of the Puruṣārthās with a comparison to Maslow's hierarchy of needs is done here to reiterate the holism of the theory of the Puruṣārthas.

Abraham Maslow gave an exposition of the theory of motivation with a new dimension. According to Maslow, a human has needs that determine his behaviour to a large extent. He says that human needs can be listed in a hierarchical manner. He enumerates them in the following way: a human's physiological needs that form the lowest level of needs; then follows a human's need for safety and security; followed by a human's need for love and belonging; which later gives rise to a human's need for self-esteem; to lead to the need for self-actualisation. Finally, a human, after fulfilling all these needs, looks for means to attain transcendence.

According to Maslow, a human moves on to the next level of needs only after satisfying the earlier level of needs. Indian thought, however, does not subscribe to this view, as it is believed that a human can progress to the higher level of needs even after giving up the lower needs. Maslow believed that a hungry individual could never be a good student. Indian thought contradicts him here and puts forth the view that one can attain even transcendence if one was able to give up the lower passions and focus on the attainment of higher pursuits. This view makes a human recognised more as a moral and spiritual being than just a biological and rational being. It helps us to understand and accept a human's spiritual needs more sensibly. A human as a purposive and conscious being, with a system of values to guide him, is clearly depicted in the Indian thought. The concept of Puruṣārthas gives us the holistic view of a human in Indian thought.

If Dharma holds such a significant place in Indian thought, let us see how our seers and philosophers have discussed it.

References

1. Maha. Santi, 167, pp. 6–9, Bible of Hinduism: A Gospel of Social Reconstruction, G.M. Ram, Allied Publishers Private Limited, 13/14, Asaf Ali Road, New Delhi, 110002.

2. Shreyashcha Preyashcha Manushyametah tou Samparītya Vivinakti Dhirah. Shreyou hi Dhiro Abhipreyaso Vṛṇito Preyo Mando Yogakshemād Vṛunite (1-2-3)]
3. Ref. *Puruṣārthas* – Datta Lakshmi Trust, 4466, Raviwar Peth, Pune – 411002, pp. 155–163.
4. Dharma and Vedic foundations: The study of Indian History and Culture Vol. IX, En 954 KUL/DHA, 11932. AIRC.
5. The Essence of Hinduism, M.K. Gandhi, Navajivan Publishing House, Ahmedabad, 380014 294.5, Gan, 10038 AIRC.

III

CONCEPT OF DHARMA

Ethics is knowing the difference between what 'you have a **right to do'** and 'what is **right to do.'** The words may be the same, but contextually and metaphorically, their implications and meanings are significantly different. When you talk of '**a right to do'** something, you are referring to the permissions and sanctions granted to you. When there is a reference to your conscience, your own internal compass, it is a reference to **'what is right to do,'** explaining Dharma, the third Puruṣārtha, of the four goals of human life, as stated in Indian ethos. Dharma is the ethical base and framework helping man to achieve Artha and Kāma, leading him to the final goal, Mokṣa. If ethics or Dharma is the lighthouse or the torch, helping man pave his path to success, prosperity, and peace, then let us understand this philosophical concept.

The word Dharma comes from the root word 'dhṛ' which means 'to uphold,' to support' or 'to nourish.' Thus, it is comprehended as the essential foundation of something or of things in general. It signifies 'truth, duty, and righteousness.' Dharma, as many feel, is said to stand for something that is established, customary, and proper. In this sense, it means that which is 'traditional' or 'ceremonial.' In some cases, it is also used to refer to 'religious ordinances or religious rites.' In the *Atharvaveda*, the word 'dharmah' is used in the sense of 'merit acquired by the performance of religious rites.' In the *Aitareya Brahmana*, the word 'dharma' is used to mean the whole gamut of religious duties. In the *Chandogya Upanishad*, the word 'dharma' includes three types of duties—that of a householder, a hermit and the brahmacharin. The first includes sacrifice, study and charity, the second has the duties of observance of austerities, and the brahmacharin has the duty of living with the teacher and learning texts and skills that include life-skills. Here, the word Dharma stands for the specific duties that are assigned to the individuals in the particular Aśramas.

In the Bhagavad Gita, the word Dharma is used to mean the duties and obligations of a man in all his roles in life, in an all–inclusive sense in the oft– quoted verse 'svadharma nidhāṇaṁ sreyah.' If understood in the right sense, the term means a man's duties and obligations towards himself, towards his caste, towards his profession or occupation and as an individual at a particular stage or Aśrama. Dharma implies the laws or principles on which society is based. According to the Vaiśeṣika philosophy, dharma is that which leads to improvement in this world and to mokṣa for the next—'Yato Abhyudaya Niśreyasa Siddhih sa Dharmah.' It shows that Dharma talks about the attainment of both outer prosperity and inner unfoldment. There is a definite injunction of attaining growth and advancement without compromising with our values.

Dhāranāt dharmamityāhuh, dharmeṇā vidṛuta prajāh:
Yasyādḥāraṇasaṁyuktāh sa dharma iti nischayah

– Mahabharata 12.110.11

'One that holds together, sustains and protects society is Dharma.' It has the quality of containing, keeping together and structuring society.

In a wider sense, Dharma is used to mean 'that which upholds humanity, society, or the world itself'—'Dhāryate Anena iti dharmah.' Dharma, in this sense, supports, sustains, nourishes, harmonises, and integrates all. It unites the inert and the sentient, the individual and the society, nation, and the world. Knowledge about Dharma is essential to achieve Mokṣa, according to Indian thinkers, as such knowledge alone leads one to the stage of liberation. It is necessary to lead life with moral values to guide at all stages. The Mahabharata also says, 'One who, by his action, attitude and speech, shows that he has always everyone else's wellbeing at his heart and is constantly engaged in the welfare of all others can be said to have "dharma".' Dharma, in this sense, represents 'correctness,' both in a descriptive sense, i.e. the way things are' and in a prescriptive sense, i.e. the way things ought to be.' It is said to reflect an inextricable and significant connection between ontology, ritual ideology, social philosophy, and ethics in the thought of India. The concept of Dharma, despite its various interpretations and connotations, still has certain consistent notions throughout history.

The term Dharma implies the observance of moral rules, norms, and commands. It gives us the direction for the right way of life, that is, Cāritra, or character-building. It includes an elaborate discussion of duties and responsibilities, which leads a man to the ultimate goal of man life. Dharma, hence, is to be understood as a prescription for a pattern or plan of action that is universally applicable. It makes it obligatory for individuals to obey as it lists down a set of rules and norms of conduct. We need to understand that a certain dharma or obligation becomes an obligation because it is valued for its intrinsic, inherent justifications.

For example, Truth has its own intrinsic value, and the obligation of speaking truth needs no justification on the basis of the consequences of such an act of truth or any other pragmatic consideration.

Dharmo hi paramo loke dharme satyaṁpratishtataṁ
dharmasaṁkṣhṛitampyetatpitrurvachanamutramaṁ:

– Valmiki Ramayana 2.21.41

'The wisdom that springs from a person's own self, tells him what truth is. Truthful behaviour/action and speech itself mean acting in accordance with Dharma. Following Dharma is practicing truth.'

As Dr Radhakrishnan said, 'Dharma or righteousness is the stable condition which gives a man perfect satisfaction. It helps a man to gain salvation as well as happiness... It always has a social implication. It is the bond that keeps society together. Dharma develops solidarity of society. It aims at the welfare of all creation.'[1] According to Indian thought, one virtue leads to another, and all are known when one is known. The ways to dharma are eight according to the epics: yajña, study, charity, tapas, truth, forgiveness, self-control, non-covetousness. The Hindu concept of Dharma thus enlisted seems very similar to the Buddhist view of the eight–fold path.[2]

Dharma is right action. In the Ṛgveda, Ṛta is the right order of the universe or 'cosmic order.' It stands for 'satya' and 'dharma,' i.e., Truth and the law of evolution. Dharma thus talks of conformity with the truth of things. Ṛta represents the Vedic notion of an impersonal and powerful force upon which the ethical and physical worlds are based, through which they are inextricably united and by which they are maintained. Ṛta is the universal truth that effectively strengthens Vedic rituals and practices. These rituals, traditions and practices are supposed to serve as the foundations for social organisation. In many ways, ṛta stands as the Vedic antecedent for the notion of 'dharma,' implying the established order of things, proper conduct, and the fitting truth. It is a concept of central importance not only to the various forms of religions, but also to our inherited culture and modern civilisation.

The term 'ṛta' is based on the Sanskrit verbal root 'ṛ' which means 'to go' or 'to move.' Thus, ṛta signifies the cosmic law or the eternal order and law. It implies the natural and moral order that helps in social order. The concept of ṛta signifies the cosmic law that allows the universe to run smoothly. It highlights the dynamic structure in which every object and all actions have their proper place. Ṛta also refers to a system in which all parts support and strengthen the whole in a flowing symbiosis. It signifies order and harmony in individual and social life, in the cosmos and in the aesthetic aspect of nature.

The conception of Ṛta is also given its due significance as it leads us to an anticipation of the Law of Karma. It connotes the experience of a 'finely tuned' universe, where everything works in perfect order, the laws of which give creative power to all gods and humans alike. According to the Vedic notion of ṛta, even gods derive their strength from their adherence to cosmic law. Any violation with regard to this system and order set by ṛta calls for a penalty. If the gods or humans were to go against the structures of ṛta, they would be said to be 'anṛta,' a common synonym for 'vṛjina,' crooked or wrong, and even 'asatya,' untrue. Throughout the Vedic period, ṛta was understood as an impersonal law and was never personified. Characteristically, the primary agent or guardian of the laws of ṛta is Lord Varuṇa, who in Vedic times at least, is an ethical Sky–God, whose omniscient judgement, the Vedic cult admired and feared. As the impersonal source of cosmic and ethical order, Ṛta includes important creative aspects.

As Dr Radhakrishnan writes, Ṛta furnishes us with a standard of morality. It is the universal essence of things; it is Satya or the Truth of things. Disorder or Anṛta is falsehood, the opposite of truth. The good people are those who follow the path of Ṛta, the true and orderly. Order in conduct is called the true vrata (vow). Vratani (vows) are the ways of life of good men who follow the path of Ṛta. Ṛta is suggestive and, at the same time, equivalent of Satya or Truth. Ṛta and Satya are born of spiritual ardour right in the beginning of things. Satya is supposed to be upholding the earth and Ṛta seems to uphold the heavens. Only a man with a pure body, pure mind, and a pure heart, leading a clean life, living in accordance with the ethical order 'ṛta,' is eligible to perform religious rites and rituals. A person, truthful in speech, thought and action has ṛta in his life.

Furthermore, the Vedic tradition held that the very structures of ṛta allow the human community access to the powers that drive the Universe itself. If the Universe is the manifestation of Reality, then Dharma or the Cosmic Order is its Will/Design, and Satya and Ṛta are its very nature. The most important ethical concept, that of Ṛta, is brought out with an elaborate exposition in the Vedās. The concept of Ṛta is seen as inseparable from the individual, social and natural aspects of the universe. It adds to the Truth, Goodness, and Beauty of the created world: Satyaṁ, Shivaṁ, Sundaraṁ.

Another concept that is closely associated with the concept of Dharma is that of Ṛṇa/ Debt. The concept of ṛna is linked to the concepts of puruṣārthas and the aṣramās, thus helping in shaping up further the ethical foundations in Indian thought. There are various types of Ṛna that are enumerated in the *Shatpata Brahmana*:

1. To gods – Deva-ṛṇa
2. To seers and sages – Guru ṛṇa
3. To ancestors – Pitṛ rṇa
4. To fellow beings – Manushya ṛṇa
5. To the environment (including all plants, animals, and elements in nature) – Bhūta ṛṇa

Ordinarily, the first three are accepted more widely in our culture. This idea of feeling indebted to the Divine, our ancestors, our teachers and seers, the nature around us, makes us realise that we are interdependent. We need to live with an attitude of gratitude and humility. The duties of children towards their ancestors and parents help in bringing in a healthy familial environment. It leads to behaviour that comes as a mark of respect, love, and affection between members in a family. As for the obligations towards sages, seers and gurus, Indian culture has always been in the forefront. Moreover, teaching-learning process is effective only if the student attempts sincerely with the right attitude. Nature needs to be nurtured so that it provides for a man in all seasons.

All our customs, traditions, rites, and rituals were opportunities for a man to repay all those he owed to in society. The debt to the divine is paid back in the form of yagnas, poojas and worship. The other way of paying back to the Divine is by being good to fellow-beings. The individual owns these ṛnas the moment he is born, as every individual carries with his spirit, the debts of the earlier birth. The idea of ṛna teaches us to be unselfish, dutiful, and responsible. It also makes it easier for us to give and share material wealth and prosperity, as we justify saying that we have probably borrowed it in our earlier birth. The idea of ṛna also helps us to learn the lessons of duties and obligations. Whatever we do in life will not seem to us as doing favours on others. On the other hand, a man will start seeking opportunities to do good deeds and help others, as it will be what he 'ought' to do.

Dharma is strongly associated with the concept of Karman/the Law of Karma, thus giving rise to the view that one's own actions in the present determine the conditions of one's life in the future. This ideological connection between two powerful concepts in Indian thought grew firmer and firmer through the generations. Manu, the lawgiver in Indian thought, asserted that only those who supported dharma as it was presented in the sacred tradition and in revelation gained fame in this world and incomparable happiness after death.[3] The term Dharma, thus, evolves with a normative dimension in which it comes to mean the sum total of one's obligations by which one fits in with the natural and particularly the social world.

As a consequence of being born as humans, everyone is caught in the endless and repeated cycle of birth and death. This is the Samsara that all humans have to endure. Liberation from this cycle of misery is the purpose of life for all, according to Manu. There are incentives to serve the rest of humanity well. Good deeds and bad deeds are counted, like a balance sheet. This law of retributive justice is called karma. Karma literally means deed or work. The cumulative effects of the deeds in this life have profound effects in the afterlife. As an outcome of his karma the body of next life is acquired. An individual's character, fortune, social class and his happiness or sorrow depends on his karma. His choice of words, actions, behaviour, intentions, and motives determines his fate and destiny, as to his opportunities, capabilities, strengths, and weaknesses in life. The body cannot escape the law of karma. However, by judgment and forethought, with wisdom and guidance, one can utilise karma to his advantage.

A human being has a free will that permits him to make intelligent choices, which in turn may alter the manifestation of karma. The ultimate goal of every individual is to reduce the bad karma that he may have to carry with him into his next cycle of birth. When good karma is accumulated over a number of lifetimes, the soul is liberated, and attainment of salvation is at hand. Every human being has the potential to eventually attain salvation by his or her deeds and this fundamental right cannot be denied to anyone. The freedom of will gives a man the right to choose his actions, whereby he is given a chance to improve his status of karma, with the repetition of good deeds and the minimising of bad deeds. The law of Karma is the Law of retributive justice.

As stated by Pitirim Sorokin, in his book *The Reconstruction of Maniti*, 'if a law or ethical norm is not deeply rooted to be in a person's convictions and in his emotional and volitional nature, becoming a potent inner mentor and guide to his actions, such a law is doomed to be ineffective, no matter how rigorous the external enforcement may be. … the enforcement of law by coercive means, when it contradicts the inherent legal convictions of the people, has never been able to prevent bloody conflict and establish lasting peace.'[4]

Even when the soul is in the embodied state during its earthly existence, the Advaita thinkers hold that a man, who is essentially a spirit, can attain the jeevan mukti state where he can live entirely in the spirit, without being affected by the evil effects of bondage, by the shackles of the body and entanglements of matter. They rely upon the Upanishadic saying: 'Ashareeram vavasantham na priyapriyosprushatah,' which means that he who is without the body, as it were, is unaffected by either priya or apriya, likes or dislikes. The ways by which such a state can be attained have also been elaborately dissussed and established. They have argued that the bondage of the soul in matter is due to beginningless ignorance or anadi avidya, as they have termed it and once this avidya is destroyed by jnana, the evil effects of karma are destroyed.

Karma is of three kinds: those actions which have been already performed in past lives and may give rise to effects in future are called 'sanchita karma'; those karmas that have already begun to fructify in the present life are called 'prarabdha karma'; and those actions, which will produce the effect in future life, are called 'agami karmas' or 'kriyamān'. Dharma sustains social order, protects people, and brings about a good amount of social cohesion. The Śrutis and the Smṛtis and customary conduct (ācāra) are major sources of morality.

Dharma has received a lot of attention from sages, seers, writers, critics, philosophers, and thinkers alike. Dharma integrates all aspects of human life. It synthesises the secular and the spiritual and provides the basis for man's comprehensive life, enabling him to fulfil all his aspirations. It makes man realise his natural self, nurturing his natural urge to grow, develop and manifest himself. It thus lends meaning to man's endeavours in life.

Dharma manifests differently in different spheres of life of the human being. Dharma of an individual is a moral obligation, characterising the essential quality of the human. When Dharma is understood in the context of society, with the human as a social entity, it reflects social solidarity. In the context of religion and faith, it spells beatitude or self-satisfaction. Finally, dharma, when systematised and structured for easy and better living, it is understood in the context of law, for fairness and justice in society.

In order to give man an idea of the vastness and true vision of reality and to help him fathom the structure and inter-connectedness of the universe, the scriptures and ethos have expounded Dharma. In addition to this, Indian culture teaches that one needs to perform his duties or Karma in order to be in tune with Dharma.

These karmas are listed as follows:

(a) Niṣidha Karma – prohibited acts
(b) Nitya karma – Enjoined regular duies
(c) Naimittika karma – Enjoined for specific occasions
(d) Kāmya karma – For the fulfilment of certain desires

(e) Prayaschitta karma – Expiations of wrong/evil acts committed earlier, atonement[5]

Today's problems in societal and managerial context for individuals stem from the fact that man is straying away from the path of Dharma and is stuck with the blind pursuit of Artha and Kama. If this can be remedied and people can be attitudinally reoriented to accept and follow dharma, society would be a better place, with better individuals and better organisations.

Paths to salvation are through three different means. Salvation attempted through the study of scriptures for the learned is Jñāna yoga. In India, an individual has other choices such as intense devotion to a personal God that he can utilise to attain salvation. This is referred to as Bhakti yoga. The third method is through selfless service to humanity called the Karma yoga, so well discussed in the Bhagavad Gita. If the essence of God or Brahman is recognised in every soul, then the service to humanity is the same as service to the Divine.

Service without regard for the fruits of action is specially extolled. A commoner can practice the latter two means of attaining salvation, even if he is illiterate and unable to study the scriptures on his own. Doing good to all is Dharma; injuring or harming others is Adharma. Strength and manliness are virtues; weakness and cowardice are sins. Independence and interdependence are virtues; dependence is a sin. Loving others is virtue; hating others is sin. Faith in God and in oneself is virtue; doubt is a sin.[6]

Knowledge of oneness between the individual self and the Cosmic self, leading to a sense of Universal Brotherhood is virtue; seeing diversity and isolating oneself from all is sin. Dharma leads to the right understanding of oneself, making one realise the Real Self through the destruction of the individual egoistic self. With regard to the aim of life, Indian ethics is appreciated as giving a very practical, socially plausible, and integral approach.

Dharma is classified into various categories:

- Varṇāśramadharma
- Svadharma
- Āpaddharma
- Sādhāraṇadharma & Sāmānyadharma
- Sanātanadharma
- Sadācāradharma and Siṣṭācaradharma

The idea of Varna has its relevance even today and it needs to be understood in the right sense, in order to justify its prevalence in

Indian culture. The concept needs to be explained contextually in order to apply it in today's organisational culture. The word 'varna' is said to have evolved from the root word 'Vri' meaning 'choice,' according to Sri Yaskācharya. Sri Yaskācharya mentions this in his work 'Nirukta', which is considered a foundational text in Vedic studies, and it is also considered to be the oldest treatise on etymology, philology, and semantics in India. According to Sri Pandurang Vaman Kane, varna' is used to refer to 'Colour,' as in 'gaura varna' to refer to fair-complexioned Aryans.

At a later stage, the term came to be used to refer to the four social classes—brahmin, kśatriya, vaiṣya and śudra—where birth determined the individual's class. This led to the anarchy in Indian society in the post Vedic times. The purpose with which the varna system began was defeated entirely; with the increase of exploitation of the lower classes (or groups?) by the higher and the rising inequality between the privileged and the deprived, the haves and the have-nots.

Varṇāśramadharma is a reference to the duties determined by one's social class (varṇa) and the stages of life (āśrama). There are four varṇas in Indian society: Brahmin, Kshatriya, Vaiśya, Śūdra. According to our scriptures, the **Brahmin** (priest) ensures the wellbeing of all with the performance of rituals and rites, thus acting as mediator between the Ultimate Reality and the individuals in society. The responsibility of the Brahmin was to see to the proper execution of works like the study of scriptures and sciences, teaching, and performance of all religious activities. The **Kṣatriya** (soldier) has the responsibility of protecting people of his land from others and from any calamities too. It becomes the responsibility of the Kṣatriya to take care of the weak, the women and children in society. The affairs of the government, the state, or defence were left to the Kṣatriyas. The **Vaiśyas** continued with agriculture, dairyfarming, and other such activities that helped people procure goods for satisfaction of basic needs. The Vaiśya (merchant or trader) produces goods that are essential for making a man's life comfortable. They work in a manner that all basic needs are provided to the people and that benefits people and society. The **Śudra** is a laborer or a menial worker who works physically to ensure the smooth functioning of society. The Śudra actually functions in a manner that allows others of the higher Varṇas to function effectively, efficiently, and smoothly, with no tension or anxiety about menial, routine, and monotonous, physical endeavours. (There is a pragmatic interpretation to this concept highlighted in a later chapter)

The aim of the social hierarchy in Indian society, in the form of Varnāṣrama, was for the purpose of division of labour, which is one of the fundamental theories of social organisation. It propounds that for an orderly progress of work in society, it is necessary that it be divided into classes according to natural tendencies. This aspect in society closely aligns with ideas found in ancient Indian texts, particularly the *Bhagavad Gita*.

In Chapter 4, Verse 13, the Gita states:

चातुर्वर्ण्यं मया सृष्टं गुणकर्मविभागशः। तस्य कर्तारमपि मां विद्ध्यकर्तारमव्ययम्।।13।।

'The fourfold division of human society was created by Me based on guna (qualities) and karma (work).'

The varna system gives the world the idea of decentralisation of power, authority, and responsibilities. In the varna system, the power of shāstra or knowledge, the power of shastra/arms and weapons, the power of wealth and the power of labour were all distributed among the brahmins, kśhatriyas, vaiśyas and the śudras, respectively.

If each individual in society has the onus of his actions, work, and duties on himself, then society moves ahead in the right direction, as all are busy with their own duties and responsibilities. It becomes difficult for anyone to shirk work that is assigned to him as his duty. In return for this, society gives him his remuneration proportionately to duties discharged. It also makes it imperative that punishment to violation of rights, shirking duties and manipulation in any manner is accorded proportionately.

According to Manu, the higher classes get special rights and privileges, but special responsibility is also given to them. He further adds that the punishment given to these classes will also vary from those meted out to the other classes. For example, the retribution made for theft should be of the value of eight times in the case of a śudra, sixteen times in the case of a vaiśya, thirty-two times in the case of a kśatriya and sixty-four or even hundred times in the case of a brahmin. This reiterates the point that Indian culture gave to its society a very fair, dynamic, and pragmatic system of rights and duties. (given what is due in terms of rights and duties).

There are similarly four āśramas too in the life of an individual: Brahmachārya, Gṛhastha, Vanaprastha and Sanyāsa. Codes of conduct (dharma) are also specifically enumerated in Manusmṛti for the four stations of an individual's life as given below:

- **Brahmachārya:** bachelor student studying scriptures under the tutelage of a Guru – In this ashram, the individual has the responsibility of his own education and enrichment. The individual learns everything that prepares him for his future life.

- **Gṛhastha:** householder, providing for his family – This aśrama is considered to be a very important one as one individual is responsible for the welfare of many others in the family. According to Manu, the other three aśramas attain fulfilment through this aśrama. The main duties of the individual in this aśrama are: marriage, reproduction, generation of wealth for the family, educating the brahmacharis in the family, rendering service to all in the family and society. During this stage in life, the virtues that are highlighted are –selflessness, caring, sharing, compassion, empathy, self – control, self-restraint, and self-fulfilment.
- **Vānaprastha:** a man preparing for speculation after his offspring is well settled – At this stage, the individual relinquishes his position as head of the family and hands over the duties and responsibilities to his son, who has proved himself capable and responsible. The individual, at this stage, is involved as a counsellor, guide, and friend, to the members in the family and society, with less active participation in worldly affairs. The family and society take advantage of the experience and wisdom of the senior family members. He renounces his passions, and desires, and moves towards activities that take him towards liberation.
- **Sanyāsa:** a stage of renunciation when a man moves away from everything he once loved and concentrates on meditation and study of the Vedas – At this stage, the individual is totally on a spiritual path, moving away from all worldly attachments. Bidding farewell to all his near and dear ones, he starts his journey towards the Ultimate Truth, thus, giving up all stored karmas and saṁskāras.

The word 'āśrama' comes from the Sanskrit root śram 'श्रम्,' meaning 'making an effort,' 'to toil,' 'to exert.' In this sense, every āśrama is a step in the life of the individual towards the final goal of mokṣa. Veda Vyasa, in the Śānti Parvan says that the āśrama system is like a four-rung ladder, that helps a man to climb upwards in the direction of Truth or the Ultimate Reality. At each stage, the individual is supposed to be preparing for the succeeding stage of life. The āśrama system is considered as a means of systematic and consistent change and development in the individual's life, all for his betterment. The concept of varnāśrama-dharma thus gives a complete, integrated, and holistic approach to a man and his philosophy of life.

It is important to note that the various obligations incumbent on members of different varṇas and āśramas mutually support each other, and that an imperfect performance of one's duties without responsibilities harms society—and thus the world—as a whole. Furthermore, these moral obligations are prescribed for the specific varṇas and āśramas and cannot be assumed by a person of another place in society. As the Bhagavad Gīta asserts: 'It is better to perform one's own obligations, svadharma, poorly than to do another's well.' The term svadharma is not to be understood as referring to one's individual or chosen personal obligations and prescribed functions that go with the chosen vocation or role. Rather, svadharma describes an impersonal generic ethical category which encapsulates one's duties determined by one's place in society. For example, all farmers will have the same svadharma and all military officers will have the same svadharma, with no farmer having the same svadharma as the military officer. Svadharma thus embodies the same ethical values as does varṇāśramadharma and the two terms are almost used synonymous.

Āpaddharma is a reference made to 'duty that is determined by an emergency,' 'āpad mūlakaḥ'. If Indian society ever experiences a situation of stress or contingency, it becomes necessary for all individuals to rise to the situation and take over certain unusual duties and help to tide over the situation. However, āpaddharma is a reconciliatory situation as one takes up certain situation-specific duties temporarily, only to go back to one's svadharma after the difficult situation is over. In such circumstances, even that which is considered wrong under normal circumstances is permitted and accepted as dharma, For example, a doctor is expected to sterilise his equipments and instruments before surgery. However, if he is operating to save a life at the battlefield or an accident, then he is permitted to do so even if the instruments are not sterilised. Similarly, the youth is expected to follow the dharma as prescribed for his āṣrama, which is study, but in times of an emergency as war, he is expected to join the army to defend his nation, as it is the need of the hour.

Spirituality presupposes certain qualities of mind, including compassion, gratitude, awareness of a transcendent dimension, and an appreciation for life which brings meaning and purpose to existence.[7]

Most authoritative texts further assert that all people, regardless of their age and occupation, should observe some common moral obligations. An elaborate listing of such responsibilities appears in the Dharmaśāstra, i.e., Smṛti-texts and Nītiśāstra treatises, which notes that everyone must refrain from certain behaviours and positively perform in certain beneficial manners. For example, it is essential that all speak the truth, live a clean and pure life, practice goodwill and benevolence, develop an attitude of forgiving, along with the practice of caring and sharing. One also needs to exercise patience, tolerance, and caution in one's behaviour, in order to avoid injury or harm to others in thought, word or deed.

Dharma in *Upaniṣads* and *Purānas*:

The *Hitopadeśa* lists eight characteristics:

ijyādhyayanadānāni tapaḥ satyam dhṛtiḥ kṣamā
Alobha iti mārgo'yaṇ dharmasyāṣṭavidhaḥ smṛtaḥ !

Sacrifice, study of scriptures, charity, penance, truth, fortitude, forgiveness and absence of greed is the eight fold path of *dharma*.

According to the *Bhagavatapurāna* there are seven characteristics that denote *dharma* in a man:

Ahiṁsā satyam asteyam akāmakrodhalobhatā
Bhūtapriyahitehā ca dharmo' yaṁ sāvavarṇikaḥ !

Non-violence, truth, non-stealing, absence of passion, anger and greed and the desire to do what is good or agreeable to beings is *dharma* for all the castes according to this *purāna*.

Finally, Manu too reduces his list to four virtues that are cardinal and almost imperative for *dharma*. They are:

vedaḥ smṛtḥ sadācāraḥ svasya ca priyam ātmanaḥ
eta c caturvidhaṁ prāhuḥ sākṣād dharmasya lakṣaṇam !

The study of *vedās*, sacred tradition and conduct, the customs of the virtuous men and what is dear to one's own self is *dharma*. Thus, Manu shifts the onus of one's actions on oneself. It becomes man's responsibility to get *vivekajṇāna* with Vedic study. The choice of one's actions as per one's own will determines his *dharmic* nature.

There are many more such lists that can be highlighted in our Indian ethos and culture, as the list is never ending. Such rules or norms of ethics that 'pertain to everybody' are 'sādharaṇadharma' and those that 'are common to all' are called 'sāmānyadharma.' Such universal values norms and duties are said to be 'sanātana' in scope. In a generic sense, they refer to mānavadharma. Sometimes, however, the oblations derived from svadharma contradict or conflict with those derived from sāmānyadharma and sādhāraṇadharma. Then it is the wisdom and maturity of the individual alone that helps in resolving this dilemma.

The best example for this kind of situation is the dilemma faced by Arjuna at Kurukshetra. Arjuna was caught in a situation where his svadharma taught him to behave like a kshatriya and fight his own kith and kin, whereas his sāmānyadharma made him think and deliberate before he fought the battle against his own family and teacher, showing him as an individual with displaced feelings and emotions.

In the managerial context, Dharma talks about justice and fair play by management systems and managerial staff. The concepts of Total Quality, the processes of recycling and waste elimination, the attitude of environmental preservation and protection, Corporate Social Responsibility, Corporate Governance, Social Audit – all display the ethics of the managerial staff and systems in corporate sector. In order to give a man an idea of the vastness and true vision of reality and to help him fathom the structure and inter-connectednes of the universe, the Sastras have expounded Dharma. In addition to this, the Sastras say that one needs to perform his duties or karmas in order to be in tune with Dharma.

The Indian value system outlined is clearly set within the frame of a transcendent ideology – the cutting edge of India's deep structure. It is considered more certain and reliable, unaffected by the changes and shifts in temporal ideologies, as it is based on transcendent realities. If the sequence dharma-artha-kāma-mokṣa is turned around to artha-kāma-dharma-mokṣa, it can lead to disastrous results in the long run. This has been proved by the steep degradation in business ethics, leading to the downfall of various industries. The degeneration of values has only resulted in a downslide in every aspect of man living, be it the family, social group, political system, education, or the nation. The ethical foundation needs to be universally accepted, understood and nurtured for the world to be a better place, with an environment of abundance for all and man wellbeing as its only concern. Indian thought has always worked with the idea of Vasudhaiva Kutumbakam as a major tenet for its core philosophy.

An individual is advised to contain and restrain all emotions that may lead him to a sinful existence or make him undutiful. Thus, he is asked to control such emotions as Kama (lust), Krodha (anger), Lobha (greed), Mada (ego, pride) and Matsara (jealousy). The moral codes of various texts repeatedly emphasize the importance of being aware of these seeming to be ordinary but strong man emotions that lead to the disruptions of a harmonious society.[8] The duties and obligations that are prescribed as guidelines in various systems help a man to be morally wise and pragmatic. As Sage Vyāsa pitifully cried out in the Mahābhārata, almost at the end of all destruction: 'Here with up-raised arms, I have been beseeching that Artha and Kāma can also be attained through Dharma. But alas! Who listens.'

Indian philosophy has always emphasised the Oneness of the Cosmic and Individual soul, leading to the idea of the Unity between all individual souls. It further helps us to understand the Universal brotherhood that is implied between all beings—not only a man and a man, but also a man and nature. Our philosophy and culture, thus, leads us to an ethical dimension of our goals in life. If one has to live with all other beings in peace and harmony, then one needs to understand one's position and role in this life. The knowledge of the dos and don'ts is also dharma, which is called vidhi niṣedhātmaka dharma.

The imperatives of dharma also come to us at times by emulating the wise and the virtuous. A study of the value systems of those who are exemplary in nature and character, and of those who are enlightened and spiritual, and those who are liberated, is of a more pragmatic and simplistic nature. Such guidance sought in the actions of those who 'practice what is right' is called 'sadācāradharma' and of those who 'act according to instructions' for decency or conformity, is called 'siṣṭācāradharma'. This kind of study of dharma is in addition to the derivatives from all sources, including Śrūti and Smṛti.

Śruti and Smṛti are the two significant authorities or sources of knowledge accepted in Indian philosophy, especially in Hinduism. Śruti is the primary authority and Smṛti is the secondary authority. Śruti literally means 'what is heard or revealed' and Smṛti means 'what is remembered.' Śruti implies revelation and Smṛti implies a tradition. Śruti is direct, divine experience whereas, Smṛti is considered to be a narration of the recollection of that experience in a parable form. As the Vedas are believed to have contained knowledge as heard by the rishis directly from the Ultimate Reality, they are called Shrutis. The four Vedās are the most ancient scriptures of the Indians.

The Vedic text comprises of the Mantra Saṁhitas, the ceremonial instructions (Brāhmaṇas), and the philosophical treatises (Āraṇyakās and Upaniṣads). Together these texts constitute the Śrutis. Not all questions of dharma could be resolved through reference to the timeless Śruti. Thus, orthodox philosophers looked to temporal literatures that were called the smṛtis. Smṛtis comprise of the six Vedāṅgas (the ancillary texts and the collections of aphoristic treatises/sūtras that interpret the Vedas), the epics Mahābhārata and Rāmāyāṇa, including the Gīta, and the Puraṇas.

Holy scriptures provide us with insights into Reality that lead us to sublime thoughts. These thoughts suggest purity of and clarity in ideas, the importance of truth and honesty in thought and speech. They also embody nobility and goodness of action. Somewhat later a new genre of literatures known as Dharmaśāstras began to appear, which were specialised works dealing with specific imperatives and problems in Vedic dharma. The most influential of these treatises is probably the Mānava Dharmaśāstra (the laws of Manu) and Yagñavalkya Smṛti which outline the various duties, rights, and responsibilities inherent in traditional Vedic society.

The Vedas are given a lot of significance as they are considered to be Apaurusheya. The Vedas influence Indian thought and culture to a large extent. The religion followed by the majority is called the 'religion of the Vedas' or 'Vaidika Dharma.' The Vedas are, hence, called the Fountainhead of Hinduism. They are supposed to be the oldest records of knowledge and the oldest authority in Indian philosophy.

According to Indian thought, the ṛṣis had a vision of ultimate reality through a penance called Abhaya Jyoti. They manifested this divine experience in the Vedas. The Vedas are thus, based on the intuitive perception of the ultimate reality. According to the Indian thinkers, the Vedas enshrine the eternal and ultimate truths. They are without a beginning and an end. They are the ultimate source to which all religious thought can be traced.

Vedic literature is extremely rich and varied in its content. It has a great significance for the study of the history of philosophy, religion, law, psychology, ethics, aesthetics, language, natural science and finally, of the forms of social life in ancient India. Many categories of modern Indian psychology, ethics and aesthetics can be traced back to the Vedic literature. The Vedās enshrine philosophical tenets which are expounded in pure philosophical form in the Vedānta, the end of the Vedās. They are also called the Upaniṣads, meaning that philosophy which is taught with the student sitting close by to the Guru.

Yoga, with its stress on the theory of Prāṇa, continues to be an established and popular system of self-development and self-realisation till date. The doctrine of the Brahman-Ātman unity lies at the base of all aesthetic theories of the Vedānta, giving a sense of the mystical and the divine in all that is beautiful. Various systems of ethical categories and 'systems of conduct' are developed by Vedānta, Buddhism, Jainism, and other schools, with the basic tenets as dharma, karma, saṁsāra etc. in mind.

A man does not survive and grow as an impersonal unit of existence, where quantitative evaluation justifies his place in the created, mechanistic world alone. He has to be qualitatively accepted, nurtured, and developed. The way a man has changed his lifestyle, his thought processes, his ways of working, his needs and wants, make us blame the sci-tech world, as it seems to have taken a man away from noble living to a world of consumption. 'Everyone has a transcendent dimension, a life of the spirit. This is most directly expressed in religion and the mystic tradition, but the frequency with which people have intense feelings of bonding with groups, ideals, or anything larger and more enduring than the person is evidence of the universality of the transcendent dimension.'[9] In this influential work, Huston Smith explores how the spiritual dimension is a universal aspect of human experience, expressed through religion, mysticism, and deep emotional connections to ideals and communities. He emphasises that spirituality is not confined to formal religious practice but is evident in the human longing for meaning and transcendence.

The ethical flaws of mechanisation were well brought out by Gandhi in his writings. He says, 'I refused to be dazzled by the seeming triumph of machinery. I am uncompromisingly against all destructive machinery. But simple tools and instruments and such machinery as saves individual labour and lightens the burden of million cottages, I should welcome.'[10] In fact, the dependence on technology and mechanisation to such a large extent has made a man seem powerless and victimised. A man should not end up looking like a material object, exclusively aiming at quantitative perfection at the cost of qualitative man excellence. He still has to be clear about his ideas of right and wrong, good, and bad, and the 'ought' and 'is.' The boundaries between the right and evil should not be allowed to disappear, in his race for material prosperity and search for power.

The ideas of Dharma and the Puruṣarthas in Indian thought, help a man to avoid getting into a stage of helplessness and void, as they balance the secular and the spiritual. The blending of the lower and higher purposes and goals in a man's living in Indian thought help him to seek guidelines whenever he is at the crossroads of life. The deterioration of values is the cause of the extinction of races, creeds, and sects in the various parts of the world, and this can be avoided if we rightly recognise and adopt what is given to us in our philosophy and culture. The wisdom of the self-realised individual in Indian society is clearly visible in his ability to discriminate the tangible from the intangible, the transient from the eternal, the phenomenal from the transcendant. Indian culture and thought, thus, has a lot to give to all those who seek. It is all there for the asking.

Today's problems in society and in the corporate sector stem from man straying away from the path of Dharma. Dharma invests well in every profession, every industry, every art, or craft with a design, meaning and a purpose. When understood in this context, earning and possessing wealth is not a crime. In fact, an individual who earns rightly, living and working in the right manner, is looked at with respect. He is said to be on the path of self-development and self-realisation. Wealth is thus, only a means to man's progress, not an end in itself. According to Indian ethos, economic justice is sought through sāmānya dharma. It implies the inculcation of various virtues such as detachment, equality, compassion, fairness, non-stealing, sacrifice and renunciation. These are the universal ethical duties applicable to all people, regardless of their social station, gender, or stage of life.

Man has a special place in Indian thought. A man is born with three things: Consciousness, Conscience, and Freedom of Will. We can understand this perspective given to a man in Indian ethos and culture only if we study and understand the picture of a man as given in the Darṣaṇās, which is discussed by me in the later chapter.

References

1. Dr Radhakrishnan, *Indian Philosophy*, Vol. I, Bharatiya Vidya Bhavan, pp. 505-506.
2. *The Indian Historical Quarterly*, Vol II 3-4, pp. 809, 814, 815, 816.
3. Reference to Laws of Manu 2.9.
4. Sorokin Pitirim, *The Reconstruction of Humanity*.
5. Kulkarni Chidambara, 'Vedic Foundations of Indian Culture'. Shree Dvaipana Trust, Bombay, October 1973.
6. *The Complete Works of Swami Vivekananda*, Volume 5, under the section titled 'Sayings and Utterances'.
7. King, D. B., & Boyatzis, R. E. (2004). Exploring the role of spirituality in the workplace. *Journal of Management, Spirituality & Religion*, 1(2), 107–35.
8. Greene, J. D. (2013). *Moral Tribes: Emotion, Reason, and the Gap Between Us and Them*. Penguin Press.
9. Smith, Huston. *The World's Religions*. Harper One, 2009.
10. Gandhi, M.K. 'The Voice of Truth, Part II, Section VII, Economic Ideas – The Place of Machinery', Navajivan Publishing House.

For Further References

'Ethics in Management and Indian Ethos – Biswanath Ghosh, Chpt 11, 'Sci-tech and Ethics', p. 129. Pub. Vikas Publishing House Pvt. Ltd., 576, Masjid Road, Jangpura, New Delhi – 110014.

Reference to 'The Indian Historical Quarterly Vol. II.3-4, pp. 809, 814-815, 816, - En 954, Law/Ind,11538 to be continued – at Anantacharya Instt.

Dharma and Vedic foundations – The study of Indian History and Culture Vol. IX. En 954 KUL/DHA, 11932.AIRC.

The Essence of Hinduism M.K. Gandhi, Navajivan Publishing House, A'bad. 380014 294.5, Gan,10038 AIRC.

Studies in the Gita Ed. M.D. Paradkar En 2 G 294.5924 Par/Stu 10679 AIRC.

A Study of Hinduism Dharmdeo N. Singh Vikas Publishing House. En 2H Sin/Stu 13312.AIRC.

IV

PSYCHODYNAMICS OF HUMAN PERSONALITY IN INDIAN PHILOSOPHY

Man has always held a special place in Indian thought. The term 'Indian psychology' is a reference to the exposition of Man as a Self, connected to other selves and the Cosmic Self. It is a major shift of paradigm from the understanding of Man as a 'person who feels, perceives and thinks' as given in Western psychology to Man as 'a manifestation of "Brahman", the Supreme Being, the Cosmic Self.' The core competence of every Indian genius is the ability to explore the inner self, going beyond the exploration of Matter and Energy.

The synthesis of scientific study and spiritual study, the study of matter and inherent energy with that of Consciousness, the study of the external world and that of the inner Self alone will lead to the development of Man in the right manner and to the right extent. The Indian insight has to ideally lead the individual self to an awareness that makes it develop, progress and contribute to the Cosmos.

Man, as understood by the *Darśanās,* is the subject matter of Indian Psychology. It is essential to understand the *Sūkṣma* of the individual as much as the *Sthūla.* This is expounded well in the *darśanās* with a shifting emphasis on some of the aspects of human personality, with reference to the essential spiritual nature of man. The differences are seen in the obvious aspects of man and the nomenclature assigned to these aspects, but the essence remains the same in all these thoughts. A majority of these schools take man beyond the temporal and the physical.

Nyāya – Vaiśeṣika: Metaphysics and Ethics

Gotama was the founder of *Nyāya* philosophy in the 4th century BC. He was also known as Gautama and Akshapada. This school of thought is also called *Tarkaśastra*, 'the science of reasoning', *Pramāṇaśāstra*, 'the science of demonstration', *Vādavidyā*, 'the science of debate', and *Anvikṣiki*, 'the science of critical study'. It is primarily concerned with the conditions of valid reasoning. *Nyāya* deals with metaphysical problems such as the nature of the phenomenal, physical world. It also discusses the nature of the human soul and the nature of the Ultimate Reality.

Gotama was the author of *Nyāya-sūtra*. Vatsayana in 4th century AD wrote a commentary on it which was the *Nyāya-Bhāṣya*. Vacaspati Miṣra later brought out a commentary on it called the *Nyāya – Vartikā – Tatparya – Tika*.

Nyāya enumerates sixteen philosophical topics, *padārthās*. They are:

1. The means of right knowledge – *pramāṇa*
2. The objects of right knowledge – *prameya*
3. Doubt – *saṁṣaya*
4. The end or motive of action – *prayojana*
5. Illustrative example – *dṛṣtānta*
6. Accepted conclusion – *siddhānta*
7. Constituent propositions of a syllogism – *avayava*
8. Hypothetical reasoning – *tarka*
9. Ascertainment of truth – *nirṇaya*
10. Debate or discussion – *vāda*
11. Disputation – *jalpa*
12. Wrangling/ / irrational argument – *vitaṇḍā*
13. Fallacy – *hetvābhāsa*
14. Quibble – *chchala*
15. Casuistry – *jāti*
16. Point of the opponent's defeat – *nigrahasthāna*

Pramāna or means of right knowledge are of four kinds –

- perception/ *pratyakṣa*
- inference/ *anumāna*
- comparison or analogy/
- *upamāna*, and testimony/ / śabda

Prameyās or the objects of right knowledge are –

- soul
- body
- sense organs
- physical objects
- apprehension
- mind
- activity
- defects
- rebirth
- fruition
- pain

- release

Saṁshaya or doubt is any knowledge of the self that one is unsure or uncertain of, any knowledge that leads man to various alternatives or options that one needs to choose from but is incapable of doing. Doubt, unlike erroneous perception, is merely indefinite or inadequate knowledge, not error or false knowledge.

Prayojana or motive is the end that induces a person to act. It is the final cause of action, not the efficient cause. According to *Nyāya*, the primary end of all action is either attainment of pleasure or avoidance of pain. But liberation from both pleasure and pain is what *Nyāya* advocates.

***Nyāya* is that philosophy that 'leads the mind to a conclusion'. *Nyāya* is normally linked with *Vaiśeṣika*, which is regarded as '*Samānatantra*', implying similarity in thought. *Nyāya* is more epistemological in its philosophy and *Vaiśeṣika* is more metaphysical and ontological. Together, the twin schools give an exposition of the entire universe of which the individual is a significant part.**

Nyāya–Vaiśeṣika reduces the Universe into seven categories/ / padārthas. They are:

1. Substance – *Dravya*
2. Attribute – *Guṇa*
3. Activity – *Karma*
4. Generality – *Sāmānya*
5. Individuality – *Viśeṣa*
6. Inherence – *Samavāya*
7. Non-existence – *Abhāva*

The Substance or *Dravya* is further classified into nine. They are:

- earth/ *pṛtvī*
- water/ *jala*
- fire/ *teja*
- air/ *vāyu*
- ether
- time/ *kāla*
- space/ *ākāśa*
- soul/ *ātman*
- mind/ *manas*

Of these, the first seven serve as the substratum for the physical or material world and the last two are depicted as constituents of human personality.

According to *Nyāya-Vaiśeṣika*, the three primary factors that are significant in the making of human personality are: *Ātman*, *Manas*, and *Śarira*, along with the organs of cognition (*jñānendriyas*) and the organs of action (*karmendriyas*). *Nyāya* advocates Naive Realism, and **its realistic ontology provides adequate basis for psychodynamics of the human personality. It hence becomes almost mandatory for one to understand the constituents that determine personality.**

Nyāya believes that human personality requires the Self/Soul (used synonymously for *Ātman*) as its pivot, as it is the substratum for all cognitions, feelings, and conations of the individual. The existence of the soul needs no proof as it is expounded that the soul's existence is indicated by man's experience of desire (*icchā*), aversion or dislike (*dveṣa*), effort (*prayatna*), pleasure (*sukha*), pain (*dukha*), and cognition. The nature of all these attributes being psychic, their mainstay, *āśraya*, has to be something other than the physical body. This leads us to the indubitable acceptance of the Soul/ Self. ***Nyāya* proves the existence of the soul with its method of inference/ *tarka*.**

On the other hand, *Vaiśeṣika* believes that the soul is directly perceived. The very intuition experienced by man of his own 'I' is proof that it exists. It signifies the egoism of the individual, where egoism is understood in the sense of 'individuation', not as is used by modern psychologists to mean an attitude. As each individual experiences the Universe and life differently, the existence of many souls is accepted in *Vaiśeṣika*. The plurality of the souls is established by the diversity and variety in experiences that are observed in individuals. Each individual feels and senses his own ego.

Nyāya-Vaiśeṣika accept that the soul is eternal, *nitya*, and indestructible, *anaśvara*. It is *vibhū*, meaning all-pervading. It has intelligence as its *guṇā*, quality and is not intelligent itself. It assumes the role of the knower, and is not the known, and is hence, identified as the subject of knowledge, not the object. As R.P. Sharma mentions in his book, *Human Personality in Ancient Indian Thought*, *Nyāya* gives us the idea of 'the Intelligised Self'.[1] This leads us to the acceptance of *Ahaṁkāra*, the ego-sense. It is neither the body, nor the mind, nor the senses. However, it has the mammoth task of controlling all these and synthesising their activities, in order to arrive at the unification and integration of all cognition and action.

Every individual is considered as unique and peculiar than the others in *Nyāya-Vaiśeṣika* as in all other schools of Indian thought. The essence or substratum of all creation being the same, the differences between the created beings is said to be determined by the *Adṛṣta*, the Unseen power of *Karma*. The Law of *Karma* determines the birth, the qualities, the capabilities and limitations, the status and positions because of the karmic residuum carried by every soul in its journey of transmigration. This lends peculiarity, novelty and particularity to every individual born, giving each one an identity.

According to the *Nyāya Bhāṣya*, it is the Self/ Soul that is seeing, enjoying, knowing, and experiencing in life. Knowing, feeling, and willing are the qualities of the Self. As the Self is the mainstay, *āśraya*, of all human endeavours and the repository of all mental propensities, instincts, desires, and mental dispositions that arise due to *saṁskārās*, it is considered to be responsible for governing the mind and the senses. The Soul perceives through the senses and functions later on the basis of its perceptions because of the intervention of the mind. This activity of the soul in conjunction with the senses and the mind, *manas*, is responsible for the birth and arousal of the individual consciousness. Hence, knowing, feeling, and willing are modes of consciousness. *Nyāya* regards the individual self as different from the Supreme Self/ Soul or God. It regards the Self as the knower or the ego. Cognition is not an activity or the *karma* of Self but is its quality/ / guṇā.

The Mind or *Manas* of *Nyāya-Vaiśeṣika* is similar to the *antaḥkaraṇa* of *Sāṁkhya-Yoga*. It is the internal sense organ or the 'sixth sense' as it is called and is responsible for the reception, assimilation, integration, and interpretation of all cognition done by the external sense organs. The Mind/ *Manas* is an intermediary organ that transmits all cognition from the *jñānendriyās* to the Soul, progressively interpreting them all in succession, facilitating the Soul to transmit back through the Mind the instructions to all *karmendriyās* and other organs to act accordingly. Mind is not, however, an independent perceiver as it is the Soul that really perceives. According to *Nyāya-Vaiśeṣika*, *Manas* is the totality of the inner organ similar to the '*antaḥkaraṇa*' of *Saṁkhya* philosophy.

Just as we accept the plurality of the Souls, we also believe that there is an independent mind for everybody. The Mind is eternal, but not all-pervading. It has no magnitude, as it is atomic. It is, hence, indestructible. The mind defies perception and as a result, constitutes the subjective side of the individual, with the body and its various senses, and the physical objects constituting the objective world.

The mind has the function of helping the soul to perceive and experience the phenomenal world. The individual has his life determined only to the extent of his birth and hereditary aspects, as earlier depicted with the influence of the *adṛṣta*. Once developed as an individual with *viveka*, he exercises his freedom of will. The mind is above and beyond the purview of volition by itself, but it can still be influenced and changed by the approach of volition. Mind is condemned as fickle and restless. It leads to changes and modifications within it, and these are the *vṛttis* that are discussed in *Yoga*. The cessation of the modifications of the *citta* self is the objective of *Yoga*. As mind is not destroyed even when the body dies, it is believed to accompany the soul on its journey while transmigrating into a new body. Hence, it carries with it the impressions or *saṁskāras* of the previous birth. The individual's instinctive behaviour and innate tendencies are normally attributed to these impressions.

There are various functions attributed to the Mind/ *Manas*. To name a few, they are recalling, storage of memories, verbal cognition, doubt, dream, imagination, inference, intuition, desire, rest and leisure, and perception of pain and pleasure. The production of cognition, pain and pleasure, desire, aversion, effort, volition, and impression after experience—all associated with the *Manas*. As the *Manas* is not all-pervading, though eternal, it leads us to accept that every individual has his own Mind/ *Manas*. This leads us to the idea that each individual has his own way of looking at objects and beings, even life situations. The subjective element in perception is revealed here. It now goes without saying that the *Manas* is very important in determining the volition and action of the individual.

The physical existence of man needs no proof. According to *Nyāya-Vaiśeṣika*, the body/ *Śarira* is an important factor in human personality. It is composed of four basic elements, namely, earth, water, fire, air. The concept of body in these schools of thought is wide to encompass even the inanimate bodies as much as the animate, including flora and fauna. Here, the reference is more to the living bodies, more specifically, the human beings that are of relevance to us.

As the body is the locus of senses and the *sukṣma śarīra*, the perception of all objects and beings that gives rise to experience is traced back to the sense organs in the *sthūla śarīra*. The *śarīra* is the field or vehicle for the experiences of the Soul. The resonance of pain and pleasure is seen in the physical body, expressed with the help of the motor organs, resulting in conation and volition.

Gotama does not recognise any difference between intellect and apprehension, i.e. between *Buddhi* and *Upalabdhi*. *Buddhi* is merely serving the Soul as an agent that manifests the object to the soul. It is hence, called as *arthaprakāśa*. Knowledge that arises is not considered as a *vṛtti* of *Buddhi* as in *Sāṁkhya*, but it is a subjective reality corresponding to the objective universe.

Nyāya-Vaiśeṣika believes that human potentiality and abilities are essential and are means to achieve liberation. **The school propounds that right volition leading to the right action at the right time can release man from the shackles of pain and pleasure.** This, in *Nyāya-Vaiśeṣika*, is *Mokṣa*, unlike the other schools of Indian thought that talk of absolute freedom. The Summum Bonum in *Nyāya-Vaiśeṣika* is the realisation that there is release from sufferings that are caused by empirical existence and worldly experience. This is possible only with valid knowledge or *pramā* that comes with the help of the accepted *pramāṇās* of the school. There has to be a proper appreciation of the good and bad, the right and wrong in life, with the awareness of the force of the *adṛṣta* that binds man in the cycle of life and death. The *kārmic* residuum in human life is responsible for all suffering. The objective of man in life should ideally be the achievement of valid knowledge that will give him the sense of discrimination. One should aim at the attainment of the highest and ultimate good, the *Nihśreyasa*.

Sāṁkhya-Yoga: Metaphysics and Ethics

Another *Āstika darṣaṇā*, the *Sāṁkhya* school, brings in a dualistic view of Reality, thus deviating from the monistic view of Reality as given in some of the schools of Indian thought.

The *Sāṁkhya* system represents one of the more interesting systems in Indian thought and religion. Although the system by itself, in its original form, is no longer a living force in contemporary Indian culture, the system has exerted a long–lasting influence in the development of thought. Moreover, *Sāṁkhya* is given its due respect and importance for the impact that it has had on the complementary system of *Yoga*, which blends the metaphysics of *Sāṁkhya* and develops its own philosophical thought and practice. Many of the terms and notions of the system are used in many other systems in Indian thought.

The term, '*Sāṁkhya*' appears to be derived from the root word, '*khya*,' together with the prefix, '*saṁ*', meaning 'reckoning', 'summing up', 'numeration', 'calculation', etc. Many thinkers see the term primarily as a designation for the notion of 'number', from which the later ideas of 'enumeration', 'investigation' and 'analysis' were derived.[2] According to Richard Garbe, *Sāṁkhya* is that school or system which emphasises the enumeration of principles, evolutes or emergents. On the one hand, says Jacobi, '*Sāṁkhya*' refers to those who define a concept by setting forth or enumerating its content. On the other hand, some thinkers propound that '*Sāṁkhya*' refers to those who investigate or analyse the various categories of existence. The term '*Sāṁkhya*' refers to those who seek the ultimate 'discrimination' or 'discernment' of the difference between *Prakrti* and *Purusa*.[3] In other words, the word is sometimes understood to mean the ultimate goal of salvation of the system. The only reasonable conclusion in all this is to suggest that the term '*Sāṁkhya*' refers primarily to the idea of 'number' or 'enumeration' but that it also signifies those who reason or analyse by means of the enumeration of categories.

According to tradition, the founder of *Sāṁkhya* is believed to be Kapila, (c. 6th-5th century BC). He is also considered to be the author of *Sāṁkhya-sutrās*. The *Sāṁkhya-sutrās* were lost, so it makes it imperative that one refers to the later sources– Īśvarakrṣṇa's *Sāṁkhya-Karika* (3rd–4th century AD), Vācaspati Miśra's *Sāṁkhya Tattva Kaumudī* (9th century) and others. One is yet to know the original texts of *Sāṁkhya* philosophy, which gives an original exposition of the thought processes of the founder. Many compilations and commentaries are more easily available on his works. The two significant and relevant compilations that I have considered here are: *Sāṁkhyakārika* of Īśvarakṛṣṇa and the *Pātañjala Sāṁkhya* by Patañjali. The philosophical system of *Sāṁkhya* as expounded by Kapila has been elaborately explained by Īsvarakṛṣṇa, in its ontological, epistemological, and ethical aspects. *Sāṁkhya* brings in a duality in the concept of Reality. According to *Sāṁkhya*, there are two all-pervasive ultimate realities or principles: Pure Consciousness, *Purūṣa* and the Pure, Primordial Matter, *Prakṛti* (also known as *mūlaprakṛti*). Primordial matter is made of three constituents called *Guṇās* – *Sattva*, *Rajas,* and *Tamas*.

Kapila's basic thesis is that the world is made of matter. Matter (*prakṛti*) is the basis of everything that is. It is omnipresent, eternal and one. The inherent motion of *Prakṛti* is as eternal as *Prakṛti* itself. Primordially, *Prakṛti* has no external cause, as there are no beginning and no end for *Prakṛti*, matter. Kapila expounds the view that the material, phenomenal world has evolved out of *Prakṛti*. *Prakṛti* may be defined as the First Cause of the world and is, hence called Primordial Matter forming the basis for the manifold universe. It is the first cause of everything except *Puruṣa*. It is the universal principle which accounts for everything physical in terms of matter and force. Even Space and Time are considered as aspects of *Prakṛti*. This is an important idea as it proves that *Prakṛti*, in its original and primary form, is beyond Space and Time. The nature of *Prakṛti* is derived from the various objects that are observed in the universe. It is hence, called as the Material and Root Cause of all things. It is also known as *Pradhāna* or *Avyakta*. It is the unintelligent but eternal principle, from where the entire creation emanates and evolves. During the stage of dissolution, at the beginning of the *Sṛśti*, *Prakṛti* is in a state of equipoise or equilibrium, *samyāvasthā*. It is non-sentient and unconscious but is active. It is the substratum of evolution.

The other parallel and co-eternal Reality accepted in *Sāṁkhya* is that of *Puruṣa*, the Pure Spirit or Consciousness. Unlike *Prakṛti*, *Puruṣa* is not matter. It is different from the body and the senses, the mind, and the intellect. It is not an object but a subject of knowledge. *Puruṣa* is not composed of any *guṇās*. *Puruṣa* is described as a discriminating but inactive, conscious but motionless ultimate principle of reality. The feeling of one's own existence is the most natural and indubitable feeling that one all have and that itself is the proof for the existence of *Puruṣa* or self. *Puruṣa* is Pure Consciousness, which implies that Consciousness is its very essence. It is beyond change or activity. It is without beginning and an end. It is subtle, omnipresent, perceptive, without qualities, and eternal. It is the seer, the experiencer, but not an agent of activity.

The relation between *Prakṛti* and *Puruṣa* is the crux of the *Sāṁkhya* philosophy. *Puruṣa* that is inactive is said to be responsible for the activity within the *Prakrti*. *Puruṣa* moves the *Prakṛti* without moving itself. The moment *Puruṣa* comes in contact with *Prakṛti*, the three *Guṇās* of *Prakṛti* are disturbed from their state of equilibrium. They form various combinations, thus giving rise to various evolutes. The question that is normally asked of a *Sāṁkhya* philosopher is: If *Puruṣa* is inactive, how is it considered to be responsible for the movement of *Prakṛti*? The answer given by the *Sāṁkhya* philosophers is thus: Just as the magnet attracts iron by its mere proximity, in the same manner *Puruṣa* disturbs the equilibrium of the *guṇās* by its mere proximity. The magnet is an unmoved mover, just as the *Puruṣa* is the unmoved mover in the case of *Prakṛti*.

Another analogy that is normally given to explain the relation of two opposed principles as *Puruṣa* and *Prakṛti* is that of a blind and a disabled man. A disabled man cannot walk but can see, and *Puruṣa* is said to be like that. A blind man can walk but cannot see, just as *Prakṛti*. *Puruṣa* is conscious but inactive and it requires *Prakṛti* to realise itself through experience. *Prakṛti* is active but unconscious and it requires *Puruṣa* to guide it in its activities.

Prakṛti is made of three constituents, the *Guṇas: Sattva*, *Rajas* and *Tamas* that are viewed not as the qualities of *Prakṛti* but as its components. *Sattva* symbolises light, virtue, intelligibility, purity, and goodness. *Rajas* stands for passion, restlessness, movement, and activity. *Tamas* symbolises darkness, inertia, ignorance, and inactivity. *Sattva* or Goodness is of endless variety, such as lightness, calmness, contentment, patience, joy etc. In short, *sattva* is anything that gives lasting happiness. *Rajas* symbolises passion of endless variety, such as excitement, restlessness, agitation, excessive activity, etc. It signifies pain. *Sattva* is regarded as something light and illuminating; *rajas*, motivating and mobile; *tamas*, heavy and restraining. Analysis of the *Sāṁkhya* philosophy shows that in effect *sattva* is potential consciousness; *rajas*, the source of motion, action, and development; and *tamas* is that which restrains action and slows down development.

In the process of evolution, matter does not increase or decrease quantitatively. Matter cannot be created or destroyed. The sum total of all matter, of all its actual or potential states, always remains constant. Matter is in a state of eternal motion. This leads us to the fact that any growth or decay, or even any withering away is nothing but the transformation of matter. There is a kind of transition from the past into the present, from the present into the future, from unmanifest to manifest and from potentiality to actuality. Redistribution of mass and energy accounts for the diversity in the created world. The idea that matter does not grow or diminish quantitatively but is merely redistributed in the process of emergence and destruction of objects is considered to be one of the strokes of genius of ancient Indian thinkers. It reflects an anticipation of the later scientific discoveries. In a more general form, this view is a distinct expression of the idea of the 'law of conservation of the mass of substance' as it is known to modern natural sciences.

The theory of evolution came to be known and accepted by the Western thinkers only in the latter half of the nineteenth century. This important principle though formulated first, with the recognition of gradation in the animal life was found to have a far-reaching application practically extending to all departments of life. The theory of evolution was known and adopted by three of the six systems of Indian philosophy, namely, *Saṁkhya*, *Yoga* and the *Vedānta*, even before the beginning of the Christian era. What is significant and relevant here is that evolution has been accepted as a principle operating, not only at the physical plane, but also in the field of spiritual living and progress. In the *Yoga* system, as in the *Vedānta*, the spiritual progress is accompanied by the psychological reconstruction of an individual.

The *guṇās* are a kind of primary principles:

- *sattva*, the conscious principle
- *rajas*, energy
- *tamas*, gross and dense mass

Everything in nature is charged with these three basic principles. The essential and necessary relation between them is evident in the fact that energy does not exist without mass, and conscious phenomena cannot exist without energy. The process of evolution begins with the individual particles of the three forces, indifferently scattered through primary matter, being gathered together into wholes with the force of natural affinity. This results in the formation of bodies distinct from one another that are gradually formed with the non-uniform pressure falling on the various parts of primordial matter.

The theory of the three *Guṇās* is peculiar to the *Sāṁkhya* school of thought. The impulse to everything in nature, the cause of all life and variety, is ascribed to the three *Guṇās*. *Guṇā* means quality in the ordinary sense of the term. However, according to Kapila, *Guṇās* are the constituents and properties themselves of the primordial matter. The significance of the *Guṇās* is that being the component constituents, they determine the essential qualities of all that has evolved from the primordial first cause. In the most general sense, they represent no more than thesis, antithesis and then something between the two. For example, they form combinations that spell cold, warm and neither cold nor warm; or bright, dark and neither bright nor dark, and so on. The three *guṇās*, constituting the basis of any object or phenomenon, are inseparably connected and mutually condition one another. They are said to be connected as closely as the flame, the wick, and the oil.

The character of all creation in the Universe is determined in accordance with the excess of one or the other of these *Guṇās*. All three *guṇās* are significant due to the role they play in the created world. Without *Sattva*, Nature/Universe would be nothing better than a blind force acting in a haphazard manner. Without *Rajas* there would be absolutely no activity or motion in the Universe, for mere *Sattva* or enlightenment would not move with inert *Tamas*. Without *Tamas*, the Universe would be absolutely an increasing round of activity due to *Rajas*, even if the activity were guided by *Sattvic guṇa*. *Tamas* alone provides the required stability to the Universe, as it comes as a restraining/ resisting agency, due to its inert tendency.

Sattva is the superlative state of serenity, selflessness, efficiency, and power. It is the state of contemplation when one attains enlightenment and discriminative knowledge. A *sāttvic* individual is normally absorbed in thoughts of the higher purposes. He will be motivated by noble intentions, continuously doing activities that benefit humanity at large. *Sattva* helps to broaden one's outlook and approach, thereby managing to break barriers that one has, emotionally and mentally. It helps man to break away the fetters of laziness, lethargy, and complacency. *Sattva* helps one to be proactive, thus helping the individual to think lateral, be creative and divergent in thought, seeking solutions to problems rather than shirking difficult situations.

A *sattvic* individual functions without agitation, stress, tension, or anxiety. He manages to achieve excellence for himself, with no personal stakes to bind him. This state of excellence comes to him effortlessly as he is self-confident and self-respecting. Work itself is worship for him. The *sāttvika* person excels due to his state of freedom, as neither does the carrot tempt him, nor is he scared of the stick. Every *sāttvika* individual feels empowered, and the more *sāttvika* individuals in an organisation, the more will the individual progress and the organisation run effectively and smoothly. It leads all to be strategic in thought and planning. Fortifying an organisation with *sāttvika* members in a majority, especially members at the top levels of management, steers the organisation towards prosperity and development. The all-round development of the individual leads to the growth of the society and organisation, thereby leading to the wellbeing and wealth of the nation. The discriminative knowledge of *sattva* helps to elicit the best in oneself and others to the maximum. If one were to be dominated by *tamas* and *rajas*, then the core competence and talents go wasted.

In Indian thought, evolution is considered to be a result of the Unseen Power consisting of merits and demerits of the individual souls, which would bear fruit as enjoyments/ sufferings to be experienced by the souls. The *Sāṁkhya* theory of evolution is not mechanical but teleological. As the *Kārika* said, the cause of the world is the relation of the *Puruṣa*, the Conscious principle, with the *Prakṛti*, the Active principle. The *Sāṁkhyas* hold that *prakṛti* is the substratum of the changing phenomena of the world. In a state of equilibrium, the *guṇās* are homogenous in nature. When *Puruṣa* comes in proximity with *Prakṛti*, this equilibrium is disturbed, giving rise to heterogeneous effects. Thus, evolution begins. The vast and varied nature of *Prakṛti* slowly unfolds itself. In the process of evolution, twenty-four principles emerge, and they form the basis of the manifold world. *Puruṣa* is always outside the realm of change, but it wrongly identifies itself with the created world, i.e. *Prakṛti* and its evolutes, namely, the psycho-physical body in which it lives. *Sāṁkhya* starts with two realities: matter and spirit. Hence, it is considered more realistic. Yet, it concludes with a state when matter, as a mutable evolvent, does not exist for the released spirit. The central teaching of the *Sāṁkhya* system is that reality is two-fold: *Puruṣa*, the Spirit and *Prakṛti*, Matter. *Puruṣa* is manifold, pure, and changeless, whereas *Prakṛti* is primarily one, ever mutable.

The individual spirit is responsible for the purpose of evolution. Evolution is undertaken for the benefit of the spirit. The spirit does not control the presence by any actual contact. The mere presence of it is sufficient to disturb the equipoise of the constituents of *Prakṛti*, thus inducing change and evolution.

Sāṁkhya lays down a four-fold classification of categories based on their respective causal and productive efficiency. They are:

- Uncaused but Productive.
- Productive and Produced.
- Produced.
- Neither Produced nor Productive.

In the first category, we have *Prakṛti*, which is itself uncaused but is the cause for everything else in this world. *Prakṛti* is the only productive agent. The cause of all causes and effects, *prakṛti*, has no cause. The products are, hence, dependent, while *prakṛti* is independent. The products are many in number, limited in space and time, while *prakṛti* is One, All-pervading and Eternal. In the second category, one classifies *Buddhi* or *Mahat* and *Ahaṇkāra*. In the third category of the produced but the non-productive, one has the sense-organs, the motor-organs, and the *Pancamahābhutās*. In the last category, of the non-productive and the non-produced, one has *Puruṣa*.

List of the twenty-five tattvas in *Saṁkhya* philosophy:

- *Prakṛti*, as *Avyakta*, the unmanifested non-differentiated principle
- *Buddhi*
- *Ahaṁkāra*
- *Manas*
- *Jñānendriyās* – five sense organs
- *Karmendriyās* – five motor organs
- The five *Tanmātras*
- *Mahābhutas* – five basic elements
- *Purūṣa*, Spirit or Self

According to *Sāṁkhya*, the entire world evolves from the influence on *prakṛti* by *puruṣa*. It is rather a sort of effective relationship through which *prakṛti* is influenced by the mere presence of *puruṣa*. Evolution cannot occur by Self/ *puruṣa* alone because the Self is inactive, nor can it be initiated only by *prakṛti* because *prakṛti* is not conscious. The activity of *prakṛti* needs to be guided by the intelligence of *puruṣa* for the evolution of the universe. With the proximity of *puruṣa* and *prakṛti*, a great disturbance arises in the equilibrium in which the *gunas* are held prior to manifestation. In this, *rajas*, which is considered the active force is stimulated and agitated, leading to the other two *gunas* activated and vibrating, with a display of energy. This vibration releases a tremendous amount of energy within *Prakṛti*, thus manifesting the universe in various grades and degrees. The process of manifestation originates from the unmanifested unity and completes its cycle in twenty-four stages. The process of manifestation begins with the proximity of *puruṣa* with *prakṛti*.

Mahat or Buddhi

The first evolute of *Prakṛti* is *Mahat* (great one) or *Buddhi* the intellect. *Mahat* is the state in which *prakṛti* receives light from *puruṣa*, the fountain of light, and sees itself, and this process of seeing is the beginning of the manifestation of the universe. The individual counterpart of this cosmic state is *buddhi*, the finest aspect of a human being that has the capacity to know the entire personality in its full purity. *Buddhi* is manifested from the *sattvic* aspect of *Prakṛti* because of the nature of *sattva*—brightness, clarity, and lightness—is affected sooner by the active force of manifestation than would be the heavy and unclear nature of *tamas*. Because of the *sattvic* quality of *buddhi*, the light of the Self reflects in the intellect similar to the way an external object reflects in the clear surface of the mirror. The Self, seeing its reflection in the mirror of *buddhi*, identifies itself with the reflected image and forgets its true nature. Thus, the feeling of I-ness is transmitted to *buddhi*. In this way the unconscious *buddhi* starts functioning as a conscious principle.

According to *Sāṁkhya* system, *buddhi* possesses the following eight qualities:

- righteousness (*dharma*)
- knowledge (*jñāna*)
- detachment (*vairāgya*)
- excellence (*aiśvarya*)
- non-righteousness/ vice (*adharma*)
- ignorance (*ajñāna*)
- attachment (*rāga*)
- imperfection or incompetence (*anaiśvarya*)

The first four are the *sattvic* forms of *buddhi* while the last four are overpowered by inertia (*tamas*).

The pure Self falsely identifies with *buddhi* and thereby thinks it is experiencing what *buddhi* is experiencing. Due to the arousal of *viveka jñāna* with the *sattvic* attribute of *buddhi*, *puruṣa* comes to realise its false identification with *buddhi's* objects and to recognise its transcendent nature in all its purity. Thus, *buddhi*, the psychic instrument, stands nearest to the Self enabling it to discriminate between itself and *prakṛti* and thereby achieve realisation of its liberated nature.

Ahaṅkāra

The sense of *Ahaṅkāra* is a derivative of *mahat* or *buddhi*. It is the property of individualisation that generates a boundary of 'I-ness'. It is often translated as 'ego', a western concept that refers to an exaggerated sense of self-importance but *ahaṅkāra* is a much broader concept. It refers to the sense of 'I' that separates one's own self from all others and creates an individual entity.

There are three categories of *ahaṅkāra—sattvika*, *rajasika* and *tamasika*—determined by the *guṇa* that is predominant in the *ahaṅkāra*. It is called *vaikārika* when *Sattva* dominates. In its cosmic form, the eleven evolutes that arise from *sattvika ahaṅkāra* are: the five sense organs—hearing, touching, seeing, tasting, and smelling; the five motor organs—speech, apprehension, locomotion, excretion, and procreation; and the mind- *manas*. When viewed psychologically, it gives rise to buoyancy and illumination. In its *tāmasiç* form, the five *tanmatras* or subtle elements are sound, touch, colour, taste, and smell are derived. When viewed psychologically, it produces idleness and sloth. The function of the *rajasic* element of *ahaṅkāra* is to energise and activate the other two *gunas*, towards evolution of the eleven organs/ *indriyās*, with the energy that it provides. It does not produce anything exclusively but is responsible for the other two functioning effectively. This explanation of the manifestation of *ahaṅkāra* is based on the *Sāṁkhya-karika*, the major text of *Saṁkhya* philosophy.

Manas

It is again a part of the *antaḥkaraṇa*, the internal organ. It has the task of synthesising the sense-data into percepts. As it has the characteristic of both the sensory and the motor organs, it suggests the course of action and exercises the volition of the individual. *Manas* is said to be the doorkeeper as it determines what to perceive, and how to interpret perceptions. Moreover, 'the decree of the will'[4] is duly carried out by the *Manas* when it turns sensations into determinate perceptions, presenting them to the *Ahaṁkāra* and *Buddhi*, with the discriminating principle as the guiding factor.

According to *Sāṁkhya* philosophy, the mind is neither atomic nor eternal, but is a product of *Prakṛti*, and is therefore subject to origin and dissolution. The cognitive senses contact their objects and supply their stimulations to the mind, which then interprets the data into determinate perceptions. *Ahaṅkāra* then claims the objects of the world, identifying itself with the desired ones while rejecting the undesired ones, and finally the intellect decides whether to pursue or avoid those external objects.

The five *tanmatras* of sound, touch, colour, taste, and smell are the extremely subtle sources of the gross elements; they can be inferred but not perceived. They evolve after the senses come into being and they are the cause of the five gross elements, which are derived in a gradual step-by-step process. First to evolve is the *tanmatra* that is the essence of sound or *sabda*, from which in turn the ether or *akasa*, the space element is derived, and its specific property is sound, sensed by ears. The air element is derived from the essence of touch or *sparsa tanmatra* that combines with that of sound or *sabda*. It has the quality of sound with its specific quality of touch, sensed by the skin. The fire element is derived from the essence of colour or *rupa tanmatra*. It combines the qualities of sound, touch, colour, and its special property is sight, which is sensed by the eyes. The water element is derived from the essence of taste or *rasa tanmatra*. All three preceding qualities—sound, touch, colour—are found in it, as well as its special quality, taste, which is sensed by the tongue. The essence of smell or *gandha tanmatra*, is produced by the earth element, whose special property is odour, which is sensed by the nostrils. The physical body is also one of the main co-ordinates of human personality. It is the *sthūla śarīra* that is said to have evolved due to the effect of *Tamas*. Thus, many thinkers opine that the objective aspect of human personality is due to *Tamas* and the subjective element of the same stems from *Sattva*.

Thus, the course of evolution takes place in stages. It starts from the root cause, *Prakṛti* and ends with the earth element, the grossest manifestation. This process is broken down into two major categories: the development of *Prakṛti* as *buddhi*, *ahankara* and the eleven senses and the evolution of the five subtle and gross elements. The mixing and matching of the three *guṇās* in the disturbed state give rise to the process of production and the resultant products. The diversity of the products is thus rendered explicable. The kind of product is determined by the *guṇa* that predominates.

Sāṁkhya philosophy, as one knows it from the *kārikās* and *sūtrās*, begins at once with the recognition of the existence of the three kinds of pains or suffering and leads to the complete cessation of all pain and suffering as its highest goal. There exists, in the normal state of the individual, identification between the embodied individual spirit and the mental processes. On the one hand, the embodied spirit appears as if it was the mental processes and manifests itself in the form of the said processes. On the other hand, the spirit identifies itself with the doer and assumes itself to be the agent of the said processes. So long as this erroneous identification persists, the individual embodied spirit remains in bondage. This erroneous identification of the Self only results in suffering.

***Sāṁkhya*, in fact, talks of three kinds of sufferings for man**. They are:

- *Ādhyātmika*
- *Ādhibautika*
- *Ādhidaivika*

Ādhyātmika pains include pains that are bodily and mental. They refer to all miseries that stem from oneself, such as physical pains, diseases, worries, anxieties, stresses, fears, desires, avarice, envy, grief, affection, love, and attachment, and all such pains, where one is responsible for oneself. They are called intrinsic as they give rise to pains that need to be treated with internal remedies. *Ādhibhautika* pains are extrinsic pains as they are caused by men, beasts, birds, reptiles, and inanimate things. *Ādhidaivika* pains are pains that are caused due to the evil influence of planets, spirits, etc.

The *Sāṁkhya* philosophers hold that there is a triad of pain that is existent. The removal of pain is desirable, and the removal of all three kinds of pain is possible through man's efforts. All physical pains and diseases can be cured temporarily with the intake of medicines and treatment that is both physiological and psychological. Mental disturbances can be treated by medicines used for calming and stabilising the individual. People with such disturbances may also seek respite by indulgence in 'distractors' that lead to temporary satisfaction and ego-boost for the individual, more so with the idea of escaping a difficult situation. Sometimes, the individual takes the help of some charms, or Godmen, or ritualistic activities to keep themselves psychologically steady and stable. But all these remedies are found to be temporary, with a recurrence of the pains.

The principal aim of life is to attain release from all these kinds of pain. The self-realised individual alone manages to escape the vagaries of life's miseries due to his freedom from the shackles of pain and pleasure. He learns to discriminate the phenomenal and the temporal from Pure Consciousness, thereby remaining unaffected.

Man manages to survive and progress despite all these pains, as he has the power of knowledge in his hands. It is, however, necessary to go beyond the knowledge that is given by the empirical sciences in order to alleviate the pain more permanently. **There has to be a cure that is more lasting and more permanent. This can come only with a study of the scriptures with a spirit of scientific enquiry.** The right way to eliminate or manage pain is with the help of discriminative knowledge, the knowledge that helps to discriminate the empirical from the transcendental, the temporary from the permanent, the transient from the eternal, and the material from the spiritual. The knowledge that one gains from this school of thought is discriminative knowledge or *viveka-jñāna*, and this knowledge helps man to exercise his freedom of will choose the right and good and eliminate the wrong and evil.

The relation of the *Sāṁkhya* school of philosophy to the *Yoga* school needs no clarification. **If *Sāṁkhya* is metaphysics and theory, then *Yoga* is looked at as a methodology of practical application given to the same philosophy. *Sāṁkhya* talks about the three kinds of pain and leads the seeker to a path that helps to eliminate pain. *Yoga*, on the other hand, gives a detailed exposition of the techniques, practices and systems that lead man to total and absolute liberation from all kinds of pain and bondage.**

The word '*Yoga*' comes from the term '*Yuj*' meaning 'union', or 'join', which implies the 'union of body, mind and soul'. Some theists understand this union to be the 'union of the individual self with the Absolute Self, the union of the *Ātman* with the *Brahman*'.

The basic text of *Yoga* is the *Yogasūtra* of Patanjali (2nd century BC). The book is said to consist of four *pādas* or parts:

- the *samādhipāda*, which deals with the nature, aims and forms of *yoga*, discusses the modifications of *citta* and elaborates on the different methods of attaining *yoga* (*samādhi* or concentration).
- the *sādhanapada*, which deals with the path of attaining *samādhi* through *kriyāyoga*, the *kleśas* or mental states causing afflictions, the fruits of actions (*karmaphala*) and their painful nature, and the fourfold theme of suffering, its cause, its cessation, and the means thereof.
- the *vibhūtipāda* gives an account of the inward aspects of *yoga* and the supernatural powers that may be acquired by the practice of *yoga*; and
- *kaivalyapāda*, which describes the nature and the attitude that is required for liberation, the nature of the goal of life and the other world, and the reality of the transcendent self.

Patanjali's *Yogasūtra* has been commented upon by Vyāsa (500 AD) and King Bhoja (1000 A.D.) among others. The former's commentary is given a further gloss by Vācaspati and also by Vijñāna Bhikṣu. The credit for systematising the available data, in the *Yogasūtra*, goes to Patanjali. Another important work on *Yoga* is that of Yogi Yagnavalkya. The *Sāṁkhya Yoga* admits a plurality of selves, called *puruṣās*. It is realistic, as it regards objects of the external world as existing independently of the mind that cognises them. The *Sāṁkhya Yoga* system derives the multiplicity and diversity of the created world from a unitary source, the *prakṛti*. ***Sāṁkhya***, as it has been handed down to us, is almost silent regarding the method of acquiring the intuitive experience that results in release, though it **mentions liberation as its ultimate objective. The school of *Yoga*, however, elaborates the practical possibilities of such release and liberation of the bound soul, with its techniques and practices**. The *Yoga* philosophy is an invaluable gift to all those who are determined to attain spiritual realisation. It is an aid to all who wish to realise the existence of the Spirit as an independent principle, free from all the limitations that come with the identification of the soul with the body, senses, and the mind.

Patanjali defines *Yoga* as '*Citta Vṛtti Nirodha*'. The concept of *citta* is of central importance to *Yoga*. *Yoga* speaks of '*Abhyāsa*' and '*Vairāgya*' as essential for the 'cessation of the modification of the mind'. *Citta* is an outward directed consciousness that is continuously distracted and disturbed by the erroneous identification of the *Puruṣa* with *Prakṛti*. The *Citta* encompasses the *Buddhi*, *Manas,* and *Ahaṁkāra* of *Saṁkhya* metaphysics. It needs to be directed to an inward journey in order to arrive at *Viveka khyāti*, where the Self establishes itself in its true nature in the state of *Svarūpāvasthā*.

There are various techniques used by this school of thought to help the individual to arrive at this state of blissful existence. They include *Pranava jāpa*, *Kriya yoga*, *Mantra yoga*, *Aṣtānga yoga*, and various other purificatory, regulatory and meditative techniques. The individual removes impediments in his development and self-realisation, alleviates the *kleśās* and culminates in enlightenment of his individual self. All these help the individual to arrive at the desired state of *Yoga*, a complete liberation or *Mokṣa*.

Other systems of *yogas* also developed such as the *Yoga* of chants and recitation (*Mantrayoga*), *Yoga* of force, (*Hathayoga*) and *Yoga* of dissolution (*Layayoga*). While *Rajayoga* teaches the *yoga* of meditation, other forms of *yoga* can be practised to realise the Absolute Truth. *Bhaktiyoga* cultivates a devotional relationship with God through prayers and rituals. *Jnanayoga* is the approach to God through discrimination and reason. This is the path of wisdom. A *Jñānayogi* sees through the miseries and delusions of life and sees God everywhere. *Karmayoga* teaches self-realisation through selfless service to others and by attaining this spirit; the God within every individual is worshipped. The *Saṁkhya-Yoga* system lays great emphasis on discriminative knowledge as the means of attaining liberation, along with a recommendation of study, reasoning, and constant meditation. It lays stress on the practicality of the *Yoga* system that leads to self-realisation.

Yoga is translated as spiritual discipline. It emphasises psychic training to attain salvation. It differs from the school of *Saṁkhya* in that it brings a deity, namely *Īśvara* to the picture. This God of *Yoga* is also symbolised in the sacred syllable *OM* (or *Aum*), which pre-empts the sublime purity of the soul and thus aided in meditation.

Yoga enjoins the path of knowledge and action, developing in the individual an attitude of devotion. It is a synthesis of *Jñānayoga*, *Karmayoga* and *Bhaktiyoga*, for the attainment of complete freedom with the isolation of the Self from the material world. This path of discriminative knowledge includes the *Ashtānga Marga,* the eight-fold path. It becomes necessary to develop mental discipline, cultivation of the right kind of knowledge, and the inculcation of right attitudes and values. The aim of *Yoga* is the control of the various modifications of the mind, with the ultimate aim being the attainment of *Kaivalya.*

Ashtānga Yoga

Yogānuśta Anādaṣudikśaye Jñānadīptirāvivekakhyāte
Yama Niyama Āsana Prāṇāyāma Pratyāhāra Dhāraṇā Dhyāna Samādhyo Uśtāvangāni: 28:29:

The training of a *Yogi* is divided into eight stages (*Ashtanga Yoga*). By practicing all these stages and techniques of *Yoga*, the impurities in the *citta* are destroyed and there is an enlightenment in the individual. The eight limbs of *Yoga* are:

1. *Yama* – (Restraints)
2. *Niyama* – (Observances)
3. *Āsana* – (Posture)
4. *Prānāyāma* – (Control of *prāna*)
5. *Pratyāhāra* – (Sense withdrawal)
6. *Dhāranā* – (Concentration)
7. *Dhyāna* – (Meditation)
8. *Samādhi* – (Self-realisation)

Yama

Ahiṁsa Satya Asteya Brahmacharya Aparigraha Yamah
Jāti Deśa Kāla Samay Anvachitrāh Sarvabhauma Mahāvratam: 30: 31:

Yama implies Restraint or the practice of the following five ethical codes.

Ahiṁsa: non-violence; not hurting or killing anyone, even self.

Satya: truthfulness

Asteya: not stealing

Brahmachārya: abstinence and chastity; self-restraint from yielding to impulses or desires

Aparigraha: avoidance of greed, non-avariceness, non- covetousness

Niyama

Śauca Santoṣa Tapah Swādhyāya Īṣvarapraṇidhānāni Niyamah

Niyama implies Observances, which is the observance of the five rules of purity.

- *Ṣauca*: cleanliness and purity, not only of the external physical body, but even of the mind. This includes personal hygiene, positivity in attitude, removal of negativity, all positive *bhāvās*.
- *Santośa*: contentment, implying that man needs to realise that he gets only what he deserves and not always what he yearns for without effort. This helps to destroy the 'keeping up with the Jones' attitude' in individuals.
- *Tapas*: penance and austerity, which implies that man needs to be perseverant in his attempts and should perform duties with a sense of detachment.
- *Swādhyay*: self-study and self-help, guiding the student to introspect, auto-suggest, and be self-reliant.
- *Iśvarapraṇidhāna*: resignation and submission to God, with faith. This is also interpreted teleologically as a submission to Divine Will if the individual does not subscribe to the theistic view in Indian thought. The individual needs to work with a sense of detachment as he realises that he has no control over the fruits of his action, but only over his actions. This leads him to the idea that his efforts alone matter, making him a *Karmayogi*.

Āsana

Sthirasukhaṁ Āsanaṁ

Posture: sitting in certain comfortable, steady postures for the purpose of relaxation of efforts or meditation on the Infinite. The most famous is the Lotus Posture (*padmāsana*). All *Āsanās* can be interpreted to instill values and attitudes while teaching or learning them. There are various benefits to the regular practice of *Āsanās*, if they are done correctly, in a disciplined manner, and religiously. The practice of *Āsanās* regularly helps to develop a disciplined mind, a kind and sensitive heart, and a rationally guided intellect, with intuition as its power. The steadiness and steadfastness that comes with this kind of practice leads man to his goals more easily as he needs to put in less effort to achieve his goals. It teaches man to conserve energy and utilise it in a stringent manner for maximum benefits. *Āsanā*, along with *Prāṇāyāma*, leads man to achieve the goal of '*Arogyaṁ ca dine dine*'. This discipline helps in keeping the various organs of the body in perfect condition, such as the heart, kidneys, lungs, stomach, liver, the *indriyās*, the brain and the spine. Practice of *Āsanās* helps to move further with *dhāraṇā*, *dhyāna*, and *samādhī*.

Prānāyāma

Tasmin asati śwāspraśwās yogārtivicendrah prāṇāyāṁ

Prānāyāma involves breath-control or the regulation of psychic *prāṇa* through the regulation of inhalation and exhalation, to enhance physical and spiritual aspects in oneself. Regulated breathing helps to manage good intake of oxygen, which in turn determines the level of energy in an individual, his tolerance to stress and strain, and his nature of managing fatigue. It helps to judge the state of mind of an individual by watching his rate and state of breathing. The technique of getting aware of one's own breathing helps to be aware of oneself. This awareness leads to heightened sensitivity in oneself towards oneself and others. The rate of breathing of individuals can be monitored, regulated, and trained for increased performance and good health. The agitated and restless mind of an individual can be calmed down by regulating and steadying his breathing. It is a good technique to manage stress. *Prānāyāma* helps in checking a wandering mind, thus leading to increased attention and concentration.

Prāṇa or *ki* is that life energy which keeps the body alive and healthy. In Greek it is called '*pneuma*', in Polynesian '*mana*' and in Hebrew '*ruah*' which means 'breath of life.' There are three major sources of *prāṇa*: solar *prāṇa*, air *prāṇa* and ground *prāṇa*, which are recognised and respected for their life-giving capacity. The three *prāṇās* invigorate the body and promote life in all forms. *Prāṇa* absorbed by the body from the various sources is absorbed directly by the energy centres of the bioplasmic body. These energy centres are called *chakras*. A reference is made to the term '*chakra*' in a different context later in the following chapter.

Prāṇāyāma helps the individual to monitor, regulate and channelise the vital energy, through techniques and *āsanās*. It is the vital force that propels life ahead and beyond the physical. It pulsates with a regular frequency and rhythm in all living beings. *Prāṇāyāma* is disciplined breathing which improves the functioning of all body systems. Special emphasis is given to the improvement of the respiratory and nervous systems in the body. It helps the seeker of Truth to arrive at it with ease and comfort, by simply blending the vital energy within himself with Cosmic Energy. It is a bridge that links the micro with the macro. *Prāṇāyāma* helps the individual to attain the state of *Samādhī*. It helps in the proper circulation of blood in the body, in the digestion of food and the elimination of waste from our body. *Prāṇāyāma* influences one's rate of breathing, thus instilling calmness in the mind. Breathing and thinking are closely related and prāṇāyāma is the best technique to understand this. By regulating one's breathing, it is possible to slow down the agitated mental state, and this helps to experience mental quietitude and concentration. *Prāṇāyāma* helps to augment a pleasant feeling throughout the body and in the mind. There is a lot of importance given to *Prāṇāyāma* in the *Gītā*, Buddhist tradition and the philosophical traditions of the various sages and seers.

Pratyāhāra

Swaswaviśayāsaṁprayoge cit swarūpa anukāra iva indrīyaṇāṁ pratyāhāra

Pratyāhāra is a technique of withdrawal, where the sensory organs are trained to ignore their perceptions and consequent feelings and look within. Every individual gets drawn to the beauty and power of the external, physical world. The colours, shapes, sizes, and variety of the objects in the world keep man trapped in sensory perceptions. Man needs to assimilate all that he gathers as input through his senses and act by volition to achieve. In order to do this, man needs to move inwards, draw himself away from the transient beauty of this world and know more about himself. The individual who knows himself well alone can be a winner and achiever, contributing to the many, as he has realised his capabilities, limitations, and needs. This process of introversion is unique and novel to Indian culture. The scientific study of an individual by himself for himself, in a holistic manner is what *Yoga* teaches.

Dhāraṇā

Deśabandhaṣchi tasya dhāraṇā

Dhāraṇā is a technique leading to steadying the mind by concentrating on a single object, an icon or a sacred symbol or a body part, such as the tip of the nose. *Āsanā* and *Prānāyāma* help in steadying and stabilising the body and mind, inciting the individual to be healthy and motivated. Such an individual now needs to focus his energies and direct them towards the goal of self-realisation. With *pratyāhāra* and *dhāraṇā*, the individual mind is introverted, attention span is increased, and concentration is also heightened. *Dhāraṇā* helps to focus on goals.

Dhyāna

Tatra pratyayaikatanta dhyānaṁ

Dhyāna is Meditation, which is a technique learnt to help the object of concentration to fill the whole mind. It can be compared to the science experiment done with children in schools, where the Sun's energy is focussed on a piece of paper through a magnifying glass, and this concentration of solar energy brings flames on the paper, thoroughly burning it. The Sun does not normally burn things such as paper or cloth when it shines regularly, but its focussed energy does so. Similarly, the energy in an individual needs to be trained to focus.

Samādhi

Tad evārthaṁātra nirbhāsaṁ svarūpa shūṇyaṁ iva samādhih

Samādhī involves deep Meditation, when the whole personality is dissolved, where the individual realises his real self and moves on the path of self-actualisation and self-realisation. *Samādhī* is not to be understood as renunciation of the physical body or even burying oneself in soil or walking down to a waterbed. It merely talks about renouncing the desire and craving for the benefits of one's efforts. It is a technique that teaches one to be detached, doing one's duty in life according to one's station in life. This is the heightened practical dimension to *Dharma* and the concept of *Niṣkāmakarma*, as given in our scriptures and culture.

The individual mind is found in the following **ever-changing states**:

1. *Kshipt*: Most of the time our mind is thrown out to some object of interest in the process of experiencing the world. Such an outgoing mind is called as *Kshipt*.
2. *Vikshipt*: Our consciousness or awareness sometimes goes outward and with effort, in turns inside. Again, it goes out. In the *Vikshipt* state, our mind plays 'in and out'.
3. *Moodha*: When the mental faculties of our awareness are not alert, it is clouded and appears to be non-functioning. This state is *Moodha*. A person who is out of his mind, in coma or in a fit has *Moodha* mind.

4. *Ekagra*: While practicing *Yoga*, you learn to concentrate your awareness on a particular object. Here the state of consciousness is *Ekagra* which is very useful for day-to-day functioning and for higher goals.

When mind becomes *Ekagra*, it is a major achievement. Man needs to be in charge of himself and should be able to manage life situations in a balanced and steady manner. Besides the ever-changing states of consciousness, there are some relatively steady and regular states as well. This is achieved by the practice of Yoga.

Relatively Steady States of Mind

- *Jagṛit*: Full awareness with conscience (*Vivek*) active all the time.
- *Swapna:* A state of dream where some people play wish fulfilment game.
- *Sushupti:* Deep dreamless sleep.
- *Tureeya*: Besides these three steady states of consciousness there is one more state called *Tureeya* where, in deep mediation, a person becomes oblivious of space and time. Suppose he sits for meditation and enters *Tureeya* level of consciousness, he will not know where he is sitting or how long he is sitting. But during that period, his consciousness becomes one with the divine or universal consciousness. As a result of that, he receives energies unheard of. If he is able to channelise this energy on waking up, then he attains the right knowledge to liberation and treads the right path.

Without going into the other details of *Aṣtānga Yoga* and the techniques of *āsanā*, let us move on to discuss the implications with regard to Management.

The eight limbs of *Yoga* are defined by separate *Sūtrās* consistent with Patanjali's practice. **The first two, *Yama* and *Niyama*,** consist of moral excellence and psycho-physical purity that needs to be observed in worldly affairs. It reiterates the fact that yogic life is integral with life in the phenomenal and physical world and the emphasis is on the need to uphold all the values of life, as a whole. **The next three limbs of *yoga*** relate to the body of the individual in attaining a level of consciousness, whereby he gets nearer to the Reality. It also assists him to learn the techniques that teach the individual to move inwards and reach that state of consciousness that gives him discriminative knowledge of the *Ātman* and the non-Ātman. It is this knowledge in the individual that becomes the first step to spirituality. The discrimination between what is real, and temporal alone leads man to the path of liberation, where the individual reaches the super-conscious state of mind. **The last three limbs** are so integrated as the ascending stages to liberation that they are given a common name, *Saṁyaṁ*, or Restraint: *Trayaṁ Ekatra Saṁyaṁ*.

Yoga is considered to be a universal art based on a very universally accepted scientific basis. **Ethical excellence is the very foundation of spiritual life. The *Saṁkhya-Yoga* and the *Vedānta*, and all other schools of thought insist on this aspect of human living**. Conquest or mastery over oneself and the worldly living, the peaceful blending with the environment, a harmonious life with society and the world are preliminary *sin qua non* to a spiritual life.

'*Yuj',* from its derived meaning 'to join' came to mean, in its extended sense, in the contemporary world, as 'harnessing oneself for work', or 'joining oneself to something that is not temporary or fleeting'. Thus, '*yuj'* came to mean 'preparing oneself for hard work' or 'preparing others for it'. *Yuj*, particularly in the *Ātmanepāda*, came to mean 'to exert oneself'.[5] The *Yoga-sutras* convey right from the beginning that *Yoga* is a system of restraining the activities or distractions of one's thoughts (*Chitta Vṛtti Nirodha*), or it is also looked at as the efforts made by one to concentrate on a definite object or idea, with an active and conscious mind. *Yoga*,[6] as Rajendra Lal Mitra, conveys is to be interpreted as 'union with Effort', not the union with God. It implies *Udyoga*, not *Saṁyoga*. It teaches one to pull oneself together, exert, and perform with dedication, concentration, and purpose.

Yoga comes only with *viveka*, the ability to discriminate between *puruṣa* and *prakṛti*, the subject and the object, the self and nature, as taught in the *Sāṁkhya*. Sri Krishna makes several references to the *guṇās* and the *Saṁkhya* literature in his sermon to Arjuna in the rendition of *Bhagavad-Gita*. The *Yoga* philosophers, after pointing the way to meditative absorption (*Samādhī*), declare that this is the best means of managing from all earthly troubles and finally their teachings culminate in the achievement of *Kaivalya* or perfect freedom of the soul.

Yoga, often termed as Indian psychology, deals with the understanding of human personality, its potential nature and constitution, as well as the basic principles relating to the very essence of its unfolding and the purpose of human existence. Thus, it differs from modern psychology, which in its attempt to look scientific divorces itself from many metaphysical quests. Modern psychology also faces another major problem as it bases its study and understanding of behaviour on merely the empirical approach.

Modern psychology, moreover, tries to highlight the aspect of 'social adjustment' of the individual in a group rather than the holistic integration and wellbeing of the individual alone. The individual's interaction with the environment, physical and social, needs to pre-empt the health of the individual. *Yoga* deals with all aspects of the individual's life more convincingly and culminates with the teaching of the highest embodiment of human existence, namely, *Samādhi*. Both modern psychology and *Yoga* help in solving the existential problems of humans, although the latter does it more intensively and extensively, keeping the man in focus in a more holistic manner.

Bhagavad Gita's Relevance to Human Personality and Work Culture

The discussion of *Yoga* is elaborately done even in the *Bhagavad Gītā*. The *Bhagavad Gita*, the 'Celestial Song' or 'Song of the Blessed', as it is called, is a celebrated religious and philosophical poem of India. It is an important scriptural testimony to the ethics of Indian thought. The *Gita* deals with eternal truths immanent in the temporal series and the historicity of the epic really elucidates a philosophy through examples. One of the most popular treatises representing and guiding Indian culture, the *Gītā*, is truly a philosophical song. In as much as the *Bhagavad Gītā* gives us guidance on all aspects of spiritual life—*karma*, *jñāna*, *bhakti* and *dhyāna*—and its message is addressed to all men without any distinction, it is considered a universal gospel.

Śrīmad Bhagavad Gītā or the Divine Song of Lord *Kṛṣna*, occurs in the *Bhīṣma Parva* of the *Mahābhārata*. It comprises eighteen chapters, from the 25th to the 42nd, in the epic. Many thinkers consider the *Gītā* as the remarkable handbook of practical living. It is said to have marked a positive revolution in Indian thought and culture, especially Hinduism. It has gained popularity and is well accepted and understood by many as it deals with human issues, with no adherence to any specific tradition or orthodox frame of thought or practice. Just as the *Vedās* are divided into three *Khaṇḍās*, the *Gītā* too can be divided into three parts. The first part, with an emphasis on *Karma Yoga,* consists of the first six chapters, beginning with the 25th chapter of the *Mahābhārata*. The second deals with *Bhakti Yoga*, expounded in the next six chapters. The last part deals with *Jñāna Yoga*, concluding with the last six chapters.

The teaching of the *Gitā* is simple and suggestive. It is said to be the quintessence of all Vedic knowledge, *samasta vedārtha sāra saṇgraha bhūtam*. There is also a verse sung in praise of the *Gītā* as follows:

sarvopaniṣado gāvaḥ
dogdhā gopālanandanaḥ!

pārtho vatsas sudhīr bhoktā
dugdham gītāmṛtam mahat

'All the *Upaniṣads* are cows; *Kṛsṇa* the cowherd boy, who is the milkman; Arjuna is the calf; the milk is the *Gītā* and the Wise man who drinks it is one who enjoys eternal bliss.' Hence, it is called '*sarva śāstra hṛdayaṁ'*, the heart of all *ṣāstras*.

As mentioned by P.N. Srinivasachari in his book, *The Ethical Philosophy of the Gītā,* 'In the *Gītā*, divinity speaks to humanity through "*nara"*, the representative of man. . . . Its purpose is not the establishment of a *siddhānta* by the refutation of all other theories but is the synthetic harmonisation of contradictory views by bringing out their common or essential features. . . . Its ethics is not speculative but is broad-based on the psychology of human nature in all its aspects of cognition, conation and feeling.' The world-famous sage-poet, Veda Vyāsa rendered into beautiful rhyme the spiritual conversation between the Lord and his chosen devotee, Arjuna. He offered it to the world out of infinite compassion for humanity that had lost its soul and was suffering. The *Gitā* teaches man to cross the endless stream of *Saṁsāra*.

The *Bhagavad Gītā* is considered the fountainhead of Indian psychology. Self-realisation is the goal of human endeavour resulting in liberation from the bondages of the phenomenal world. **The purpose of religion, philosophy and psychology in India is to realise the goal of liberation. Ideally, in any individual, there should be no contradiction between thought, will and feeling.**

The similarity of metaphysics and ethics between the *Sāṁkhya-Yoga* and the *Gītā* is clearly seen in the exposition of the ethical bases of *Gītā*. The *Gītā* traces the transition from the popular idea of conduct as the ethics of sensibility to the morals of niṣkāmakarma arising from self-knowledge. The essential part of the ethics of *Gītā* is the ascent from sensibility to spirituality. It paves the path for moral fulfilment and moral freedom. As brought out in the metaphysics of *Sāṁkhya*, the *Gītā* too accepts that the senses, *Jñānendriyās*, relate to the transitory, phenomenal world and get drawn to the temptations of this world. The sensory world is colourful, pleasant, and distracting. The *Manas* is then drawn to this world by the senses, and it seeks the help of *Buddhi* to exert a steadying influence on itself. The *Buddhi* then needs to step in to control and guide the *Manas* and manage the senses. The *Karmendriyās* then act as per the guidance of the *Manas*, guided by the *Buddhi*. Moral freedom thus depends on self-determination.

Morality is discussed only in relation to voluntary actions in all schools of thought, Eastern or Western. The *Gītā* too follows the same principle of moral judgement. It analyses voluntary action into five factors. They are:

1. *Adhiṣthāna*
2. *Kartā*
3. *Kāraṇa*
4. *Ceṣṭāḥ*
5. *Daiva*

Every moral act is a combination of all these five factors. The first is the *Adhiṣthāna*, the Body, which is a conglomeration of all elements, the *mahābhūtasaṅghātarūpa*. It is called the *kṣetra* or field of action. The *karta* is the doer or the finite self. The *kāraṇa* is constituted by cognitive and the conative aspects of the human, the *jñānendriyās* and the *karmendriyās*. *Ceṣṭāḥ* denotes the various activities of the prāṇa, which sustains the body and its functioning. *Daivaṁ* is the *Adṛṣta* or the Unseen that implies the divinity that is present in the Cosmos and the individual self that guides, nurtures, and protects the dhārmic value of an act and the doer. All these factors need to be recognised in *Karma*.

The concept of *Dharma* is entirely dependent on *Viveka Jñāna*, the ability to discriminate. It also largely depends on the individual's capability to think rightly guided not by Reason alone, but by moral and spiritual injunctions. Real knowledge comes only with the realisation that the soul alone is real. In this context, *Gītā's* reference to *Karma* brings out two interpretations. *Karma* means the actions of the mind, speech, or body. Good or bad *karma* depends on the things one thinks, says or does. Secondly, *karma* can also be interpreted as the force or energy created by one's actions and the impressions of these actions that condition or influence one's lives. Rebirth is thus defined and determined by one's *karmās*.

Aniṣtamiṣtāṁ Miśraṁ Ca Trividhām Karmaṇaḥ Phalaṁ

– Bhagavad Gītā, Chapter 18, Verse 12

Karma is three-fold according to the results or consequences of the act itself: positive, negative or both, ie. pleasant, painful, or mixed. *Karma* is said to be of the following kinds:

1. *Sancita Karma*: Summation of *karma* performed until date, stored as *Saṁskāra*.
2. *Prārabdha Karma*: *Karma* which results in one's enjoyment or suffering in this life. The *karma* which has been selected for *Bhoga* through one's experiences in this life belong to this category. These *karmas* determine one's birth in a family, one's environment where one grow (physical and social), the profession, the possessions, etc.

3. *Kriyāmāna* or *Āgami Karma*: *Karma* that the jīva will be accumulating for the future.

Whenever *karma* is performed with a sense of attachment or with a desire for its fruits, it leaves an impression on the soul that is called *Saṁskāra*. The tendency to repeat these *karmās* are called *Vāsanās*. The dominant *guṇa* in every individual, *Sattva*, *Rajas* or *Tamas*, determines the substance and energy that give rise to tendencies of *Karmas*. These *karmas* determine the *Saṁskārās*. The *Samskārās* in turn again determine the *karmas* of the present birth. Here it is evident that *Guṇās*, *Karmas* and *Saṁskārās* are related and intertwined.

Every individual's perception of the universe will be determined, to a large extent, by his *Saṁskārās*. Hence, his worldview or Weltanschauung is limited. This limited vision and worldview is a major cause to man's problems. A limited vision of the world and oneself, due to the finitude of one's faculties and perceptions, leads one to believe that one is independent of others and exclusive in oneself. This erroneous and faulty idea of oneself leads to suffering and misery. The objective of all the schools of thought in India is to remove such erroneous, incomplete, and deluding perceptions that man carries with him while functioning in this world.

The *Śāstrās* convey the interconnectedness of everything in this universe and the interconnectedness of all the various universes that one can know of. Man is inextricably connected with the universe. The *Chandogya Upaniṣad* is said to have brought in the effect and influence of everything in the universe in the birth of every child. This view is an extension of the tenet of Oneness and Unity in the Cosmos that every scripture and testimonial conveys in our culture. Once man realises the interconnectedness and interdependence of each and everything in the Universe, he will realise that as a speck in the universe, he has no right to have an *Ahaṇkāra* that makes him conduct himself wrongly. The Law of *Karma* too, works as a deterrent to man's wrong or sinful deeds.

In the *Gītā*, the Ultimate Reality is viewed as One, Immutable, Imperishable and beyond change. In Chapter IV of the *Gītā*, Lord *Kṛṣnā* himself says, 'Though unborn and immortal, and also the Lord of all beings, I manifest myself through my own *Yogamāya* (divine potency), keeping my nature (*Prakṛti*) under control.' *Bhagavad Gītā*, Chapter IV, Verse 6. In Chapter VIII, it is said 'Beyond this unmanifest, there is yet another eternal, Unmanifest, that Supreme Divine substance, which does not perish even though all beings perish.' *Bhagavad Gītā*, Chapter VIII, Verses 20–21. And Chpt. XII, Verse 3, Chpt. XV 18. If this reality is beyond change and perish, and is known as all-pervading, then it leads us to believe that every object of this universe is pervaded by this same Consciousness. The Lord further goes on to say, 'He whose Self is harmonised by *Yoga* seeth the Self abiding in all beings and all beings in the Self; everywhere he sees the same.' Chapter VI-29.

The *Gītā* talks about the three paths that lead to liberation of the individual soul in great detail, with equal emphasis to all paths: *Bhakti Yoga*, *Karma Yoga* and *Jñāna Yoga*. The path of devotion to God is *Bhakti Yoga*. The path of action, *karma,* or duty, where the doer is not interested in the results of fruits of action, but merely the performance of duties, is *Karma Yoga*. The path leading to knowledge of God is *JñānaYoga*. All three paths are paths to liberation, the ways to free oneself from the attachments to transitory and temporary things. They lead to self-realisation and God-realisation, according to *Gītā*.

The *Gītā* defines *Tyāga* as the surrender of the fruits of one's actions and efforts. Man needs to surrender the fruits of his deeds to the Lord. The individual has no right to give up his duties or work assigned to him, but merely to give up attachment to the fruits of his actions. This is the core philosophy of *Niśkāmakarma* as expounded in the *Gītā*.

Lord *Kṛṣṇā* brings out a new interpretation to the term *Saṅnyāsa*. He says that giving up the worship of the sacred fire or sitting idle without doing any work, claiming to renounce this phenomenal world, is not Saṅnyāsa. It is the giving up of attachment to the fruits of karma and duty that is true Saṅnyāsa. One need not leave his home, family, job, attire, food, and one need not go into a forest or hermitage to be a Saṅnyāsi. There is no need to go into seclusion and live in solitude. A true Saṅnyāsi is one who is able to live with society, fulfilling all his duties, and working for the benefit and well-being of others. To be a part of the same tempting and distracting world, and yet not be bound by it is Saṅnyāsa.

Moreover, *yagna* is also an act of sacrifice in our scriptures. It was always felt that the Gods could be pleased with the performance of a *yagna*, a religious ritual and a prescribed duty for all the wealthy and the wise to win the benevolence of God. The performance of a *yagna* in the earlier days involved a lot of expenditure and as it was always beyond the reach of certain classes and castes, this brought in a distinction in society.

Gītā gives this ritual a new interpretation. It brings out the meaning of *yagna* as the act that is done with the philosophy of *Niśkāmakarma*. This made it easier for all to perform *yagna*, the poor, the rich, the illiterate or the literate, the weak or the strong, the man or the woman. Even the student who is studying with an aim to progress in life and contribute to society is doing *yagna*. Hence, *yagna* came to mean any activity or endeavour of man that is done with no attachment to its fruits. In order to perform this type of *yagna*, man needs to depend on none other than himself. Man's self-reliance and self-sufficiency is well brought out here. The performance of such *yagnās* will help humanity to free itself from the bondages of *karma*. It raises man to the higher levels of consciousness.

Yoga is the entire philosophy of *Gītā*. The concept of *Yoga* as interpreted in the *Gītā*, however seems more relevant in modern context. In the *Gītā*, *Yoga* is understood as equanimity of *Manas* and *Buddhi*, with the subjugation of *Ahaṁkāra*, in the performance of duties. The individual who is a real yogi will merely perform with *Dharma* in mind, with no other expectation from others or even the Lord. Even if he feels that he does not get what he deserves and what is due to him, he continues with a calm mind and contented attitude. This is called *Yoga* in *Gītā*. All work that is conducive to self-realisation and God-realisation is *Yoga*. In other words, it is a reiteration of the tenet of *Niśkāmakarma*.

There is a new interpretation given to the term '*tapas*' in Gītā. Normally, as understood by the common person, performance of feats that display masochistic tendencies in an individual are expressions of *tapas*. It was earlier believed that the individual needed to walk on fire, or stand in ice cold water, or perform feats of physical endurance to do *tapas*. The entire interpretation was overhauled. Today, the term is interpreted in three ways: *tapas* for purity of body, purity of speech, and purity of mind. The various conditions that are mentioned by *Kṛṣṇā* for performance of *tapas* are: worship of God, reverence and service to humankind, reverence for the wise and the learned, cleanliness/ *Śauca*, integrity, celibacy, and *Ahiṁsā*. In addition to these, *Kṛṣṇā* also said that it was mandatory for man to speak truthfully, study scriptures, work with detachment and not malign or harm others. Purity of thought, feeling, action and intention alone will give man the tapas for the mind. Man needs to have good control on his *Indrīyās,* both *Jñānendrīyās* and *Karmendriyās*. Silence is virtue, but not at the cost of giving up Truth. *Tapas* when understood in this context, seems attainable and possible even to the common person.

The teachings of *Gītā* are perennial in their relevance and significance. The cardinal tenets of the *Gītā* guiding humanity even today, helping man to resolve contemporary issues and problems are the following:

1. *Gītā* emphasises on self-awareness and self-realisation, which signify inner religion, rather than religious creeds and conflicting dogmas.

This forces man to put in conscious effort in attaining wisdom, *prajñā*, and working towards achieving goals in life. Man realises his inner nature that is divine.

2. *Gītā's* emphasis on work and duty needs no further elucidation. It has always laid stress on man's performance of duties. One cannot reach perfection by giving up work. The concept of *Niśkāmakarma* is unique to *Gītā*. It emphasises on the need to perform one's duties with no desire for the fruits of one's efforts. The motive in doing one's duty should be the performance alone, not the consequences and benefits of the work. When a man fails in his duties, he is not only harm himself, but he becomes a liability to others around him. Moreover, his share of the responsibility will have to be borne by others then, the benefits of which he will enjoy without his own contribution.
3. Detachment is an attitude that is encouraged by *Gītā*. The modern, scientific world with its increased inventions, discoveries and knowledge bank, has made man more attached to material and transient things. Man is unable to escape the temptations that stem from the comforts and conveniences coming with the technologically advanced society. With the rising standard of life, there is seen an inverse resultant in the decline of peace and happiness in man's life. Man needs to learn to give up the need for acquisition and possession and adopt a life of realisation and renunciation. This alone will lead him to a life of peace and serenity. He should learn to balance the material and the spiritual, enjoying work and duty as much as he enjoys the pleasures of life.
4. The *Gītā* believes in an integration of the various aspects in an individual, further leading to an integration of the individual with the society in which he lives. Man's attitude of selflessness alone will help him to draw away from the externalised aspects of life and move inwards, as he frees himself from the trappings of the external world.
5. *Gītā* does not limit its teachings to any particular religion, cult, sect, or faith. It talks about humanism which breaks barriers and helps build bridges among people. Spirituality highlights the essence on man. This spiritual nature of the human is elaborated with ethical practices advocated in the *Gītā*. Service of humanity is prescribed as a form of worship making it easy for all to practise religion. If man follows and understands humanitarian ideals, it binds man to man. This helps to avoid conflicts of any kind in life.

The study of *Gītā* helps to inculcate the right values in life. Man is enabled to choose his priorities rightly. It helps in eradicating fear of all kinds in life as man realises his true self. The knowledge man has of oneself and the world around him helps him to interact in a healthy manner. It teaches man to do his duty for duty's sake, thus helping him to release himself from the bondages of life, including that of work. Man learns to enjoy his work rather than consider it a burden. The acceptance of the divinity in all beings fosters a sense of security and wellbeing in every man.

Man faces problems in life today as he is unaware of his real self. He has wrong ideals and values, giving rise to lopsided priorities. Man falters in his decisions and fumbles on his path in life. He fails to plan his daily activities, making him feel that time is elusive and scarce. He seems lost in his own world. Such a faceless man needs to establish his identity. He has to read the scriptures, learn from authoritative sources and seek the right role models in life. A role model is one who has the right philosophy of life, with steady wisdom, the right values and one who can be a (beacon) torchbearer to others.

Thus, one reads in the *Bhagavad Gita*:

Buddhiyukto jahātiha ubhe sukṛita-duṣkṛite Tasmād yogāya yujyasva yogaḥ karmasu kauśhalam

A person endowed with wisdom renounces both good and bad actions in this life. Therefore, strive for yoga, for yoga is skill in action. This verse is from the *Bhagavad Gita*, Chapter 2, Verse 50 (BG 2.50).

This verse, when related to human intentions and proficiency in performance of work or activity done by the individual, indicates that he is endowed with a discriminating intellect. Such an individual works selflessly, with the objective of achieving universal welfare.

It is necessary to have the right role models in life. This is so as emulation and imitation have always been important factors of learning. Man learns faster by watching others than by reading or accepting instructions. This is so because it becomes easier to see the results of the actions of the role models, helping others to decide whether to follow or not. Our values, ideologies, outlook, bias, misconceptions, attitudes, prejudices are determined by our role models. A role model should be one who leads others to greater heights and better levels in life. This makes the rightness and appropriateness of the role model more significant.

The *Gītā* offers a role model that is ideal, a *Stithaprajña*.

duḥkheṣhv-anudvigna-manāḥ sukheṣhu vigata-spṛihaḥ vīta-rāga-bhaya-krodhaḥ sthita-dhīr munir uchyate

– Bhagavad *Gītā*

'He whose mind is not perturbed by adversity, who is free from desires for pleasures, who is devoid of any attachment, fear and anger – such is indeed to be of steady wisdom.'

This verse is from the *Bhagavad Gita*, Chapter 2, Verse 56 (BG 2.56)

In today's world, the ideal man is one who possesses the maximum, has a fat bank balance, has an enviable lifestyle, and is garbed in riches. He is assumed to be the most successful and happiest man in life. Unfortunately, what is seen in reality is sometimes just the converse. It is also paradoxical that an individual may have many degrees and certificates to his credit but may not have the wisdom to lead life well. He is indecisive and confused. He may be successful in the material world but may be miserable from within. His interpersonal relationships are also not healthy and successful. Such an individual who has his life in shambles can never be a role model for others.

In order to relieve man of the stress of looking for the right model of humanity, *Gita* presents the ideal of *Stithaprajña* within the parameters of the *Purushārthās*.

Lord *Kṛṣṇā* replies to Arjuna regarding the traits of a *Stithaprajña* in the *Gītā*. According to the Lord, an ideal man is one who has destroyed the ego/ *Ahaṁkāra*, performs his duty for duty's sake, with no expectations of the fruits of his efforts coming to him. He plays the various roles in his family, society, or organisation very diligently and devotedly. He leads life selflessly and moves away from attachments of any kind that can bind him. He gives up all his desires, leading a life of simplicity and piety. He has no selfish goals, but he endeavours to excel. He will not try to achieve anything at the cost of his values and principles.

'*Sukhaduḥkhe same kṛitvā lābhālābhau jayājayau Tato yuddhāya yujyasva naivaṁ pāpam avāpsyasi*'-

'Treating pleasure and pain, gain and loss, victory and defeat alike, prepare yourself for battle. In doing so, you will not incur sin.'

That line is from Bhagavad Gita Chapter 2, Verse 38 (BG 2.38).

A *Stithaprajña* has realised his real self. External events and trifles in life do not affect him as he is confident about himself. He performs his duty in the same manner whether he is gaining rewards or experiencing losses. He is free from all attachments and is neither rejoicing in good fortune nor lamenting his misfortune. He is aware that there are many external factors beyond him that affect and influence his life. But he tries to keep a check on those factors within him in control. He accepts the Law of *Karma* and its dictates with a pleasant and cheerful attitude. The awareness that one determines one's own extent of happiness in life helps him to walk the ethical path more confidently.

A *Stithaprajña* is a man of wisdom. He stays calm and composed even in difficult situations. He will have no confusion in thought and action, as he is aware of his goals. He is free from cravings, desires, and passions. The control of desires helps to control negative emotions. Even when he is faced by trials and tribulations, he is unaffected. He rises above the world of plurality, trying to realise the essential oneness of all creation. He is said to have waged a war against *Kāma*, won it, and restored *Dharma*.

A *Stithaprajña* is different from the rest of humanity as he tirelessly and ceaselessly puts in efforts to better himself. His aim in life is to self-actualise and self-realise. His attention and energy are well channelised and he aims to excel in all his efforts. He sets his own standards and outperforms every time to better his own performance.

A *Stithaprajña* is an ideal man as he plays every role in life determined by the āṣraṁās well and to perfection. His sense of duty and commitment makes him work ungrudgingly and unflinching. He is the architect of his own life and takes the responsibilities of his family and society without a whimper. He accepts accountability for his own actions. He rises due to his efforts and fails too due to his follies and faults. His life is an expression of the divine. Such an individual is creative, good, peaceful, and productive. His purpose in life is to achieve bliss and contentment. He strives for spiritual enrichment and a state of sovereign freedom. He adds value to life with every thought or deed in life.

A *Stithaprajña* practises yogic contemplation to purify his mind. He, moreover, dwells in a universal point of view, where the wellbeing of all beings is the motivator. This universal point of view is described as '*sarva-bhūta-hia-rati*'. This point of view is differentiated from the universal point of view that takes justice as its ethical base for determining and promoting wellbeing. The former view highlights the moral along with the emotional and benevolent dimension in man, whereas the latter talks about the more legal or moral aspect. In the case of the latter, the individual will not exploit others for his own wellbeing. But he will put himself on par with others and see that all get the benefits equally. In the case of the former, the individual will subjugate his desires, wants and needs for the sake of others. There is seen the domination of the sattva guṇa in him. He works within the parameters of *dharma*, with the qualities of *tyāga*, *ahiṁsā*, *satya*, *dayā*, *vairāgya* as his guiding principles. He will never act on the dictates of *kāma*.

A *Stithaprajña* is one who lives life in the same phenomenal world as all others. He is not a '*mukta*'. He looks at himself as one among the others, without any *ahaṁkāra*. He works with the objective of alleviating the suffering of all around him. His only motivation for action is the welfare of all. He belongs to all, and all are his. He is lead by *dharma* and he walks on the path leading to *samādhī*. The concept of *Stithaprajña* as given in the Indian tradition is a combination of moral discipline and mental training which is also found in Buddhism and Jainism as in the *Gītā* and *Advaita*.

'ātmanaḥ pratikūlāni pareṣaṁ na samācaret':

Finally, we have the *Mahābhārata* declaring that there is only one common and primary factor that is essential as a categorical imperative to guide all human actions. It is necessary for man to learn the essence of *dharma*, the *dharmasarvasva*, which teaches that one should not do to others what one would not like to experience oneself. This dictum is very similar to the Biblical Commandment: 'Do unto others what one would like others do unto you.'

Upaniṣads: Tenets and Ethics

The *Upaniṣads*, the *Gītā*, and the *Brahmasūtrās* constitute the *Prasthānatraya* of Indian testimonial knowledge. It is said that it is not possible to attain spiritual liberation without an understanding of the *Prasthānatraya*. The subtle principles of *Dharma* are expressed well in these three testimonials in very simple and lucid manner, making profound truths easier for people to learn. Thus, the *Upaniṣads* too, need to be understood with the basic tenets made relevant for today's man. From these scriptures are drawn Indian ethics that help in guiding the Indian through his daily as well as spiritual journey. Though *Vedānta* currently is the favourite of English-speaking Indian intellectuals, it was from the wisdom of the *Upaniṣads* and *Bhagavad-Gita* that the ancient Indians set forth their ethics in a practical way, expected to be followed by all. The Laws of Manu (*Dharmashastra* or *Manava Śāstra*) gave details of societal rules and *Arthaśāstra* of Kautilya detailed the politics and economics.

The *Upaniṣads* are the quintessence of Vedic thought. The word '*Upaniṣad*' is etymologically derived from three words put together: '*upa*', '*ni*' and '*ṣad*', meaning 'nearby', 'with devotion and determination' and 'sitting' respectively. The indicative meaning is that a student has to develop the right qualities of the head and the heart, develop a burning desire for knowledge, approach a teacher, sit at his feet with sincerity and tune his mind to the teachings given by the expert. He needs to absorb the knowledge given in its entirety. He has to assimilate and imbibe it all, leading to the practice of virtues. Sitting at the feet of the teacher is symbolic in many ways. Just as the flow of water from a higher to a lower level is mor natural and faster, the flow of knowledge too is faster from the teacher of a higher calibre. Moreover, another interpretation given is that the student at a lower level will sit automatically looking up at a teacher, with respect and reverence. It is also implied that the student sitting at the lower level will have an attitude of humility and devotion.

The other meaning of '*ṣad*' is to 'destroy' and 'to lead'. The *Upaniṣads* help the seekers of Truth to realise the real Self, hence, destroying ignorance or *Ajñāna*. The study of the *Upaniṣads* leads the student from the lower levels of knowledge and living to higher levels. This study also leads the seeker to the truth of the Ultimate Reality. The word '*ni*' is understood to mean 'determination'. The student must approach the teacher with a determination to gain the knowledge. The student should be so determined that he is ready to abide by the instructions of the teacher in order to achieve his goals and not give up midway.

The four *Vedās* have epitomised Indian thought, culture, and religion, incorporating the philosophy that is spiritual in its basic essence. In all the four *Vedās*, there are three sections: *karma khanda*, *jñāna khanda* and *upāsana khanda*. The *Upaniṣads* constitute the *jñāna khanda*. There are more than 108 *Upaniṣads* in the *Vedās*, all giving to man the 'knowledge of the Self'. This addresses common questions about existence, the world's origins and substance, and its purpose.

According to the *Upaniṣads*, the world has evolved out of *Brahman*, the Ultimate Reality. As it is a result of an evolutionary process and not creation, the world is made of *Brahman* by *Brahman*. Hence, *Brahman* is looked at as the Efficient Cause as well as the Material Cause of the World. If this view is accepted then the world has to be as spiritual and holy as the Creator, who is Pure Spirit and Consciousness.

Accepting this view drives us to the query: Can such a world be anything but pure, holy, good, righteous, and spiritual? This leads us further to the idea that all forms of life will have a part of the same Spirit as denotes the Reality. If *Brahman* is responsible for the evolution of all forms of life and there is a part of this Spirit in all beings, it implies that there is Oneness and Universality in the Universe. This part of the cosmic Spirit that is found in all forms of life is the *Ātman*.

The *Brahman-Ātman* unity makes it imperative for the human soul to accept the unity between all forms of life. The ethical connotation to this is significant. Can one man harm or hurt another when there is a sense of belongingness and unity among them? The destruction of one part of the Reality by another part of the same Reality seems absurd. This idea has given rise to environmental ethics too. If all beings have evolved from the same Reality, *Brahman*, it automatically follows that there is Universal brotherhood between Man and Man and also between Man and other beings.

The idea of *Brahman* as given in the *Upaniṣads*: *Nirguṇa Brahman* is accepted as the Reality from whence all creation came forth. '*Nirguṇa*' implies 'with no attributes'. The common person did not grasp the concept of a reality that was described as Pure Consciousness or Spirit. The idea of *Nirguṇa Brahman* was then explained with certain attributes, both metaphysical and moral, giving rise to *Saguṇa Brahman*. *Brahman* was said to have the attributes of Omnipresence, Omnipotence, Omniscience, All-pervading, Eternal, Infinite, Holy, Pure, Benevolent, and so on. This made it easier for all to understand the magnificence of the Reality.

It was however difficult for a commoner to accept a Reality to which one could not relate. Then emerged the idea of *Īśvara*, a Personal God. This idea of reality seemed more acceptable as one could relate and identify more easily. All the attributes of *Saguṇa Brahman* were personified and given a *naam-rūpa*. This form of Reality gave rise to rituals, prayers, and worship. Man found it easier to relate to and accept this reality. He could share, ask, plead, request, convey, feel for, worship and revere such a reality. This gave rise to the *Karma khānda* and the *Upāsana khānda* of the *Upaniṣads*.

The need to live life in its true essence makes it necessary for all to understand this philosophy and spirituality. The term '*upaniṣad*' itself is believed to connote a '*rahasya*' or 'secret'. In short, the *Upaniṣads* have been taken to be the authoritative sources of the secrets of right living. It thus, became necessary for all to sit close to an authority, with devotion and sincerity, to understand life and its secrets. The *Upaniṣads* are thus considered to be philosophical treatises that help man to realise his essential nature and live his life rightly and rightfully.

Upaniṣad means 'to sit down near' because the main teachings of the *Vedās* were explained to the students, who sat at the feet of their teachers. In general, *Upaniṣads* proclaim salvation by knowledge and realisation, i.e., *Jñāna* and *Samādhi*, rather than by faith and works. Selfish desires are obstacles in the life of the seekers of Truth (the Higher- Self, also called as *Brahman*). A seeker of true Divinity will attain salvation when he realises the Truth, the all-pervasive *Brahman*. The universe came into existence because of a primeval desire of *Brahman*. Now it is the duty of the humans to restore it to the state of things at the time of creation. This can be done by sacrifice, benevolence, study and even ascetism, which in turn will permit the seeker of truth to attain bliss. Honesty is especially extolled. He who has not denounced evil will never obtain *Brahman*. The worldly perceptions of smell, taste, touch, hearing, and sight make one separate from the true self. When one can transcend these perceptions there is no consciousness of anything other than Self. This is immortality.

There are six great sayings, *Mahāvākyas*, from the *Upaniṣads* that give the basic insight into its philosophy. They are as follows, with a brief analysis of each:

- *Ahaṁ Brahmasmi* or 'I am *Brahman*': Vedic knowledge teaches that our own 'Self' is the true Divinity. The Truth is within us, in our own heart. This states the identity of the innermost consciousness of the individual with the Supreme Divine.
- *Ayaṁ Atmā Brahmā* or 'The Self is Brahman': This states that not only individual soul is Divine, but all beings are identified with the Absolute Truth.
- *Tat Tvam Asi* or 'That art Thou': Whatever we see or think about, we are That. We are the ultimate Thou and I in all.
- *Prajñānam Brahma*: 'Knowledge is Brahman': Supreme intelligence is present inherently within us and is capable of returning us to the Divine.
- *Sarvam Kalvidaṁ Brahma*: 'The whole universe is *Brahman*': Not only the consciousness in you and me but also the 'principles of being' are all Divine. The entire universe is Divine, which includes our Self.
- *So'haṁ*: 'Here am I': This identifies the Divinity in our Self as something that happens naturally like breathing. '*So*' is inhalation and '*Ham*' is the natural sound of exhalation.

These are the six statements of the identity of individual consciousness with the Divine reality. They all merge into and derive from the word '*Om* (*Aum*)', the Divine word meaning 'I Am All'. All of these statements point to the fact that whatever or however we worship, be it an image, book, an idea or even a God, it is the knowledge that the Truth is within ourselves, and that will ultimately lead to self-realisation. Self is the true Divinity. This is the essence of the *Upaniṣads*.

That because of which there is life in this body is *Brahman*, the Self. Its existence cannot be denied by anyone as it leads to a denial of one's own existence. To know that this reality is 'Me' is the highest achievement that a human being can gain. There is nothing greater than this as the knowledge of the Self appearing as many in this Universe leads to a change in vision for oneself.

The unity in diversity breaks all barriers, changes the sense of limitation that one ever felt. It also helps to discard the sense of finitude that one feels about oneself. The entire vision of the Universe changes, enlarging the canvas of life for all beings. The perception of the individual as dark, unholy, vicious, impure, and destructive can never be true, with the origin determined. This leads one to accept that there is inherent divinity and goodness in all beings, with the essential spirit that lies embodied in all.

The *Kena Upaniṣad* says:

'That which is not seen, but because of which the eyes are able to see; that which cannot be described by words, but because of our speech is able to describe other things; that which is not heard by the ears, but because of which our ears are able to hear; that is *Brahman*.' (I:4-7)[7]

The ethics of a philosophy always follow its metaphysics. The study of human conduct involves the consideration of the same from two standpoints: one from the standpoint of the individual himself and the other from the standpoint of the society. There are various virtues that are highlighted in the various *Upaniṣads*. To cite a few examples:

The *Brihadāraṇyaka Upaniṣad* enumerates the virtues of exercising control on oneself, charity, and mercy as the higher virtues.

The *Taittriya Upaniṣad* talks about the following virtues that need to be cultivated by every individual. An individual should always speak the truth, practice penance, learn to restrain himself from indulgence due to temptations and pleasures, develop a tranquil and contented attitude. He is also enjoined to look upon his father and mother as gods and admonished that he should not do anything that is blameworthy. He should also develop the attitude of giving without expecting in return for it. The act of giving should be done with joy and kindness, not with egoism.

The *Katha Upaniṣad* begins with the deterrent. It propounds that one who has not turned away from his wickedness, is not tranquil or subdued in nature. He is not peaceful and will never be able to grasp the truth about the Self. It emphasises the need to have the right knowledge along with the right character. Unless a man has ceased to commit sins, is of good character and has the right knowledge, he can never attain liberation. The distinction between the '*preyas*' and the '*śreyas*' is brought out in the form of a story of Nachiketa and Yama, the Lord of

Death. Every individual should learn to distinguish the 'good' from the 'pleasant' and the 'right' from the 'good'.

The idea of penance in the *Upaniṣads* is not to be understood as oppressive asceticism. The *Upaniṣads* teach man to lead a life of wellbeing and fullness, with the maximum utilisation of one's potential for a balanced life. There is no need to restrain oneself to the extent of self denial even if ethically justified. This would lead to perversion and repression in an individual. The idea of penance merely means leading a life in which the disturbing passions are kept in check and duties are performed well. The individual is asked to lead a life that has simplicity and piety as against ostentation and hedonism.

All *Upaniṣads* talk about values and virtues that a man should follow in order to lead a life of fulfilment and actualisation. The list is never ending and the exposition of moral teaching in the *Upaniṣads* are well brought out in parables.

The ***Vedānta*** **tradition** evolves and revolves around three basic tenets:

1. *Vivek*: which gives the individual the sense of discrimination between the temporary and the permanent, between the eternal and the transient, between the real and the unreal, righteous and the unrighteous, the good and the evil, the necessary and the unnecessary. This kind of wisdom helps the individual to prioritise in life, take decisions wisely, and be consistent in behaviour.
2. *Vairagya*: Developing an attitude of detachment, with a scientific approach to everything in the world. This does not mean the lack of spiritual initiative. On the other hand, it implies a spiritual inclination, helping him to accept all beings as part of the same reality. It merely implies the control of senses when dealing with the phenomenal world. There is detachment from everything except the final goal of Self-realisation.
3. *Śad-Sampat* – the six virtues that are man's treasures. They are:
   - *Shama* – Control of the senses
   - *Dama* – Resilience
   - *Shraddhā* – Faith
   - *Sādhanā* – Eight-fold yogic discipline
   - *Uparatī* – detachment from the others and ignoring the negative
   - *Titikṣā* – sustained, continuous yearning for right knowledge
4. *Mumukṣatvaṁ*: the earnest desire for Mokṣa, leading the individual to progress on the ethical path, towards self-realisation.

An individual is both a citizen and a worker. He has various roles to play in society. He/ she has to take the responsibility for self-development on himself as a primary responsibility. The environment and society can only help and assist in various ways by providing the opportunities and the inputs. The individual needs to realise that it is only through a healthy body that one can perform well—*shariram adhyam khalu dharma sādhanām.*

The self is realised in five ascending Kośās steps: *anna* (food), *prāna* (breath), *manas* (mind), *buddhi* (intellect) and *ātman* (self/ soul). The five *kośās* are:

- *Annamaya kośa* – the layer in man's being which is made of the physical body, which is nurtured by the food that is taken in by the individual.
- *Prāṇamaya kośa* – determined by the breath taken in by the individual, which is the source of vital energy. The proper intake of oxygen and the right extent to which the exhalation of carbon dioxide and other elements from the body is done determines the status of health of the individual. Breath or *prāṇa* signifies the inevitable link between the microcosm and the macrocosm.
- *Manomaya kośa* – which is the psycho physical aspect of the individual. It determines the emotional, affective, and conative dimensions of the individual. It decides the level of emotional intelligence that is exhibited by the individual. The various bias, misconceptions, ideas, beliefs, etc., are placed in this *kośa.*
- *Vijñānamaya kośa* – This is where the intellect predominates to help the individual to use his faculties of reasoning, logic, intuition, and insight. All valid *pramās* are at play here to give the individual the Reality in its pure form. A seeker of Truth realises his oneness with the Ultimate Reality due to the *Vijñānamaya kośa* in himself.
- *Atmanomaya kośa* – It is the kośa where the micro meets the macro, the individual spirit identifies itself with the Ultimate Spirit, disengaging itself from the bondages of the temporal, phenomenal world.

All the *kośas* that go into making of the individual need to be accepted and understood well. Self-development needs to be life-long, proceeding through the various stages or *āṣramās*. All *kośās* are integrated to give the individual his existence and identity. The success level of one's development can be evaluated by the measure of *sat* (truth), *cit* (consciousness) and *ānanda* (joy) in one's life.

Śramaṇa Traditions: Buddhist and Jaina Ethics

Buddhism and Jainism are studied under the category of non-Vedic or *Śramaṇa* tradition. The schools categorised under this tradition do not accept the authority of the *Vedās*. The scriptural texts of this tradition are in *Prakṛt*, *Pāli* and *Ardhamāgadhi*. In *Prakṛt*, the tradition is called '*Samāna*', derived from the word '*Saṁ*', meaning restraint, effort, and equality, all in one. The Sanskrit equivalent for '*Saṁ*' are three words: *Śrama*, *Ṣama*, and *Sama*, meaning effort, restraint or constraint, and equanimity or equality, respectively. The *Śramana dhamma* has for its basic tenets the values and virtues of self-control, self-effort, equality of *Jivās* and also the equanimity of mind. ***Śramaṇa* traditions give importance to one's elevation to higher spirituality.**

Buddhism

As in the case of the *Āstika darśanās*, the *Nāstika darśanās* also began their study with an analysis of Reality. They too begin with the realisation that man is trapped in an endless, painful cycle of birth and death. This bondage that man wants to release himself from, is a resultant of the very nature of the human constitution. Hence the need to study Self, its nature, and the epistemology and ethics in a tradition arose.

Buddha never wanted to start anything new. His intention was to revive what was already there but was forgotten or ignored. Buddha, too, like *Saṁkhya*, began with the idea of *Dukha*, Sorrow. On his tour of his father's kingdom, as a prince, Buddha saw life with its sickness, aging, and death. This brought in him a distress and disturbance that made him go in search of Truth, a Truth that was ultimate and universal, that would help man to eliminate his miseries and pains.

Although Buddhism is today looked at as a world religion, it began as a mere ethical teaching of Buddha. Buddha laid an ethico-spiritual path for man to follow that would lead him to liberation. According to Buddha, man had to free himself from all sufferings, which meant he had to release himself from all bondages. Man suffered only because of his attachments to people, things, possessions, wealth, name, fame, status, and recognition. Man is bound to the ephemeral and transient world, which is temporary and distracting. He needs to realise himself as a spiritual being, going beyond the physical and the rational.

Buddha's main teachings begin with the 'Four Noble Truths' They are:

- There is Suffering – *Dukha*
- There is a Cause for Suffering – *Dukha Samudāya*
- There is an end to Suffering – *Dukha Nirodha*
- There is a way to end Suffering – *Mārga*, the Eight-fold Path

According to Buddha, every event or occurrence in man's life shows immense possibilities of producing *Dukha*. Man's suffering begins with birth, leading to sickness and death too that become factors leading to misery. If man does not get what he wants, it is suffering and if man gets what he does not want, even then it leads to suffering. Thus, Buddha says that man's life is 'Sarvaṁ *Dukhaṁ*'. Suffering and misery in man's life seem almost inevitable.

Buddha believed that there was a cause for everything in the Universe. This gave rise to the doctrine of '*Pratityasamūtpāda'*, the Law of Dependent Origination. Buddha believed that there was a cause for everything in the Universe. This gave rise to the doctrine of '*Pratityasamūtpāda'*, the Law of Dependent Origination. According to Buddha, no individual remains the same at two points of time. The individual is only a continuous series of consciousness or states of the changing consciousness. The Self is considered to be a psycho-physical aggregate, the '*Naam-rūpa-skandha sanghat*'.

The human personality is analysed in terms of the aggregate of the five *skandhās* related in time by the causal chain. These five *skandhās* are: Nāma-rūpa (Name and Form), Vedanā (Sensation), Saṃjnā (Perception/Recognition), Saṃskāra (Mental Formations/Volition), Vijnāna (Consciousness). According to him, man's suffering due to age, sickness and death is primarily due to *tṛṣṇā*, craving, which originates right at birth. This suffering of man can be traced to *Avidyā*, ignorance. As mentioned in all the earlier schools of Indian thought, Buddha too reiterates man's ignorance with regard to Reality. Man's attachment to things temporary and fleeting is due to ignorance.

As Heraclitus once remarked, 'One cannot step into the same river twice,' Buddha too considers life as a stream of consciousness.

Buddha traces the development of man's ignorance to the final destination of death and enlists them as the Twelve Links. These twelve links (nidānas) form the backbone of Buddhist philosophy on the origin of suffering and the cycle of samsāra:

1. **Avidyā (Ignorance)** – which leads man to misunderstand Reality, the Four Noble Truths and the nature of impermanence, and suffering
2. **Saṃskāra (Volitional Formations)** – which refers to the karmic impressions and tendencies formed by past actions, leading to the present consciousness
3. **Vijnāna (Consciousness)** – which is the link between past karma and present existence, creating an awareness to shape the present life
4. **Nāma-rūpa (Name and Form)** – signifying the psycho-physical organism, the created life form, the basis for experience

5. **Ṣaḍāyatana (Six Sense Bases)** – The six faculties: eye, ear, nose, tongue, body, and mind, which are the tools through which we perceive the world
6. **Sparśa (Contact)** – or the interaction and experience of the external world, with the help of the sense organs
7. **Vedanā (Sensation)** – the pleasure or pain that arises from sense experience
8. **Taṇhā (Craving)** – incessant desire and craving for pleasure and avoidance of pain which is the root of all attachment and bondage
9. **Upādāna (Clinging)** – bondage that leaves man dependent, unable to achieve freedom, Mukti
10. **Bhava (Becoming)** – The process of existence and continuous change, leading to karmic momentum, in turn, leading to rebirth
11. **Jāti (Birth)** – The beginning of a new life, conditioned by past karma
12. **Jarā-maraṇa (Aging and Death)** – The inevitable outcome of birth, which includes pain, misery, despair, aging, and death

Man begins his journey of life with ignorance, *Ajñāna* that seems inevitable. The next link in this chain is *Saṁskāra*, the tendencies that are predispositions due to *Karma*. This leads to *Vijñāna*, Consciousness, followed by the awareness of the Mind-Body Complex, *Nāmarūpa*.

Buddha, in his deep insight into the nature of existence, unravels the cycle of suffering through a series of probing questions. Each answer reveals a link in the chain of **dependent origination**, ultimately pointing to **ignorance** as the root cause.

- He asks – What is the cause of old age and death? The answer: Birth.
- He asks – What is the cause of Birth? The answer: *Bhāva*, desire to exist.
- He asks – Why does one want to exist? The answer: *Upādāna*, clinging or attachment.
- He asks – Why attachment? The answer: Due to Cravings, unfulfilled desires.
- He asks – Why craving? The answer: Due to *Vedanā*, Sensation and resultant pain.
- He asks – Why the sensation? The answer: *Sparsh*, between the sense organs and external objects.
- He asks – Why the *Sparsh*? The answer: The six sense organs have their own fields, *Shaḍāyatan*, inviting *sparsh*.
- He asks – Why do we have the senses? The answer: As we have the mind and the body, *Nāmarūpa*.

- He asks – What operates behind the mind-body complex? The answer: *Vijñāna*, Consciousness.
- He asks – Why do we have consciousness? The answer: Because of predispositions/ tendencies due to previous karma, *Saṁskāra*.
- He asks – then ultimately, what is responsible for man's suffering? The answer: *Ajñāna*, ignorance.

The removal of the cause for suffering is the only way to end man's misery. In order to achieve this the wheel of *Dhamma* needs to be operated which revokes or reverts the wheel of transmigration and birth and death of every soul. The two important limitations that man can control to save himself from misery are *Ajñāna* and *Tṛṣṇā*, where the individual is expected to stop himself from developing attachments and thus curb cravings.

The path to end cravings and reverse the wheel of life is called the 'Noble Eight-Fold Path', the *Ārya Aṣtānga Mārga*. The eight Virtues that Buddha highlights are the following:

- Right Faith – *Saṁma Dṛṣṭi*, (*Saṁyag Dṛṣṭī* in Sanskṛit)
- Right Resolve – *Saṁma Sankalpa* (*Samyag Sankalpa* in Sanskrit)
- Right Speech - *Samma Vācha*
- Right Conduct – *Saṁma Kamanta*
- Right Livelihood – *Saṁma Ājīva*
- Right Effort - *Saṁma Chyayāma*
- Right Mindedness – *Saṁma Sati*
- Right Meditation – *Saṁma Samādhī*

The first two stages are steps leading to 'Wisdom', *Prajñā*. The next four are attitudes and approaches in social life that help to develop Character, called *Sheel*. The last two are steps that culminate in *Samādhī*, where the individual liberates himself.

According to Buddhism, one has the free will to choose one's course of action. The free will is given as much significance in Buddhism as in any other tradition of Indian philosophy. Buddhism preaches a way of life that gives individuals a choice and various options that are very pragmatic and plausible.

There are certain ethical principles that stand out as universally acceptable. They are:

1. Avoid evil and instill goodness to purify one's mind. Be generous, learn to care and share whatever be one's capacity to give.
2. Develop a positive attitude, with an open approach to all in life.
3. Have a tranquil and calm mind, with a readiness to accept whatever be life's situations.

4. Develop the habit of concentration and focus on the right things to the right extent, to conserve energy for the right purpose.
5. Live with prudential wisdom, not theoretical knowledge. Buddha felt it is a waste of time and effort to discuss philosophy, without understanding its pragmatism and relevance.

As every individual lives in society and is not isolated from social environment, it is essential to follow certain disciplines in life. It implies the inculcation of values and practices that makes him aware of himself, with a realisation of the need to have self-control. It helps to develop adaptability, self-control, and restraint. One needs to live with goodwill in order to be acceptable in society.

Buddha gives us the five precepts that help to lead life ethically. The 'dos and don'ts' in the Buddhist way of life are as follows:

1. To abstain from killing, and develop love, kindness, and compassion to all living beings.
2. To abstain from stealing and develop right means of livelihood.
3. To abstain from sexual misconduct and develop restraint of the senses.
4. To abstain from lying and develop truthful speech.
5. To abstain from intoxicants and develop restraint and mindfulness.

The more one can observe the above Five Precepts and Five Virtues, the happier and more peaceful is one in life. Then the idea of peaceful co-existence of all beings does not seem utopian.

To be a real Buddhist is just to take the Triple Gem as one's guide in life. For one to adopt the Buddhist philosophy and way of life, one needs to embrace the Dhamma and Sangha, ie. the ethical code and the community feeling prescribed by Buddhism. There is advice for the progress in practice called the Basis of Merit Making as taught by the Buddha as follows:

1. Charity or generosity (*Dāna*)
2. Morality (*Śila*) and
3. Development of meditation which is of two kinds, namely: tranquillity of the mind and spiritual insight (*Bhāvanā*).

From the above-mentioned principle, it is clear that charity and serving society in the way of giving a helping hand and other spiritual practices are regarded as the additional practices of being a Buddhist.

To be a virtuous being in life, one needs to qualify with the listed virtues:

1. To be accompanied by moral shame (*Hiri*) and moral fear (*Ottappa*) for doing wrong or immoral acts.

2. To be accompanied by reasonable faith (*Ṣaddha*), morality (*Śila*) learning (*Suta*) sacrifice or generosity (*Caga*) and wisdom (*Panna*).
3. To be endowed with these four divine states of mind: Loving-kindness (*Metta*), wishing happiness to others as opposed to ill-will, Compassion (*Karuna*), wishing others to be free from suffering as opposed to violence, joy over others' achievement (*Mudita*), as opposed to jealousy, Equanimity (*Upekkah*), being impartial as opposed to prejudice.

The four states of the mind that are referred to here are similar to the bhāvās that are discussed in the Yoga system.

In order to give a more definite framework to guide man in his everyday living, Buddha gave the Eight-Fold Path, similar to the *Aṣtangika* Mārga of Yoga. The three learnings of Buddhism, '*ṭrisikṣa*', are discipline, contemplation, and wisdom.

Buddha insists that man should learn to accept this world full of suffering and despair as the only reality. According to him, those who regard this earthly life as pleasant (optimists) are ignorant of the disappointment and despair yet to come. On the other hand, those who succumb to the pains and miseries in life and regard them as unavoidable but inevitable, and they try to escape these situations in life. Buddha abhors them both.

According to him, man should accept the suffering and work his way out by conducting himself well ethically. This alone will lead to man's liberation. The extremes of both hedonism (as in the case of an indulgent lecher) and asceticism (such as a saint renouncing even his actions and efforts) need to be avoided. According to Buddha, in such extreme cases, a lecher is as much a sinner as a saint. He further goes on to say that it is not enough to merely avoid both extremes and take a Middle Path but is more important to transcend both extremes and go beyond.

Buddha believes that the best and simplest start to happiness is in 'Knowing and regarding Reality as it is.' It is imperative to realise the world as full of hardship and regulate one's daily conduct of life according to this knowledge and standpoint. Hence, he emphasises on developing traits such as perseverance, fortitude, and forbearance. It is also important for man to develop confidence to be bold and courageous to face life situations. Hence, diligence (*virya*) and bravery (*dhairya*) were included among the various virtues. The extremes of materialistic indulgence and ascetic self-mortification are both despised by the Buddhists.

Buddha accepted life as one full of suffering and he appeals to man to use his faculties of reasoning and emotionality within the ethical framework to deal with life. The first tenet of Buddhistic teaching for man is that he is egoless and selfless. This would definitely shock the *Vedāntin* who believes that all beings have a unity due to the Self or Spirit that is embodied in them. Buddhism is of the view that all things in the Universe being selfless have no original self or real being. A man does not have a core or a soul that he can consider his own core. A man exists, but he cannot grasp his real self as he has none. Buddhism believes that the existence of a man is nothing but an existence depending on a series of causations.

There is normally a tendency to see Buddhistic traces of ethics in Gītā ethics. There are similarities between the various concepts brought out in Buddhism and Gītā as both talk about man's position in life which is full of choices and dilemmas. Man can eliminate his suffering only with right, discriminative knowledge, where man realises the difference between the permanent and the transitory. All schools of thought in India show the path to liberation.

The Gītā theory of *rāga*, *dveṣa* and *moha* explained in the twelfth chapter is likened to the Buddhist theory of suffering due to attachments. The five steps of liberation mentioned in the Gītā are similar to those stated in Buddhist ethics. The idea of Niśkāmakarma as given in the Gītā is even more austere in Buddhist thought, as Buddhism believes that the love of humanity stems from disinterested motives of nobility and divinity, not from sentiment. To the Buddhist, the Summum Bonum of life is the extinction of sense and sensibility and the attainment of Nirvāṇa. The way to Nirvāṇa is contained in simple and eternal truths and techniques. The Four Noble Truths and the Aṣtāngika Mārga of Buddhism sum up the entire ethics of the school.

The relevance of Buddhist ethics needs no reaffirmation with regard to the management scene. It is mandatory that man follows the ethical path in order to enhance performance and rightfully gain what is due to him in life. In order to be excellent in his own endeavours and to be contented in life with his gains and achievements, man needs to understand and accept the truths revealed by Buddha. The teleological explanation to the four Truths and the Eight-Fold Path leads man to liberation, Nirvana.

The CEO of every organisation, in order to be exemplary, has to live life ethically, no matter what faith or religion he follows or what thought he subscribes to. Every executive has to achieve his goals in life through the achievement of the organisational goals. Following the path prescribed by Buddha, every individual attains his liberation through work and duty alone. The need to be rightful in speech, deed and thought is emphasised here as in all other schools of Indian thought.

Jainism

Jainism is an ancient tradition and school of thought with twenty-four leaders to their credit. The last of them, Mahāvira, was born in the 6th century BC. The religious and philosophical leaders of Jainism were called the *Tirthankārās*. The name 'Jainism' comes from the term *'Jinā'*, meaning 'conqueror'. The *'Jaina'* is one who has conquered his passions and emotions, has achieved liberation and attained perfection. *'Jina'* is the 'conqueror' who is victorious over the inner enemies of an individual, the *Kashāyas*:

Anger – *Krodha*
Pride – *Maan*
Deceit – *Māyā*
Greed – *Lobha*

So, the very name Jainism indicates the ethical character of this religion. The philosophy of Jainism is based on Life and Experience. It is a realistic school as it believes that whatever is in the Universe has an existence of its own. Existence is Reality and Reality is Existence. According to Jainism, God does not exist as the Creator of the Universe. The world or universe just exists as it is *Anādi*. The Universe is governed by the Law of *Karma* and no interference in the working of the laws of nature is required by any divine being.

Jains have two components of Reality: Soul/ / Jiva and Matter/ / Pudgala. The Soul is pure, all-knowing, energy and a life-force, and perfect happiness. This free Soul gets associated with Matter, and as a consequence, becomes limited and bound, only to experience unhappiness. Matter is viewed as both the atoms that constitute it and the forces that give form to those atoms. The Jains believed that matter could be both gross and subtle- gross, when visible as in the case of physical objects and subtle, as in the case of the Soul. Thus, the Jains held the view that the Soul is also Matter, albeit of a different composition, due to the chetana lakṣaṇa inherent in it, making it a Conscious Spirit.

Reality, according to Jainism, is complex. It can give rise to different perceptions and hence, no single perception of reality can be considered complete by itself. If one insisted that his view alone is the entire truth, then it would be a dogmatic assertion and a partial truth. This is the *Anekānta* view of Jainism, giving us an idea of the Jaina view of life. It presents intellectual non-violence vital for the right understanding of life.

When Mahavira was asked about the problems of eternality and immortality of souls, he said, 'Gautama, souls are eternal from the point of view of Substance and non-eternal from the point of view of modes.'[8] The problems of finiteness and infiniteness of the world is explained with reference to Substance, Space, Time, and Modes. Jainism needs to be looked at, neither as a code of conduct, with norms and rules, nor as a set of metaphysical principles, but as a way of life.

The existence of misery and suffering is as much recognised by Jainism as by the other schools of thought. 'The world is afflicted, miserable, difficult to instruct and without discrimination,' says the *Ācārangasūtra*.[9] This view of the Jainas was commented upon by Śilānka in the following way: 'All creatures, overcome by attachment, aversion and delusion, tormented by various, excessively bitter physical and mental miseries should try to know what is good and what is bad for the removal of that misery, and this is not possible without a peculiar type of discrimination.'[10]

Jainism has made a profound influence on the lives and culture of this country. It is very much essential for us to understand the effect of this school of thought, going beyond its religiosity, in order to understand the basic tenets and principles laid down by the *Tīrthankarās*. Jainism has contributed to literature, philosophy, and culture. Its contribution to Indian logic is to be found in the doctrine of *Anekāntavāda* and *Syādvāda*. The most characteristic feature of the Jaina ethics is the clear demarcation between the householder's duties and the ascetic's or monk's duties. The distinction is mentioned as '*muni dharma*' and '*śrāvaka dharma*', individual ethics and social ethics. Jainism teaches that the householder has his life rooted in compromise and hence, needs to learn to live with moderation as his keynote of existence.

Jaina doctrines may be broadly divided into (1) Philosophical and (2) Practical. Jaina philosophy contains metaphysics, epistemology, and psychology. Its practical doctrines relate to ethics, asceticism, monasticism. Jainism believes that every soul is potentially divine and can achieve Godhood. Every soul can become a God if it follows the ethical path prescribed by the Jaina philosophy, is what the Jainas believe. This is the idea of '*Saṁbhava*' as explained in Jainism. The ideal of life is liberation or mokṣa from suffering and man has to achieve this by his own efforts. Human existence is considered to be the highest form of existence, and this is a view that all other schools of thought in India too concur with. Every soul has to carve its own path through efforts or *Purushārthās* as understood in Jainism.

The soul exists, is eternal and immortal. It merely transmigrates from one body to another and getting embodied in a human body is considered to be a result of good *karma*. The soul has the following characteristics:

Infinite Knowledge – *Jñāna*
Infinite Faith – *Darśan*
Infinite Energy – *Vīrya* or Shakti
Infinite Bliss – *Ānanda*

The soul when born is impure as it has on itself the *kārmic* matter that is residual of the earlier births. It is hence necessary for the soul to know its true nature and by its own efforts discard the residual matter and attain *mokṣa*.

The Jaina theory of *Anekāntavāda* is a theory of liberalism. It is a special feature of Jainism. It actually implies that Reality is not one-sided but has many sides. It further elaborates on this view by saying that Truth (that is used synonymously with Reality) needs to be looked at from various angles. The perception of Reality by any individual from one angle is one-sided and hence, incomplcte. *Anekāntavada* is the opposite of *Ekāntavāda*. '*Aneka anta*' implies 'infinite ends' and it leads to the idea of looking at something from various points of view. Any object, thought, situation or subject needs to be looked at from different angles. Only then can a more truthful and complete picture of the same be obtained. Anekāntavāda is more popularly known as the Jaina theory of '*Syādvāda*'. '*Syat*' means that little is known and leaves scope for much more to be known. *Anekāntavāda* is the principle and the way to implement this principle is called *Syādvāda*.

What develops from this understanding of Reality and perception may be extended to the contemporary scenario of management. The theory of *Anekāntavāda* clearly emphasises on the need to develop lateral thinking and divergence in thought. It is necessary for all individuals to accept individuals with their differences and cultivate an attitude of tolerance and non-violence despite different people with divergence in thought and attitudes. If one is able to look at something differently from what one normally does, with a diametrically opposite standpoint, then it becomes easier and right to analyse something. There comes a judicious and justified understanding of the situation or object. The decrease of controversy in one's own mind leads to a clarity of thought which helps one to convince the others involved. Truth needs no justification, but it needs to be grasped rightly in order to be conveyed rightly. Thus, the theory of *Syādvāda* or *Anekāntavāda* helps in decision making and problem-solving. Thus, the theory of *Anekāntavāda* is expounded as the theory of Peaceful Coexistence.

The theory of *Anekāntavāda* leads us to Jaina ethics, giving us more clarity on the way of life prescribed for every individual in Jainism. The duty of man to himself is not alienated from his duty to society. There can exist no conflict between the duty of man to himself and society. According to Jainism, the highest good of society and community is the highest good to himself. Jaina ethics needs to be understood against the backdrop of Jaina metaphysics.

The scheme of Jaina ethics put forth certain rules of conduct that all individuals find it easy to understand and follow. Accordingly, rules and norms are divided into two categories:

1. Those prescribed for the householders or the *Śravakās*
2. Those prescribed for the ascetics and sages, *Munis*

The *Śravakā* is defined as '*Śrunotī iti Śrāvakaḥ'*, which means that a *Śravakā* is one who listens to and accordingly follows religious and ethical precepts. The ethical code prescribed for the *Śravakā* includes twelve *vratās* or vows, eleven *Pratimās* or stages of life, six *Avaṣyakās* or daily duties and the general principles of right conduct.

Let us see what Jainism has to offer us in the ethical dimension which can be applied to modern day's industrial set-up.

Vrata is a solemn oath taken by the individual after deliberation, in order to observe a code of conduct, and not merely obey as it has come from an authority. **The householders are expected to observe in their daily lives the following twelve *vratās*: five *anu-vratās*, three *guṇa vratās*, and four *śīla vratās*.**

The *Anu-vratās* are:

1. *Prāṇātipata Virmana Vrata*: *Ahiṁsā* or Non-violence: A Jaina can never harm or destroy a *Jiva*. The vow also forbids the killing of weak creatures and any other troublesome insects. One needs to treat animals well and with compassion. The individual also has the duty of respecting himself well and work towards his well-being. Taking care of oneself also implies non-violence.
2. *Mriṣāvāda Virmana Vrata*: *Satya* or Truth: This vow implies that one should never tell a lie. The vow is also concerned with commercial honesty. It forbids a person to tell lies for business and profit. This *vrata* includes the avoidance of certain habits such as speaking rashly to others, revealing secrets if something has to be kept confidential, giving false advice, cooking up accounts, etc.
3. *Adattadāna Virmana Vrata*: Non-stealing: No individual has the right to use another's property without the other person's consent.

Moreover, no individual has a right to expect what is not due to him or what he does not deserve. Every individual is allowed to rightfully ask for what he has put in efforts. Assuming ownership over anything that is not one's own is considered a grave sin that is punishable even under law. Even if the man escapes legal penalties, he will not escape divine justice, according to Jainism.

4. *Maithuna Virmana Vrata*: Chastity is a virtue that carries with it a lot of penance, austerity, and faithfulness. Refraining from legitimate copulation, indulging in illicit sex etc. are considered as sins. Excessive sexual indulgence and the perverted attitude towards women, evil talk about a different sex, marriage brokerage–all these are unpardonable acts. This particular *vrata* is relevant and significant in today's corporate scene where reports of cases of sexual abuse, and sexual exploitation of sexes for the sake of pleasure are abundant. Such reports expose the culture of the organisation as much as that of the individuals involved in such cases. The need to be chaste is emphasised with regard to both the sexes, with no sexist view encouraged or tolerated.
5. *Parigraha Virmana Vrata*: Non-avariceness, limiting possessions, not hoarding are traits that are encouraged by Jainism. *Jainas*, who are primarily involved in business and commercial activities, and who handle a lot of finance, shrewdly realised that the true way of increasing wealth is by curbing desires and passions. It becomes necessary to limit the necessities of life, resist temptations and ensure peace of mind.

All *Jainas* along with the observance of the *Anuvratās*, need to stay away from the four '*Makaras*': *Madhya* (wine), *Māṁsa* (meat), *Makhan* (butter) and *Madhu* (honey). These are considered to be the Mūla guṇās to be observed by every *Jaina*. *Madhya* and *Maṁsa* are avoided as one is considered to be intoxicating and the other unhealthy for man. In addition to this, the killing of animals for the sake of one's own palate is considered a sin for two reasons- one, as no man has the right to use another form of life for self-gratification and two, as it violates the norms of environmental ethics.

Guṇā Vratās

In addition to the five main *Anuvratās* and the four '*Makaras,*' there are three special vows relating to the limitation and determination of his daily work, food, and enjoyment. Jainism believes that it is possible to restrict the extent of sin by restricting the motives for sinning. It is possible to do so by restricting one's area of functioning with a focus on certain goals that are determined within the ethical framework. This includes *Digvrata*, *Deṣavrata* (according to some *Jainās*, it is *Shikshā vrata*), and *Anarthadandavrata*.

The first *Guṇā Vratā* talks about restricting one's worldly activities to fixed areas geographically. It is believed that unnecessary travel should be avoided, as it will keep one away from distractions and pleasures. The second *Guṇā Vratā is* to be understood as living with discipline and restraint in speech, conduct, and duties. The need to develop oneself with the attitude of gratitude, compassion, humility as a continuous learner, with the persistence to evolve as a good soul is the second *vratā*. The third *vratā* refers to refraining from sadistic actions that result in pleasure for the individual at the cost of others' pain. This reiterates the need to respect life in all forms in the created world.

Shikṣa Vratās

Disciplinary or Educative Vows: A householder is also required to practice the following vows devised specially for householders in consonance with the discipline of the ascetics.

1. *Sāmāyika*: taking a vow to devote some time for contemplation and meditation for self-development and spiritual enhancement.
2. *Pausadhopavāsa*: taking a vow to fast on four days of the month, the two eighth and the two fourteenth days of the month.
3. *Upabhoga-Paribhoga Parimāna*: taking a vow of restraining oneself with regard to everyday enjoyment of consumable and non-consumable pleasures.
4. *Atithi Saṁvibhāga*: taking a vow to take one's food only after feeding the ascetics or other pious and elderly in the household.

In general, it will be observed that Jainism teaches primarily to respect life in all forms. The universality and unity of the Spirit in all forms of life accepted by Jainism is very similar to the Advaitin's view of life. The dignity of each individual is well protected in Indian thought. This is evident in all the ethical teachings, no matter which school of thought is referred to.

In the course of this study of ethical viewpoints in Indian philosophy, it has been observed that the concept of human rights is clearly a Western and more contemporary concept. The idea of instigating to fight against atrocities due to violations of rights is not seen in Indian thought. This is so because the idea of duty is overemphasised in all schools of thought, which leads to the protection of the other's rights automatically. If each one performed his duties well, there will never be a need to fight for protection of rights be it for oneself or for others.

Accommodating all mutual metaphysical differences, all major schools of thought that represent Indian thought, grapple with the exposition of human personality, the suffering of man and his liberation from it all. The schools give a detailed description of human personality, with a prescriptive techniques and methods that lead man to self-actualisation and self-realisation. The merging of the individual, phenomenal self with the cosmic self is also mentioned in most of the schools. The philosophical endeavours in India begin and end with a teleology.

References

1. Sharma R.P., Human Personality in Ancient Indian Thought, Kanishka Publishers and Distributors, New Delhi, p. 11.
2. Garbe Richard, Die Sāṁkhya Philosophie, pp. 189–191, cf. Also, Mircea Eliade, Yoga: Freedom and Immortality, Trans. W.R. Trask (New York: Pantheon Books, 1958) pp. 367 – 368.
3. Hermann Jacobi, Review of Second Edition of Garbe's Die Sāṁkhya Philosophie, in Gottingsche gelehrte Anzeigen, 181 Jahrang (Berlin, 1919) p 28.
4. Sharma R.P., Human Personality in Ancient Indian Thought. Kanishka Publishers and Distributors, New Delhi, p. 39.
5. Muller Max, The Six Systems of Indian Philosophy, Associated Publishing House, New Delhi, pp. 290–291.
6. Rajendralal Mitra (1822–1891), *Yoga: The Science of the Soul*, p. 291.
7. Hindu Culture – An Introduction. Swami Tejomayananda, The Hindu Culture Series, Central Chinmaya Mission trust, Mumbai-400072, 1993, p. 43.
8. Kalghatgi Dr. T.G. Jainism – A Study, Department of Jainology and Prakrits, University of Mysore, 1976, Mysore.
9. Ācārāngasūtra, SBE, Vol.XXII, 1.1.2.1. Jaina Ethics, Dayananda Bhargava, Motilal Banarsidass, Delhi, 1968. p. 3.
10. Ibid. p. 4.

V

YOGA: THE MAGIC TO SELF-MANAGEMENT

Yoga is a school of thought that constitutes the perennial wisdom of India. The Yogic culture is evident in all aspects of life in India, be it food, dress styles, communication, postures, activities, habits, and attitudes. It is expressed in all art forms such as music, dance, and sculpture. All through the years, yoga has remained as one of the most important facets of Indian Culture and has managed to remain vibrant and responsive to the changing times all through this period. As it developed in India, it came to be associated with the development of Hinduism and its philosophy. Yet, in its essence, it has always remained away from any religious doctrines or dogmas and never demanded acceptance of any specific belief system. It has always remained as a pathway to realisation of Truth, open for all the people professing different faiths belonging to different religions and different races. In essence, it is a path of spiritual enquiry, awakened by the earnest desire for having a deeper understanding of Life and the entire phenomenon associated with it.

The literal meaning of the word Yoga in Sanskrit is Integration. In this sense, Yoga represents a process through which one can learn how to live in the most integrated way. It involves therefore the process of identification and then elimination of all that would contribute to disintegration. It teaches one to integrate the body, mind, and soul in oneself. It further goes on to teach integration of individual goals and objectives with the social and organisational goals. It is also a way of life that integrates the phenomenal with the transcendental, the individual soul with the Divine. When taken in this sense it becomes a continuous process, requiring constant vigilance and involving all the aspects of life.

The process of identification of all the elements causing ill health and the use of appropriate techniques to neutralise their ill effects is one of the primary concerns of Yoga. When Yoga is used as a science of health and healing, all its techniques and methods that are meant for the spiritual experiences automatically get geared to do their job for the promotion of the wellbeing of the individual. Yoga is a way of life. This lifestyle includes Āhara (food), Uccāra (Right Speech), Ācara (routines and relationships), Vihāra (relaxation and recreation), and Vicāra (thought processes). As major aspects that determine individual health and wellbeing, Indian thought has discussed them in detail.

Determinants of Lifestyle: Āhara, Uccāra, Ācara, Vihāra, Vicāra:

Āhāra

As the food, so the mind.
As the mind, so the speech:
As the mind and speech, so the action.
As the action, so the lifestyle.
As the lifestyle, so the man.

There can be no life without food, water, and air. The ancient yogis have given enough thought to this aspect of man's life and they have suggested food habits that can help to preserve and protect health. Their analytic mind has led to the categorisation of food into three kinds: Sāttvic, Rājasic and Tāmasic. These categories come from the Sāṁkhya analysis of Matter as having three guṇas: Sattva, Rajas, and Tāmas.

Āhāras tvapi sarvasya trividho bhavati priyaḥ
Yajñas tapas tatha dānaṁ teṣaṁ bhedam imam ṣṛṇu.
– Chapter XVII, Verse 7.

In the Bhagavad Gītā, Lord Kṛṣṇa discusses the three kinds of foods that are dear to different kinds of men, classifying them on the basis of the Guṇās: Sattva, Rajas and Tāmas. According to the Lord, food is of great importance as the mind is formed by the food that is taken by the individual. It is only pure food that helps to develop pure mind, and it is only the pure mind that grasps the spiritual truth.

On the hypothesis that spiritual excellence depends largely on mental efficiency and steadfastness, which in turn depends on physical fitness, the ethics of Gītā proceeds to distinguish various kinds of foods and their effect on human nature. For the support of life and the maintenance of a healthy body, food is significant. According to the Gītā, the sāttvika kind of food is the best for the individual with the higher goals in life who desires peace, tranquillity, and contentment. It nurtures life, provides energy and vigour, promotes positivity and joy, is simple and palatable.

Āyuḥ sattva balārogya sukha prīti vivardhanāḥ
Rasyāḥ snigdhāḥ sthirā hṛdyā āhāraḥ sāttvikapriyāḥ
– Chapter XVII, Verse 8.

Foods which augment life, vitality, purity, strength, joy, and cheerfulness are foods that are sāttvic in nature. These foods give health and good appetite. They are substantial, savoury, agreeable and oleaginous. Sāttvic food is natural and is therefore, easily digestible. There is generally a preference for vegetarian food under this category. It is required to generate energy, rejuvenate weary and tired bodies, and create alertness in the minds of individuals. Sāttvic food, moreover, does not tax the individual's digestive system and makes the individual feel light, relaxed, and peaceful. This kind of food makes the individual feel contented, bringing in an attitude of Santośa.

Yad tad agre viṣaṁ iva pariṇāme 'mṛtopamam
Tat sukhaṁ sāttvikaṁ proktam ātmabuddhiprasādajam.
– Chpt XVIII, Verse 38.

That pleasure which is like poison at first but in the end is like nectar, born of the purity of one's own mind of Self-realisation, is declared to be Sāttvic.

Certain foods are not tasty to the tongue but are good for health of the individual. A taste for such healthy, nutritious food should be cultivated in the individual from childhood. Moreover, bitter medicines are administered for certain diseases. The taste of the medicine should not prevent the individual from taking it for his own good. When extended to the aspect of self-realisation, the verse discusses the need for practicing self-denial and sacrifice to attain Brahmānanda. In spiritual life, the need to endure and the significance of determination to persevere is highlighted.

Kaṭvāmla lavaṇātyuṣna tīkṣna rūkṣa vidāhinaḥ
Āhāra rājasaye 'ṣṭā duḥkha śokāmaya pradāḥ
– Chapter XVII, Verse 9.

Foods that are bitter, sour, saline, excessively hot, pungent, dry, and causing thirst are rājasic foods. They produce pain, sorrow, and disease according to the Lord. These foods immediately produce discomfort in the body of the individual who has consumed it and consequently the individual feels mentally uncomfortable. If the Sādhaka is in the quest of spiritual progress, he should avoid such foods. Rājasic foods are said to produce diseases, 'amayapradāḥ', as they are tough on the digestive system but good for the palate alone.

The Lord explains how rājasic foods are delusive. They are tasty, and good for the palate. They are tongue-ticklers. Such foods are, however, difficult to digest and give rise to various kinds of diseases. They produce grievous discomfort to the body and disturb the Dhyāna Sādhana of the individual. The mind becomes agitated and distracted. It cannot remain steady in contemplation.

Rājasic food is as its name suggests includes food that creates the need to act and move. As rajas, the guṇa, suggests energy, similarly the food that is rājasic makes a person active, to the point of restlessness, aggressiveness, angry, anxious, and even irritated. Rājasic food is preferably taken in cold weather, as the body requires energy to keep itself warm and active. It is also prescribed for all those who do manual or physical work.

Yātayāmaṁ gatarasaṁ pūti paryuṣitaṁca yat
Ucchiṣṭam api cā 'medhyaṁ bhojanaṁ tāmasapriyam

– Chapter XVII, Verse 10.

Food, which is stale, dry, rotten, and putrid, refuse and impure is classified under this category. These foods are harmful to anyone and hence not advised for consumption at all. They not only damage the system, corrupt the blood, and disturb physically, they also disturb the mind. It makes individuals live under a delusion as it keeps them totally in the dark about themselves and others. Tāmasic food, as the name suggests, is food that makes an individual slothy, lethargic, inert, lazy. It is normally food that is difficult to digest and is not energising. Such food is said to produce a lot of gas and phlegm.

It needs to be noticed that the various food patterns that have been adopted by people in India have been determined by the station (varna) and the stage (āṣrama) that the individual belongs to. The age of the individual, his role in society and family, the kind of activities that he engages in and the extent to which he exerts himself determines his diet. Moreover, students, scholars and academicians, sages and seers, pious people and men of character observe strictly sāttvic diets, in order to foster peace, contentment and mental energy to help the study of arts, sciences and scriptures. On the other hand, the army, the protectors, the manual labourers, and the householders are allowed to have rājasic foods as they needed to exert themselves physically. Tāmasic food is generally avoided by all, as there is never a need for slothful, lazy, and lethargic people in society.

There is another justification given for the preference of sāttvic food, which is predominantly vegetarian food in Indian culture. It is considered unethical to kill life for the sake of the gratification of one's needs. All forms of life are respected and worshipped, and the worship of animal-forms only reiterates the idea of divinity in all forms seen in Nature. Since the general masses find it difficult to understand and grasp the inner deeper significance of the scientific and hygienic reasons of these observances, they were prescribed and recommended as part of religious duties.

The moral justification for this belief is based on the theories of Ahiṁsā and Karma. Ahiṁsā teaches the values of non-aggression and non-violence of any living creature. Ahiṁsā aims at non-hurting, non-injury, and non-killing. The law of Karma teaches that one is the maker of his own destiny and good deeds alone will result in happiness and bad deeds bring forth misery. Taking away someone's life for the satisfaction of one's own need is considered immoral anyway. Meat eating would necessitate the slaughter of animals which is a violation of the principle of Ahiṁsā. Moreover, those who believe that they do not want to increase their kārmic residual on their soul which will determine their next birth also abstain from non-vegetarianism.

The physiological reason justifying this teaching is that most meat increases the acidic content and stress hormones in the blood. This results in lowering of oxygen content in the blood giving rise to a situation of lessened resistance and immunity in the body. According to the yogis, the intake of vegetarian food is conducive to meditation as the five senses, the mind, the brain, and the heart are kept healthy due to the right extent of oxygen in the body. Intake of Sāttvic food is a prerequisite for meditation and spiritual development, as the type and quality of food determines mental and emotional stability and health.

In the modern world, the choice of food is primarily based on taste, the time taken for its preparation, and the convenience in packaging while travelling. The industrial world has made it mandatory for people to manage with ready and fast foods that come in 'easy to use' packs across the counters. All it requires is a little heating and boiling. The new approach to food is to break it into proteins, carbohydrates, vitamins, fat minerals etc. food value. People who are very fastidious about their diet and health with a modern approach tend to calculate calories before consuming anything. In Yoga and Ayurveda, it is a tendency to select foods based on the gunās, with a consideration of the effect that the food has on the body and mind of the individual. What is necessary is to understand the nutritive value of the food, its resultant psycho-spiritual value, not just the caloric value.

Another important fact to be understood is that one's diet should be in accordance with the geographical, climatic, and ethnic factors of the place where he lives and the constitution one inherits as a member of the native land. If observed carefully, it will be found that the local people eat what is locally and seasonally available. The choice of foods ought to be determined by its agreeableness to the individual constitution. This is actually Nature's way of looking after humans, which man has failed to decipher and value. It provides for man in consonance with his bodily needs by growing in Nature what is ideal for him, by changing crops, fruits, and vegetables seasonally.

This idea of Āhāra, when understood in this perspective leads us to the ethics of Environment, where man needs to sustain and nurture the environment in order to save himself. When man looks after and protects the environment, it should be done as an obligation and duty to himself. He is not obliging anyone else in doing so.

In the study of man and his daily requirement of nutrition, it has been observed that man needs a replenishment every four hours. Thus it is almost mandatory that man eats every four hours to provide for the body in the form of breakfast, lunch, snack with tea and dinner. The body clock gets used to the diet if the individual is regular with his food habits and this helps in avoiding indigestion, gas, and acidity. As the body is rested during the night and fresh to start work in the morning, it is advisable to start the day with a heavy breakfast, slowly reducing the quantity during the day, ending with an early and light dinner.

Natural hunger is looked at as a healthy sign for good health. If the individual feels normally hungry with a gap of four hours between meals, it is considered ideal. Eating less or overeating should be avoided. In order to improve the resistance and to increase immunity, it is important to understand one's own body well and its requirements need to be met. In every aspect of the human being, there are individual differences which need to be accepted. Hence, what is good for one cannot be imposed on another, as each body demands specifically.

Each aspect is inter-related and is of paramount importance. A life full of joy, serenity and good health will be attained only when the diet is well planned and well balanced. In order to respect the food eaten by one, it is necessary to observe Mauna or silence while eating food in cheerful mood. It is also advisable to avoid drinking water before, during or immediately after meals, as it dilutes the digestive secretions leading to indigestion. It is not considered a healthy practice to eat in haste, eat while busy or preoccupied, or to eat while engaged physically or mentally, indulging in anything other than food. The posture adopted while eating, the peace in the atmosphere, the joyous and pleasant attitude, and the reverence to the food in front of one—all these factors need to be kept in mind for good digestion and absorption of food. A positive attitude towards oneself and the world, and the right food that one consumes hastens digestion of food and absorption of nutrients. The habit of saying a prayer before meals is basically to still the mind, develop an attitude of positivity, with feelings of gratitude and humility towards the one who has given us this daily meal. Such practices though found outdated and redundant today have immeasurable benefits.

Yoga does not support the idea of Fasting if it involves starving totally. According to this school of thought, the body requirements necessarily have to be met at regular intervals, with caution exercised to avoid overeating or poor eating. Nutrition has to be provided regularly and systematically to keep the body fit and the mind stable. In case of overeating on some occasion, the individual may skip his next meal to substitute it with a fruit diet or a salad or even just soup. Fasting or taking light food helps to give the digestive system rest. It gives the digestive system enough time to throw out toxins from the body. Then at least the body will get its nutrition, and some fibre for clearing the system. This helps the digestive system to recoup from the stress it has undergone and regain its normalcy. Denial of nutrition to the body will only lead to depression in the individual. Such practices lead the individual to compulsive eating habits in order to overcome the depression set in due to denial of food to the body when required.

Various psychosomatic diseases are traced to such practices that may be done with the right intention but wrong techniques. In order to avoid such faulty food habits and to be healthy, one needs to know oneself, one's body requirements and adjust food patterns accordingly. Fasting too needs to be done scientifically, with abstinence of specific kinds of foods to the right extent for a stipulated period of time, under the guidance of an expert. Fasting done mechanically as part of a ritualistic practice is condemned. It is more a sort of self-discipline. Fasting depends on faith and faith is positive thinking. This itself helps the individual to be healthy.

Śariramādhyaṁ khalu dharmasādhanaṁ.
Kalidāsa Kumārasaṁbhavaṁ – 5/33.

This psychophysical body is the best means to realise the goal of dharma.

The individual should realise that it is his duty to keep himself healthy and fit. Thus it comes under the purview of Dharma, to provide for oneself and the others who are dependent on him. It is in conformity to the dharmic principles that an individual should be regular and disciplined regarding intake of food. Moreover, the knowledge of the right kinds of foods to be taken at the right time and the right quantity is equally important. This wisdom or Jñāna also implies that the individual should know himself well, his physiological requirements, the availability and suitability of the food that he chooses to consume.

Yoga teaches the attitude of Vairāgya with regard to food too. The individual needs to look at the intake of food more as a matter of dharma, whereby he is able to choose what is right for him and not what he likes. He is then able to restrain himself and his cravings with regard to food. This helps to avoid indulgence in food that is tasty but necessarily not nutritious and agreeable. This detachment brings in clarity and confidence regarding food, giving it the necessary significance for personal growth. He must free himself from all attachment and destroy in himself all desire and all craving for certain foods. The intake of food should be well planned, the diet so designed that it leaves the individual contented and satisfied. The individual has to be mentally equipoised to manage the best assimilation of the food. The right kind of food taken to the right extent will definitely keep the individual charged for the entire day, leading to a calm and stable mental disposition. The individual starts his day ready to take charge of his own life and duties. The end of the day does not see him fatigued and exhausted but rested and satisfied. He experiences a feeling of Santośa.

Uccāra

The Gītā discusses the austerity of speech in Chapter XVII, Verse 15 in the following manner:

Anudvegakaraṁ vākyaṁ satyaṁ priyahitaṁ ca yat
Svādhyāyābhyāsanaṁ cai 'va vāṇmayaṁ tapa ucyate

The right kind of speech is that which does not excite others, which is truthful, delighting to the listener, beneficial to those who listen. Speech should convey that the speaker has studied the Vedas, Upaniṣads and the Purāṇas. He should be interested in sharing his knowledge with others.

'Anudvegakaraṁ vākyaṁ' implies that the refinement and austerity of speech is seen if it fulfils the four conditions mentioned in the above referred verse:

- not exciting or inciting, pleasant to the ears, soft and gently spoken.
- adhering to truth, with the right choice of words, and the right manner of conveying
- beneficial to those who listen to the speaker
- conveying truths and knowledge.

The Gīta emphasises on the need for Svādhyāya and Satsaṇga as it is necessary for the individual to know his real self and the Reality around him. If the individual takes to meditation and reading of the scriptures, he develops the right attitudes, learns to discriminate and this vivekajñāna helps his communication. He develops mysterious powers that enable him to speak the truth fearlessly and directly. He also conveys to the listener that he expects nothing in return for what he has shared. His clarity of thought improves and his inspiration and enthusiasm becomes contagious. This will inspire others to follow his path of svādhyāya and meditation. The speaker with just the weapon of his speech can motivate others to seek Truth.

Many underestimate the power of speech. But Indian culture has always given importance to sounds and speech, as is seen in chants, mantras, and recitations. The power wielded by music on health has been accepted long back in our culture, which is now being talked about in other cultures. The very acceptance of 'Śabda Brahman' in our philosophies shows how the power of sound is significant for us. Moreover, the mythological origin to the world is shown as it emerges from the mouth of Brahma with the utterance of a syllable 'AUM'.

Speech that provokes others to act wrongly is definitely considered wrong. Conveying what one does not know, or mean is again considered a sin. Gossip, slander, untruth, lies, provocation, incitement, ridicule, and mockery are all characteristics of speech that is wrong and vicious.

It is important to keep the mind still, serene and calm, with a lot of clarity in thought and speech, before conveying what is one's thought or feeling. It is not only what is conveyed that is important. The manner is equally significant. The speaker should have a pleasant facial expression and look serene. He should have self-control and be pure in thought and feeling. There should be no ill will or cruelty displayed while talking.

Ācāra

When it comes to ācāra, Indian philosophy needs no certification or authentication externally, as the entire philosophical trend seems pervaded by the theme of Dharma. As expounded in the Smṛti śāstras, ācāra is the ability to discriminate between dhārmic and adhārmic actions. It is the enhancement of the ability to discriminate whether our actions are in accordance with the ethical norms and standards of the society in which we live.

The Smṛti śāstras say – 'Ācāro prathamo dharmaḥ', which implies that the first and foremost duty in man's life is good conduct by following dharma. His likes and dislikes, bias, prejudice and his whims and fancies, normally guide man. This leads to our discrimination getting clouded. The above-mentioned spiritual injunction thus leads to two major guidelines: (1) that one needs to be aware of one's station in life and be following one's duty well, with no external force or coercion required;

(2) that in being a spiritual being, one needs to lay stress on good behaviour and conduct, with internalisation of values and disciplining oneself. Good conduct should be given foremost significance, with no subjugation of ethical values to any material achievement.

In Indian culture, an individual is honoured and respected for his conduct than his scholarly persona. The fact that he is wise and dhārmic elevates an individual in society rather than his knowledge of the various scriptures, arts, or sciences. If the individual is a scholar with a lot of knowledge with bad conduct, he is looked down upon much more than an individual who is primarily ignorant or 'mooḍa' and is bad in conduct. In the case of the latter, his ignorance is not excused but he is looked at with more compassion, as there is a hope in his case that he could be taught to change. Nevertheless, the individual who is scholarly is clearly aware of the right and wrong and deliberately chooses to be bad or immoral, thus warranting no compassion or sympathy.

Talking of vidyā or knowledge as essential for good conduct or ācāra, it needs to be quoted from Swami Tejomayananda's book, *Hindu Culture-An Introduction*: 'Akṣara refers to the alphabet and literature and Sākṣara means one who knows the alphabet, who is an educated, literate person.' So ironically it is said, 'When literate people, Sākṣarās, become perverted in their minds, they become Rākṣasās.' Every man needs to realise that he lives in society with accountability to society and there is no one who can claim to be above or beyond law.

The four determinants of good conduct and dharma as accepted by our seers are: 'śruti, smṛti, sadācāra, and svasya ca priyam ātmanaḥ'

1. Śruti (श्रुति) – 'That which is heard' – this gives divine law
2. Smṛti (स्मृति) – 'That which is remembered' – offers practical wisdom
3. Sadācāra (सदाचार) – 'Good conduct or customs'– experiential knowledge, even customs and rituals
4. Svasya ca priyam ātmanaḥ (स्वस्य च प्रियं आत्मनः) – 'What is pleasing to oneself', ensures personal authenticity

Śruti and smṛti are scriptural and testimonial authorities that are accepted in our culture. Sadācāra implies the conduct that is accepted as good and noble in accordance with ethical norms by society. This is the individual conscience or inner sense of right and wrong, which recognises that personal integrity and self-reflection are vital in ethical decision-making. Moreover, it encourages one to act in ways that resonate with one's inner values, provided they do not contradict the other three sources.

Dharma, according to Manu, is 'what is done by persons well-versed in the Vedas and always approved by the conscience or reason of virtuous persons'. What is approved by the conscience is universal and hence, accepted as right, and whatever is disapproved is wrong. As Manu says, 'What gives satisfaction to the soul is right and what gives dissatisfaction is wrong... The traditional good conduct of generations (pāramparyakramāgataḥ) of virtuous persons in a country is called sadācāra or ācāra. It constitutes the Ethos of a community.'[1]

Ācāra thus becomes a major source of Dharma, be it customary morality or reflective morality. The last determinant implies one's choices determined by the joy and pleasure that results from one's actions. If an individual cares for his happiness and tries to avoid sorrow, then he should learn to respect the fact that others also want happiness in their lives. One does not have the right to achieve or enjoy at the cost of others. The idea of dharma when understood with its pragmatic dimensions leads us to realise its extent beyond legality or illegality of actions. An action that is legal is within the purview of ethics but an action that is moral goes beyond its legality.

The four factors that are determinants are thus called 'caturveda dharma lakṣaṇa'. The recognition and acceptance of one's own dignity and that of others is itself a sure and certain guideline for dharma. Respect for life in all forms and value for human dignity is a major dictum that comes with this injunction. Dharma is the permanent excellence of character, which is the result of the prolonged performance of duties by an individual.

Vicāra

The term 'vicāra' is understood as 'thought', 'reflection', 'discrimination', 'clear vision' and 'thought processes leading to vivekajñāna'. According to Patanjali, 'vicāra is a mental activity related to subtle objects', in which there is analysis of all experiences in his life. According to Vācaspati Miśra, 'vicāra is a mental activity by means of which the subject brings before consciousness all the "subtle" particularities and constitutive parts of a "subtle" object. It is the "making evident" of the sūkṣma, the subtle.'

As mentioned in the Gītā:

Manaḥ prasādaḥ saumyatvaṁ maunam ātmavinigrahaḥ
Bhāvasaṁṣuddhir ity etat tapo mānasam ucyate

Keeping the mind serene, untroubled, and unexcited is important. It is equally important to be calm and composed. The individual should be pleasant, with no cruel thoughts in his mind. He should observe silence, meditate and contemplate well to gain that for which he is striving. He should have self-control. These help to develop purity of thought and feeling. Anger, hatred, lust, fear, and greed darken and twist the countenance of the individual. Fleeting thoughts and passions darken the mind and face of the individual. All these need to be avoided. It is hence necessary to be Sāttvic in thought and feeling to develop the right attitudes and behaviours.

The yogi is first taught to realise what are his weaknesses/Kleśas. He has to learn to practice techniques and develop attitudes/Bhāvas that will help him eradicate these weaknesses. The yogi thus adapts himself better to change that is inevitable and adopts a way of life that, to a large extent, helps him to express his life philosophy.

Kleśās and Bhāvas: Acquired Deficiencies in Human Personality:

Constitutional defects in individuals that lead to actions resulting in pain and misery are called Kleśās. There are **five such defects in humans that need to be corrected: *Avidyā, Asmitā, Rāga, Dveśa, Abhiniveśa.***

Avidyā, Ignorance

This includes ignorance not only about the world, but also about oneself. It is important that the individual has discriminative knowledge that helps him to understand the Reality. Moreover, an individual has to accept his dharma, duty, and live his life with a purpose. For this, man has to have the right kind of knowledge. The information that man collects from various sources about the various aspects of life, and the created world needs to be comprehended rightly. This information with its teleological steering leads him to lead life wisely. Avidyā or ignorance clouds his mind, not allowing him to think or act rightly. Such Avidyā needs to be eradicated as early as possible as man lives under delusion with this Kleśa.

Asmitā, Ego

Egoism leads man to believe that he alone is real and supreme. All others are looked down upon as incapable, with inadequate knowledge or resources. The egoistic individual believes that he is indispensable, and his absence makes a big difference to the work done. Looking at oneself as superior to the others alienates him from groups and this hampers his social development. He ends up being isolated and lonely. Man needs to realise that every individual is special and unique. All have their special qualities and potentialities. It requires people and opportunities to tap these abilities in others. This can be done only with an open approach, cultivation of humility and an altruistic attitude. Humility dawns upon a man when he learns to see his faults and insufficiencies along with the good qualities and virtues in others.

Rāga, Attachment

Man's suffering, according to Indian thought, is due to attachment. Man is drawn to things fleeting and temporary. He needs to know and understand the Real in order to eliminate suffering in life. Man's attachment is normally to his own bodily self, his family, his groups, his peers, his kith and kin, his wealth, and his organisation. The sense of belongingness is not decried here, but the sense of possession that comes with attachment is criticised. It is good to possess but it is bad to get possessed by the possessions. When man starts possessing, then he has expectations that give rise to frustrations and misery when left unfulfilled. Hence, it is advised that man function with a sense of detachment, with the idea of duty as the prime motivator. Man realises that he lives in society with a purpose, and this purpose has to be the attainment of liberation.

Dveśa, Hatred

The earlier kleśas lead him to the development of feelings of love and hate. The more a man is attached to someone or something, the more he has the feeling of possession. The more this feeling, the more he tries to exercise control. Self-love, ego and perceiving others as below/ failing in one's expectations, gives rise to dislike, hostility, and hatred. This need in him to control results of others' actions leads to negative emotions if he is unsuccessful. Without understanding the purpose of others' actions, he develops a feeling of hatred for all those who are contrary or dissenting to his views. According to Yoga and the Gītā, any excess of emotion is detrimental. Hatred as a negative emotion is destructive in nature. It destroys not only the others around but also the one who hates. It affects physical health, disturbs mentally and emotionally, leaving the individual weak and sick. Hatred breeds revengefulness. Nothing positive can be achieved by hating someone or something. The realisation that all are part of the same Reality and essentially have the same cosmic energy in each should help discard such feelings.

Abhiniveśa, Fear of Annihilation, Loss, Vanish (from the scene) or Death

Abhiniveśa is a kleśa resulting in fears and anxieties. The kleśa egoism does not allow an individual to lose face in any situation. The egoistic individual will not take loss or failure very well. Moreover, his attachment to things and people make him feel dependency on them all. His possession gives a sense of security to him. There is no self-confidence and self-reliance that has developed in this individual that can make him feel independent and detached. Thus, the constant fear of losing his securities leave him anxious and depressed. He loves himself too and almost looks at himself as immortal. Death is an eventuality that needs to be understood and accepted. Loss is one side of a coin, which shows gain on the other. Man needs to accept both loss and gain with a sense of detachment. In order to eliminate all fears in life with vivekajñāna, man needs to be detached.

Patanjali names certain dispersions of the mind that are obstacles to man's development and progress in life. He calls them the '*vikṣepa*' of the mind.

The various *vikṣepās* are:

Vyādhistyāna saṁśaya pramādālasyāvirati
Bhrānti darśanā labdha bhūmikatvānavas
thitatvāni cittavikṣepās te'ntarayaḥ

- ***Vyādhi,*** sickness: physiological disorders, disorderliness of the secretions, and malfunctioning of the organs of the body, disorder of structure or function of the human body or mind.
- ***Styāna,*** apathy: 'the inability of the mind for action.' This leads to inactivity, incompetence, mental laziness, lack of enthusiasm, debility, dullness, etc.
- ***Saṁśaya,*** doubt thought which oscillates between two extreme alternatives or options, making it difficult for the individual to decide.
- ***Pramāda,*** negligence, heedlessness, carelessness, 'the disposition to non-performance (anānusthāna), indifference to the means which lead to samādhi'.
- ***Ālasya,*** laziness, lethargy, or idleness; indolence and inertia produced by the heaviness of the body and of the mind. Patanjali explains this inertia as 'heaviness of the body due to 'kapha' and 'heaviness of the mind due to tamas.' These two can cause inertia which result in inactivity and listlessness, making the individual lazy and slothy.
- ***Avirati,*** non-cessation of wants: the greed of the mind, the essence of which is the contact with sense-objects and the mind's ceaseless desire for the acquisition of objects. This creates a yearning for sensual pleasures and the individual clings to enjoyment derived from sense-objects.

Patanjali explains this *vikṣepa* in the following manner. According to him, every individual mind is always agitated due to the onslaught of ideas, thoughts, sensations, and emotions. These give rise to human activity. Such individuals are always rājasic in nature. They are restless, involved in constant activity and motion, with the idea of attaining something more physical and material. Avirati is the non-cessation and non-detention of such mental and physical activity that results in the individual getting tired and fatigued. There may not be great productive or contributive activity done by such individuals. A yogic individual would work to the optimum extent for a maximum output, actualising his potential, without exerting in futile activities.

- ***Bhrānti*** darśana, erratic perception: erroneous knowledge arising out of wrong understanding, false notions, illusions, delusions, misconceptions, etc. It could be either incomplete or partial perception or erroneous perception.
- ***Alabdhabhūmikatva,*** lack of initiative: 'the fact of being a person for whom a bhūmi has not been attained', which implies that the individual has not yet worked enough to attain the degree, state, position, stage, or situation that he deserves and requires. This is the 'bhūmi' that is referred to here. Vyāsa explains it as 'not attaining the stage, bhūmi, of the concentration of the mind, samādhī'. Patanjali however explains 'bhūmi' as the stage of attaining strong base or foundation and the individual being firm, dṛdha, in whatever he thinks.
- ***Anavasthitatva,*** inconstancy: 'the fact that the mind does not maintain itself in the stage, referred to as bhūmi, that it has attained.' There is a reference to the general weaknesses of human nature, which hinders the realisation of Truth for the seeker. This *vikṣepsa* leaves the individual unstable and fidgety.

All these vikṣepās are obstacles for the individual who wants to attain samādhi through the path of Yoga. They are obstacles in man's progress towards the realisation of both the individual and cosmic self.

Yoga talks of **purification of the mind through the development of four positive feelings**. They are:

- ***Maitrī*** – Friendliness
- ***Karuṇā*** – Compassion
- ***Muditā*** – Joy in the joy of others
- ***Upekṣā*** – Indifference, non-attention, non-violence, non-involvement, and non-co-operation in the wrong. Giving up the negative. Develops a proactive but detached attitude in the

individual. Helps to understand the negative of an individual and situation and try corrective measures instead of merely criticising.

These four feelings and attitudes are called social attitudes. They help us in developing good relations with all around us, including nature. An individual who sees the divine in all will naturally consider all as friends. With this attitude, it becomes easier to belong. For such an individual, home is where the heart is. So the feeling of belonging will help him to reach out, help and be sensitive to all. He feels joy in the joy of others and pain in their suffering. Such individuals can never be contributing to situations that give misery to others. He is compassionate and accepts individuals with their differences. The need to belong makes such individuals relate to others with no expectations. They make efforts to develop long lasting relationships which are meaningful.

Finding joy in others' achievements and gains requires an attitude of magnanimity. It is normally found that one individual finds it difficult to take the other's success well, leading to envy and jealousy. Muditā helps to develop positivity in oneself, which automatically generates positivity around oneself. An individual with the attitude of Muditā will never let someone else destroy his peace of mind or state of joy. The ability to maintain one's own peace and joy without letting the others' affect him is due to Muditā. Peace and happiness are within the individual himself, and he needs to realise this. External situations are bound to be different, sometimes even negative. But one determines one's own life.

Upekṣā helps one to move away from the negative tendencies, feelings, thoughts, and people. The individual has the freedom to choose what he wants in life, happiness, or misery. He can choose the see the good and ignore the bad in life or even vice versa. But according to Yoga, one should develop an attitude of indifference to joy or pain. Happiness should not give the individual an emotional high and make him depressed in a negative situation. He needs to develop an attitude of detachment, not indifference, to people and life though. This sense of detachment keeps them involved in everything and everyone around, without any strings attached. The sense of detachment helps him to do his duty sincerely and with devotion. It is an art to see the good and the positive in life at all times. Upekśa helps one to develop an attitude that will enhance relationships. It will help the individual to attain goals, help perform duties and lead life fruitfully.

The 'śāstras identify six weaknesses or enemies—arishadvargas—that block the development of the individual and impel him into doing the wrong. These are: kāma (lust), krodha (anger), lobha (greed), moha (infatuation), mada (arrogance) and matsarya (jealousy). The individual needs to overcome these obstacles in the path of self-development and get into a life of discipline that spurs development in the right and spiritual path. This can be done with kauśalam, with dexterity in action, and a will to enjoy samatva, a balance, in all situations to help man to learn and progress. The individual learns to act rightly and to avoid certain actions and behaviours. A person engaging in lokasaṅgraha, the welfare of all, will grow in competence and stature. Growth and development of one takes place through abhyāsa, practice and vairāgya, detachment. This comes with vivekajñāna in accordance with dharma, which is the objective of the various schools of thought in our philosophical heritage, especially Yoga.

Vihāra

Rest and relaxation are considered to be as important as work in Indian philosophy. Every individual needs to use his leisure time well. Man needs to replenish the energy used by the body and here, tāmas helps in giving a break to man's activities. Recreation has been given its due significance as is seen in the encouragement of arts, performing or otherwise. 'Indian culture has always kept an open forum for display of individual creativity and imagination.' Art and Architecture have opened vistas for man to express his aesthetic sense in a utilitarian manner. This is also seen in the colour and structure of dress styles and housing in India, where utility matches aesthetics with the available resources.

Moreover, music and dance of Indian culture need no further exposition. There is seen global acceptance and interest in Indian performing arts. The various skills and arts and crafts of tribals and villagers too are welcomed in global markets, thus showing the credibility and feasibility of Indian goods that are made Indigenous, more as outcome of recreational activities.

All festivities and celebrations in the name of religion are recreational activities that are done with a purpose. Religious occasions are celebrated with a higher purpose in mind, and the individuals also have an attitude of sincerity and humility in them. The sanctity of such recreational activities gives the mind enough rest and relaxation. These celebrations help to bring together people of a particular faith, acting as socialising agencies. The individual enjoys with a different attitude, as it is a scene different from a social party. He is reminded of the divine in every act that he performs. The attitude of charity, giving and sharing develops with such activities.

Vihāra is given its due importance, and this is clearly seen in the various festivals, religious occasions and social functions that are encouraged in our culture. Festivals and celebrations help to break the monotony and pressure of routine work. They help the individual to rejuvenate and get revitalised in the name of the Divine. These occasions are significant not only as socialising agents but also as developing brotherhood and kinship.

Vihāra plays an important role in developing the 'let go' attitude. Man feels small and egoless, especially when he is in a group of like-minded and similarly people. While getting together for recreation and entertainment, he chooses his group. He belongs to the group more easily and is spontaneous and natural with them. This approach of being oneself is very relaxing, and the individual feels at ease with himself. There is a reduction or elimination of stress in his life. His approach to life changes and he lives more joyful and happy. Vihāra helps to maintain the sanity of the individual, as certain activities become means to express or vent out his repressed emotions. Vihāra is a technique of conscious and planned relaxation for rejuvenation of the body, mind, and soul.

Yoga: Its Socio-Cultural Dimension

For the purpose of helping an individual to attain liberation, Yoga advocates certain techniques. These can be grouped together in the following manner.

1. **The practical discipline**, which involves the practices of Āsanās, Prāṇāyāma and Meditation.
   - Āsanās involve the increased awareness of various physical and physiological processes, which are influenced by controlled stretching, contraction and relaxation of various muscles, their co-ordination in balancing, during maintenance of Posture, etc.
   - Prāṇāyāma practices similarly involve the regulation of breathing mechanism along with the increased awareness of the pressure changes within the lungs and abdomen.
   - Dhyāna and Samādhī, or the Contemplation and Meditation practices, increase the awareness of one's mental processes including the thoughts, emotions, memory etc. It can make one aware how the constant restlessness at the level of mind contributes to the feeling of emotional stress feeling of constant fear and insecurity. This increased awareness combined with the manipulative techniques of Dhyāna practices gradually restore the psycho-physiological functions back to its healthy, harmonious, and balanced state.

2. This section is concerned with the **regulation of Diet as well as regulation of daily habits** involving the pattern of sleep, recreational activities and working habits. This helps in removing all those irritants, which are responsible for the imbalance in the functioning of body-mind complex.
3. This section concerns itself with **changes in one's attitude, behaviour, and lifestyle**, which would help in inducing the feeling of sharing, feeling of warmth in friendship and concern, love, and respect for the whole beautiful world. This acts as an antidote for the feeling of hopelessness, and loneliness, which may come in the absence of proper relationship with the world around.

Sattva is the superlative state of serenity, selflessness, efficiency, and power. It is the state of contemplation when one attains enlightenment and discriminative knowledge. A sāttvic individual is normally absorbed in thoughts of the higher purposes. A Sāttvic individual is motivated by noble intentions, and he will be continuously doing activities that benefit humanity at large. Sattva helps us to broaden our outlook and approach, thereby managing to break barriers that we have, emotionally and mentally. It helps man to break away the fetters of laziness, lethargy, and complacency. Sattva helps one to be proactive, thus helping the individual to think lateral, be creative and divergent in thought, seeking solutions to problems rather than shirking difficult situations.

A sāttvic individual generally functions without agitation, stress, tension, or anxiety. He manages to achieve excellence for himself, with no vested interests to bind him. This state of excellence comes to him effortlessly as he is self-confident and self-respecting. Work itself is worship for him. The sāttvika person excels due to his state of freedom, as he is neither tempted by the carrot, nor is he scared of the stick. Every sāttvika individual feels empowered, and the more sāttvika individuals in an organisation, the more will the individual and organisation run effectively and smoothly. It leads all to be strategic in thought and planning. Fortifying an organisation with sāttvika members in a majority, especially members at the top levels of management, steers the organisation towards prosperity and development. The all-round development of the individual leads to the growth of the society and organisation, thereby leading to the wellbeing and wealth of the nation. The discriminative knowledge of sattva helps to elicit the best in oneself and others to the maximum. If one were to be dominated by tāmas and rajas, then the core competence and talents go wasted.

Many times, when people talk about Yoga, they focus their attention only on the first component involving varieties of āsanas, prāṇāyāma and meditational techniques. Thus, they confine Yoga to a small period of their daily life as if the rest of the day has nothing to do with Yoga. But really speaking the Yogic way of living in the rest of the day is not only equally but more important from the healing point of view. Whatever skills one has learnt from the Yogic practices need to be used throughout the day. In this sense the **Upayoga** i.e., the use of the Yogic skills, through the day needs to be given proper attention. The last two components attend to this Upayoga aspect of Yoga.[2]

Practical Implications and Relevance to Corporates

If one undertakes Yoga with this spirit kept in mind and comply with all the instructions given, one will find that Yoga not only gives relief from problems but actually opens up a new way of enjoying your life. Yoga is today found to be very popular in the corporate sector. It is incorporated in many training programmes. The rising stress levels of the top management staff necessitates the practice of Yoga. The various benefits, facilities and perquisites given to all in the corporate sector makes it easier for people to manage their families. Yet the stress that arises due to the ever-rising inflation, work, responsibilities, the pressures of educating the children and the consumerism that needs to be understood can never be denied. 'Keeping up with the Jones' is an attitude that is evident in every individual and his family members. The workers and the manual labourers, along with the non-management staff need to be physically fit and mentally peaceful, as they shoulder the responsibility of their large families entirely by themselves.

Yoga contributes to the corporate world in many ways. Firstly, a search that is undertaken by an individual to know himself well happens with the practice of yoga and development of a yogic attitude. There are questions that he asks himself and finds answers himself, without waiting for a guide or counsellor. The management schools and the consultants and trainers boast about SWOT Analysis, conflict management, management of stress, motivational programs, problem-solving techniques and attitudes, Input-Output systems, and personality development. Any recruitment agency uses various testing techniques, such as psychometric tests, behavioural assessments, interviews, personality, and aptitude tests. Situational judgement tests are given to candidates before recruitment and to employees before promotion. Such tests are solved successfully by yoga practitioners as response to ethical dilemmas, disputes and disagreements, compliance and adaptation are natural to an individual who is capable and sure of himself. Moreover, regular yoga practitioners are normally successful due to their clarity in thought, high competence at work, excellent communication due to their steadfastness, consistency in approach and their deep-rooted values.

All these and more come naturally to the individual with the practice of Yoga and the adoption of yogic approach in life, as everything stems from self-development and self-management, which is the basis of Yoga. He learns to maintain his work-life balance and copes with the demands of his family, workplace, and community to the right extent in the right manner. The wellbeing and mental and physical health, and emotional and spiritual intelligence is natural with Yogic practice. Such individuals, employees, employers, CEOs, and leaders can only work in the best possible manner for the best of an organisation. Their suitability and sustainability is unquestionable, provided they learn and practice yoga with the right approach and goal.

In the next chapter, we explore the lives and legacies of a few great spiritual luminaries whose teachings illuminate the path of yoga. These remarkable individuals not only spoke of higher ideals—they lived them. Their wisdom offers us a blueprint for cultivating a yogic mindset that leads to inner growth, purposeful living, and lasting success. Through their inspiring journeys and timeless guidance, we are invited to walk the same path—with clarity, courage, and compassion.

References

1. 'The Foundation of Hinduism', Jadunath Sinha, p. 46; Pilgrims Book Pvt. Ltd., 414-416, Express Tower, Commercial Complex, Azadpur, Delhi. 1999.
2. Tola Fernando & Dragonetti Carmen, 'The Yogasūtras of Patañjali on Concentration of Mind', Translated into English from the revised original Spanish by K.D. Prithipaul, Motilal Banarsidass Publishers, Delhi.

VI

SOCIO-CULTURAL FOUNDATIONS OF GOVERNANCE

Shruti and Smriti are two sources of knowledge in Indian philosophy. Smritishastras are secondary Hindu scriptures that supplement the Vedas, focusing on **dharma** through codes of conduct, laws, and social obligations. The term is a Sanskrit compound of *smriti* (remembrance/tradition) and *shastra* (science/treatise), referring to texts that are **remembered and transmitted** through human intellect, unlike the *Shruti* (heard), such as the Vedas. Vedic knowledge when taught by sages and seers through chanting, meditation, recitation, and emulation is Shruti. The Vedas are Apaurusheya and are seen as the primary source of divine knowledge. Man gains knowledge with regard to righteousness, duties, moral conduct with the help of both, Shrutis and Smritis.

Smritis are considered secondary sources of knowledge to the Vedas. The Smritis focus on the ethical and traditional guidelines spelling out Dharma in various texts, rituals, and traditions. Legal and ethical guidance and framework of modern society is also based on knowledge from the scriptures, and the Gurukuls of ancient times, which were documented for generations to come. providing laws and ethical guidance for individuals and communities. Vedic knowledge and wisdom shared as compositions, texts, and shared experience in the form of narration and stories constitute the Smritis. This category of knowledge includes texts such as *Dharmashastras* (books on right and wrong, good, and bad, law), *Itihasa* (epics depicting moral issues, and leading to their solutions, like the Mahabharata and Ramayana) *Puranas* and other literary texts. Many seers, gurus, sages and social thinkers in India were yogis. They were looked at as *Smṛti Kāras* who have given us various texts called *Smṛti Śāstras*. To name a few, we have *Manu*, *Yajñavalkya*, *Gautama*, and *Cāṇakya.*

Manu's Concept of Dharma

The most famous of these and probably the pioneer exposition on duties was given to us by *Manu*. There is an interesting story that was told to us to emphasise the significance of the teachings of *Manu*. As the story goes, *Manu* is considered to be the 'mind-born' son of Lord *Brahma*, the Creator of the universe. The words '*Manuṣya'* and '*Mānava'* are believed to be derived from *Manu*. The same name is said to be etymological for the English word 'Man' referring to all humans. When Lord *Brahma* decided to create, he had *Manu* taking birth from one half of his mind and from the other half came *Shatarupa*, a woman. When *Manu* and *Shatarupa* married, they became responsible for the creation of the entire human race. An analogy can be drawn here with the Biblical story of Adam and Eve. The story that Adam was created by God, and Eve from Adam's rib, and the union of the two led to the creation of the human race seems very similar. The idea of leading the entire human race to such a parentage is probably to strengthen the idea that man is born with divinity and inherent goodness.

Lord *Brahma* is said to have assigned the task of teaching *Dharma* to the human race to *Manu*. Hence it is believed that Lord himself taught *Manu* the *DharmaŚāstra*. The *Manusmṛti* is an exposition of the *Dharmaśāstra* as taught to him by the Lord and as required to be conveyed to the humans. Maxmuller expresses his opinion that *Manusmṛti* is based on an ancient *Dharma Sūtra*. The *Manusaṁhitā* appears to be prior to the *Mahābhārata*. There are many common verses that occur in the *Manusaṁhitā* and the *Mahābhārata* with similar ethical implications. 'Both inculcate mental purity, and both condemn ritualistic morality. It is however believed that the ethics of the *Bhagvad Gītā* is more comprehensive, personal and reflective than *Manu*'s ethics.'[1]

Manu states in the *Manusmṛti* that all men behave due to needs and desires and engage in activities that lead to their fulfilment. *Manu* explains how man is prompted by some desire or the other when he chooses to act. It is an erroneous belief in the mind of man that he gets happiness when fulfilling desires. As *Manu* says in his *Manusmṛti*, 'Desires are not satiated by their fulfilment; the more one tries to satisfy them, the more they grow.'[2] According to *Manu*, the fulfilment of desires is similar to fuelling a fire, which only asks for more fuel every time it is burning. The only way man can rid himself of this anxiety and desperation is by breaking free of the bondages that come with attachment to material and transient things.

In order to realise the need to break free, man needs to first learn to discriminate the phenomenal from the transcendental, the eternal from the temporal. This leads us back to the goals prescribed in Indian thought, the *Puruṣārthās*. *Manu* suggests that the best way for man to enjoy freedom is to give up all desires, be it physical, mental or emotional. The only aim of man should ideally be spiritual growth and evolvement. The realisation of the spiritual self in man is the key to his liberation.

Manu realises that it is not easy for man to be desireless, as achieving this state almost seems impossible for one who lives and survives due to his desires. It becomes necessary to resolve this paradoxical situation by finding a viable path. Man needs to satisfy his needs and fulfil his desires but the extent of freedom he enjoys will depend on the level of needs. If man has needs related to the lower self, then he gets his gratification by performing certain acts with the help of his senses and his physical body. If man decides to choose the higher purposes in life, then man finds himself less frustrated and anxious, calmer and more contented.

Sukha, *Shānti* and *Santoṣa* fill up his life as he is constantly in need of activities that take him to excellence. The evolvement of man as a conscious and purposive being is the only way to free oneself from bondages. This leads us back to *Dharma*. *Manu* emphasises on leading a life of discretion, of righteousness, of discipline, and of restraint. *Manu*'s concept of *Dharma* is anti-hedonistic. Desire, according to him, can never be pacified by gratification. The more it is gratified, the more it is intensified. He considers the renunciation of desires better than their fulfilment.

The *Manusaṁhitā* is mainly concerned with an exposition of duties, responsibilities and virtues, thus closely relating itself to the concept of *Puruśārthās* in Indian thought. As the onus of the action is solely on the individual himself, who works within a framework given by authority, be it human or divine, it can be said that *Manu*'s ethical treatise is a blend of customary and reflective morality. His ethics is considered to be more rigid and authoritarian than rational and personal. He regards the Divine Law as the supreme *Dharma*, regarding ethos, custom and social law as subordinated and derived from this universal source. *Manu* with all this dogmatism regarding the supremacy of the conscience gives due respect to the authority of reason in morality.

Manu, the lawgiver of Indian thought, has enumerated ten virtues or values that characterise a virtuous or *dhārmic* individual, the ideal *Mānava*. They are:

Dhṛtiḥ kṣamā damo steyaṁ śaucam indriyanigrahaḥ
Dhīr vidya satyam akrodha daśakaṁ Dharmalakṣaṇam
– *Manusmṛti* 6.9[3]

1. ***Dhṛti* – fortitude or forbearance:** This is a virtue that allows man to hold on to something. There are three kinds of *dhṛtis*—*tamasic*, *rajasic*, and *sattvic*—which are discussed in the eighteenth chapter of the *Gītā*. ***Tamasic dhṛti*** is the tendency to hold things that are detrimental such as sleep, food, bias, prejudices and wrong notions.

Rajasic dhṛti is holding on to money, power, position, pleasure, name and fame. Here, achievements are not valued for their own sake, but for the sake of the other benefits that come with them. A hedonistic attitude with egoism is displayed by people with *rajasic dhṛti*. ***Sattvic dhṛti*** is the ability to rise above all obstacles, difficulties, hurdles and problems in life in order to achieve a noble goal. People with *sattvic dhṛti* are interested in actualising their potential for its own sake, with no strings attached. The goal or purpose keeps him going even if he is physically tired and mentally fatigued. They are individuals who will function with higher purposes.

2. ***Kṣamā* – forgiveness or the ability to endure cheerfully:** Forgiveness is considered one of the highest virtues in our culture. It is very important to forgive an individual for the wrong that he has committed. It is more important to forget that he has been forgiven for what he has done. That's why the dictum 'Forgive and Forget'. If one keeps reminding oneself and the other that he has been forgiven, then the goodness of the forgiver is lost. It will only make the forgiven write in guilt and will make him diffident the next time.
3. ***Dama* – control over our organs of action:** It is necessary to have restraint over our senses and feelings. One cannot be impulsive and reactive in behaviour as it is harmful for oneself and others. Such individuals are shunned, and these individuals find it difficult to develop good interpersonal relationships. Their behaviour is uniformly brazen and they become unpredictable.

   In order to develop healthy and mature relationships with all around, it is necessary to exercise control on one's senses and action. Restraint as mentioned earlier has always been the keyword in our culture. This kind of self-restraint should not be mistaken for tolerance that leads to submissiveness.
4. ***Asteya* – non-stealing:** It is a virtue that needs no elaboration as it has already been discussed in an earlier chapter. It is the attitude of not trying to or not even thinking of taking what is not one's own. No individual has the right to take or desire what is not his own. In the management scene, it can be interpreted as not vying for what one does not deserve. It can also be interpreted as not coveting somebody else's position or grade.
5. ***Śauca* – purity:** Another virtue that needs no further exposition is *Śauca* as it been discussed under *Yoga*. The need to be clean and pure is not only applicable to physical or bodily cleanliness but also mental and emotional purity. The need to be pure in thought and feeling that leads one to purity of motive is overemphasised in our

culture. Actions done with volition are judged as right or wrong, good or bad on the basis of motive and intentions of the doer.

6. ***Indriyanigraha* – mastery over sense-organs and restraint of perception:** The need to restrain our senses from getting drawn to the external world is important for self-awareness and self-mastery. If one needs to keep away from the distractions and temptations of the external world, then it is necessary to monitor and control the sense organs. Withdrawal of the senses and turning them inwards helps introspection and contemplation, a practice that is central to spiritual practice. Yama and Niyama in yogic philosophy are techniques that help to develop discipline. Pratyahāra is a technique in *Yoga* that teaches one to withdraw and restrain the senses. It does not mean repression of desires and greed, but it is a pointer to a conscious choice of thoughts, words and deeds by limiting sensual input. It is considered a step to prepare oneself for spiritual realisation, with the achievement of inner peace.
7. ***Dhī* – using the faculty of discrimination:** *Manu* stressed the need to have the right knowledge of the Real. In order to lead a stress-free and blissful life, full of contentment, it is imperative for an individual to develop the right attitude that comes with *vivekajñāna*. Once the individual knows what is eternal and infinite, what is real and permanent, he stops hankering after the fleeting. The knowledge of the 'right' and the 'wrong' also helps one to lead stress free life, as there is no conflict of motives in the individual in his choice of actions. It implies the ability to control oneself, as the individual learns to practice *dama*. The supreme ends of life need to be realised with the senses completely controlled and the mind totally disciplined. *Manu* recognises the importance of freedom of will in an individual. Man needs to learn to walk on the path of *Dharma*, by the right choices that he makes.
8. ***Vidyā* – knowledge:** Education is distinguished from literacy here. It is not enough to have the ability to read and write. It is more important to assimilate what has been learnt than accumulating information to become encyclopaedias. Discriminative knowledge that helps one to lead a simple and healthy life is the objective of all learning. As the scriptures say, Knowledge that liberates one from all psychological entanglements is the only real knowledge.
9. ***Satya* – truthfulness:** Truth understood as a synonym to God or Godliness has exalted this virtue. It is necessary to speak the truth at all times. It is imperative that one needs to be honest, committed to one's word, keep up one's promises. It is also necessary to verify facts

before speaking about anyone or anything, or else it is against the principle of truth. For *Manu*, truth is subordinated to humanitarian considerations.

10. ***Akrodha* – absence of anger:** Anger is an emotion that makes a slave of an individual, making him irrational in his behaviour. An angry man loses control totally over himself, behaving in a manner similar to animals. In order to avoid this situation, man needs to exercise control on negative emotions and regulate his behaviour to be socially acceptable. Moreover, no individual is in the right frame of mind to take right decisions when angry. This will lead to situations that are hampered due to man's own folly.

    Anger is justified by many as a natural emotion in man. It, however, needs to be realised that even natural emotions need to be expressed in socially acceptable manner. The aggression and violence normally exhibited by an angry individual can only be destructive. Nothing productive or constructive comes with anger.

In the *Manusaṁhitā*, there is a reference to '*Śreni Dharma*', where the functioning of the guild or organisation is shown as following a 'law'. It lays down the following injunction: 'If a man belonging to a corporation inhabiting a village after swearing to an agreement, breaks it through avarice, the 'king' shall banish him from the realm'. *Manu* feels that happiness and misery depends on oneself. Happiness is subjugation to oneself. Misery is subjugation to others. Self-reliance and self-dependence makes one happier. Dependence on others all the time makes one miserable for all factors that lead to satisfaction and realisation are external. This leads us to believe that *Manu*'s ethics almost seems ascetic. He differentiates between pleasure and happiness well. One who desires the happiness and good of all attains supreme happiness.

Manu enjoins performance of five kinds of sacrifices—***pancayajña***. The five kinds of sacrifices are:

- ***Brahmanyajña*:** the study of the scriptures and undertaking the teaching of scriptures to others, along with a recitation of the name of the Lord.
- ***Pitṛyajña*:** the performance of *Śrāddha*, as a mark of reverence to the departed souls in the family.
- ***Devayajña*:** the performance of religious rituals, sacrificial rites, and chanting of *mantrās*.
- ***Nṛyajña*:** the conduct of the householder towards guests, *athithi*, where he treats them as personification of the Divine.

- ***Bhūtayajña***: tending to the various elements in nature and the flora and fauna in the environment.

Here the word '*yajña*' is taken to mean 'duty' and 'responsibility' in a figurative sense. *Manu*'s description of the '*yajñas*' seem very similar to the *Upaniśadic* notion of '*Ṛṇa*'.

In the *Manusṁṛti*, *Manu* says that all actions spring from the individual's mind, speech and body. They produce good or bad results, the *karmas*. These *karmas* are causal to the conditions of life (*gatayah*) for any individual. While discussing the sins committed by people, he enumerates three kinds of sins:

- bodily or physical sins that include theft, killing, physically harming others or oneself, and adultery.
- verbal sins like speaking harshly, talking irrelevant, gossip, slander, speaking lies, speaking ill of others in their absence.
- mental sins like wrong and bad intentions, thoughts of injury to others, attitudes of jealousy and negativity, wishing ill for others.

Yagñāvalkya agrees with the exposition of *Dharma* and *Karma* as given by *Manu*. He strongly believes that *Dharma* and karma lead to the formation of the seeds of *Karma*. From this *Karmasaya*, the individual's life in this birth is determined, with regard to his *jāti*, *āyuḥ* and *bhoga*. Similarly, the *Yagñavalkya Saṁhita* also prescribes that if a man steals the property of a guild or any organisation, or breaks any agreement with it, he shall be banished from the realm and all his property confiscated.

When discussing social ethics, it is impossible to overlook the profound contributions of ***Cāṇakya***, whose influence spans both economic thought and political strategy.

Cāṇakyasūtrās: Ready Reckoner for Management and Leadership

Cāṇakya, also known as Kautilya and Vishnugupta, authored the *Arthaśāstra* and the *Nītiśāstra*, foundational texts in economics and political philosophy. His work *Cāṇakyasūtras* distils essential principles of conduct and governance, offering a concise framework for managing the affairs of a kingdom. There is an elaborate exposition of all the aspects of administering a state: from taxes to hierarchical positions, to laws and policies, to rewards and punishments. It was during 150 AD, though the date has not been conclusively established yet. Though there is a lot of mystery about his origin and region, and his works are not yet dated with certainty, it is certain that *Cāṇakya* is the man who destroyed the Nanda dynasty and installed Chandragupta Maurya as the King of Magadha.

He is considered a master strategist, well versed in the Vedas. Adept at creating intrigues and devising strategies for solving political issues, *Cāṇakya* 's genius is well recognised through his works. The *Arthaśāstra* is widely regarded as the most comprehensive treatise on statecraft from classical India. Primarily composed in prose, it also includes 380 shlokas, blending analytical discourse with poetic expression to articulate its principles of governance, economics, and diplomacy.

Artha, literally wealth, is one of the four supreme aims or *Puruṣarthās* prescribed by Hindu tradition. In accordance with this philosophical base of our tradition, *Cāṇakya* maintains in his *Arthaśāstra* that the state or government of a country has a vital role to play in maintaining the material status of both the nation and its citizens. 'The *Arthaśāstra* deals with both the science of economics and the science of politics.' The significance of an efficient administrative machinery along with the emphatic demand for the maintenance of law and order in a nation and its various organisations cannot be undermined.

In Sanskrit, the word *Artha* has an interesting dual meaning. It means 'meaning' but also means 'money' like in *Cāṇakya's 'Arthaśāstra'* or economics. In fact, the term 'Economics' itself is derived from the Greek '*Oikos*' meaning Household and '*Nomos*' meaning Management.

Arthaśāstra, the treatise on Economic Administration was written by *Cāṇakya* in the 4th century before Christ. It consists of 15 *saṅgrahas* (chapters), 380 *ślokas* (verses) and 4968 *Sūtras* (aphorisms). In all likelihood, the *Arthaśāstra* stands as the earliest known text on the practice of management, offering a systematic and strategic framework for governance, administration, and economic planning that remains relevant even today.

It is essentially on the art of governance and has an instructional tone. *Cāṇakya* wrote this treatise for his *Swamy* (the king) Chandragupta Maurya and stated in its preface that it has been written as a guide for 'those who govern'. *Cāṇakya* was interested in establishment and operation of the machinery through which the king preserves the integrity and solidarity of the State and generates power.

Some of his sūtrās that are found relevant for the present-day management teachings are elaborated here in the following paragraphs. These sūtrās are then interpreted with reference to the context.[4]

Sukhasya mūlaṁ Dharmaḥ (asti)
The basis of happiness is ethics.

– *Cāṇakyasūtrās, Sūtra* 1

Cāṇakya believed that ethics is the root, '*mūlaṁ*', for all happiness. '*Sukha*' implied not only happiness as a state of mind but also prosperity, welfare, good health, comfort and convenience. '*Dharma*' implies duty and code of conduct. *Cāṇakya* lists out three kinds of duties that are mandatory for human beings who follow the path of *Dharma*. They are the duties that have to respected due to one's varna, the duties that have to be followed in the four *aṣramās* by all, and the various virtues that are listed for the benefit of all civilised beings. The six virtues are *ahiṁsā* (non-violence), *satya* (truth), *śauca* (cleanliness), *anasūya* (non-jealousy), *anṛsansya* (compassion) and *kṣamā* (forgiveness).

According to *Cāṇakya*, management should ideally work with the objective of giving all happiness. Happiness needs to be differentiated from pleasure. In today's industrial world, what is evident is the abundance of material prosperity and comforts. The organisation tries to bind the employee by exploiting his weaknesses, by giving him more and more perquisites and facilities that make his life comfortable and pleasurable. Every organisation follows the hedonistic philosophy while dealing with its employees. It only triggers an increasing pressure in the employee for achieving things that temporarily satiate his needs. The sense of false security and well being that is given to the employee leads him to a sense of being deceived and exploited. This slowly sets in a feeling of disgust as his self-esteem is at stake.

Thus, the *Sūtra* mentioned above talks about *Dharma* as the only source of happiness, which is a state of mind within the individual. Ethical practices are more universal and eternal, leading to happiness that is more lasting and permanent, keeping the individual's dignity intact.

At the same time, *Cāṇakya* also realises that an individual whose basic needs are taken care of well will presumably be more ethical than one who is in poverty. This leads one to the second *Sūtra* in his work.

> *Dharma*sya *mūlaṁ arthaḥ*
> Basis of ethics is wealth/ resources.
>
> – *Cāṇakyasūtrās,* Sutra 2

This makes it clear that *Cāṇakya* does not believe that man needs to deny himself or others the satisfaction of his basic needs. The organisation has to take care of him, providing him with all that can relieve him of the stress of his basic needs. Moreover, the employees can be expected to follow rules and codes of conduct only if their basic needs necessary for survival are satisfied.

In order to provide the individuals with opportunities the actualisation of their potential in the right manner, there has to be some enterprise or task assigned. These areas of enterprise and work should ideally have the objective of wealth generation, both for the individual himself and the organisation too. Considering today's world of technological advancement, there are two major areas of wealth generation: the industry and the service sectors. This renders his third *Sūtra* explicable.

Arthasya mūlaṁ rājyaṁ

– Basis of resources is a kingdom (enterprise or organisation in this context). *Sūtra* 3.

Rājyamūlaṁ indriyajayaḥ

– Enterprise is rooted in gaining victory over one's sense organs (*indrīya*). *Sūtra* 4.

Indriyajayasya mūlaṁ vinayaḥ

Moral training and discipline alone helps to conquer the senses.

– *Cāṇakyasūtrās, Sūtra* 5

For an enterprise or an organisation to be successful, the individuals involved at all levels, within and without the same, need to be resourceful and effective. With the holistic approach of Indian ethos and *Cāṇakya*'s understanding of human behaviour, the fourth *Sūtra* talks about the victory that is essential over one's own sense-organs and motor organs. Traditionally, man has been taught to exercise control over his organs and channelise his mental energy for good purposes. Indian culture has emphasised control on the Self, with the individual focussing on the Ultimate Reality. Control, however, should be in moderation and exercised with discretion, for it should not lead to repression or suppression of the individual.

One's control over the organs implies that the individual has the qualities of self-restraint, moderation in indulgence sustained channelising of energy and actualisation of potential. The six enemies of the mind: *kāma*, *krodha*, *lobha*, *mada*, *moha* and *matsara* can be conquered only with the victory over the organs. An individual needs to exercise control over his organs in order to 'realise his long-term goals with regard to his Self. The gratification of desires and the resultant feeling of pleasure is temporary and short-term. Man yields to temptation more easily if he has the position of power, according to *Cāṇakya*. 'Power corrupts' is an observation that is universally accepted. 'The philosopher-poet-king Bhartruhari has propounded an excellent hypothesis on why 'good advice' does not get used, though really useful to those in need.' As quoted by Ashok Garde, Bhartruhari says, 'the learned are smitten with jealousy, those in power positions are spoiled by arrogance, and the rest are too badly hit by ignorance.'[5]

Cāṇakya advises his teams to inculcate the values of tolerance and patience while dealing with people. It is also necessary to cultivate an attitude of humility to avoid hurting others around oneself. This is one way of giving a sense of belongingness to all around and keep them motivated. *Cāṇakya* uses the word '*vinaya*' to refer to humility and modesty, which is later expounded by him as 'training in morality' and 'self-discipline to be ethical'. In fact the first chapter in his book is called as '*vinaya-adhikārikaṁ*', 'the book of moral training'. *Cāṇakya* opines that one has to have basic, built-in humility. If otherwise, the individual will neither see nor observe occurrences around one in their true perpectives: an arrogant mind will either filter uncomfortable observations or distort them to suit one's intentions and views.

The next five *sūtrās* discuss the sources of training and their benefits:

Vinayasya mūlaṁ vruddhopasevā

Moral training comes from the service of the elders (seniors and experienced).

– *Cāṇakyasūtrās, Sūtra* 6

Vruddhopasevayā vijñānaṁ

Right knowledge comes from the service of the learned.

– *Cāṇakyasūtrās, Sūtra* 7

Vijñānena ātmānāṁ saṁpādayet

It is necessary to equip oneself with worldly knowledge, which comes from the experienced.

– *Cāṇakyasūtrās, Sūtra* 8

Sampāditātmā jitātma bhavati

One who has acquired right knowledge alone is the one who has conquered himself.

– *Cāṇakyasūtrās, Sūtra* 9

Jitātmā sarva-arthaiḥ sanyujyeta

The one who has conquered himself shall endow himself with all resources.

– *Cāṇakyasūtrās, Sūtra* 10

Training in organisations normally focus on enhancement of skills. But *Cāṇakya* believes that training needs to be holistic. It is necessary to realise oneself as a potential, competent and capable being. However it is more important to realise oneself as a spiritual being with all these potentialities, that will lead him to be a moral and effective individual for the progress of the organisation. Only one who has conquered himself can be trusted with all resources, meaning benefits and facilities here in the context. If otherwise, the resources provided will be abused or misused. The value of what is received by him from the organisation will not be truly understood by him. Hence, *Cāṇakya*'s insistence on training from the learned who will teach him to recognise what is more lasting and permanent.

It is remarkable to note that many principles found in contemporary management theories were clearly articulated by The *Amātya*, or chief administrator, oversees the daily functioning of the state by coordinating a council of key officials. This council includes the *Mantris* (Ministers), who advise on policy; the *Senāpati* (Commander or Defence Minister), responsible for military affairs; the *Purohit* (Chief Justice), who upholds legal and ethical standards; and the *Yuvarāj* (Heir Apparent), the designated successor to the throne. Together, they form the backbone of governance, ensuring stability, strategic decision-making, and continuity of leadership. *Cāṇakya* centuries ago, in his writing shared insights into leadership, strategy, governance, and organisational behaviour which continue to resonate with modern-day practices, underscoring his timeless relevance. As in the current day management, the importance of vision, mission and motivation was captured in *Arthaśāstra*. *Cāṇakya* advised his *Swamy* to rule through *Prabhu Śakti* (vision), *Mantra Śakti* (mission) and *Utsah Śakti* (motivation). *Cāṇakya's* articulation of a king's objectives—centred on strategic governance, economic prosperity, and societal welfare—appears strikingly aligned with the principles outlined by Peter Drucker in *Managing for Results*. Both thinkers emphasise purposeful leadership, goal-oriented planning, and the importance of aligning actions with long-term outcomes. Though separated by centuries, their frameworks converge on the idea that effective management is rooted in clarity of purpose, ethical conduct, and measurable impact. Drucker proposed Economic Performance as the corporate objective and highlighted the constituents of Economic Performance as:

- Making present business effective.
- Identifying the potential and realising it; and
- Making it a different business for a different future.

Cāṇakya reminds his *Swamy* that his objectives for his rule are:

- Acquire power.
  (Making present business effective)
- Consolidate what has been acquired.
  (Making present business effective)
- Expand what has been acquired; and
  (Identify potential and realise it)
- Enjoy what has been acquired.
  (Making it a different business for a different future)

Cāṇakya recognised that the efficient functioning of a state required the establishment of a well-structured administrative machinery. He demonstrated a keen understanding of organisational dynamics, emphasising not only structural and procedural aspects but also the human elements—such as motivation, ethics, and interpersonal relationships. His insights extended to the qualities and responsibilities of leadership, advocating for rulers and administrators who are strategic, disciplined, and morally grounded.

Cāṇakya defines management in his own inimicable manner. According to him, one needs to begin with the social aspects of human living. Then he discusses the role of a manager, the various resources and skills, and the policies in an organisation. All these factors are important for initiating an enterprise.[6]

This is well brought out in the following *Sūtra*:

a-labdha-lābhādi catuṣṭayaṁ rājya-tantraṁ

These four, starting from gaining the non-possessed, together constitute the technology of enterprise.

The management of an organisation consists of four elements:

- gaining possession of the non-possessed
- protecting that which is gained
- making the protected grow
- through deployment of employees

On the organisational aspects, *Cāṇakya* evolves an elaborate hierarchy under the king. The king appoints Amatya, the Prime Minister. The *Amātya*, or chief administrator, oversees the daily functioning of the state by coordinating a council of key officials. This council includes the *Mantris* (Ministers), who advise on policy; the *Senāpati* (Commander or Defence Minister), responsible for military affairs; the *Purohit* (Chief Justice), who upholds legal and ethical standards; and the *Yuvarāj* (Heir Apparent), the designated successor to the throne. Together, they form the backbone of governance, ensuring stability, strategic decision-making, and continuity of leadership. *Cāṇakya* weaves a design of a tall hierarchy for governance going down to the level of village through his concept of Mandalas. Gram Panchayats and Panchayati Raj set up that was adopted by the Government of India can be considered as a logical derivative of *Cāṇakya* 's attempt to bring administration to the lowest appropriate level in the machinery of State.

It is indeed interesting to note that *Cāṇakya,* having woven an elaborate organisation, moves to set up policies and procedures i.e. business processes.

Arthaśāstra has detailed policies for the society, individual industries, labour and employment, calamities and control of vices. At this stage, he shows the depth of his knowledge of the major element of effective and efficient implementation of business processes, namely, the human aspect of management. He observes that the State, as an organisation, is a social organisation with economic aim. Here again, Peter Drucker and *Cāṇakya* go hand in hand as Drucker defines an organisation as having 'social dimension and economic objective'. *Cāṇakya* at this stage, reminds his *Swamy* that sound knowledge of complex human nature is essential in effective, efficient and honest running of the State machinery. He warns of two undesirable attitudes of human nature, *Pramada*, meaning excess and *Ālasya*, meaning inactivity, to be watched for and avoided. This is where, according to *Cāṇakya,* the leadership counts.

The essence of leadership, he stresses, lies in its acceptance by the subjects. He, therefore, advises the *Swamy* never to forget the two pillars of the art of governance: *Nyāya*, justice and *Dharma*, ethics. He also decries autocratic behaviour as a leader is visible, and people follow the leader. Hence, he advises the *Swamy* to introspect to identify his *atma dośas*, i.e. deficiencies to improve or develop himself. He further advises his *Swamy* to study deficiencies of his cabinet members and take steps to improve upon them. He states that Mantris could be incompetent, Senapati could be over ambitious, Purohit might not consider the present-day practices or traditions while enacting laws or justice, which might lead to injustice. As regards Yuvaraj, he advises specific training to prepare him for the eventual succession. He states that the Yuvaraj should be trained in three specific areas: *Arthaśāstra* (economic administration), *Nitiśāstra* (foreign affairs) and *Daṇḍanītī* (political science).

Cāṇakya seems to have given a lot of thought to human resource development for the government machinery. He is specific about the qualities Mantris must possess. He writes about these qualities as qualifying standards for appointment as a Mantri. These qualities are:

- *Drudhachitta* (power of concentration)
- *Shilavan* (character)
- *Pragna* (thinking capability)
- *Vangmi* (communication skills)
- *Daksha* (observation / vigilance)

Anantaśāstraṁ bahulaśca vidyā
Alpaśca kālo bahuvighnatā ca,

Yatsārabhūtaṁ tadupāsanīyaṁ haṁso
Yathā kshīramivāṁbumadhyāt. – ***Cāṇakya* Neeti ṣāstrās 4.13**[7]
The scriptures are countless, knowledge is in abundance,
Time is short, many a hindrance.
Their essence only is worth your pick,
Like milk is extracted by a swan from the water-mixed milk.

Simhādekam bakādekam śikṣeccatvāri kukkkuṭāt,
Vāyasātpañca śikṣecca ṣat śunastrīṇi gardabhāt.
– *Cāṇakya Neetiṣāstrās* 4.14[7]
One virtue from the lion, one of the heron,
Four of the cock, six of the dog,
And three of the donkey one should learn.

Etān viṁśatiguṇācariṣyati yo janaḥ,
Karyāvasthāsu sarvāsu ajeyaḥ sa bhaviṣyati.
– *Cāṇakya Neeti ṣāstrās* 4.15[9]
These twenty virtues if picked by anyone,
He turns out invincible, In every situation.

Prabhūtakāryamalpam va yannaraḥ kartumiccati,
Sarvarambheṇe tatkāryaṁ siṁhādekaṁ pracakṣate.
– *Cāṇakya Neeti ṣāstrās* 4.16[10]
A work whether big or small, one intends to do must be done.
Doing the same with full strength,
Is a quality the lion declares to everyone. (Virtue of the lion)

This *Sūtra* primarily reflects the significance given by an individual to any activity that he does as his duty. If the individual learns the dignity of labour, he will do even the most insignificant job with the same seriousness and sincerity as the lion, which treats every prey and every prowl with the same seriousness.

Indrīyāṇi ca saṁyamya bakavat paṇḍito naraḥ,
Deśakālabalam jñātva sarvakāryāṇi sādhayet.
– ***Cāṇakya Neeti ṣāstrās* 4.17**[11]
A person turns Paṇḍit
If as a heron he keeps his senses under control.
And after evaluating the place, time and strength,
Achieves every goal.

Cāṇakya basically talks about the need for concentration and focus, which alone can lead an individual to success. His insistence on the virtues of character and self-esteem are well brought out in his sūtrās. According to him, man can learn a lot from animals and birds, watching them as they function in tune with the environment. These animals do no harm to others for the sake of pleasure, and they live in accordance with their essential traits and purposes. They do not transgress but do not permit others to do so too, when their security is threatened. This is well brought out in the following sūtrā.

Pratitthānaṁ ca yuddhaṁ ca saṁvibhāgaṁ ca bandhuṣu
Svayamākramya bhogaṁ ca śikṣeccatvāri kukkuṭāt.

– *Cāṇakya's Neeti śāstras* 4.18[12]

Rising against hostility, encountering, Sharing with birds of the same flock.
And eating the self-earned food, these four qualities are taught by the cock.

What *Cāṇakya* is trying to say is that one should learn to be amicable when working together as a team, a department or an organisation. But teamwork should be with the focus on the goals that are commonly to be achieved. One should share the credit, the benefits and the blame equally while working together. At the same time, if it is for the betterment of the group and there is a deviant present to create obstacles in the path of achievement, then one should learn to be courageous enough to face the hostility of such members in the group. One has a right to take only what one deserves and what one has earned.

In addition, he highlights the competencies that a Mantri/ Chief must possess. These competencies are the same as the competencies advocated by the management gurus of the present times, namely, Knowledge, Skills and Attitude.

Gūḍhamaithunacāritvam dākshyam kāle ca saṁgraham
Apramādamviśvāsam pañca śikṣecca vāyasāt.

– ***Cāṇakya's Neeti ṣāstrās* 4.19**[13]

Love-making in privacy, Skillfulness, timely-stow.
Circumspection and non-trust, These five qualities teaches the crow.

The crow teaches man to be discreet and cultured in behaviour. It is important to respect one's own need for privacy as much as the others' too. The crow makes one realise that blind faith is harmful and it is necessary to exercise caution in business or any enterprise that one is involved in. Non-trust here, in the context, does not imply lack of trust. It merely highlights the need for caution and elimination of a lackadaisical attitude towards anyone or anything. This teaching can actually be more applicable for people who work in the security forces/ departments, vigilance and enquiries, and the maintainance and safety sections of organisations.

Bahvāśī svalpasantuṣṭaḥ sunidro laghucetanaḥ,
Svāmibhaktaśca śūraśca ṣaḍete ca śuna guṇaḥ.

– Cāṇakya's Neeti ṣāstrās 4.20[14]

A glutton but content with little,
Deep sleep but awake at short call.
Faithful to the master and bold,
Take these six virtues from the dog's fold.

Loyalty and dedication have always been attributes glorified in a dog. These are virtues that are necessary for the growth of the individual along with the growth of the organisation. In the absence of these values, individuals with vested interests will exploit the others and the organisation, with an eye for personal gains and benefits. The alertness that is normally appreciated in a dog leads us to believe that even when the physical body requires the rest, the purposive, conscious self needs to be active and awake. *Vivekajñāna* as discussed in all systems of thought in India, highlights the need for this alertness which alone develops in man a foresight and helps him to plan the future. The officials who are responsible for planning and designing HR policies, marketing strategies, and training programmes for the employees should necessarily be dedicated, loyal, committed to organisational goals, fair and just in any deal, with a keen foresight, and acumen to help envisage problems. By failing to plan, one plans to fail. Every effective performance is based on thorough preparation. One should be firm about the goal, but flexible about the process of reaching the goal.

Suśrānto(a)pi vahedbhāraṁ śītoṣṇe naiva paśyati,
Santuṣṭaścarate nityaṁ tṛṇi śikṣecca gardabhāt.

– Cāṇakya's Neeti ṣāstrā 4.21[15]

Though tired but carries load, Indifferent to heat and cold.
Grazes always with ease,
Learn from the donkey these three qualities.

'A beast of burden' is what the donkey is looked at as by one and all. The animal that does not shirk from heavy burden and work is appreciated for its perseverance and diligence. The learning from this example is clear and well spelt out. It is imperative that each one should shoulder one's own responsibilities in life, as given in our scriptures, in the form of *varṇāṣrama Dharma* and *svadharma.* The responsibilities have to be shared in any organisation in order to ensure the growth of the same. This is true for any individual in an organisation, irrespective of his position or authority.

Cāṇakya's knowledge about human behaviour is really astounding. He advises his *Swamy* about six emotional devils that he should avoid and ensure that his cabinet members also avoid. He makes it amply clear that at times, these six emotional devils do not allow appropriate decision making in any operation. This holds true for the CEOs of organisations, too. The emotional devils identified by *Cāṇakya* are:

- *Kāma* (lust)
- *Krodha* (anger)
- *Lobha* (greed)
- *Māna* (vanity and conceit)
- *Mada* (arrogance and haughtiness)
- *Harsh* (overjoy and resultant foolhardiness)

Having looked at the key areas of an efficient and effective organisation, *Cāṇakya* looks at external realities that the government machinery would face. He starts systematically studying what he calls 'the essentials' of an organised State. He identifies the essentials as the territory of the kingdom, the population of the kingdom, the organisation through which the kingdom is being run and last but not the least, the unity within the kingdom.

According to *Cāṇakya,* the essentials of the State should be taken care of through 'constituents of the State' identified by him. These constituents are *Swamy* (King), *Amātya* (Prime Minister), *Janapada* (populated territory), *Durga* (fort), *Kośa* (treasury), *Bala* (force/ army) and *Mitra* (ally). His choice of *Mitra* as a constituent of the State is interesting. He thinks of a network of allies to fortify a kingdom. *Mitra* is a king who would come to the support of *Swamy*, if *Swamy*'s kingdom is attacked by another king. It will also be the duty of the *Swamy* to extend all help if the *Mitra* is attacked by another king. In today's world of globalisation, the same concept is applied when corporates form alliances to fortify their territories from external dangers such as cheap imports and the entry of strong competitors.

At this stage, *Cāṇakya* refers to diplomacy as an important element in *Nītiśāstra* (foreign affairs). His clarity of thought is evident from the identification of six attributes of diplomacy. The attributes he talks about are Intelligence, Memory, Cleverness of Speech, Knowledge of Politics, Morals and Readiness to provide resources. Though he is not shy of launching an attack as an external strategy, he also advises the use of diplomacy as a useful strategy to be explored showing his pragmatic approach to the external realities. He identifies the external threats as the superiority of strengths of other kingdoms as well as ambitions of other kingdoms. If one replaces the word 'kingdom' with 'corporate', *Cāṇakya*'s advice makes sense in today's corporate turf battles.

It is interesting to note the advice *Cāṇakya* provides to handle a strong king who has evil designs as well as a weak king who has catapulted easily. To defeat designs of a strong king, *Cāṇakya* advises networking with other kings defeated or threatened by the strong king on one hand and develop nuisance value through 'nibbling by the sides'. He also advocates the concept of *Upekṣā*, the studied indifference, in the face of strength as a diplomatic move. To a weak king who easily catapults or surrenders, *Cāṇakya* advises his *Swamy* to give the king his dignity and not to rub his nose in the defeat. This way, he suggests, *Swamy* will have a useful friend who will never forget the treatment received and will remain ever so grateful.

Finally, from the point of view of management of the kingdom, *Cāṇakya*'s advice to his *Swamy* is indeed insightful and valid to the corporate world of the 21st century. It can be an effective guideline for all in an organisation if the term *Swamy* is substituted by CEO and the term 'kingdom' with 'organisation'. His advice is as under:

1. *Swamy*/ CEO should run a diversified economy actively, efficiently, profitably and prudently.
2. Diversified economy should consist of productive forests, water reservoirs, mines, productive activities, trade, markets, roads, ports, and storages.
3. Efficient management means setting up of realistic targets and meeting targets without using overzealous methods.
4. Wealth lies in economic activities. Proper direction and guidance from *Swamy*/ CEO will ensure current prosperity and future gains. Inactivity of *Swamy*/ CEO in the economic sphere will bring the kingdom/ organisation close to destruction.
5. *Swamy*/ CEO must bear in mind that a Chief of any organisation with a depleted treasury is weak and the easiest target for a takeover. As *Cāṇakya* says in his sūtrās:
   '*Artha-saṁpat prakṛti-saṁpadaṁ karoti*'
   '*prakṛti-saṁpadā a-nāyakaṁ api rājyaṁ nīyate*'[16]
   which means that 'Wealth of resources leads to wealth for the people, and through excellence and abundance of resourceful people, the enterprise flourishes.
6. *Swamy*/ CEO should ensure enactment of prudent policies. Prudence should be based on *Dharma* and *Nyāya* that will ensure equal opportunity for all to earn a decent living.

7. Profitability should not only mean surplus over costs. It should also mean provision of investment for future growth.
8. Availability of resources and other facilities is important. It is practical to acquire a smaller base for investment with resources in abundance than a large venue that would need substantial investment to generate revenue.
9. An ideal *Swamy*/ CEO is the one who has the highest qualities of leadership, intellect, energy and personal attributes.
10. *Swamy*/CEO can reign only with the help of others. He should appoint the required number of people 'second-in-line' to look after the governance of the 'State machinery' or organisation.
11. While limiting the span of control for the *Swamy*/ CEO, *Cāṇakya* warns against centralisation of power in the hands of the *Swamy*/ CEO by stating 'one wheel alone does not move a chariot'.
    Cāṇakya gives this message in the following *Sūtra*:
    'Na ekaṁ cakraṁ bhramayati' [17]
12. *Swamy*/CEO should take proper care in appointing advisors and consultants. He should have clarity in terms of qualities an advisor should possess, most important being practical experience, thinking prowess, sound judgement and ability to differ while keeping total devotion to the kingdom/ organisation.
    Throughout *Arthaśāstra*, *Cāṇakya* makes some really thought-provoking observations. They are listed below as Pearls of wisdom from *Arthaśāstra*:
    Avinīttaṁ snehamātreṇ na mantre kurvīta[18]

Do not seek advice from/ consult with an arrogant/ morally untrained person only because of friendship.

A confidante should necessarily prove himself worthy of being told secrets or plans yet to be realised. Such a person in whom one would like to confide and would like to consult should have the qualities of humility, self-discipline and moral rectitude. Even if the person has great knowledge and is humble to some extent, it is necessary to let him pass the integrity test. This idea is further reinforced in the next *Sūtra*.

Śrutavantaṁ upadhā-śuddhaṁ mantriṇaṁ kurvīta[19]

Make him a minister (consultant and confidante) who is learned and who has passed the integrity tests.

Cāṇakya believes that the learned are the worldly wise who have seen and experienced the world. '*Śrutavān*' could also be a reference to the one who has 'listened' to the wise and learnt the *Vedas*. He advises that such individuals should be put through 'upadhā', which is a procedure to test the integrity of the person. If a man is tempted with money, wine, women, power and position and he overcomes them to come clean, 'śuddha', then he ought to be placed in positions that are befitting him.

For the growth of an enterprise, there has to be a wealth of policies, which are well protected. He brings it out in the following sūtrās thus:

'*Mantra-rakṣaṇe kārya-siddhiḥ bhavati*'
'*Mantra –saṁpadā rājyaṁ vardhate (Sūtra 1/ 27)*
'Śreṣṭhatamāṁ mantra-guptiṁ ahuḥ (Sūtra 1/ 28)[20]

Protecting policy/ strategy leads to work accomplishment.

Wealth of policies/ excellence in strategies makes the enterprise grow and prosper.

Pre-eminent amongst means of protection is said to be the policy, and confidentiality of strategies is said to be the most important.

This leads to fairness in dealing with the personnel in an organisation as there can be no decision taken on the basis of a personal discretion, or a preconceived bias. It is also essential to maintain secrecy of certain policy matters as the lack of confidentiality may be detrimental in certain areas or functions such as vigilance enquiries, tenders, and bids for sale and purchase. Policies that are already established and implemented make it easier for managers to take effective actions and there is uniformity in the functioning of the managers in similar situations due to the guidelines of the policy. A manager can avoid getting into a blind spot with a policy to guide him.

'*Rājya-tantra-āyattaṁ nīti-Śāstraṁ*' [21]

The science of ethics/ politics depends upon the technology of enterprise (management).

Following the ethics in business is the job of the top management who 'call the shots' on 'how an enterprise is managed'.[22]

In conclusion, it may be said that a treatise written ages ago still has relevance even today. *Arthaśāstra* written in the 4th century BC, is a work whose relevance has not faded even after 24 centuries have gone by. *Arthaśāstra* is the evidence of the intellectual capital India possessed in its glorious past. It is the tradition of the past and what is needed is the attitude for resurrecting and recreating the intellectual capital for the future.

In the *Arthaśāstra*, the crux of his teaching is 'control over mind and senses'. If one looks closely into his teaching, it is seen that *Cāṇakya* advocated moderation in material pleasures and adherence to the path of righteousness. He himself lived such a life, refusing all adornments or riches. His constant exhortation to give up sensory pleasures, and cultivate qualities like kindness, patience etc may sound hypocritical coming from a man who overthrew governments. But it is not so, as he lived a life of purpose and discipline himself. In talking about the four stages of life, the *Āśramas*, he propounds the mixing of spiritual and sensual aspects of life, with the former slowly displacing the latter in stages. One can go on and on with illustrations from his life proving *Cāṇakya*'s farsightedness, keenness of perception, and infallibility.

Cāṇakya lived life in a manner that made all envious of him. He displayed the three marks of a superior man which are 1) being virtuous and thus free from anxiety, 2) being wise and thus free from perplexity, 3) being brave, and thus free from fear.

In India, there are many thinkers who can be talked about with reverence and affection for their contribution to social welfare and wellbeing. Vivekānanda and Gandhi too did colossal work for the liberation and upliftment of the Indians, both individual and collective. Their ideologies were deeply rooted in Indian philosophy and ethics. The universality of their teaching needs no further exposition.

Vivekānanda on Ethics and Conduct

Swami Vivekānanda is looked at as an important link between India and the Western world. He emphasised on the consciousness of the spiritual unity and the solidarity of humanity taught by our ancient thinkers. Indian thought reached across the shores of the world mainly due to the travel undertaken by Vivekānanda to the various parts of the globe, conducting lectures and conferences on Spirituality. Vivekānanda felt that life in India was almost stagnating as a result of the fears that the Indian mind experienced. These fears stemmed from insecurities, lack of self-confidence and irrational beliefs.

Vivekānanda worked with one objective in life and that was 'for the welfare of the common masses, for the happiness of the common masses' just as Buddha preached '*bahujana-hitāya, bahujana-sukhāya*'.

One of his favourite utterances was: 'All expansion is life; all contraction is death. The first manifest effect of life is expansion. You must expand if you want to live. The moment you ceased to expand, death is upon you, danger is ahead.'

Vivekānanda's theory of education is ideal and significant as it emphasises on all-round development of the individual. To quote Vivekānanda, 'The end of all education and all training should be **Man-making**. The end and aim of all training is to make men grow. The training by which the current and expression of will are brought under control and become fruitful, is called Education.... The reason for man's successful conquest over nature and the animal kingdom is his tremendous will. Those who have shaped the world have not only been men with muscles of iron and nerves of steel, but of tremendous will which nothing can resist.'[23]

His theory of education is very relevant to the Management scene, where training is a major requisite for the organisation. It is necessary to understand that training programmes that are organised by the organisations should focus on the development of the values of the members in the organisation, without emphasising on the mere training of skills. What is required of the staff and the management today is the all-round development of the individual, in body, mind, and soul. Training of skills alone leads to lop-sided growth of the individual, where the knowledge of the 'how' of technology, industrial functions, and products will lead to *Ahaṁkāra*. If the individual is trained in various skills along with the development of his character, with a channelising of his will, he is an asset to the organisation. 'Man-making' clearly talks of the process of building up a man's character, as it is not the physical or mental attributes alone that make him humane.

Vivekānanda stressed the need for a positive approach in life. He believed strongly that one should have positive ideas as negative thoughts only weakened men. Kind words encourage and harsh words mutilate human souls. It is necessary to provide an environment of nurture and care for all individuals to grow. Every individual is born unique, and every individual has been blessed with a potential. It is for the organisation to tap the talents and capabilities of the individual in order to benefit both the individual and the organisation. One should not grow at the cost of the other but should provide for the simultaneous growth of both.

Teamwork is greatly stressed in his philosophy of education. Vivekānanda believes that no great work is ever done by mere individual effort. All achievement, physical, mental or spiritual, is possible only with co-operative and co-ordinated efforts. The organisation needs to encourage and motivate people within the organisation to work together in order to achieve success in the competitive world. Values of co-operation and mutual trust and respect need to be cultivated in individuals from the childhood itself. Continuous reinforcement of positive values and weeding out of negative thoughts and feelings is a must for organisational and national growth.

Swami Vivekānanda had tremendous faith in the potentialities of man. According to him, man's powers and potentialities are unutilised, underutilised or misused. If man has blundered in life with respect to his capabilities, the only factor that can be responsible is the ignorance in his mind. Man has yet to realise his own powers. Man's success lies in removing the darkness that has set in due to *Avidyā* and kindle the latent spirit in himself. For this, he needs to develop concentration, for which Vivekānanda recommended regular meditation. The secret of man's success lies in his ability to focus and concentrate. Man needs to realise the spiritual core within himself and express it through his skills.

The key to develop good concentration, according to Swamiji, is *Brahmacarya*. According to him, *Brahmacarya* is chastity in thought, word and deed, always and in all conditions. The chaste brain has tremendous energy and gigantic will power. Without chastity, there can be no spiritual strength. *Brahmacarya* is not only restraint over the bodily impulses and urges. It implies restraint over mental modifications, speech, and feelings. It is necessary to develop an attitude of detachment in oneself to keep the distractions of the phenomenal world at bay.

Swami Vivekānanda never felt that religion could have a degenerative and detrimental effect on man and society. He always said that religion was the innermost core of true education. He emphatically said that Religion was not in doctrines or dogmas, nor in intellectual argumentation. It was realisation in one's life and experience of the Supreme Love, which transcended the bodily limitations and became identified with all humanity.

'Indian philosophy, Indian religions and Indian culture were powerfully influenced by the traditional vision and bore the stamp to universality and humanism. Through them, India seeks to demonstrate to the world that to be strong need not be fearful, to be peaceful need not be weak, but that strength and peacefulness can co-exist in a nation as much as a person.'[24] He believed that it was necessary for Indians to sound the 'drums of *Dharma*' proclaiming the message of 'co-existence, friendship and peace'. '

Vivekānanda's teachings lead us to a philosophy where there is a wonderful synthesis of *jñāna* (discriminative wisdom), *karma* (duty and action), *bhakti* (devotion) and *yoga* (contemplation).

Vivekānanda made *Upaniṣadic* thoughts simple for the young minds. Vivekānanda believed in the inherent goodness and divinity of man. He always expressed the view that man was primarily selfless, loving, peaceful and virtuous. All scientific and philosophical discussions on man portray him as an intelligent being with a pure soul. He has immense powers within himself, and he has knowledge that is in consonance with the well-being of all around him.

Vivekānanda's teaching is an exposition of *Upaniṣadic* thought in simple terms, mainly directed at the youth. He felt that the youth had to be shaped at an early age as the future of every nation rested on them. Man is like a coiled-up spring waiting to unfold. When released from the pressure and strains of the phenomenal world, man becomes a potential soul unfolding all his capabilities, moving towards self-realisation. Vivekananda believes strongly that the *Vedānta* rightly claims that what is expounded as ethics and morality is a manifestation of the inherent goodness in man and also the oneness and unity of the created world. This expression of oneness is summed up in the Chaṇdogya Upaniṣad, as '*Tat Tvaṁ Asi*', 'That Thou Art'. The *Ātman-Brahman* unity is the rationale for all ethics and spirituality in Indian culture, according to Swami Vivekananda.

Vivekananda's simple and profound thinking appeals easily to the common man who leads life with aspirations, dreams and goals. The primary goal of every individual should ideally be the establishment of a character and to obtain '*pratishṭa prajñā*', prudential and established wisdom. Truth, purity in thought, word and deed along with a selfless attitude will help man to vanquish all his enemies and eliminate all his miseries. His philosophy will definitely guide the man in a corporate set up, as it equips every individual with the required competencies. He motivates the man of today with the following line- *udyogīnāṁ puruṣasimhaṁ upaiti lakṣmiḥ*, which means that Goddess Lakshmi visits only those who work hard and have a heart like that of a lion. He does not rebuke people who would like to earn wealth but in fact goads them to work, in order to earn peacefully and ethically.

To sum up his philosophy for the corporate world, Vivekananda implores man to have three essentials for self-growth and collective growth:

- Love, which makes one feel from the heart and opens up even the most impossible gates
- Will, which drives and motivates one to act
- Steadfastness, which keeps one going on the path of truth under any circumstances.

Gandhi's Philosophy of *Sarvodaya*

The word '*Sarvodaya*' is a little word implying a profound thought and philosophy. The word '*Sarvaṁ*' means 'all' as well as 'wholesome'. The word '*Udaya*' means 'rising' or 'the holistic emergence'. 'Figuratively, the word "*Sarvodaya*" came to mean "the wholistic growth and all-round development of all the sections of global humanity".'[25]

Gandhi presents a model for development that is an all-inclusive one for the benefit of the individual. His idea of development was the all-round development of an average Indian's quality of life. Nobody has emphasised the need for ameliorating the economic condition of the economically depraved Indians more sincerely and aggressively than Gandhi. But Gandhi never believed that economic well-being of an individual could alone make the quality of his lifestyle commendable. It is more important to see that the individual is culturally enriched and morally sound than economically supported. An individual's quality of life is determined by a number of factors. His economy is very important but not sufficient to crown it with all that is desirable. Some of the other necessary factors are his attitude towards his way he spends it, his ability to fulfil his needs, his capability to do well the job he is assigned to do, his education, his reading habits, his sense of self-respect and self-dignity, his dealings with the other members of his family and society, the freedom he has to function as a viable member of his society, etc.

Gandhi's model of economic development is found to be more qualitative in nature, spirit and objectives. The sole guiding principle in Gandhian thought is ethics and religion. It aims at the self-realisation of the individual, where happiness that is sought is not achieved with a compromise on morality. It is rationally justifiable in the language of modern ethical terminology. Gandhi urges the individual to give up his prejudices and wrong beliefs. He asks him to discard all his superstitions and develop a scientific attitude. The scientific temper in man alone can keep alive the spirit of enquiry, leading him to right knowledge.

A visit to Gandhi Ashram at Ahmedabad gives further access to his writings and philosophy. What seemed very theoretical, and abstract is made so profound and practically applicable by Gandhiji. He brings down the Utopian to a very pragmatic level. As a further elaboration of the five vows of *Satya*, *Ahiṁsā*, *Brahmachṛya*, *Aparigraha* and *Asteya* which are Patanjali's '*Yamas*', Gandhiji added the following six:[26]

- *Aspṛushyatānivaran*: Eradication of Non-touchability
- *Swāśraya*: Bread by one's own labour
- *SarvaDharma Samabhāv*: Respect for all religions
- *Swadeshī*: Use of indigenous goods
- *Abhay*: Fearlessness
- *Aswād*: Control of the palate

Gandhi's interpretations of these vows made them relevant to contemporary society and industry.

- '...without *ahiṁsā*, it is not possible to seek and find truth.... Nevertheless, *ahiṁsā* is the means and truth is the end.'

- '*Brahmacharya* means giving up all pleasures of sense, i.e., control of all sense-organs.'
- '*Aswad* means not to enjoy the pleasure of the palate. Food has to be taken as we take medicine, without thinking whether it is palatable or otherwise, only in quantities limited to the needs of the body.'
- 'It is theft if one takes anything over and above one's minimum needs.'
- 'Non-possession is allied to non-stealing.... A seeker of truth cannot hold anything against tomorrow.'
- 'A seeker after truth must have no fear of caste, government or robbers, nor of poverty or death.'
- 'Untouchability implies pollution by touch. Removal of untouchability spells the breaking down of barriers between man and man.'
- '(Physical) Labour is a must for all men, ... how can a man who does not labour have a right to eat?'

Gandhi gave a lot of importance to these vows. He felt that these 'vows should be taken in observance of universally recognised moral principles which we do not habitually act upon.... A vow means unflinching determination. They are necessary for overcoming the difficulties in adhering to moral rule. Determination is nothing if it bends before temptation.' Gandhiji projected as social values the vows that had hitherto been associated with personal values.

In his plan for constructing a developed society, with indigenous resources, Gandhi insisted on constructive criticism as an important component of his programme. He chided the people who blindly followed what was doled out to them in the name of culture or religion. He firmly believed that personal morality had to be coherent with social ethics in order to promote wellbeing of the majority.

Gandhi's mantra for social development and individual liberation from the shackles of materialism is: '*Īśā vāsya idaṁ sarvam yat kinchit jagatyām jagat, tena tyaktena bhunjithaḥ mā grudhah kasyasvit dhanaṁ*', which means that one can enjoy one's wealth only by renouncing it. He explains it thus: 'Earn your crores by all means. But understand that your wealth is not yours; it belongs to the people. Take what you require for your legitimate needs and use the remainder for society.' According to Gandhi, one has a right to live an honourable life and hence, one can rightfully take only that part of the wealth that is needed for a livelihood. The rest of the money belongs to the community and should be ideally used for its welfare.

He firmly believes in the goodness of mankind which forces him to live in an illusion that all would contribute equally towards wealth generation. In reality, however, this does not happen in many cases. Gandhi replies to this question of inequality in work and equality of benefits in the following way, 'The question is of conviction. If you accept the principle of *Ahiṁsā*, then you have to strive to live up to it, no matter whether you succeed or fail . . . . My theory of trusteeship is no makeshift, certainly no camouflage. I am confident it will survive all other theories. It has the sanction of philosophy and religion behind it. No other theory is compatible with non-violence.'[27] 'With non-violence as the rule, life will no doubt be a series of compromises. But it is better than an endless series of clashes.'

Gandhi believes in making an appeal to the goodness in all human beings, which is the premise with which Gandhi begins his theories of education and economic development. Every individual should use his talents and potential for the good of all, not merely for personal aggrandisement.

The apparent snag in the Gandhian model is the impossible looking task of impressing upon a rich landlord, or a factory owner, to behave in the manner of a trustee of people's property, without seeming a master. If this attitude can be developed by adopting some governmental, legislative, social or political, measures to stop exploitation of the poor workers, rural or urban, the Gandhian model would be decidedly the best. It would not have any undesirable ethical fallout and will be very greatly favourable to those who cherish the sentiments of national self-respect and rational self-confidence.

The idea of trusteeship, among Gandhian ideas of social reconstruction, is a novel idea. It is a unique way of keeping the dignity of every human being intact, although it is an idea which has been considered to be impracticable by many. It is also true that in his theory of social reconstruction the two building blocks are non-violence (*ahiṁsā*) and truth (*satya*), whereby Gandhi has taken care to protect all alike. 'The word "*Satya*" is derived from "sat" which means "that which is". *Satya* means a "state of being". Nothing is or exists in reality except Truth.... Without truth it is impossible to observe any principles or rules in life.'

Making profit in business and enterprise is not ethically undesirable. A businessman has the right to make profit, but he has to keep his profit-making endeavour within the bounds of morality. He will do that marvellously well if he treats himself as the trustee of the property from the use of which he earns his profit. Gandhi himself always kept his personal or public operations well within the bounds of morality. In the present industrial world, the idea of trusteeship itself was considered impractical. A businessman can be expected or required to earn his profit only in a morally desirable manner. He has no right to exploit those who work for him. He is also denied the right to possess or hoard by depriving benefits to those who have worked to enable him to prosper.

The axiom of the Gandhian model is development of the nation along with the preservation of the cultural ethnicity and the upholding of the principle of *Dharma* as given in our scriptures. Gandhi insists that the ethical soundness of Indian tradition cannot be questioned and predicts that it will last for eternity. 'There is no salvation for us without true *Swadeshī*.... Its observance is a moral duty for us.'

For Gandhi, Truth is God. His idea of religion thus transcends all divisions that arise in the name of caste, creed or race. He followed and practiced humanitarian values, which gave a different connotation to religion entirely. '*Ahiṁsā* teaches us to entertain the same respect for all religious faith of others, as we accord our own.' For Gandhi, an individual was religious if he performed his duties according to his station in life unflinchingly.

The great sages, seers and social activists have all worked in tune with Indian thought and culture. They seemed to have a foresight and a deep grasp of the various problems that Indians could face if they failed to recall their rich cultural heritage. The constant reiteration of the teachings in the ancient texts and the obvious anxieties in the mind of the great thinkers of India with regard to its future needs no more elaboration. It is necessary for any Indian citizen, especially the youth of India to definitely read and understand the scriptures, epics and texts in order to reconstruct the edifice of our glorious culture. The Indian philosophical systems give deep insight into the ethos, ethics and the management systems, without spelling them out as essential for learning and development. The necessity to blend economic growth with spiritual growth is an eye-opener for the youth of today.

Understanding the various aspects of Indian culture, including religion, as a catalyst to growth becomes mandatory for today's generation. There is an attempt made to expound religion in its pure sense, with a view to re-establish the ethics and sanctity of religion as practised in India. The next chapter is an attempt to discuss religion and its significant contribution to the glory of a moral society, highlighting the aesthetics and customary aspects, leading it all to good management.

References

1. Sinha Jadunathan, *The Foundation of Hinduism*, Pilgrims Book Pvt. Ltd., Delhi:1999, p. 43.
2. Swami Tejomayananda, *Hindu Culture: An Introduction*, Central Chinmaya Mission Trust, Mumbai: 2002, Chapter IX 'The *Śāstras*', p. 84.
3. Ibid. p. 96.
4. Narayana G., *Strategic Leadership: A Journey through Chaanakya Sutras and Kautilya Artha Shaastras*, Ahmedabad Management Association, Ahmedabad: 2002. p. 27.
5. Garde R. Ashok, *Cāṇakya's Aphorisms on Management*, Ahmedabad Management Association, Ahmedabad: 2003, p. 21.
6. Ibid., p. 76
7. Sharma R.K, *Chāṇākya's Neeti Scripture:The first English Translation in Verse*, Bharatiya Vidya Bhavan, Bombay: 1994, p. 75.
8. Ibid., p. 75.
9. Ibid., p. 75.
10. Ibid., p. 75.
11. Ibid., p. 75.
12. Ibid., p. 76.
13. Ibid., p. 76.
14. Ibid., p. 76.
15. Ibid., p. 76.
16. Garde Ashok R., *Cāṇakya's Aphorisms on Management*, Ahmedabad Management Association, Ahmedabad: 2003, pp. 35, 36.
17. Ibid., p. 41.
18. Ibid., p. 44.
19. Ibid., p. 44.
20. Ibid., p. 59.
21. Ibid., p. 81.
22. Ibid., p. 81.
23. India's Contribution to World Thought and Culture, Vivekananda Rock Memorial Committee, Madras: 1970, p. 340.
24. Ibid., p. 347.
25. Dharmadhikari Acharya Dada, *Philosophy of Sarvodaya*, Translated by S.S. Pandharipande, Popular Prakashan Pvt. Ltd., Mumbai: 2000 pg.vii.
26. Visit to Gandhi Ashram, Ahmedabad, Gujarat.
27. 'Trusteeship' by M.K. Gandhi, Compiled by Ravindra Kelekar, Pub. Navajivan Publishing House, Ahmedabad 380 014, 1960, pp. 6, 9.

VII

EASTERN THOUGHT INTERWEAVING FAITH AND ETHICS

Another important aspect that influences and determines man's philosophy of life is Religion. Religion, as mentioned earlier, is an integral part of Indian culture and ethos. It is inseparable from the philosophical basis that determines man's living. In order to understand the ethos of Indian culture, it is important to study the various aspects that influence man. Contrary to popular belief, the religion of India does not repudiate the world, negate social values, or forbid the enjoyment of legitimate pleasures for man. Religion, in fact, points to the path that leads to enduring happiness, both here and hereafter. It leads man to the highest truth in his life. There is no exaggeration in saying that the very life of India is centred in religion and religious beliefs, expressed through religious practices.

Religion, in India, was never given a specific name. The way of life that was prevalent in India at that time was known by the name '*Sanātana Dharma*', meaning 'eternal virtue', which clearly indicates the emphasis on ethics and morality. It existed to unite people in a shared experience and explanation of life. Man's ceaseless quest for the Absolute Truth is like searching for something precious, either that has been lost or not found yet, which is necessary for peace and happiness. The study of religion helps us to understand human behaviour and its various patterns, which come as response to the situations and hazards of life. It also provides an agreed way of looking at the world, giving the individual a sense of purpose and meaning. The study of religion leads to a knowledge that is profound and subtle, if understood in its true essence. This knowledge leads to ethics and special acts of worship. Religion helps man to deconstruct, construct, and reconstruct his own character and personality. As it is prescriptive in nature, it effectively works to introduce discipline in man's life.

In India, the relationship between philosophy and religion is like that between science and technology. Religion is philosophy applied to everyday life. A philosopher is not one who reads, talks or teaches a particular philosophy, but one who lives it and becomes a model for others to emulate. The roots of Indian philosophy are in the *Vedās*. Thousands of years have passed since then. During the course of history of Indian philosophy and religion, several ideas and sects have formed, established, merged and assimilated. Thus, the philosophy and religion of India has been very dynamic, and it continues to be so.

The concepts of Indian philosophy, though rooted in the *Vedās*, are not limited by them or to them. There are new sects being formed regularly and some old sects being assimilated into others. New religious ideas are always welcomed with open hearts and minds. The *Vedās* proclaim, 'Truth is one. The wise call it by various terms: *Ekam Sat, Vipra Bahudhā Vadanti.'* In India, the students of philosophy and the followers of religion are encouraged to question everything. If a system does not answer the questions, it deserves to be re-examined or thrown out. If a new idea answers all the questions in a rational way, it is accepted. A religion is approachable through various sects, paths, gurus, saints, etc and a person is free to choose any of them that enables him to reach the Truth. The only requirement is the zeal to know the Truth and the sincerity towards the zeal. This rational and open attitude is the hallmark of Indian philosophy and religion.

In order to show the relevance of religion in this study of management, the purpose and significance of religion and religious symbols is brought out. To quote Ninian Smart, from his work, *Religious Experience*, 'No one can understand mankind without understanding the faith of humanity. Sometimes naive, sometimes penetratingly noble, sometimes crude, sometimes subtle, sometimes cruel, sometimes suffused by an overpowering gentleness and love, sometimes world-affirming, sometimes negating the world, sometimes inward-looking, sometimes universalistic and missionary minded, sometimes shallow and often profound-religion has permeated human life since early and obscure times.'[1].

Somewhere in the materialistic progress and acquisition of knowledge and skills to maintain a more than comfortable lifestyle, man has lost his sense of orientation. He is not insane, mad, or bad in terms of personality and character. It is just that man has turned out to be an 'incomplete' human being because he is unable to properly link the goals of life with his actions and ambitions. At times, his rationality is coloured with frivolous sentiments. There is nothing wrong with knowledge, skills, or ambitions per se, as long as these are beneficial to oneself or one's family and community. But if this comes at the cost of someone losing out on his entitlement, society will necessarily have to put up with inequality, and social strife as its corollary. This is the cause of violence of some kind in the people's mind. Almost the entire world is in a state of turmoil because there does not seem to be a strong and solid value-system to back-up mankind. All value-systems have broken down and need a healthy revival.

All the developed religions of the world emphasise that human life and endeavours have to be seen, understood and acted upon by taking a holistic view of the universe. Man, no doubt, tends to think himself to be God's most important creation, primarily because of his capacity for logical thinking. Man has to accept that there is a much higher level and kind of intelligence that goes with creation. The Creator's gift of giving man a degree of intellect not given to other living things necessarily makes it incumbent upon man to think and act with a deeper sense of responsibility and circumspection. There will be no value to life if man lives only for the day, like animals do.

Man lives with a presumption—that a truly purposive life is possible only with a total belief in the existence of God and a profound faith in divinity. But it is not so. This is because blind performance of rituals in the name of religion does not imply true religiosity. **One should know the basic tenets of one's religion**, and the significance of the rituals and relate these to the essence (philosophy) of the religion and then reason out one's response.

As Vivekananda said, 'Religion is a manifestation of the divinity already present in man.' Religion is a human creation, and all religions are specific responses by people of different cultures to the peculiar conditions that they find themselves in. It is an outcome of the economic, moral, intellectual, social, cultural, and psychological fabric of the people of a particular geographical location at the material time. As the conditions and standard of living evolve, religious consciousness also transforms with the needs of the time of the people within a cultural milieu.

Keeping this definition in mind, let us now understand the influence of religion and religious values and symbols in India.

The distinction between sign and symbol needs to be made clear here. A sign is an indicator whereas the symbol is a representation. There is a certain amount of arbitrariness about signs and the word that is a sign of something can be easily swapped with another word. But in the case of a symbol, it is more intimately involved in that to which it refers. It participates in what it symbolises and cannot be swapped for another symbol. Any explanation of a symbol destroys its meaning and essence, as it will not carry the same power. A symbol is, hence, a thought in action.

Religious symbols help the believers in many ways. These symbols help them to understand their faith in profound ways. They tend to unite the intellect and the emotions of the individual or group. They also integrate the personal and the social dimensions of the religion of the individuals. They help to form groups enabling individuals to share certain commonly held beliefs. These common beliefs are expressed by symbols. Religious symbols are significant in this context as these symbols enshrine and express the highest values and relationships of life.

In India, the whole of nature is seen as vibrant with life and everything around man is considered to be a representation of divinity. Trees, rocks, rivers, animals—all provide a focus for the sacred that man seeks to realise. The devout make these symbols of divinity by worshipping them and seeking the meaning of life in them. These symbols speak of the powers that confront human endeavour. They serve as signposts pointing to the constant struggle experienced in the tugs of the good and the evil. Everything in nature is symbolic of the spiritual aspect in life, and they are major sources of support to mankind.

Of the various symbols that are used in religious practices in India, a few that are mentioned here are the more significant and the more utilised ones. To name a few, there is a mention of the *Cakra*, the *Sūrya*, the *Swastikā*, the *Rudrākṣa*, the *Śaṇkha*, the *Padma*/ *Kamala*, *AUM*, etc. It needs to be accepted that each symbol has a role to play in our faith and belief.

Cakra

The concept of *Cakra* has an important part to play in Indian culture. This concept gives rise to many other symbols. It is generally translated as the 'wheel'. It is sometimes translated in English as the 'lotus', the 'plexes', or the 'circular diagram'. When understood in this context, it is used for concentration on cosmic or psychic energy. Indian philosophy and religion accept the divinity of all creation. This divinity is symbolised as the circular halo over and around the head of a being, which is called the *Sahasrāra-Cakra*. It is considered the highest spiritual attainment by an individual.

The entire phenomenal world is depicted as resembling a wheel. This is an indication of the dynamism of the world. It also symbolises the cyclic nature of all worldly processes— the seasons, the occurrence of day and night, the movement of heavenly bodies, the cycle of birth and death, the causal chain, the succession of involution and evolution, including the alternation of happiness and misery.

In *Sāṁkhya* philosophy, the term '*Cakra*' is used in the sense of cyclic processes in the phenomenal world. Creation itself is depicted with the symbol of a wheel, showing that the wheel of creation has three tyres, representing the three *guṇās*, *Sattva*, *Rajas,* and *Tamas*. They are also understood as time, space, and causation. The sixteen extremities of *Sāṁkhya* are the *vṛttīs* mentioned in its philosophy. The eleven *indrīyās* and the *Pancamahābhūtās* evolve to complete the evolutionary process.

In Hinduism, Buddhism, and Jainism, the Cakra (wheel) is recognised as a symbol of the Law of Karma. It represents the continuous cycle of actions and consequences that shape human experience. The wheels are shown as revolving on three paths: the path of righteousness (*Dharma*), the path of non-righteousness (*Adharma*), and the path of knowledge (*Jñāna*). All beings move through these paths in a circular pattern. Each rotation of the Cakra produces pairs of opposites—such as merit and sin, joy and suffering, freedom, and bondage. These contrasts help explain the ethical and spiritual effects of one's actions. Through this symbolism, the Cakra offers insight into the principles of Karma and the moral responsibilities it implies.

The concept of *Cakra* is widely used in all religions and systems of philosophy in India, which includes Hinduism, Buddhism, Jainism, or even *tāntrik* religion. It is also used in *Sāṁkhya*, *Yoga* and *Vedānta*. In Hinduism, the *Cakra* is a representation of cosmic manifestation and also of individual life. Here an explanation of the *Cakra*s in relation to the individual is given in an interesting manner. The flux of man's actions is known as *karma-cakra*. The wheel of time that governs man's life is the *Kāla-Cakra*. The *Cakra* that denotes the moral order in man's life is the *Dharma-Cakra*. The *Cakra* that denotes a perfect and beautiful lifecycle is named the *Sudarṣan Cakra*, which is the one shown as carried by Lord *Kṛṣṇa* himself. The *Sudarṣana Cakra* symbolises the source of unlimited energy that is utilised for protection from the evil in every form.

The Buddhist symbol is in the form of a wheel with eight spokes representing the Noble Eight-fold Path, which means the way leading to the cessation of suffering. This Path consists of the following: Right View, Right Motive, Right Speech, Right Action, Right Means of Livelihood, Right Effort, Right Mindfulness and Right Concentration. This symbol is called '*Dhammacakka*' or the Wheel of *Dhamma* and has been adopted as the seal of the World Fellowship of Buddhists.

The spokes in the wheel or *Cakra* symbolise the diversity within the unity of a circle. Man, his society, his life, his activities, the resultant joys, and sorrows are all discussed in Indian tradition in the form of a wheel or *Cakra*. All these diverse factors have the underlying principles of activity and rhythm. Metaphysically, all ideas and speech/ sounds of the individual are within this *Cakra* called the *Sahasrāksarāvāk*. Buddha too talks of the *Dharma-Cakra*, which determines man's state in this world. *Cakra* as a symbol of perennial motion denotes the necessity for industriousness and perseverance in any endeavour undertaken by man.

*Cakra*s or energy centres are very important parts of the energy body of the individual. The physical body has various organs of different sizes and shapes, and in the same manner, the energy body has minor, major and mini *Cakra*s. The *Cakra*s are energy centres or plexus that whirl and are in constant rhythmic motion. They control and energise the organs of the visible physical body. They are like power stations that supply life-energy to the vital organs, keeping them healthy and active. These organs become diseased and sickly if they do not get enough life-energy to function rightly. These *Cakra*s are also the centres of the psychic faculties. People with highly activated *Cakra*s tend to be energetic, healthy, and active, while those with less energised *Cakra*s end up fragile, weak and lethargic.

The *Cakra* as a symbol of rhythm and activity is said to be responsible for the harmony between the inner and outer of a human being. The *Cakra* is considered to be lead the human from the physical to the astral, to the psychic to the spiritual dimension of life. The potency of the *Cakra* determines man's state of being in birth, childhood, youth, and old age. It leads from birth to decay. The understanding of the *Sūkṣma śarīra* is possible with the understanding of the *Cakra*s.

The human body is depicted in *Yoga* and *Ayurvedā* as having various *Cakra*s. The *Cakra* has its significance as it shows the centre of energy points of the various organs in the human body. The stimulation of these *Cakra*s energise the individual. *Prāṇāyāma* is a technique in *Yoga* that helps to energise and stimulate the *Cakra*s within the human body. The *prāṇa* that is channelised to these various organs of the human body excite the *Cakra*s, giving them the essential power to function effectively. The *Cakra*s thus, help to keep oneself holistic and healthy. there are seven main chakras that run along your spine. These are the chakras that most of us are referring to when we talk about them.

Each of these seven main chakras has a corresponding number, name, colour, specific area of the spine from the sacrum to the crown of the head, and health focus. The seven chakras in yoga are energy centres along the spine that influence physical, mental, emotional, and spiritual well-being. Each chakra has a unique role and balancing them supports overall harmony and health. Here is a simplified yet holistic overview of each chakra:

1. ***Muladhara (Root Chakra):*** which is at the base of the spine and represents the element Earth. Its function is to maintain stability, help in survival, and keep man grounded. If it is energetic and healthy, it governs our basic needs like food, shelter, and safety. A balanced root chakra brings a sense of security and connection to the physical world. A blocked root chakra can manifest as physical issues like arthritis, constipation, and bladder or colon problems, or emotionally through feeling insecure about finances or basic needs of wellbeing. When it is in alignment and open, we will feel grounded and secure, both physically and emotionally. Issues with this chakra can be seen via problems with the associated organs, like urinary tract infections, lower back pain, and impotency. Emotionally, this chakra is connected to our feelings of self-worth, and even more specifically, our self-worth around pleasure, sexuality, and creativity.
2. ***Svādhiṣṭhāna (Sacral Chakra):*** It is located in the lower abdomen, below the navel. It represents the element Water, which is fluid in nature, thus epresenting creativity, aesthetics, and sensual and emotional expressions. It is responsible for emotional balance, creative and free expression of talent and emotions, and deep relationships. When it is blocked, it manifests as menstrual problems, urinary tract infections, and unnecessary and negative feelings of guilt, shame, fear and resultant unhealthy relationships. Participation in creative activities like music, dance, painting, and sports activities can help remove blockages.
3. ***Manipura (Solar plexus Chakra):*** which is located in the upper abdomen, near the stomach, representing the element Fire. It symbolises power, willpower, determination, and confidence. This chakra motivates the individual, boosts confidence and self-esteem, and helps in decision-making and problem-solving. Blockages in the third chakra are often experienced through digestive issues like ulcers, heartburn, eating disorders, and indigestion. It is the chakra of our personal power. This means it is related to our self-esteem and self-confidence.
4. ***Anahata (Heart Chakra):*** which is at the centre of the chest, representing the element Air. It majorly seeks to bridge the physical and the spiritual realms of creation. As the name suggests, it signifies love, compassion, empathy, forgiveness, goodness, and sensitivity. This helps to connect easily with all and build relationships. Blocks in our heart chakra can manifest in our physical health through heart problems, asthma, and weight issues. But blocks are often seen even more clearly through people's actions. People with heart chakra

blocks often put others first, to their own detriment. It is the middle of the seven chakras, so it bridges the gap between our upper and lower chakras, and it also represents our ability to love and connect to others. When out of alignment, it can make us feel lonely, insecure, and isolated.

5. ***Vishuddha (Throat Chakra):*** at the throat, representing the element Ether or Space. This chakra manages the energy for communication and expression and governs speech and articulation. As one would expect, this chakra is connected to our ability to communicate verbally.' Voice and throat problems as well as any problems with everything surrounding that area, such as the teeth, gums, and mouth, can indicate a blockage. Blocks or misalignment can also be seen through dominating conversations, gossiping, speaking without thinking, and having trouble speaking your mind. When in alignment, you will speak and listen with compassion and feel confident when you speak because you know you are being true to yourself with your words
6. ***Ajna (Third Eye Chakra*:** which is between the eyebrows, representing the element Light, symbolising clarity, intuition, deep insight, imaginative thoughts, perception—all leading to wisdom. Since this chakra is physically located on the head, blockages can manifest as headaches, issues with sight or concentration, and hearing problems. People who have trouble listening to reality (who seem to 'know it all') or who are not in touch with their intuition may also have a block. When open and in alignment, it is thought that people will follow their intuition and be able to see the big picture.
7. ***Sahasrara (Crown Chakra)*:** which is at the top of the head, representing the element Cosmic Energy. The vibrancy and energy at this point is a symbol of spiritual enlightenment, depth of personality, and sustained enlightenment. It shows that the individual is connected to a higher consciousness and lives with inner peace and contentment, is detached and mindful, living life with a deep purpose. The crown chakra is linked to every other chakra (and therefore every organ in this system), and so it affects not just all of those organs, but also our brain and nervous system. It is considered the chakra of enlightenment and represents our connection to our life's purpose and spirituality. Those with a blocked crown chakra may seem narrow-minded, sceptical, or stubborn. When this chakra is open, it is thought to help keep all the other chakras open and to bring the person bliss and enlightenment. As these are all energetic centres of the body that correspond to feelings, one of them

probably resonated with you as you were reading. A different one may resonate with you tomorrow. It is likely that one resonates with you more than any others as a continuous problem, a chakra where you often deal with blocks. Other blockages may pop up every now and then. In the chakra system, these patterns have specific terms and there are recommended treatments.

In the study of the psycho-physical aspect of man, it can be interpreted as the interdependence of the human race. The integration of the individual himself in all aspects of his personality can be well brought here. The *Cakra* is a symbol of the temporal and the spatial, which is ever-changing. When extended to the psychological dimension of human personality, it refers to the ever-changing mental states of the individual. It is also significantly a symbol implying change, growth, development, movement, and transformation. It is a symbol of adaptability. This reiterates the teaching of Indian culture where the individual needs to have an all-round development. He is taught to be flexible enough to adapt, yet firm enough to be stable and consistent in his behaviour. The *Cakra* can, hence, be looked at as a symbol of hope and faith for the betterment of humanity.

Surya

Surya is considered to be the source of life, light, and energy. It has naturally become the symbol of Creation and the Creator. It is believed to be representing the cosmic sacrifice from which the entire creation has taken place. It is placed at a pedestal as it is considered to be the celestial door leading to immortality. *Surya* is the ātman, the Ensouling principle, of the whole creation: '*Surya ātmā jagatastasthaṣaśca*'.

Udaye savita raktaḥ, raktaścāstasamaye tatha.
sampatau ca vipatau ca mahatāmeka rupatā.[2]

At the time of dawn and at the time of dusk, the *Surya* is red-bright; so are the great men and the stable-minded persons who are peaceful and cheerful in all conditions of happiness and misery. The *Surya* thus becomes a symbol of the nature and attitude of the stable and successful individuals in society and thus, the organisations in an industrialised society.

During the Vedic era, Indians were sun worshippers. A verse from the *ṚgVedā* says that the *Surya* (Sun) is a farsighted God, whose chariot is drawn by seven horses. The wheel of the chariot and the seven horses have a special significance. As *Surya* is the Lord of time, the wheel is said to symbolise the wheel of time, the seven horses symbolising the seven days of the week. The spatio-temporal phenomenal world is perceived due to the light of the *Surya*.

Surya signifies life, light, and energy, which is present in all beings too. At the micro level, the individual aura is an emission of the light and energy that inheres in him. The vibrations from the individuals are transmitted and conveyed to other beings around him, allowing him to establish the identity between beings. This leads to the realisation of one's own spiritual self along with that of the others. It is this realisation of the spiritual core in all that reinforces the ethos of Indian culture, stemming from the *Ātman-Brahman* unity.

Surya signifies light, which is also interpreted as Knowledge, *Jñāna*, that dispels the darkness of ignorance and erroneous knowledge, *Avidyā-Māyā*. The devout Indian always seeks Truth. The realisation of one's inner core is the realisation of the Ultimate Reality. In order to grasp this Truth, the devotee seeks the grace of the *Surya*, the giver of life and light. The lighting of a flame, be it a lamp, candle, or a 'Havan' (sacrificial fire), signifies the invoking of the energy and grace of the *Surya*. The symbol of *Surya* renders the lamp or *Deepaṁ* significant in our religious and cultural practices.

In Yoga, the *Surya Namaskār* is an exercise that gives the required stretch and pull to the individual's physical body, with a tug at his mental and psychological aspects too. This exercise helps the individual in developing an attitude of submission to the greatness of the *Surya*, with an attitude of humility and devotion. In fact, it teaches the individual to look up to anyone and anything that is in the environment who is better and greater than himself. It also inculcates in him the readiness to put in efforts to achieve one's goals. The physical and mental wellbeing in the individual can be enhanced by just this one single exercise.

The *Surya* in the human personality is evident in his readiness to work, his eagerness to learn, and his positive attitude to life. An individual with such traits will have an aura around his physical body that seems fluorescent and glowing. This makes the individual light and subtle, closer to the Ultimate reality. The *Surya* bestows its light, heat, and energy on all alike. The individual too should be impartial, just and fair in his dealings with all. Only then can he be a *Stithaprajña*. Moreover, the *Surya* exhibits a power enough to protect the good and destroy the evil.

As the *Surya* is the representation of creation and its force, it symbolises all that is born, that grows, that evolves. While discussing *Cakra*s and the vital energy, *prāṇa*, the significance of the *Surya* and solar energy is well brought out. Thus, the *Surya* in our culture is significant as a symbol.

Swastika

The symbol of *Swastika* is as old as the history and culture of India. Since the time of Indus Valley civilisation, this symbol was very popular among the people. Etymologically, the word '*Swastika*' signifies 'happiness, pleasure and good luck'. 'It has the prefix "*Su*" meaning "good" and "*asti*" meaning "being or existence". In Vedic texts, it occurs several times as a noun in the sense of happiness and as an adverb "well" or "hail".' It is looked at as an emblem of the *Surya*, as a solar wheel with spokes. It is considered to be an auspicious symbol amongst many religions in India, as a symbol of fortune and good luck. The cult of *Surya*-worship is probably the most ancient cult. The *Surya* is the dispeller of darkness. It brings joy, light, and life for mankind.

Being the symbol of the *Surya*, the *Swastika* (just as the *Cakra*) is believed to represent the principle of life and movement. It is 'named *Ṛkvān*, that is, the rhythmical movements'.[3]

The *Swastika* is also considered to be representing the world, which is dynamic and continuously moving because of its spokes. At the same time, it is fixed on to the unchanging and stable centre, which is understood as Brahman, Pure Consciousness or the theistic God. Thus, creation is said to be both dynamic and stable.

The *Swastika* as a symbol of auspiciousness justifies its prevalence on many doors or walls of buildings. It is also looked at as a symbol of protection against evil spirits. The *Swastika* drawn on a constructed structure, be it a home, school, organisation etc, invokes the blessings of Lord *Śivā*, the destroyer of all evils and the protector of all good. It is also worshipped as the symbol of *Ganeṣā*, the '*vighnahartā*', to ward off or eliminate all obstacles before engaging in any auspicious ceremony.

If human personality has to be understood in this perspective, then its relevance to management too can be established. Man needs to be flexible enough to adapt, adjust and evolve. At the same time, he needs to be consistent in his behaviour, with a strong and stable ethical base. His character has to be morally and emotionally stable, mentally, and physically growing and developing, and his sociability meaningful. He needs to live with a purpose and set his goals with wisdom. He has to be realistic in goal setting, with *Jñāna*, right knowledge. He should exhibit the integration of the various aspects of his personality. It is also important to be altruistic in nature, as the general well being of the maximum should be his guiding principle.

The word '*Swastika*' in Sanskrit is differently put in *Pāli*. In Buddhism, the term is taken as '*Sūti*',' and the *Swastika* cross is a combination of two symbols, '*sutti-sūti*', which means that contentment and peace of mind are the only two ideals of life.

In Jainism, the cross of *Swastika* is a representation of both the male and female principles. In addition to this, Jainism also believes that the horizontal and vertical lines crossing each other at right angles represent the soul and matter. Jainism advocates that there are four grades of the existence of soul in the material universe. The first level is recognised as the protoplasmic or archaic life. The next level is that of the earth with its plants and animal life. The third stage is the celestial, which is a reference to life in the other worlds. The final stage is the spiritual stage in which the soul is entirely freed from the bonds of pudgala: the *kārmic* material particles to attain the goal of liberation. This stage is reached only with the help of the three jewels—right belief, right knowledge and right conduct.

This affirms the tenet of Indian philosophy and ethos that it is necessary to follow the paths of Karma, *Jñāna* and *Bhakti* in order to attain liberation. Moreover, the integration of opposites to create a 'whole' is well brought out here. The significance of the rhythm and movement in life for the progress of the human race needs no further clarification or exposition. The necessity for organised and disciplined motion to attain goals is well brought out here as the four arms of the *Swastika* that move cyclic are anchored to the epicentre just as the matter in the human being gets its essence from the spiritual core.

Rudrākṣa

The *Rudrākṣa* are beads, which are the seeds of the tree by the same name, which grow in the Himalayas and the far eastern countries. There is a mention of the liberation attained by the *ṛṣīs* in the *Ṣāstrās*, the '*Upadeśa Khanḍaṁ*' and the '*Suta Samhita*'. These seeds are generally of four colours: white, reddish, golden and the dark. The white and the golden are rare varieties and the other two are said to be more common. Etymologically, the '*Rudrākṣa*' comes from two Sanskrit words '*Rudra*', meaning '*Śiva*' and '*Akṣā*' meaning 'eyes. Hence, *Rudrākṣa* means the third eye, the eye of *Śiva*. This mythological third eye is the spiritual insight or realisation of the individual.

In relation to the size, the *Rudrākṣa* gets its significance. The smaller the size of the bead, the greater is said to be its efficacy. Similarly, the more subtle and intuitive in perception, the more self-realised is the individual. Moving from the gross to the subtle, the *sthula* to the *sūkṣma*, is depicted in the *Rudrākṣa*, as mentioned in the '*Rudrākṣa Jabalopaniṣad*. It is mentioned in it that 'in the crust of the *Rudrākṣa* dwells Lord *Brahma*, in its hollow rests Lord *Viṣnū*, and in its mouth is located lord *Śivā*, while in its *Bindu* abide all the celestials.' If the Creator, Sustainer, and the Destroyer of the Universe reside in this bead, then its efficacy and powers need no more justification.

The importance given to the enhancement of the intuitive and spiritual powers of the individual with the practice of meditation and tapa, along with the power of Truth, is brought out here. The *Rudrākṣa* is considered to be a symbol of goodness prevailing over the evil, with the efficacy of the spiritual powers of the individual endorsed.

Śaṇkha

The *Śaṇkha* or the conch has the form of a multiple spiral evolving from one point to ever-increasing spheres. It thus symbolises the origin of the universe from a single source, vis. God. As it is found in water, it symbolises the causal symbolism of water from where it evolved and to which it will dissolve. When a *Śaṇkha* is blown, it produces a deep, intense, and mystical sound, which represents the *Śabda Brahman*. Indian thought and religion believed that the world has evolved from a single syllable *AUM*, which is the sound that comes from the *Śaṇkha*. It thus represents the *Praṇava*.

Lord *Viṣnū* is depicted as holding the *Śaṇkha* in one of his four hands, as a symbol of *Nāda Brahman*, another name for *Śabda Brahman*. The *Śaṇkha* is said to be a symbol of Goddess Laxmi too as the Goddess resides wherever there is Lord *Viṣnū*. The mere presence of the *Śaṇkha* is said to be dispelling all obstacles in the life of an individual, opening the doors of opportunity and fortune for him. The blowing of the *Śaṇkha* too is significant. It is believed to dispel all sins committed by the individual, as it is believed to be an invocation to the Supreme for forgiveness.

The therapeutic properties of the *Śaṇkha* are also highlighted. According to old texts, the disturbing effects of *pitha* and *vatha* are curbed due to the presence of the *Śaṇkha* close to the individual. It is also said to endow man with strength and beauty.

The *Śaṇkha* is said to be a call to the human race to pursue higher and nobler goals and values in life. It represents the multi-faceted being in the world, created from a single source. The various dimensions to man's personality also can be raced down to a core character, just as the various spirals end in a single point in the *Śaṇkha*. The sound of the Creator that emanates from the small *Śaṇkha* shows the power of sound and speech in the created world. Thus, *Uccāra* is given a lot of significance in Indian culture. The blowing of the *Śaṇkha* is considered as effective as the chanting of *mantrās* to appease God.

Padma

The lotus unfolds itself into a beautiful flower, with the roots and stalk in water and just the flower seen above the water. It is taken as the symbol of the universe coming out of the *Surya*. It rises from the navel of *Viṣnu* and is also the seat of *Brahma*, the creator. Hence there is a lot of sacredness attached to this flower. Psychic centres in the body that are associated with the rising of the *kundalini* are symbolised as Lotuses.

The deep-rooted sanctity of everything in the phenomenal world and inherence of divinity in every reality is signified in the Lotus. It is considered a symbol of beauty, purity and perfection. Although it grows in muddy waters, it still remains clean and shows no trace of the mud on itself. This is to signify the detachment of an individual from the temptations and distractions of the sensory world. Man should not let anything tarnish his essential spiritual nature and should develop his character in such a way that others look at him with awe and envy. This detachment allows him to live in bliss in this world, with nothing affecting him, joy or pleasures, or miseries. He lives unruffled, merely concerned about his *Dharma*.

The roots of the Lotus are deeply embedded in muddy waters, with the thick mud nourishing the plant. This is an indication of the need for problems and challenges in man's life that make him realise his real self and purify himself. The deeper and thicker the swamp, the more beautiful is the flower that blooms. Similarly, the more difficult life seems, the more man puts in efforts and the more refined and holistic he becomes.

The deity in the Indian pantheon is shown as standing on the full-grown lotus, which represents the Truth. It shows that the 'man-of-perfection' is ever rooted in the Supreme Truth, who is symbolic of Brahman. The Lotus indicates the final goal of human evolution.

The Lotus symbolises the simultaneity of cause and effect, as it bears its flower and sheds its seed at the same time. Every act of man leads to an effect, which is a cause to something else simultaneously. This principle is brought out well, as if explaining the Law of *Karma* to humanity.

The Lotus is a symbol of the beauty and freshness in creation, which is continuously sustained by Lord *Viṣṇu*. Moreover, as it is associated with Goddess *Lakṣmī*, it also symbolises the abundance in the phenomenal world in the form of resources and the abundance in man, in the form of potential talent and skill.

There are many more that can be added to this list of symbols, relating them to human behaviour and the higher purposes in life.

Personification of Virtues from *Purāṇās*:

Rāmāyaṇa

The *Rāmāyaṇa* is an epic that deals with the story of Lord *Rama* and his exile for fourteen years in the forest. He is talked about as an epitome of virtues and personifies all those values that are prescribed in the concept of *Dharma* elaborated in our *Śrutīs*. The various characters in the epic are personifications leading the common person to introspect, observe, learn, and imbibe.

Rama is considered to symbolise the values of Knowledge, Devotion, Obedience, Duty, Purity, and Selflessness. Sita is a personification of Duty, Purity, and Devotion too. The difference that is brought out between the two characters with similar traits is in the small and nondescript incident when Sita asked Rama to get her the golden deer. When Sita asked Rama to get her the golden deer, Rama hesitated initially – for two reasons – one, that he felt there was no need to desire something that was not one's own (avarice), and two, that he did not feel it safe to leave Sita alone to go hunting for the deer (duty). The results are known to all those who have read the *Rāmāyaṇa*. Here it is shown that even a slight deviation from *Dharma*, in the form of greed and desire, with the attraction for material possession signifies the lack of Knowledge. Thus, all virtues need to be channelised with the Right Knowledge and the realisation of the Pure Spirit which is the highest realisation for man.

Lakṣmaṇa as a symbol of duty, perseverance and dedication and unquestioned co-operation is well brought out here. In relation to the same incident, *Lakṣmaṇa*, in order to protect Sita, stays back with her at the hermitage. When he heard Rama shouting for help, he is torn between two duties. In order to still keep Sita protected, before he leaves to help Rama, he draws a line that he pleads Sita not to cross over. This was a line that demarcated the area of protection for Sita, which in the epic is called the *Lakṣmaṇa Rekha*. Transgressing this line led to Sita's abduction by *Rāvaṇa*, the evil one. This symbolically determines the path of *Dharma* or virtue that one needs to abide by. One needs to live within the bounds of *Dharma* in order to lead life peacefully and successfully.

When right knowledge, *Jñāna*, and true devotion, *Bhakti* are separated, it leads to misery. This is symbolically shown in the separation of Rama from Sita. Spiritual knowledge without devotion is incomplete just as devotion without spiritual knowledge is.

The brothers also symbolise similar characteristics as *Lakṣmaṇa* follows Rama to the forest for fourteen years giving up his comforts of the palace. His sense of duty seemed greater to him than his own life's desires and passions. His recognition of the need to support one in distress and suffering clearly proves that *Dharma* along with *Karma* alone makes deeds superior. Bharata too renounces the throne offered to him as he felt that he had no right to accept what was rightfully his brother's. This selflessness or altruism displayed by the brothers needs no further justification and can be very well emulated. The *Vedānta* clearly advocates that high thinking is important, along with simple living. But high thinking alone, with no corresponding action along the same lines is as criminal and sinful.

Aṣokavāṭikā or *Māyāpuri* at Lanka, as it is called, is symbolic of the world of *Māyā*, illusion. The phenomenal world is material, transitory and short-lived, but is extremely disturbing and distracting. *Rāvaṇa* denotes evil and his ten heads denote the various forms of evil and the numerous ways of deceit. *Rāvaṇā* abducting Sita denotes the attempt to subjugate devotion to vice. This led to a chaotic situation, bringing misery to all involved, leading to total doom and destruction. This world of *Māyā* needs to be transcended and the epics and scriptures show us the path. The techniques of self-awareness and self-realisation are well expounded in our scriptures and ancient texts. Man chooses his life and his path in life. The philosophy of life determines man's choices. So, the onus for man's liberation from the world of misery and suffering is on man himself.

Happiness inherent in devotion needs to be restored and here faith plays a part. This is characterised by Hanuman. Hanuman also symbolises power, the strength that is derived from goodwill and good intention, along with a conviction in oneself. Hanuman symbolises determination and dedication that stems from the choice of duty, along with a sense of loyalty. Faith is required in all endeavours of the human being. It plays a major part in motivation as man lives and works with the hope of getting his emoluments for his efforts, if not immediately, then sometime thereafter. The belief in a life hereafter gives man hope and it is faith that keeps him active.

Even the smallest of beings that gathered to help Rama was rewarded and appreciated by him. This talks of the goodness, gratefulness, and magnanimity of Rama. The little squirrel in its own way carried little pebbles while constructing a bridge to Lanka. In order to show his appreciation of the efforts of this little being, Rama is said to have run his fingers over its back. The three dark lines seen even today on its back are said to be the marks of Rama's fingers.

Mahābhārata

Bheeshma is considered to be a character of extraordinary deeds and valour. He lived an exemplary life, leading man on the path of duty and selflessness. He represents *Dharma* in all ways. In fact, *Dharma* itself is said to have found its explanation in him. He managed his life in a manner that created envy and fear in the minds of many. His discipline and austere lifestyle evoked in him divine and mystic powers that helped him to destroy the evil and wicked. His self-sacrifice is always at its zenith. The wisdom that one can get from a study of his character is a treasure to posterity. He is looked at as enthroning the virtues glorified in our culture.

Yudhiṣtīra represents Truth/Satya, Bhima stands for strength/Shakti, Arjuna stands for fearlessness/Nirbhaya, Nakul for Knowledge/*Jñāna,* and Sahadeva for devotion/ Bhakti. Draupadi was shown as married to five husbands, which implied that all these qualities were essential in a man for a woman to be happy and successful in life.

Wisdom and character of the woman helped to maintain the peace and comfort of any family, society or organisation. The egoism displayed by Draupadi and the vicious remark made by her at Duryodhana led to the *Kurukṣetra.* This teaches us that egoism can lead one to make impulsive, unmindful utterances that can lead to permanent devastation.

Dhritarashtra was the blind prince of Hastinapur. He marries Gandhari, a good-looking and capable princess. In order to deny herself the pleasure of seeing and enjoying a world that her blind husband could not see, she blindfolds herself. They have a hundred sons, who were called the Kauravas. The Kauravas were responsible for a lot of wrongdoing in the kingdom. Instead of being the wisdom and vision for Dhritarashtra, she neglects her capabilities and adds to the limitations of the blind king. One's capabilities should be used to overcome another's limitations.

The victory of good over evil as anticipated is evidently portrayed in all Indian epics. This helps to keep one's faith in the goodness in the human race and also to believe in the ultimate triumph of goodness and morals in every situation in the created world. Every character in the epics and scriptures can be interpreted to suit modern psychological theories and modules. The segregation of 'Types and Traits' as done by modern psychology in the study of Personality is already well researched by our ancient thinkers. This leads us to accept that management as an art or science can be well developed from our *Purāṇās* too.

Summum Bonum of Life

The culture and ethos of India basically gives man a way of life. It embodies all the eternal moral values or the Universal principles with an aim to bring about the spiritual unity of humankind. Religion as a major component of Indian culture also worked towards this goal. What is being discussed is not a particular religion but the Indian way of life. The seers of India through the ages perfected this by intuitive vision and which has been described as *Sanātana Dharma*. The followers of this *Dharma* were called Hindus by the Westerners, who did not know the significance or implication of the religion itself, or the name given to it. Indeed, Indian philosophical thought arose from the outgrowth of the spirit via the temporal life. Having fully probed the contents of the *Vedās*, it braced itself as a result to divinise human life and emancipate it from miseries so that man can become immune to them. This is the *raison d'être* behind the *saṁskārās*, rituals and traditions. In Indian thought and ethos, misery and bondage stem from ignorance, *Avidyā*. This ignorance could be either intellectual, psychological, and spiritual.

To awaken the spirituality in the individual, it is necessary to make efforts to arouse him at the level of the mind and intellect. Spiritual practices, which are more translated in daily living as religious practice, help to generate devotion and reverence for the divine. In order to help the aspirants of liberation find the path of right discriminative knowledge and inculcate in them a sense of devotion and sincerity, religion played its own role. Moreover, religious practices help to destroy the ego in the individual as he has to necessarily bow down to the God he sees in the icons and idols he worships.

Fleming's survey amongst fifty US scholars in the field of business ethics revealed a clear opinion about the relation of religion to business. He revealed that '. . . religious concepts are important in business ethics for two reasons. First, since many managers are religious, there is a need to connect religious values to business practice for them. Secondly, the religious community can be more sensitive than philosophers in such areas as moral obligations and human dignity.'[4]

Spirituality is to rise above all religions marked by purely ceremonial aspects of the church, mosque, or temple. It is to understand and then experience that the Creator and his Creation are One. The following observation by Sai Baba makes the process and the end of spiritual growth absolutely clear: 'It is good to be born in a religion, but not good to die in one. Grow and rescue yourself from the limit of regulations, doctrines that fence in your freedom of thought, the ceremonies and rites that restrict and direct. Reach the point where 'places of worship' do not matter, where all roads end from where all roads began.'[5] Spiritual growth can be achieved if we live our worldly life in accordance with Basic Human Values.

Vivekananda rightly says: 'Religion is philosophy concretised through rituals and symbols.'[6] The religious symbols, rituals and religious scriptures and epics, help to inculcate these eternal values that were prerequisite for man's liberation. In Indian ethos, problems of philosophy and religion are not divorced but are almost clubbed together under one compact tenet called *Dharma*. The ethos primarily acts as a bridge between the micro and macro, the temporal, and the eternal. It primarily beseeches man to be, not a God, but godly. This is the crux of all Indian thought and philosophy, with its emphasis on spirituality.

In short, India's socio-cultural structure expounded the native philosophy and ethos, which believed in a Universal moral order both in the microcosm and the macrocosm.

References

1. *The World Religions: A Lion Handbook, A Comprehensive Guide*, Lion Publishing, Oxford, England, p. 11.
2. Subhāṣita Ratna Bhāṇḍāgāra. Gorakhpur: Gita Press, 1998, p. 112.
3. Sudhi Dr., *Padma: Symbols of Art, Religion and Philosophy*, Intellectual Publishing House, 23, Ansari Road, Daryaganj, New Delhi.
4. Fleming J.E., 'Business Ethics: Diversity and Integration', *Business and Professional Ethica Journal*, Vol. 6, No. 4, p. 82.
5. Chibber *Padma* Bhushan Lieut Gen. Dr. M.L., *Sai Baba's Mahavakya On Leadership: Education in Human Values*, Sri Sathya Sai Books and Publications Trust, Andhra Pradesh.
6. Swami Vivekananda, *Complete Works*, Calcutta: Advaita Ashrama, Vol. VIII, 1959, p. 356.

VIII

SPIRITUAL DIMENSIONS OF PROFESSIONAL PRACTICE

As we saw in the earlier chapter, Spirituality refers to 'energy or force or breath of God in man'. Man has within him two sets of forces working: the Material and the Spiritual. The Material may be understood as the *Prakṛti* and the Spiritual as the *Puruṣa*, as given in *Sāṁkhya* school of thought. Apparently, the two forces seem to work at cross-purposes. *Prakṛti* is said to keep the individual entangled in the temptations of the senses and keep him away from the Spiritual and make him struggle to free himself. The spiritual forces, *Puruṣa*, endeavour to free him from the clutches of the material world. These spiritual forces try to raise the individual consciousness beyond the material, to help him seek the Truth.

Human existence is a paradox. Within each individual, two forces operate in constant tension—one that asserts 'I' and another that whispers 'not I'. These forces are not merely psychological quirks or moral dilemmas; they are the very fabric of our being, woven into the structure of life itself. They manifest as selfishness and selflessness, acquisition and renunciation, desire and sacrifice. This duality is not unique to humans. It pulses through all living beings. Consider the predator that kills to survive yet risks its life to protect its young. Or the human who may commit acts of violence, yet willingly dies for love, family, or principle. These contradictions are not anomalies—they are expressions of the two fundamental forces that shape the universe.

At the heart of this paradox lies the tension between individuality and universality. The force that says 'I' seeks to preserve, protect, and expand the self. It is the drive behind ambition, survival, and possession. It builds empires, accumulates wealth, and defends boundaries. Yet, the force that says 'not I' dissolves those boundaries. It gives, forgives, and sacrifices. It is the source of compassion, empathy, and transcendence. It leads man to the beyond.

This duality is not a flaw—it is a feature. It is what makes humans capable of both cruelty and kindness, destruction and creation. It is why we struggle with moral choices, why we feel torn between duty and desire, and why we are capable of both profound love and deep hatred. To live wisely is not to eliminate one force in favour of the other, but to harmonise them. It is to recognise when to assert the self and when to surrender it.

Man has a *Kurukshetra* within him due to these two forces within him. These two sets of forces are ever at war with each other, contending for victory. Thus, we see the clash between the two forces within man. For ages, it is believed that man was kept in the dark about his own essential nature. He was hypnotised by the glamour and colour of the phenomenal world, unaware that he is the Spirit. His identification with the body made him believe that he was the senses, but he is actually the eternal and immortal Spirit. If the forces of the senses be decreased and the strength of the Spirit be realised, then man will discover and/ or rediscover the Truth about himself.

Creation is necessarily a coming together of opposites. It is seen everywhere in the created world that the pairs of opposites come together to express the eternal Truth—spirit and matter, male and female, ascent and descent, positive and negative, light and darkness and so on. The list of such pairs is never-ending, and it is mentioned here only to reinforce that man is also a reality with inherent opposites within him. Even in the conception of God in a theistic sense, the modern temper tends towards a divide. That is why Lord *Śivā* or the Goddess *Kāḷī* in Indian mythology, who symbolise both protection (of good) and destruction (of evil) in a holistic synthesis, are much misunderstood by the modern mind. The 'warring' traits in the human being are the diverse aspects in his personality, presenting him in a more holistic and complete manner, making him a genius.

A human genius can be easily identified by the three major characteristics: greatness of purpose, the optimum utilisation of limited means and the astounding results that emerge from his actions. These are characteristics that are evident in a self-realised individual. In order to develop in oneself the right attitude and the right abilities, one needs to realise the essential spirit within oneself. The liquidation of the ego, the channelising of one's energy, the right goals in life and the means adopted to achieve one's ends determine the extent of spirituality in an individual.

In order to understand and evaluate oneself and to be compassionate to all others who are different, the distinctive features of spirituality and materialism are enumerated in this chapter.

The contemporary world looks at materialism as opposed to spirituality and the apparent differences between the two are projected as inherent contradictions. The idea of *Purūṣārthās* in Indian thought, however, has made it clear that both materialistic values and spiritual values, *artha* and *dharma*, are required for the individual to be holistic, along with the acceptance of two more goals in life, *kāma* and *mokṣa*. It is, however, necessary to understand that extreme materialism can take man away from his inner core.

The various traits of the materialistic and that of the spiritual being are elaborated here to bring out the difference between the two. It is also significant to have no preconceived notion about the materialistic and the spiritual, and to realise that the term 'spiritual' is not understood in relation to religiosity or ritualism. 'Spiritual' here is mentioned more with reference to 'value-based' behaviour and principles. The materialistic individual too is not necessarily one without any values. It merely implies that such an individual has his priorities in life different from the others, whereby he lays stress on the physical world alone as real and the economic values as the only guide to life. Pleasure becomes his sole objective in life.

Value-driven individuals approach people and situations with an open and universal approach. There are various attributes that are 'essential' traits in such beings. Some of the evident ones are mentioned here.

A spiritual being does not believe in excessive indulgence in any pleasurable activity, thus being free from the shackles of the attractive and distracting phenomenal world. At the same time, he does not behave indifferent to the world and its inhabitants. The idea of renouncing is accepted well by him, where he learns to renounce his excess needs, greed and desires. He, however, does not renounce people, roles, duties and responsibilities, knowing well that the purpose of life needs to be realised. *Karma* within the framework of *Dharma* is his principle of functioning.

On the other hand, in a materialistic being, there is maximisation of 'individualism'. There are certain consequential attributes that are evident in such a being. A materialistic individual believes in '*artha*' and '*kāma*' as the only sources of happiness. He mistakes pleasure for happiness. Desires and wants can never be satiated permanently. All that leads to sensory pleasures in the materialistic world leads to gratification of needs and wants. It does not give the individual a sense of fulfillment that is more lasting and meaningful, but the materialistic individual is unaware of it. There is excessive indulgence in *kāma* and the growing need for *artha* leads him to a path that deviates from *dharma*.

The spiritual being will never allow exploitation of oneself or others. He lives with dignity and protects his self-esteem. He considers everyone, including himself, as an 'end-in-oneself'. No individual has the right to use another as means to achieve or gain something for oneself. The spiritual individual lives life with a purpose and his goals are more meaningful. He does not work to seek gratification of wants alone, but functions for fulfillment. He has higher order needs, in concordance with his innermost core, the Spirit.

On the other hand, the materialistic individual functions with an urge to possess and hoard, transgressing all limits of ethics at times. For him, everything and everyone needs to be perceived as means to his ends. His goal in life is to gain materially, profit and possession being his primary motivators. The materialistic individual is led by egoism that is greed-based whereas the spiritual being is guided by altruism, which is more fulfilling.

In the case of a materialistic individual, the driving force is the reach that he has in the market, both in terms of purchase and supply. He markets not only ideas and products. He succumbs to the pressures of the competitive market economy and trades himself, becoming a means. He lives with the delusion of a halo around himself created of his own. He is more interested in creating and maintaining an image of himself as successful and happy. He thus starts living up to standards set by others with regard to pomp, splendour and prestige that are temporary and finite. His false ego is satisfied temporarily, in the process of creating more needs and wants for himself. The process is never ending. This ultimately leads to consumerism, where goods are produced for satisfying artificially created needs and desires. Production of goods for the satisfaction of a select group in society is unjustifiable.

A spiritual individual has a lot of *Saṁyaṁ,* i.e., self-restraint, where there is proper channelising of his energies, and this results in fairplay. The guiding factor for all actions in the case of such an individual is *Dharma*, Righteousness. The idea of duty is well understood by such individuals. On the other hand, if the individual is very indulgent and passion-driven, then there is freeplay, which leads to expansion of ways and means of satisfaction of needs. There is a definite deviation from *Dharma* for the purpose of satisfying basic instincts.

A spiritual individual will function for self-development and self-actualisation. He will not deny himself pleasures of life, but he will definitely fulfil his needs ethically. He will, moreover, enjoy the benefits that he reaps for the efforts that he puts in, which will be well earned by him. He will not work with the remuneration, position, status and power as his motivators. If an individual has his bodily needs and material gains as priority in life, he will plan his activities only if he stands to gain something in return. His returns are more tangible and have a price tag attached to them all. His activities are more towards self-aggrandisement.

Indian culture provides a strong ethical base to the self-realised individual who sets his goals in life within the framework of the *Puruśārthās*. With the *Yama-Niyama* of the *Yoga* system, the *Pañcasheela of Buddha*, the *Vratas* and *Anuvratas of Jainism*, and the basic concept of *Dharma* that is elaborated, Indian culture does not give any sanction to moral deviations. Both means and ends are significant and both need to be ethically monitored. Moral values need to be kept in focus while determining the goals and the means of attaining them. Man, as a spiritual being should work for achieving higher purposes at every stage in life. If the individual is driven by a hedonistic philosophy, then he will determine his goals in life on the basis of his needs and desires that are more instinctual. The guiding factors are his needs and his resources. He justifies his actions with the convenience of a popular principle, that 'the end justifies the means'. Moral integrity is the last in his list of priorities. All other factors are given undue importance, such as prestige, position, resources, ambitions, possessions, etc.

The individual, as is mentioned in the earlier chapters, is a conglomeration of different attitudes, capabilities, likes and dislikes, views and opinions. It is necessary to understand that man, with a pair of opposite forces within him, has to function as a whole, towards common goals, guided by universal values. In order to help man achieve his goals in life, man has to harness the physical energy within himself, and channelise it rightly to realise the inherent Spirit. This is possible only if materialism and spirituality are not considered as opposites and mutually exclusive. Materialism needs to be kept in its rightful place, utilising the knowledge available to transcend the physical and economic reality to attain the spiritual reality. Materialism is thus to be understood as a step that leads one towards the highest goal of Self-realisation.

Philosophically, the opposites are mutually complementary and supplementary and coexist in every being. Man needs to understand this Truth and transcend the opposites to grasp the Unity that lies beyond. Man is conscious of his essential nature and is at the same time aware of his phenomenal existence. Hence, he is different from the other beings in the phenomenal world. This knowledge leads him to gain mastery over his limited environment and the urges of his senses. He develops within himself a growing need to be powerful enough to direct his own ascent.

Spirituality is thus his life Force. It continuously transforms and reshapes inert matter into an integrated whole. In the process, spirituality gives dimension to man's living, becoming both his purpose, goal and end along with paving him a path that leads to the said goal or end. Man becomes a 'co-partner' in the execution of a plan to fulfil the purpose of his own existence and Being. **The central theme of all Indian thought is 'the essential unity of all beings'**.

Rtasya srungamurviya vi paprathe – *Ṛgveda* 8/86/5
The rule of cosmic order pervades everywhere.

Rtasya pathaa preta – *Shukla Yajur veda*. 7/45
Therefore, live life in tune with the cosmic order.

Having accepted that the majority of philosophical schools and religions in India accept spirituality as their essential characteristic, it is time to understand spirituality at the workplace. The nexus between Spirituality in Indian thought and Management in the Industry is explored here.

Management implies the co-ordination of the various resources in the organisation, with a focus on human resources. The significant role of Human Resource in an organisation needs no justification or clarification. At the organisational level, HRD may be understood as including activities and processes undertaken to promote the intellectual, moral, psychological, cultural, social and economic development of the individuals in an organisation, in order to help them to achieve highest human potential as a resource for the community.

HRD may be looked at as a system and process concerned with an organised series of learning activities. It is organised within specified time limits with the purpose of producing behavioural changes in the learner or available human resource in such a way that it acquires a desired level of competence, preparing him for the present or future role. HRD, ideally speaking, should bring about 'total all-round development' of all those people who are included under the 'resources' of an organisation. HRD is not to be looked at as a piecemeal or a one-time exercise. It needs to be a continuous, sustained and ongoing process of growth and change. It needs to keep pace with the changes and developments taking place in an organisation, community, society and the nation. It has to be abreast of the current developments at a global level and also update itself on the current issues and needs of the local and regional community.

In an ideal organisation, with an ideal HRD setup, the individual employed is helped to plan his life and growth. This can be done by

HRD, with the individual in focus, by providing opportunities to all, with the following objectives:

- To help acquire or sharpen capabilities required to perform various functions associated with their present or expected future roles.
- To develop their general capacities and abilities as individuals and discover and exploit their own inner potentials for their own and organisational purposes, to help actualise what is latent and potential.
- To develop an organisational structure in which relationships within an organisation are not determined by hierarchies, but by functions, recognising the interdependence and mutuality and accepting the need for a healthy interaction.
- To develop an environment where teamwork and collaboration among units and sub-units, departments and business units are strong and contribute to the professional well-being of employees, in addition to the growth of the organisation itself.

HRD mechanisms are designed on the basis of certain beliefs and assumptions. They are:

- Human resource is the most important resource and asset of any organisation.
- Human resource, unlike other resources, can be developed and increased to an unlimited extent. For man, sky is the limit when it comes to growth and excellence.
- A healthy environment that is characterised by values of openness, trust, and transparency is essential for development of both the individual and organisation.
- The levels of motivation and enthusiasm need to be constantly maintained at a peak, generating mutuality, interdependence and collaboration among members in an organisation.
- The development of human resource needs to be planned, monitored and catered to, for the benefit of the individual and the organisation.
- Employees feel committed to their work and the organisation if the organisation perpetuates a feeling of belonging, which depends on how well the organisation provides for the satisfaction of the basic needs of the individual and his family.
- In addition to this, the organisation needs to provide opportunities for the individual to develop himself and fulfil his higher needs through the appropriate management styles and systems.

Indian thought, with its balanced view of the needs, goals and ethical framework determining man's behaviour, gives us an ideal framework, within which HRD can formulate its policies and strategies. The elaborate exposition of the *Puruśārthās* and *Dharma*, and the significance of the idea of Duty in our culture, makes it clear that Management has a lot to gain from Indian philosophy. The spiritual foundation on which the superstructure of our personal and social life is built, makes it conducive and possible for us to enhance and enrich our individual and organisational culture. The essential element in the nature of man is the spiritual principle within him and the ideal of moral life is the realisation of this principle. Taking this as the highest goal of his life, man needs to live in a manner that he balances his sentient and his rational self. For this, he needs to monitor his desires, instincts and feelings.

Spirituality at the workplace implies an environment that nurtures, caters to and facilitates the functioning of individuals. The fast-paced, demanding, stressful work atmosphere creates chaos, which forces one to seek value–based answers to difficult situations. All in the organisation seek ways of personal stability, which, in the long run can only be achieved from within. No external factor is permanent enough to last a lifetime to sustain stability in the individual.

An individual with a spiritual attitude will attach significance to each and every object that he possesses and utilises as he finds them all sacred. His attitude of looking at 'Work as Worship' makes him look at all equipments, instruments, appliances and tools as his personal belongings. This sense of possession and belongingness makes him take care of and maintain these tools and equipments. Thus, the infrastructure of every industry or organisation will be kept in order. The damage to any tool or infrastructure in the organisation or industry will disturb and depress him.

A spiritual individual will look at all beings as an 'end' in himself. This helps him to accept people as they are and not try to put people into slots made by him or others. The acceptance of individuals with their imperfections and limitations makes it easier for him to function as his expectations from others are lower. This, in turn, leads to less frustrations and reasons for depression in him. This approach makes the individual foster an atmosphere of belonging among people, thus helping to form teams and groups. The idea of Universal Brotherhood and Oneness of Being that is conveyed in Indian thought is well brought out here. The trait that is evident here in the spiritual individual is that of open acceptance of alike.

The other aspect that can be highlighted in a spiritual individual is the adherence to standards and quality. The spiritual individual would not like to compromise on his quality of work and output as he feels it is a commitment to himself that he is fulfilling at work. The spiritual being will try to excel at every activity and at every stage in life. He will not like stagnation as he realises that it is necessary for him to progress to realise himself and reach the stage of liberation. So, his commitment is more to himself than others. One would not like to fail then as he is an individual with self-respect and self-esteem. A spiritual person will strive for Quality in all aspects of his living.

Another feature that is very obviously observed about a spiritual being is his recognition of himself as a part of a Whole. This leads him to believe that he alone is not powerful, but he is dependent on many others similar to him. The concept of inter-dependence is more significantly highlighted here, as many fail to understand this and tend to have egoistic representations of themselves, leading to conceit and vanity. The spiritual individual will always live with an attitude of humility and gratitude, thus paying homage to the potential in himself as much as in others.

An individual who lives with a spiritual attitude will be aware of oneself, with strengths and limitations and aim at being self-realised. He will be well aware of his own strengths and limitations, thus actualising his potential to the optimum extent to reap maximum benefits for one and all. Such individuals are natural leaders. The quality of leadership is expressed in their ability to take decisions and accept the responsibility of the consequences of their decisions too on themselves. The onus of every decision and action is on them, and they shoulder it well. Leadership and the sense of responsibility are well evident here.

When the spiritual being is known to identify all beings as part of the Holistic Divine, then the idea of universal brotherhood needs to be respected. Such individuals would always like to share the benefits of their actions. The sense of belonging that they advocate will be well expressed only if they encourage the partaking of the benefits reaped by an agency or organisation by all who belong. Spirituality here is seen expressed as Generosity and the thought of the Wellbeing of all.

A spiritual being, at work, functions with an integrity that is admirable. He functions in alignment with people, other resources and his own responsibilities, for achieving the objectives of an organisation. He is self –motivated and displays a natural desire to learn, grow and succeed. He also takes it as his responsibility to see all others around him are nurtured in the same manner, helping them to utilise their capabilities as well. He respects and values individual and group dignity.

When a spiritual individual completes his purpose and achieves his goals in life to the right extent and in the right manner, he develops a universality of outlook. This is a mark of or the characteristic of perfection. What is unique about him then is that he still retains his individuality, without letting it make him egoistic.

If man needs to feel in complete control of his life, he needs to realise the importance of controlling and managing his time. Controlling one's time means controlling the events in one's own life by one's volition to a major extent. This is where the prerequisition of self-awareness and self-development needs to be recognised. Man can achieve inner peace in life only through the appropriate control of events, which, in turn, leads to serenity, balance and harmony in his life.

There is direct relationship between self-esteem and productivity, which is well accepted by all management experts. In order to make one feel better about oneself, to build one's own morale and esteem, one needs to be highly productive. Every activity of a spiritual individual who recognises this fact will then be directed towards contributing for the growth of the organisation, society and nation, in turn, helping him to grow.

In order to be effective and efficient in life and at work, one needs to be in charge of oneself. A winner is one who does not merely do different things but is basically one who does even ordinary things differently. If a man wants to be a winner and he wants to achieve in life, he needs to have a unified expression of all three- body, mind and soul. The body (*Śarīra*) is responsible for action, *Karma*. The mind (*Manas*) and intellect (*Buddhi*) relate to cognition, *Jñāna*. The Self/ Soul relates to Being (*Sat*). This unified expression is the *Sat-Cit-Ānanda*. Action, Cognition and Being together denote the humanness of mankind.

A winner is one who not only manages himself but is one who leads others to manage their lives too. Such a winner in the corporate world is a Leader, whom others respect, and emulate. The culture of any organisation depends on the values of the leader and the work-culture created by him.

Let us now understand the concept of leadership as expounded in Indian ethos.

Leadership: An Indian paradigm of ethical governance

In order to be a leader in life, one needs to first have control on oneself. Self-restraint becomes the keyword as mentioned in the earlier chapters. One has to necessarily be pure in thought, word and action. This is referred to as '*Trikarna Śuddhī*'. A leader has to possess certain qualities that are life-sustaining and eternal, such as Adherence to Truth, Control of Senses, Equanimity, Forbearance and Compassion.

He also needs to be knowledgeable. He needs to know himself well, with a complete awareness of his own strengths and weaknesses. This knowledge should be supplemented with knowledge of his occupation and its demands. Thirdly, he should have adequate and right knowledge of his environment, both physical and social. An integration of all virtues and right knowledge makes one invincible.

Leadership is considered an inevitable and integral part of social living conditions. A leader is one whose ability to lead the survival of the others depends. As a social animal, man is comfortable living in groups. In any group there will always be people who will lead and others who will follow. Leadership takes on varied forms—a religious leader, a spiritual leader, a political leader, or a social figure.

In the business context, leaders comes in various forms:

- an entrepreneur who has a start-up and sustains business
- the leader of a Workers' Union
- the leaders representing Dealers, Customers, Consumers, Suppliers, Agents
- trainers who prepare leaders
- consultants who guide and suggest for better working conditions
- Advisors and Board members, for problem-solving and decision-making

The list is long, showing multi functions and traits of leaders.

There is a great difference between a leader, a successful leader and a good leader. A leader is one who plays his role on the basis of his position and authority and is for himself. A successful leader is one who plays his role well and manages to achieve what he is expected to by the others and the organisation. A good leader is one who plays his role well, manages to gain for all and the organisation, and who leads ethically. Successful leaders are even humans like Hitler who led people to suffering. Hitler had the entire nation doing what they wanted them to do. But he was not bothered about them. He fought as a leader to boost his own image and like a megalomaniac, he was a prisoner to his own ego. A good leader is one who bases all his activities and thought processes on the welfare of the masses. His concern is not only himself but is the 'many'.

Leadership depends greatly on 'Character'. A good leader builds his character on Universal Human Values, which becomes a cardinal need. If this criterion is met, he becomes a good and great leader. The basis to good leadership is a sound character with adequate knowledge of oneself and one's position, which brings along with it knowledge of one's duties and responsibilities. Leadership cannot be superficially acquired as a skill.

There can be four basic types of leadership styles in business houses. They are:

- **Autocrat:** Here the decisions are made alone, with not much information or data requested from the other staff or subordinates.
- **Consultative Autocrat:** This kind of leader seeks and collects lot of data from his staff and subordinates, but ultimately takes a decision by himself, with no need for consensus felt.
- **Consensus Manager:** In this style of leadership, the leader not only encourages input from the groups but discusses it all with an open approach. He also encourages group decision making.
- **Shareholder Manager:** The leader in this case is hardly a leader. He neither encourages nor does he feel the need for any discussion or data collection. He does not require any information exchange. He merely allows the group to make decisions and implements them. His chair and position is important for him.

Of these four kinds of leaders, the last type can be totally given up as he is not even worth being called a leader. He is merely absolving himself of his responsibilities and passing on the authority to others. In this way, he puts the onus of the consequences of the decisions on others all the time. It is very misleading with a leader like this. It will seem initially that he is democratic and allowing the subordinates to grow. But in reality, it is not so.

If one looks at the first kind of leader who is a manager, then it goes against the principles of democracy. There is no participation by the others as the manager of this kind merely instructs them to get jobs done. In this case, the manager runs the risk of taking a decision without getting the support and points of view of others. The onus is entirely on him. In the second and the third types, the manager runs the risk of sharing information with those who need not know certain things about the organisation, thus giving them the advantage of knowing more than needed by them. He ends up taking a decision on the basis of information provided by the others without a check on the data. In the leadership style, where consensus is sought, there can be a faulty decision due to group pressure and group conflicts.

The best style of leadership is thus a mixed style. The leader has to decide on his style of leadership depending on the situation, the people involved, the time factor, the objectives of the action and the long-term consequences of the decision taken. He has to fluctuate ideally between the three leadership styles, adapting himself to the situation, depending on the need of the hour. In order to be absolutely free of riddles and to sketch a picture of an ideal leader and manager, what is most required is his character-sketch. In the later part of the chapter, the reference to a leader presupposes the goodness in him and thus is a mention of a 'good' leader.

Unfortunately, emphasis is laid on personality today and not character. What is studied by western schools of psychology is superficial behaviour and not the core inner self of the individual. Today,'personality has dominated the scene in the design of evaluation tools, with 'character' is relegated to a backseat. Personality is the exteriorisation of the individual's physical traits, capabilities, skills, talents and aptitudes. These need to be observed and the individual should be given the opportunities to develop and hone what is already inherent in him. But what gives this exteriorised self an identity and individuality is his inner core, the 'Self'. The essential spiritual nature of man transcends the limits of the mind, the intellect and the *ahaṁkāra*. This transcendence by an individual takes him closer to the Real Self, which is ethical and value based. Management of Self is the first step to growth, progress and success.

The leader is very important in an organisation as he has a major role to play in the growth and success of the business. He has the following functions to fulfill in the organisation:

- Motivate and guide the personnel
- Influence and shape the social system
- Understand subordinates and secure their cooperation
- Create a climate for performance

Nature and Importance of Leadership

A leader is one who has earned the respect, loyalty, devotion and confidence of the others in a group. Leadership cannot be conferred or imposed on someone. It needs to be earned by the individual who wants to lead. There has to be a co-existence with the fellow beings as there is no leader without followers.

A leader has to be compassionate and empathetic to the others in the group. He should have the capability to understand the feelings and problems of all, in order to facilitate the satisfaction of both individual and social needs. He should be a dependable friend, trustworthy, confidante, and a good guide. A good leader is one who keeps his team members informed of all developments in the organisation.

The model of leadership emphasises three major skills that are needed in a leader: conceptual skills, technical skills and interpersonal skills. Conceptual skills are skills concerned with planning and policies. Technical skills enable the leader to deal with things, machines, anything to do with technology. What is, however, most important is the skill of managing people. The art of enhanced interpersonal relationships fosters an atmosphere of understanding of human feelings, attitudes and motives. The leader has to develop a positive attitude, sensitivity to individual and social issues, good communication skills, tact, and a pleasing personality. This enables him to be popular and powerful, both at the same time. A leader can be effective only if he is powerful.

The Indian model of leadership emphasises on the character and wisdom of the individual, thus laying stress on the all-round development of a leader. The ethical strength of his character is what makes him deal with all situations in life wisely. The principles and values followed by such a leader are universally and consistently applied to all people and situations alike. While the Western model manager is what Peter Drucker calls the "knowledge worker", the Indian model is what S.K. Chakraborty calls the "wisdom worker".[1] While the 'knowledge worker' knows what 'is', the 'wisdom worker' knows what 'should be'. If the Western model lays emphasis on 'policies and people', the Indian model respects 'principles in people'. Einstein had rightly observed that knowledge of what 'is' does not automatically lead to knowledge of what 'should be'.

The ideal leader who is a 'wisdom worker', effective with all skills well developed, is the **Stithaprajña of the Gītā.** The Stithaprajña is established in Sattva, with a fusion of mind and matter, the temporal and the eternal. He relates to the phenomenal world in a manner of detachment, doing his duties as expected by dharma. As he functions with an attitude of Niśkāmakarma, he does not have expectations that need to be fulfilled by others around him. Gita advocates non-covetousness and relinquishing of attachment. As Gītā points out, 'Wise men endowed with equanimity, renouncing the fruits of actions and freed from the shackles of birth attain the successful supreme state.' [Chapter II, Verse 66] To quote Gītā, 'He, who gives up all desires and moves free from attachment, egoism and thirst for enjoyment attains peace...' [Chapter II, Verse 71] These are traits of an ideal leader, who is free from sense of pleasure, has stability of mind, is self-controlled,

Gītā lays a lot of stress on effectiveness and importance of the role of management leadership. In Chapter III, verses 21 and 22 talk about the importance of a good leader. A good leader is one who would live life with Sattva dominating all his thoughts and behaviour. He would inspire his teams to internalise the values needed for leading life ethically. He would be a role model, motivating them to attain the goal of self-realisation, keeping in mind the other three puruṣārthās. He would also guide them to achieve artha and kāma within the framework of dharma.

Work itself will be worship for the one who believes in Niśkāmakarma, the ideal of Lokasaṁgraha being the main motivator. A leader, in Indian thought, is a 'giver' instead of a 'receiver'. The consolidation and welfare of society as a whole is the goal of all activities for such a leader. Leadership in this sense is 'leadership through renunciation' not 'leadership with appropriation'. They lead by letting go of personal desires, not by collecting power or wealth. To be a good leader, they must be free from attachments like greed, ego, or personal gain.

Āruruksor muner yogaṁ karma kāraṇam ucyate
Yogāruḍhasya tasyai 'va śamaḥ kāraṇam ucyate. – Chapter VI, Verse 3

As expounded in the Gītā, 'For the sage (leader) aspiring to ascend to yoga, action is said to be the means, and for the same sage (leader) enthroned in yoga, serenity is called the means.'

The Gītā enumerates the qualities of a leader as well as the leadership styles as that of Duryodhana, Yudhishthira, Arjuna and Kṛṣṇā himself. The leadership style that would be most productive would be the one that is most productive. It emphasises that only democratic leadership can help one to lead well and succeed in achieving organisational goals along with personal development. The ideal leader has to be people-centred, more than task-centred.

The Gītā talks of the leader as one who sets examples and urges the others to follow his path in the following verse:

Yadyadācarati śreṣthastattadevetaro janah
Sa yatpramāṇaṁ kurute lokastadanuvartate – Chapter III, Verse 21

Whatever a leader does, another person too follows the same act. Whatever he upholds as authority, an ordinary person follows that too.

As Arjuna explains to Arjuna at the battlefield, 'If you run away from the battlefield, all others too will follow you. If you fail to do what is expected of you because you are a śreṣta puruṣa, then all others too will fail in their duties. So do your duty, whether you like it or not'. The śreṣta is one who is self-realised and leads by example. Spirituality is his essence and universal values, his guide.

The various aspects of Spirituality can be studied from the scriptures, from religion and tradition, and from various epics and ancient tests. The *Vedās*, *Upaniṣāds*, *Cāṇākya*, *Arthaśāstra*, *Dharmaśāstra*, *Jaina-Bauddha* traditions, and the various religious practices and texts enshrine the eternal and universal values. The study of man as a holistic being, differentiated from other beings due to the essential Spirit in him, is extolled. The study of the various sciences in their own way, lead us to the knowledge that man is a higher order creation, unlike many other beings, and that man's rationality puts him at this level in the hierarchy of evolution. The study of man and his place in modern management is considered a part of modern scientific study. The modern management theories depict man as a resource, studying him merely in the light of industry and trade, which needs to be rectified.

The study of Spirituality involves the study of man for what he 'ought' to be, and what he 'is' in relation to the ideal. The ideals that are emphasised upon are those leading to eternal Bliss and Tranquility. The existence of man as a holistic being needs no further justification as denial of the spirit in him will mean the denial of his own existence. Sat-Cit-Ananda is the highest personification of the human being. In the eyes of the physicalist and the economist, man is merely respected for what he is capable of producing, whether his Spirit is realised or not. The externalised aspect of man is alone the subject of study in such sciences. Values that are extolled here are those related to the sensory world, leading to feelings of pleasure. The goals that direct man's behaviour in this case are short-term and set without much foresight.

'A time will come when science makes tremendous advances, not because of better instruments for discovering and measuring things, but because a few people will have at their command great spiritual powers, which at the present are seldom used.' ".

Change is inevitable. The world as we see it is constantly changing and in a state of flux. As the world is not to be considered Real, it is labeled as 'illusive reality' or 'relative truth'. The only unchanging reality that Indian schools of thought accept is the Essence of all beings, the Consciousness, *Chaitannya*. This consciousness principle is addressed as Brahman, Self, Ātman, Īśvara or God. The Seers call it *Sat-Cit-Ānanda*. The ideal individual is one who lives close in reality to this concept of *Sat-Cit-Ānanda.* He has to be rooted in the real, be conscious of the real and live with the goal of attaining bliss in life.

The ideal CEO has to be rooted in the reality of the situation. He has to live in the present, learning from the past and looking ahead at the future. Basking in past glory or mourning for what is already a bygone is the sign of a loser. The ontological concept of *Sat-Cit-Ānanda* is to be considered as an ideal present before the entrepreneur for developing foresight, positivity, realistic perspectives and be wise in all decision-making and problem-solving. The ideal of *Sat-Cit-Ānanda* is an ideal that man can aspire to reach through finer aspects of his nature developed and refined.

In an attempt to probe into the Reality, the human mind reaches higher levels of consciousness. The mind becomes refined, pure, and subtle. During this process the person acquires certain characteristics in his personality. He becomes calmer, collected, their desires become less, and they become kind, compassionate, and generous. At the final stage of realisation, the person crosses over/ transcends the limitations of mind and words and comes face to face with Reality. As his consciousness has transcended the language function of the mind, no words are available to describe his experience at that level of Realisation. When the person comes to human level of consciousness, the Divine Realisation withers away. Thus, while the person is at human consciousness he cannot experience the Reality and while he is experiencing the Highest the function of the mind including those of language and speech is suppressed. Therefore, the Reality cannot be described in words. Whatever description we get from the great Seers, saints, or Avatara Purusha is at the best close approximation of that Reality. In order not to be deluded by what is not real, one has to root out all evil tendencies from one's mind. The veil of ignorance needs to be cleared, and the light of discriminative knowledge be kindled. Love, fear, jealousy, hatred, passion, anger, infatuation, and so on surface only because of our mistaken belief about Reality as something else. Living life with the true spirit guided by reason and intellect, in the wake of spiritual wisdom is a man's saviour.

Asato ma sat gamaya,
Tamaso ma jyotir gamaya,
Mṛtyoma amṛtam gamaya.

From the unreal, lead me to the Real.
From darkness lead me to light.
From death, lead me to Immortality.

This is a prayer recited by many that indicates the desire in man to be closer to Truth and Reality. What is indicated here is that man needs to be led to the Real, the Wisdom and the nectar of Immortality. The only way man can achieve his ideal is by being a *Karmayogi*, with *Bhakti* in his attitude and *Jñāna* to guide him. In the corporate world, man can avoid all stress and strain of work, to live as a winner in the contemporary society if he grasps these truths given by Indian thought.

References

1. Peter Drucker, 'The Landmarks of Tomorrow, 1959 and S.K. Chakraborty, Wisdom Based Management: A Cross Cultural Perspective (1995) and Management by Values (1991)
2 Dr. Chibber M.L., Padma Bhushan Lieut Gen (Retd.), Sai Baba's Mahāvakyas on Leadership – Education in Human Values', Sri Sathya Sai Books and Publications Trust, Prashanti Nilayam, Andhra Pradesh, 1993.
3. Kumar Arun, *Management Leadership through Bhagwat Gita*, Shubhi Publications, Delhi, p. 6.

IX

MODELS OF MANAGEMENT: THE INDIC WAY

Philosophy ought to translate into life. The relationship between metaphysical realities, ontological concepts and epistemological theories on one hand, and the ethical and aesthetic values on the other is very similar to the relationship between science and technology. The scope of philosophy remains incomplete and inadequate, if it does not guide mankind to lead his life successfully. The philosophical tenets and ethical values that are highlighted in the earlier chapters merely pave the path for applied philosophy.

Indian philosophical schools, as *darśāṇās*, give us a vision. They need to be understood and valued for what they are – 'storehouses of prudential wisdom'. The application of the ethical and aesthetic values in the life of man gets him closer to the metaphysical reality, *Brahman*. These values are expressed through the various activities of man, to fulfil the corresponding needs in him. Along with various needs, there are the economic needs of man that dominate his activities. The basis for all these needs may be attributed to his survival instinct. Instinctual behaviour is involuntary. But behaviour that is done with a Design is voluntary and reflects the Will and Intention of man. Prudential wisdom stems from philosophical tenets and theories. The induction into the domain of philosophy needs to be carefully and wisely done.

One major area where man exhibits his voluntary behaviour is his area of work. The contemporary industrial world takes away the spirit in man to make him function as a mere rational being, working almost logically, and at times, mechanically. This illusory success makes him eulogise himself. This temporary self that is created to satisfy his ego is also, unfortunately, lost today. Man is at the crossroads searching for himself. This is more evident in the industrial world where man is valued for what he gives and what he seems to be, not for what he 'is.' The real man is still to be found among the many faces at factories, workshops and in executive cabins.

The realisation that industry and business can co-exist with the Spirit in man evoked chuckles. The need to re-establish this Reality and accept the industrial world for what it is worth is the driving force of this study. Can spirituality survive with the throngs of materialism glaring at its face?

Based on this theme, here is an attempt to search and save the Spirit that was throttled in the wake of the curses of automation. It is necessary to realise that automation and technology are required for faster and better work and more success. But it is more important to accept that they can be mere tools, not substitutes for humans. Man has to be himself, using these tools and techniques for better products and productivity. The profound teaching of the sages and seers, and the authority of the scriptures are revived and re-established, with certain aspects of specific institutions chosen for case-study.

Here is a sample survey done with a few organisations and their leaders talking about the management style and the ethical model applied in their organisations. Leaders of institutions were selected for a study on the culture and practices that were prominent in their area of work. It was necessary to understand the approach, the practices and the codes that were followed by them. It was kind of these leaders to share with me their observations, views and thoughts about themselves, their organisation, and their work culture.

A questionnaire was given to them and in a discussion that followed, a few key points were noticed. The response to the questionnaire is only a pointer for further discussion and curiosity. Institutions selected belonged to various sectors – an MNC, a private institution, an educational institute and two recognised NGOs.

Kubota is a multinational corporation from Japan with headquarters in Osaka. It is one of the leading tractor manufacturers. Kubota Agricultural Machinery (KAI), the Indian subsidiary of Kubota Corporation, Japan which started their operations in India in December 2008, with the goal to offer agricultural machinery products with advanced Japanese technology to improve farm productivity. Kubota has more than 300+ dealers spread across India.

Mr. G.S. Grewal, Managing Director, Kubota Agricultural Machinery India Pvt. Ltd. spoke about his passion and commitment for excellence and growth. He shared how he led a talented team of professionals, empowering them to work towards the goals of the organisation. Managing business growth and overseeing financial and operational aspects of the organisation were his major responsibilities and he succeeded in fulfilling them due to his belief in human values and competencies of his teams. He talked about the systems, structures and values in the organisation proudly, stating that values are the basis for the sustenance and success. He strongly believes that values that are taught and propagated in our ethos and culture are naturally imbibed and followed in our work style and approach. This is what Mr. Grewal had in response to my queries, that I share here.

Mr. G. S. Grewal, Managing Director
Company: Kubota Agricultural machinery India Pvt Limited

Organisational Culture: Administration & Management

(a) What management philosophy or leadership approach guides your organisation today?

- The management philosophy that guides and directs our organisation is tosupport the future of the earth and humanity by providing products and services that are focused on agriculture, food production, water, and the environment. The culture of mutual respect, trust and teamwork is promoted.

(b) What are the core values that define your organisation's identity and purpose? (both economic and ethical dimensions)

- The core values centre on supporting life by innovating solutions for food, water, and the environment through a commitment to customer-centricity, innovation, agility, and excellence.
  - Integrity
  - Innovation
  - Customer-centricity
  - Sustainability
  - Teamwork

(c) To what extent are these values understood, embraced, and practiced across all levels of your organisation?

- Very well cascaded, understood and practiced across the organisation at all levels.

(d) When behavioural norms or policies are violated, what kind of consequential / corrective action is taken by the leadership? (Is it guided by policy, values, or situational judgment?)

- In case it is an unintentional violation, counselling is done by the HR and leadership team. If it is an intentional major violation of policy, strict action is initiated.
- It is always guided by policy and values and based on collective judgement by leadership and HR.

(e) Is disciplinary action applied consistently across roles and hierarchies? How do you ensure fairness and transparency?

- If it is an intentional and serious violation, the action is taken irrespective of level or grade of the individual.

(f) In your view, what constitutes a holistic approach to management in today's interconnected world?
- Employee engagement, empathy and focussing on the reason, rather than the person. Holistic approach to business, which benefits the society and brings happiness to employees.

Leadership and Change Management

(a) How long have you been associated with your organisation? How would you describe its approach to HR, governance, and policy implementation during your tenure?
- 14 years. Creating a culture of mutual respect and trust. Collective decision making and ensuring proper corporate governance.

(b) Would you recommend any changes or improvements to current systems and practices? If yes, what would they be?
- NA

(c) In your opinion, what drives meaningful change in an organisation today?
Through systems, strategies, and structures?
Or through people, processes, and purpose?
- People, processes, and purpose.

(d) How resilient is your organisation in adapting to global shifts, such as AI disruption, MNC influence, BPO culture, and digital transformation?
- The organisation is quite agile to change as per the changes in the VUCA world.

Values, Ethics and Conflicts

(a) Do you believe economic value systems and ethical value systems can co-exist in business? Are they complementary or contradictory in your experience?
- Ethical value systems are essential for having a sustainable business and hence, they are complementary to each other.

(b) Is it possible to uphold moral values while pursuing aggressive growth and profitability? Where do you draw the line? (Turnover, profit, and moral values)
- The moral values must be maintained at all times while pursuing aggressive growth. It is better to sacrifice growth if it cannot be pursued using moral means.

(c) Can you share examples of goal or interest conflicts you've encountered? (a) Between personal and organisational interests, (b) Between leadership and staff, (c) Between customer expectations and organisational priorities, and (d) Between departments or teams

- Not that I can remember.

(d) How did you navigate these conflicts? What guiding principles or frameworks helped you resolve them?

- In case of any conflict, I would refer to the core values of the organisation, and they would become the guiding principles to resolve the conflict in the right direction.

Customer Centricity and Talent Practices

(a) How central is the customer to your organisation's strategy and culture? How do you balance customer satisfaction with internal priorities?

- We always follow the 'customer first' approach and all action are prioritised towards creating higher customer satisfaction and create value for the customer.

(b) What are your recruitment policies? How do they reflect your commitment to diversity, inclusion, and Indian entrepreneurial spirit?

- The recruitment process looks at the attitude of the person. Female diversity is driven as a policy, and an all-inclusive cultural approach is taken irrespective ethnicity and religion of the person.

(c) How do your hiring practices embody both economic goals and moral values - such as fairness, opportunity, and social concern?

- The hiring process looks at the person's capability and past performance and hence, giving him/her a fair chance to contribute to the economic goal of the organisation. It is not dependent on his social status, ethnicity or gender.

(d) Does your performance appraisal system reflect and reinforce your organisation's core values? How is it perceived by employees?

- Yes, the performance appraisal system is based on the results against the objectives set for the individual at the beginning of the year and the challenges faced. The objectives are guided by the core values of the organisation. The appraisal is perceived as a fair and transparent process by employees.

(e) Are appraisal outcomes used for the following decisions? Please elaborate on each: (a) Role placement, (b) Promotions, (c) Transfers, (d) Incentives, and (e) Termination

- The appraisal outcome is used for the career growth of the person and to give the relevant feedback on improvement areas and appreciation for the good work done.

- The Role placement, promotion, increment are decided accordingly. Appraisal process does not lead to termination as it is a process to improve the performance of the employee and guide him in the right direction.

Transparency and Governance

How transparent is your organisation in sharing the following types of information with stakeholders?

(i) HR policies and guidelines
(ii) Placement and transfer decisions
(iii) Appraisal and promotion criteria
(iv) Financial policies and disclosures
(v) Information required by internal vigilance teams
(vi) Information required by external auditors

- Full transparency is maintained, and all relevant information is shared with stakeholders, as required.

Corporate Governance

(a) How does your organisation ensure accountability, fairness, and transparency in its governance practices?
   - We follow robust corporate governance practices. Through periodic internal and external auditors, the processes and policy adherence is reviewed. These are reviewed by the board and the management as per the corporate governance guidelines.

(b) What role does the Board of Directors or senior leadership play in upholding ethical standards and stakeholder trust?
   - The auditors' reports are reviewed by the board and action taken reports are asked for by the board members on a periodic basis. These are shared with the stakeholders during the AGM.

(c) How do you manage conflicts of interest, insider risks, or governance lapses - especially in high-stakes or cross-border operations?
   - NA

(d) Are your governance practices aligned with Indian regulatory frameworks and global benchmarks? How do you stay compliant and agile?
   - The governance practices are reviewed by external auditors and consultants to ensure regulatory compliance at all times.

Corporate Social Responsibility (CSR)

(a) What are the key CSR initiatives undertaken by your organisation? How do they reflect your values and commitment to society?

  - Education for underprivileged children, water ATMs for rural areas and improvement of rural infrastructure. Various livelihood projects are undertaken to support the socially downtrodden, providing opportunities for means of employment and earning.

(b) Do your CSR efforts align with Indian ethos and values /principles? (e.g.: dāna (generosity), seva (service), and lokasangraha (collective upliftment), Karmayoga).
  - Yes, as explained above.

(c) How do you measure the impact of your CSR programs — economically, socially, and environmentally?
  - We measure the impact by social impact and environment impact Assessment tools.

(d) In what ways do you engage employees, communities, and partners in co-creating CSR outcomes?
  - The employees attend the implementation of CSR initiatives and hence they are involved. The CSR initiatives undertaken are shared with channel partners during annual conferences.

Futuristic and Contextual Reflection

(a) In light of rising technological influence, cultural shifts, resource constraints, and domestic market challenges—how does your organisation stay rooted in indigenous values while remaining globally competitive?
  - We focus on our customers, and all actions are taken focused on becoming a trusted brand for our customer and this helps us to stay competitive.

(b) What would you like to suggest for an ideal organisation and nation?
  - An organisation should stay focused on its purpose and the problem it solves for the society.

(c) How relevant do you feel Indian Ethos is relevant, suitable and applicable to management dynamics?
  - The Indian ethos emphasises the values of mutual respect, integrity, self-discipline, making them highly relevant in professional settings.

With this interaction with the Managing Director of Kubota, I came to know that the culture in an MNC too can be related to Indian work culture, more so as the Japanese culture had a likeness and similarity with Indian ethos. In the Japanese culture, IKIGAI refers to a reason and a meaning for living. It is important to find one's reason for being and to determine one's purpose for living. The moment you learn to love, be it someone close to you, be it your work, be it your duty and obligations in life, or even the environment around you, you will definitely be happy. The secret to happiness in the IKIGAI philosophy is to choose what you love, what is your capability and strength, what the others need from you that you are capable of giving, and what you can get for your efforts. If you are seeking something that is material and temporary, you can never get happiness. Seek some purpose or goal that is eternal and everlasting.

In tune with the IKIGAI and the Purushārthas of each individual, it is important to realise that life is not always about oneself. Happiness is amazing. It is so amazing that it doesn't matter if it is yours or not. It is so truly said that a society grows great when old men plant trees the shade of which they will never sit in. Ikigai is a Japanese concept that means 'a reason for BEING'. The entire cultural ethos of Indian philosophy discusses nothing but the concepts of 'BEING' and 'BECOMING'.

Transitioning from an MNC to a Private Limited firm, I'd like to share the insights and experiences I gained through my interaction with Mr. Abhishek Rathi.

Mr. Abhishek Rathi
Designation: Founder and CEO of VCreaTek

Abhishek Rathi is the Founder and Chief Executive Officer of VCreaTek Consulting Services Pvt. Ltd., a Pune-based data analytics and information management firm. With a B. Tech in Computer Engineering and early career experience as a Business Intelligence consultant at L&T Infotech, Rathi combined technical expertise with entrepreneurial vision to launch VCreaTek in 2014.

Leaving a family business in Kolkata and a corporate role behind, he started VCreaTek with just five team members and a mission to help businesses harness the power of data. Over the past decade, Rathi has grown VCreaTek from a startup into a thriving organization of over 350+ professionals. Under his leadership, the company has expanded its services from core data warehousing and analytics to a broad suite of offerings including healthcare analytics, business intelligence consulting, and academic mentorship initiatives. VCreaTek today serves clients across industries such as retail, supply chain, and healthcare, delivering technology-driven solutions that drive decision-making and efficiency.

Rathi's accomplishments as an entrepreneur have earned wide recognition. He was honoured as one of the top five finalists of the Mahesh Idol Award 2024, a prestigious accolade celebrating excellence in entrepreneurship within the Maheshwari professional community. Under his guidance, VCreaTek has also been lauded for its corporate social responsibility, receiving special recognition at the Rotary CSR Awards 2025 for the company's contributions to social causes. Beyond steering a successful business, Abhishek Rathi is deeply committed to community service and inclusive leadership. He served as the President (2024-25) of the Rotary Club of Pune Professionals, where he spearheads initiatives in children's education, water conservation, and other community projects. Within his organization, Rathi has championed an inclusive hiring initiative—pledging to recruit at least one specially-abled individual every six months.

By bringing on board visually impaired talent and providing mentorship, he has fostered a more diverse workplace and set an example for the industry. Through his leadership, Rathi exemplifies how entrepreneurial success can go hand-in-hand with social responsibility and inclusivity, positioning him as an inspiring role model.

He is keen to contribute to nation's mission of fostering entrepreneurship by actively mentoring startups and supporting the growth of SMEs through strategic guidance and hands-on collaboration.

Mr Abhishek Rathi's Special Skills:

- Management Consulting
- Thought Leadership
- Strategic Planning, Budgeting
- Leadership skills
- Quantitative and Qualitative Analysis
- DW BI Architect
- Dimensional Modelling
- Dynamic Dashboards, KPIs, and Metrics
- Six Sigma
- Business Analytics
- Technologies – Hadoop Ecosystem, AWS Big Data Stack, Teradata, Oracle, Salesforce. Tableau
- Qlikview, Cognos, Informatica, MuleSoft, Open-Source Technologies

- **About VCreaTek:** a young, vibrant and specialized company (started in 2014), providing analytics and information management services. It focuses on helping organisations to derive maximum value from their growing assets.
- **Goal:** Creating Technology Solutions for Actionable Insights
- **Company Profile:** Developing Data and Analytics led technology solutions for Retail & Supply Chain
- For further information on the organisation: www.VCreaTek.com

My interaction with Mr Abhishek Rathi was very pleasant and enjoyable. Creating technological solutions to simplify solutions business needs, work preventive strategies for any forthcoming problems, solve business issues with the idea of preventing recurrence and keeping the organisations and their teams happy and successful is the vision of VCreaTek. As a part of the entrepreneurial team at LinkedIn and other professional media groups, Abhishek has been on the go, with upskilling and networking.

The biggest asset in this organisation has been the induction of youngsters with diversities. Such employees are involved and included in the mainstream, giving them a sense of belonging. The regular young staff in the organisation are taught sign language to help them communicate easily and effectively with the few others with special needs. Such employees are involved and included in the mainstream, giving them a sense of belonging. The regular young staff in the organisation are taught sign language to help them communicate easily and effectively with the few others with special needs. He believes in inclusion, and he organises training programs for his staff, including technology related, personality development and communication skills.

As a private firm, VCreaTek assists with Data & Cloud, Design, Research Labs, Smart Analytics, & Chauffeur Cabs. The services provided speak about the diverse area of function and resources.

Their most recent milestone achievement was embarking on the Stanford Seed Transformation Program (2026) by the Stanford University Graduate School of Business, reflecting the vision and commitment of the leadership of Mr. Abhishek Rathi. His initiative keeps him and his teams ready for eternal learning, powered by growth, deeply rooted in purpose.

In a conversation with Mr. Abhishek, he states that "this tie-up with Stanford University is the beginning of a deeper journey, where insights power progress and learning become the foundation for creating a lasting impact." He says that he "looks forward to explore new ways to think, lead, and grow" and looks forward to "grow while translating strategy into action and data into direction". His aim is to "build an organisation that learns faster, leads with purpose and leaves a strong footprint on the world around".

Mr. Abhishek is also a mentor with Disha Cohort 8, an opportunity provided to him by NASSCOM. The mutual learning and positive outcomes of the Disha initiative synergized with VCreaTek efforts inspired all to continue sustained learning with innovation-driven frameworks.

Mr. Abhishek believes in building an organisation that is always challenging limits, embracing change, breaking set barriers, and displaying a liberal attitude. This has helped to amplify development and progress at every stage and age of the organisation.

His response to the questionnaire made me realise that he works with very simple work philosophy, focussing on his teams, and his clients. He believed that he would achieve his goals and fulfil his dreams with the support of his teams alone. He gave them a lot of opportunities for upskilling and personal development, making it a win-win situation for himself and them. He believed that there is still a lot of scope for improvement and hence, he rates his success ratio much below what it actually is. His incessant travel and resultant exposure to varied cultures and people have helped him to be a continuous learner, with regard to human psychology and work ethics. His positivity and sense of humour, his open attitude to work and people, and his faith in the goodness of humans help him to accept situations as they come and people as they are. Driving himself and people to excellence is his philosophy of work.

Questionnaire

Organisational Culture: Administration and Management

(a) What management philosophy or leadership approach guides your organisation today?

- "Creating Opportunities and Sharing Success" has been our philosophy which guides our organisation. We believe that our organisation is a platform where people can join and use their capabilities to give it back to community thus following the philosophy of sharing the success.

(b) What are the core values that define your organisation's identity and purpose? (both economic and ethical dimensions)

- Our services should be economically viable, value creating, aligned with customer vision and done ethically (virtuous) with all togethe (we) as single team.

(c) To what extent are these values understood, embraced, and practiced across all levels of your organisation?

- Understood – 60% among folks who are more than 2 years with us Embraced & Practiced – 25 to 30%

(d) When behavioural norms or policies are violated, what kind of consequential / corrective action is taken by the leadership? (Is it guided by policy, values, or situational judgment?)

- Guided by policy. Since we are young and growing firm, we do understand that acceptance of policy is some challenge, so we, do take some situational judgement for sensitive issues.

(e) Is disciplinary action applied consistently across roles and hierarchies? How do you ensure fairness and transparency?
- Yes. Based on guided policy the action is taken. Based on situational judgement, an independent committee is formed to investigate and gather all information, which is further discussed and debated in a common room.

(f) In your view, what constitutes a holistic approach to management in today's interconnected world? (Consider emotional intelligence, sustainability, mental health, social well-being and spiritual quotient)
- Holistic Approach should consist of Value Generation, Alignment of all Stakeholders on the Value to be created and the associated challenges for that journey.

Leadership and Change Management

(a) How long have you been associated with your organisation? How would you describe its approach to HR, governance, and policy implementation during your tenure?
- 11 years.
- I have been associated since inception of the company so the approach of the organization in last 10 years has been to make it more process oriented and policy driven.

(b) Would you recommend any changes or improvements to current systems and practices? If yes, what would they be?
- More stringent as well as inclusive way to implement the actual policies beyond the paper purview of those.

(c) In your opinion, what drives meaningful change in an organisation today?
1. Through systems, strategies, and structures?
2. Or through people, processes, and purpose?
- In my opinion, it is through, purpose, process and people.

(d) How resilient is your organisation in adapting to global shifts — such as AI disruption, MNC influence, BPO culture, and digital transformation?
- 70% to 80% resilient.

Values, Ethics and Conflicts

(a) Do you believe economic value systems and ethical value systems can co-exist in business? Are they complementary or contradictory in your experience?

- Yes. They can co-exist and they are complementary.

(b) Is it possible to uphold moral values while pursuing aggressive growth and profitability? Where do you draw the line? (Turnover, profit, and moral values)

- Yes. It is possible to uphold moral values while pursuing growth and profitability. The mindset of aggressive growth is incorrect. The business plan should be of sustainable growth. And that rate can either 200% or 20% depending on the business / industry line. And that 20% may be aggressive for a particular industry whereas 200% may be below normal growth for another. And hence, organisation should chase sustainable growth within the moral and ethical values. Thereby removing the need of "where to draw the line"

(c) Can you share examples of goal or interest conflicts you've encountered? (a) Between personal and organisational interests, (b) Between leadership and staff, (c) Between customer expectations and organisational priorities, (d) Between departments or teams.

Examples:

(i) Between Personal & Organisation => Withdrawal of higher salary from company for personal house purchase would have been conflict of interest. This was resolved by taking the amount as loan from company and not increased salary.

(ii) Between leadership & staff => Having different benefits for leadership and staff seems to be justified based on roles. But in our organisation, we do have policy of same tickets and same gifts for all employees all across.

(iii) Between customer and org => Customer expectation was to have all team members work over the weekend and specifically during the festival holidays. Was tough but we managed to get this resolved by ensuring only the critical team members work and that too with rotation. Organisation priority was to ensure that customers don't just look at "hours" spent during work but more on quality.

(d) How did you navigate these conflicts? What guiding principles or frameworks helped you resolve them?

- Most of them do get resolved by following the guiding principles. We try to see if our decision has any red flag on one of the principles. – we, value, viable, virtuous and vision.

Customer Centricity and Talent Practices

(a) How central is the customer to your organisation's strategy and culture? How do you balance customer satisfaction with internal priorities?
- By communicating our priorities with the customer. And if not then we have let go some of thc projects / customers where our org priorities are not aligned with customer expectations.

(b) What are your recruitment policies? How do they reflect your commitment to diversity, inclusion, and Indian entrepreneurial spirit?
- Our recruitment policies are simple – should be an internal reference or at most 2nd degree connect. We hire based on roles for which we have work for at least one or two years of work. We don't hire only for a project.

(c) How do your hiring practices embody both economic goals and moral values — such as fairness, opportunity, and social concern?
- Unfortunately, there have been cases where references were hired only because they were referred by senior folks from company. Eventually, all hiring has been objective based with proper test and interview for ALL Candidates

(d) Does your performance appraisal system reflect and reinforce your organisation's core values? How is it perceived by employees?
- Not yet. It is more quantitative based on projects. For Employees, it is a part of regular exercise. Unfortunately, it is not treated as a component for reflection and growth.

(e) Are appraisal outcomes used for the following decisions? Please elaborate on each: (a) Role placement, (b) Promotions, (c) Transfers, (d) Incentives, (e) Termination
- Role placement – Yes
- Promotions – Yes
- Transfers – Haven't been used so far.
- Incentives – Yes
- Termination – Yes

Transparency and Governance

How transparent is your organisation in sharing the following types of information with stakeholders?

- HR policies and guidelines – Fully shared with all employees and updated regularly.
- Placement and transfer decisions – Communicated openly and applied consistently.

- Appraisal and promotion criteria – Clearly defined and accessible to all staff.
- Financial policies and disclosures – Fully transparent and compliant with regulatory requirements.
- Information required by internal vigilance teams – Shared completely and promptly.
- Information required by external auditors – Provided in full, ensuring accuracy and compliance.

Overall, we try to maintain 100% transparency level – which reflects our integrity driven culture.

Corporate Governance

(a) How does your organisation ensure accountability, fairness, and transparency in its governance practices?

- Regular and complete communication with all stakeholders along with expectations. Review with the auditors and board members

b) What role does the Board of Directors or senior leadership play in upholding ethical standards and stakeholder trust?

- Regular Review, Messaging, and re-enforcing the importance of ethical methods/actions, governance and compliance

c) How do you manage conflicts of interest, insider risks, or governance lapses — especially in high-stakes or cross-border operations?

- So far only through direct communication, involving the senior leadership and then taking actions immediately

d) Are your governance practices aligned with Indian regulatory frameworks and global benchmarks? How do you stay compliant and agile?

- Indian Regulatory Frameworks – Yes. Auditors and Compliance Consultants for various regulatory needs
- Global Benchmark – Yet to be reviewed. But I guess we are only halfway.

Corporate Social Responsibility (CSR)

(a) What are the key CSR initiatives undertaken by your organisation? How do they reflect your values and commitment to society?

- Volunteering by team members for various activities. Donation of some amount for various initiatives of Rotary Club. Donation to NASSCOM Foundation. Guest Lectures and Sessions to various colleges from Tier 3 or Tier 4 cities.

(b) Do your CSR efforts align with Indian ethos and values /principles? (eg.: dāna (generosity), seva (service), and lokasangraha (collective upliftment), karmayoga).
- I think yes

(c) How do you measure the impact of your CSR programs — economically, socially, and environmentally?
- Economically and socially.

(d) In what ways do you engage employees, communities, and partners in co-creating CSR outcomes?
- Interested Employees do participate in various activities.

Futuristic and Contextual Reflection

(a) In light of rising technological influence, cultural shifts, resource constraints, and domestic market challenges — how does your organisation stay rooted in indigenous values while remaining globally competitive?
- Direct communication, leading from front, re-enforcing the principles and values throughout the year.

(b) What would you like to suggest for an ideal organisation and nation?
- Equal Opportunities

(c) How relevant do you feel Indian Ethos is relevant, suitable and applicable to management dynamics?
- People related dynamics are 100% relevant / connected with Indian Ethos

As a response to my questionnaire, his views about people, work, success and happiness seem to be in consonance with values in Indian Ethos. Creating Opportunities and Sharing Success aligns beautifully with the idea of 'collective upliftment' and 'selfless service', in sync with the Indian concept of Lokasangraha and Seva. The very idea of sharing success and the resultant benefits reflect his magnanimity and spirit of non-possessiveness (Aparigraha). All collective achievement is redistributed and enjoyed collectively. Mr. Rathi's assertion that economic value systems and ethical value systems can co-exist and are complementary directly challenge the view that profit and ethics are in conflict. This aligns with the Indian concept of Purushārthas (the four aims of human life).

Individual success and organisational prosperity along with communal benefit is not utopian. The use of five guiding principles (we, value, viable, virtuous, and vision) to resolve conflicts acts as a moral compass, akin to adhering to one Dharma. The resolution where a higher salary was forgone for a company loan to purchase a house is a powerful example of prioritizing organizational interest and ethical conduct (virtuous) over personal immediate gain, demonstrating a commitment to Yogakshema (welfare of the whole). VCreaTek, as an organisation, has established a powerful, value-driven philosophy, showing a strong commitment to sustainable, ethical growth over aggressive, amoral growth which is commendable, truly embedding the Indian Ethos into the organisation work-culture.

This brings us to a critical question: Is ethics confined to corporate management and industrial enterprises alone? Or can it be evaluated across other functional domains and organizational types as well? To explore this further, let's pivot our focus and examine how ethical principles manifest within the education sector.

Dr. Aruna M. Katara
President, Hope Foundation and Research Centre, Pune (www.hfrcpune.org)

Dr. Aruna Mukesh Katara, President of the Hope Foundation and Research Centre, Pune, a Public Charitable Trust championed by the renowned FINOLEX Group, stands as a beacon of transformative leadership and enduring vision. Under her aegis, the Hope Foundation, founded in 1979 by her father, the venerable Shri Pralhad P. Chhabria, has transcended its original mission to become a formidable force in enhancing medical health accessibility and fostering quality education and research across both rural and urban landscapes in India.

Under her leadership, the Foundation has expanded its institutional footprint through three key educational initiatives:

- **The International Institute of Information Technology (I^2IT), Pune** – an autonomous engineering and research-driven institution offering undergraduate and postgraduate programmes in technology with a strong emphasis on innovation, industry relevance, and ethical governance.
- **The Finolex Academy of Management and Technology (FAMT), Ratnagiri** – an AICTE-approved and university-affiliated institution supporting technical education in the Konkan region.
- **The Pralhad P. Chhabria Research Center (PPCRC), Pune** – a research-focused initiative promoting interdisciplinary science, deep-tech development, and industry partnerships.

With over 25 years of experience in management, institutional development, and academic administration, Dr. Katara has played a central role in establishing and strengthening these institutions through a philosophy that integrates professional excellence, social responsibility, and value-based education. Her vision continues to shape HFRC's mission of creating equitable access to learning opportunities for students across urban and rural India.

Dr. Katara's leadership approach places emphasis on innovation, participative decision-making, ethical systems, and a strong belief that education must serve both individual aspiration and national development. As a response to the questionnaire, she displays her prime focus on empowering the youth through education and research, leading these institutions towards becoming preeminent knowledge hubs, thus contributing to the nation's growth.

Organisational Culture: Administration and Management

(a) What management philosophy or leadership approach guides your organisation today?

- I²IT follows a **participative and transformational leadership philosophy** guided by the belief that **"Innovation and Leadership is our mantra."** As an academic institution, we operate on the principle that **we learn and grow together**, with equal importance given to **students, faculty, and ethical governance**. Our leadership framework blends **transformational vision**—inspired by the legacy of our Founder Chairman Late Shri P. P. Chhabria—with **participative systems** that empower departments, clubs, cells, and student teams to take ownership of initiatives. We focus on three institutional pillars:
  1. Quality education and industry readiness for students
  2. Professional growth and research encouragement for faculty and staff
  3. Ethical, transparent, compliance-based administration

The leadership style ensures that **creativity is not restricted by hierarchy**, and decision-making is rooted in **dialogue, accountability, and institutional values**, aligning modern academic governance with Indian ethos.

(b) What are the core values that define your organisation's identity and purpose? (both economic and ethical dimensions)

- At I²IT, **Innovation and Leadership is our mantra**, reflected in all academic, administrative, and social initiatives. Our core values integrate **economic purpose**—industry readiness, entrepreneurship, employability, research impact—with **ethical commitment** to transparency, fairness, and social responsibility. We uphold values such as **equity in admissions and hiring,**

integrity in evaluation, responsible use of technology, and fair-pay structures. Social responsibility is embedded through **NSS activities, NGO collaborations, community STEM outreach, and socially relevant projects**. The campus culture encourages **continuous learning, merit-based recognition, respect for diversity, and ethical decision-making**. We believe education must serve **societal upliftment, not just individual advancement**, aligning institutional growth with **Seva (service), Dharma (responsibility), and Lokasangraha (collective good)**. Thus, economic value and ethical value are not separate goals, but **complementary anchors of our institutional identity**.

(c) To what extent are these values understood, embraced, and practiced across all levels of your organisation?

- I²IT ensures that institutional values are **communicated, internalised, and practiced at every level**—students, faculty, staff, and leadership. These values are introduced through **orientation programs, policy manuals, Code of Conduct, and Founder Chairman's value-based message video**, and reinforced through daily academic and administrative practices. Students live these values through **hackathons, innovation projects, environmental campaigns, social internships, entrepreneurship cells, and transparent evaluation systems**. Faculty demonstrate them through **diverse pedagogies, research contribution, continuous upskilling, and student-centred mentoring**. Administration upholds them through **ethical compliance, transparent procedures, and fair documentation**. Leadership models them through **policy-based decision-making, accountability, and open communication**. The shared culture of **ownership, responsibility, and service** ensures that values are not ceremonial—they are **actively practiced and institutionally reinforced**.

(d) When behavioural norms or policies are violated, what kind of consequential/corrective action is taken by the leadership? (Is it guided by policy, values, or situational judgment?)

- Corrective action at I²IT is based on a **combination of documented policy, value-based judgement, and situational understanding**. Violations are assessed by considering **intent, impact, repetition, and scope for improvement**. Minor concerns are addressed through **counselling, verbal warnings, or memos**, while serious or repeated violations are handled by **formal committees such as the Disciplinary Committee, Anti-Ragging Committee, ICC, or Grievance Cell**, ensuring neutrality and confidentiality. Decisions follow **institutional policies, 360-degree fact verification, and due process**, not personal discretion. The institute follows a **reform-first approach**, prioritising **learning, accountability, and behavioural correction** over punishment. However, in cases involving harassment, academic malpractice, or ethical breach, sanctions are **firm, documented, and policy bound**. Thus, discipline at I^{2}IT is **consistent, compassionate, and principled**.

(e) Is disciplinary action applied consistently across roles and hierarchies? How do you ensure fairness and transparency?

- Yes. At I^{2}IT, disciplinary action is uniform, non-discriminatory, and evidence-based, irrespective of an individual's role, seniority, or designation. We ensure fairness through committee-based decisions, written documentation, opportunity to be heard, and policy-linked outcomes. No action is taken without formal inquiry, proof, and recorded minutes, which prevents bias and protects both institutional integrity and individual dignity. Students and employees are informed of rights, appeals, and review mechanisms, ensuring transparency. Multiple levels of checks—policy manuals, grievance redressal forums, HR rules, and statutory bodies—prevent misuse of authority. The institute's guiding belief is that ethical consistency builds trust, and therefore accountability increases with hierarchy rather than diminishing. Discipline is not punitive control, but a marker of institutional credibility and equal treatment.

(f) In your view, what constitutes a holistic approach to management in today's interconnected world? (Consider emotional intelligence, sustainability, mental health, social well-being and spiritual quotient)

- A holistic management model must combine **emotional intelligence, sustainability, mental well-being, social purpose, and spiritual grounding** with operational efficiency. At I^{2}IT, this is reflected through **empathetic mentoring, inclusive governance, wellness initiatives, ethical tech education, and NEP 2020–aligned creative learning spaces**. Stakeholder well-being is supported through **counsellors, mentor systems, yoga and fitness events, trekking groups, and cultural/artistic expression platforms**. Sustainability is addressed through **green campus drives, waste audits, and eco-themed student projects**. Professional growth is complemented by **value education, reflective practice, and community participation**, ensuring that education produces **competent professionals and responsible**

citizens. A truly holistic institution is one that gives **equal weight to people, purpose, performance, and planet**, rooting modern innovation in **timeless human values**.

Leadership and Change Management

(a) How long have you been associated with your organisation? How would you describe its approach to HR, governance, and policy implementation during your tenure?

- I²IT has consistently demonstrated a **professional, transparent, and policy-driven governance culture**. Over the years, the Institute has strengthened its approach to **HR, compliance, academic autonomy, and performance-linked accountability**, while ensuring that **Innovation and Leadership remains our mantra**. HR policies are based on **merit, equal opportunity, skill development, and evidence-based appraisal**, while governance is enabled through **structured committees, documented minutes, internal and external audits, and statutory compliance**. Faculty are encouraged to **pursue higher education, publish research papers and books, file patents, and participate in FDPs and conferences**, reflecting a growth-oriented HR outlook. With autonomy status, I²IT is now transitioning toward **industry-aligned curriculum design, sponsored research labs, LMS adoption, and flexibility in academic frameworks**, reinforcing the shift from **rule-based functioning to value-based institutional maturity**. Governance has become increasingly **collaborative, data-backed, and student-centric**, ensuring long-term credibility and academic excellence.

(b) Would you recommend any changes or improvements to current systems and practices? If yes, what would they be?

- Yes. As I²IT advances into its **autonomous era**, a few strategic enhancements will strengthen academic and administrative growth. First, the adoption of a **full-scale Learning Management System (LMS)** can improve digital pedagogy, feedback systems, and student tracking. Second, we can accelerate the establishment of **industry-sponsored research labs and incubation centres** to deepen the industry-academia connection. Third, as autonomy expands academic freedom, **curriculum revision cycles can become more agile**, enabling rapid integration of AI, Blockchain, Cybersecurity, AR/VR, and emerging technologies. Strengthening **data-driven dashboards** for academic performance, placement analytics, and resource utilisation will support smarter decision-making. Additionally, **structured mentorship for new faculty, mental well-being policies, and outcome-linked faculty incentives** can further support professional satisfaction. These improvements do not replace existing systems—they **extend them into a more future-ready, research-oriented and learner-driven institution**.

(c) In your opinion, what drives meaningful change in an organisation today?

1. Through systems, strategies, and structures?
2. Or through people, processes, and purpose?

- Meaningful change begins with **purpose**, but becomes sustainable only when **people, processes, and systems align with that purpose**. At I²IT, we believe that institutional change succeeds when stakeholders understand the **"WHY" behind the change**, not just the "what" or "how." Strategies and structures create stability, but **people create ownership**—which is why transformation at I²IT is rooted in **transparent communication, participative planning, student and faculty buy-in, and phased implementation models**. Change is introduced through **clear policy, documented processes, measurable outcomes, and supportive handholding**, rather than enforcement. When purpose is shared and people feel valued, **innovation becomes cultural, not forced**. Thus, change is not a "top-down announcement," but a **collective transition where systems support progress and values sustain momentum**.

(d) How resilient is your organisation in adapting to global shifts — such as AI disruption, MNC influence, BPO culture, and digital transformation?

- I²IT demonstrates strong **academic and operational resilience**, adapting continuously to **AI-driven industries, global workforce models, and digital culture**. The Institute has integrated specialisations in **AI, Data Analytics, Machine Learning, Cybersecurity, IoT, and Cloud Computing**, supported by hackathons, internships, and industry projects that expose students to **real corporate environments and MNC expectations**. Digital transformation is embedded in **teaching-learning methods, online evaluations, blended learning, and administrative automation**. Entrepreneurship is encouraged through the **Industry–Institute Interaction Cell, start-up mentoring, and MoU-based collaborations**. I²IT remains responsive to global change because it treats **learning as a lifelong process, not a curriculum-bound exercise**. Our resilience comes from **future-**

skilling, value education, and a culture that welcomes innovation rather than resists it.

Values, Ethics and Conflicts

(a) Do you believe economic value systems and ethical value systems can co-exist in business? Are they complementary or contradictory in your experience?

- At I²IT, we firmly believe that **economic value and ethical value not only co-exist but must co-exist** for long-term institutional credibility. Economic value helps us achieve **institutional growth, placements, employability, research visibility, and financial sustainability**, while ethical value ensures **fairness, transparency, and trust among stakeholders**. We follow the principle that **growth must never violate dignity, equity, or educational purpose**. Ethics is not a restriction—it **guides how goals are achieved**, ensuring that processes remain just, policies remain transparent, and outcomes remain stakeholder-centric. Whether in **admissions, hiring, collaborations, financial decisions, or student evaluation**, we uphold merit, fairness, and honesty. In Indian ethos, **Dharma (right action) and Artha (economic pursuit)** are complementary, not contradictory. At I²IT, **Innovation and Leadership is our mantra**, but integrity is the compass that ensures innovation never loses direction.

(b) Is it possible to uphold moral values while pursuing aggressive growth and profitability? Where do you draw the line? (Turnover, profit, and moral values)

- Yes. **Moral values must guide growth—not get sidelined by it.** At I²IT, growth is encouraged through **quality education, industry relevance, faculty development, research culture, and student success**, not through shortcuts that compromise ethics. We draw the line wherever growth threatens **academic integrity, student rights, work–life balance, equality of opportunity, or institutional reputation**. For example, **merit-based admission and hiring** prevents commercialisation of education. Employee well-being, professional dignity, and ethical teaching–learning processes remain **non-negotiable**, even in competitive environments. The Institute rejects models that trade values for revenue, such as **unfair fee practices, biased recruitment, or grade manipulation**. Aggressive growth is justified **only when it respects people, purpose, and policy**. A culture becomes toxic when profit overrides principle—therefore, at I²IT, **values set the boundary, progress moves within it**.

(c) Can you share examples of goal or interest conflicts you've encountered? a) Between personal and organisational interests b) Between leadership and staff c) Between customer expectations and organisational priorities d) Between departments or teams

- Conflicts arise naturally in any institution, and I²IT resolves them through **dialogue, documentation, and policy clarity**.
  1. **Personal vs organisational:** Faculty research timelines vs academic workload are balanced with flexible scheduling and workload adjustment.
  2. **Leadership vs staff:** Differences in pace of implementation are resolved through **consultative meetings and phased rollouts**.
  3. **Customer expectations vs institutional priorities:** Student/parent demands for grade relaxation or attendance waivers are declined to protect **academic integrity and fairness**.
  4. **Department vs department:** Resource conflicts (labs, budgets, events) are handled through **coordination committees and priority-based scheduling**.

Across all conflicts, decisions follow **institutional values, AICTE norms, and documented policy**, preventing emotional or hierarchical bias.

(d) How did you navigate these conflicts? What guiding principles or frameworks helped you resolve them?

- Conflicts at I²IT are resolved through **policy-based evaluation, ethical reasoning, and fair process**, not personality or power. The institute follows a **committee model** to ensure neutrality—whether the issue involves students, faculty, or administration. The principles guiding resolution include:
  1. ***Fact verification, not assumptions***
  2. ***Right to be heard (natural justice)***
  3. ***Documented decisions, not verbal directives***
  4. ***Confidentiality and non-retaliation***
  5. ***Restorative action before punitive action***

The **Universal Human Values (UHV) framework** strengthens conflict handling by reinforcing empathy, mutual respect, and shared responsibility. Leadership ensures **transparent communication of what, why, and how decisions are made**, reducing misunderstanding and power imbalance. Conflicts are treated as **opportunities**

to strengthen culture, not weaken relationships, ensuring that institutional values are protected even during disagreement.

Customer Centricity & Talent Practices

(a) How central is the customer to your organisation's strategy and culture? How do you balance customer satisfaction with internal priorities?

- At I²IT, the **student is the primary stakeholder**, and therefore the central "customer" of the institution's academic, administrative, and developmental ecosystem. The institute ensures **student-centric governance** through feedback-driven curriculum revisions, placement-oriented skill programs, mentoring systems, and grievance redressal mechanisms. Parent expectations, alumni inputs, and employer demands are also integrated into decision-making through **industry advisory boards, internship partners, and alumni interactions**.
- However, customer satisfaction is balanced with **non-negotiable pillars**: academic standards, ethical policies, and long-term learning outcomes. For example, while students may demand grade leniency or attendance concessions, the institute prioritises **academic integrity and fairness** over convenience. The balance is maintained by ensuring that **short-term satisfaction never compromises long-term professional readiness**. Thus, I²IT treats stakeholders with **responsiveness, not indulgence**—ensuring that education remains **student-focused, value-driven, and institutionally disciplined**.

(b) What are your recruitment policies? How do they reflect your commitment to diversity, inclusion, and Indian entrepreneurial spirit?

- I²IT follows a **merit-based, transparent, and diversity-conscious recruitment process** for both students and employees.
  1. Admissions follow **MH-CET/DTE/AICTE norms**, ensuring equitable access across **gender, regions, socio-economic backgrounds, and linguistic identities**.
  2. Faculty recruitment focuses on **subject expertise, research output, pedagogical skills, and ethical commitment**, not just credentials.
  3. The institute encourages applicants from both **industry and academia**, supporting cross-pollination of knowledge.
  4. Hiring reflects the **Indian entrepreneurial ethos** through support for **start-up founders, research innovators, and patent contributors**.

5. Special consideration is given to candidates aligned with **NEP 2020, Outcome-Based Education, and UHV/ethics-based teaching**. Scholarships, fee concessions, and **earn-while-you-learn models** support inclusion of first-generation learners.

Recruitment at I^{2}IT is not just about filling positions—it is about building a **responsible, future-ready academic community**.

(c) How do your hiring practices embody both economic goals and moral values — such as fairness, opportunity, and social concern?

- Hiring at I^{2}IT is structured on the belief that **competence and conscience must coexist**. The institute does not encourage **influence-based hiring, informal appointments, or unequal pay structures**, ensuring fairness and dignity of labour. Economic sustainability is maintained through **efficient staffing, workload-based allocations, and research/industry-funded positions**, reducing unnecessary financial burden while maintaining quality. At the same time, the institute reserves opportunities for **research scholars, women returning to work, early-career educators, and socially committed professionals**, reinforcing **inclusion and mobility**. Hiring panels include **multiple reviewers, documented scoring rubrics, and interview audits**, ensuring that no selection is based on bias or hierarchy. In doing so, I^{2}IT demonstrates that **ethics is not a cost—it is a safeguard for institutional credibility**.

(d) Does your performance appraisal system reflect and reinforce your organisation's core values? How is it perceived by employees?

- Yes. The performance appraisal system at I^{2}IT is aligned with **Outcome-Based Education, research contribution, student engagement, institutional service, ethical conduct, and professional development**. Faculty evaluation includes **classroom innovation, student feedback, publications, patents, mentoring, committee work, industry exposure, and value-based teaching**. The appraisal process is **documented, review-based, and multi-layered**, reducing subjectivity. Employees view the system as **transparent and growth-oriented**, since appraisals are linked not only to financial increments but also to **responsibility assignment, leadership roles, FDP opportunities, and recognition programs**. The presence of **feedback cycles, self-assessment forms, and review committees** ensures that appraisal is ** developmental rather than punitive**, reinforcing the institute's values of **fairness, accountability, and continuous improvement**.

(e) Are appraisal outcomes used for the following decisions? Please elaborate on each: (a) Role placement, (b) Promotions, (c) Transfers, (d) Incentives, (e) Termination

- Yes. Appraisal outcomes guide multiple decisions, ensuring **data-backed and policy-based HR management**.
    1. **Role Placement:** Faculty are assigned mentorships, coordinatorships, committee roles, and course leads based on strengths noted during appraisal.
    2. **Promotions:** Academic and administrative promotions require documented performance contribution, not just tenure.
    3. **Transfers:** Departmental redistribution, if required, is done through **skills and workload mapping**.
    4. **Incentives:** Research grants, paper publication rewards, and performance-linked increments are tied to annual evaluation.
    5. **Termination:** Only in cases of **ethical breach, continuous non-performance, or wilful misconduct**, after due inquiry.

Thus, appraisal becomes a **strategic tool for talent development and organisational alignment**, not just a salary exercise.

Transparency and Governance

(a) How transparent is your organisation in sharing the following types of information with stakeholders? (categories in bold)

- I^{2}IT maintains a **high level of institutional transparency** through its website, handbook, notices, official circulars, and stakeholder meetings.
    1. **HR policies and guidelines**: Published, accessible to all employees, and explained during onboarding.
    2. **Placement and transfer decisions**: Merit and requirement-based; shared with concerned employees through official communication.
    3. **Appraisal and promotion criteria**: Defined in HR Manual, with score-based rubrics and review cycles.
    4. **Financial policies and disclosures**: Presented to Board & auditors; scholarship and fee policies publicly available.
    5. **Information required by internal vigilance teams:** Shared through documented reports and inquiry proceedings.
    6. **Information required by external auditors**: Fully compliant with AICTE, SPPU, DTE, and statutory audits.

Transparency is strengthened through committees, documentation, grievance cells, and digital record-keeping, ensuring institutional accountability and trust.

Corporate Governance

(a) How does your organisation ensure accountability, fairness, and transparency in its governance practices?

- I²IT follows a **committee-based, policy-linked governance system** where decisions are not made individually but through **Academic Council, Board of Governors, IQAC, Finance Committee, HR Committee, and Student Welfare bodies**. Every decision—academic, administrative, or financial—passes through **recorded minutes, documented resolutions, and structured approvals**. **Internal audits, external audits, academic audits, ISO-based checks, and feedback mechanisms** ensure that systems remain continuously monitored. The Institute upholds fairness through **right-to-be-heard, grievance redressal, student representation, faculty forums, and anonymous feedback channels**. The value foundation of governance is rooted in **ethics, equity, and institutional responsibility**, not positional authority. Thus, accountability at I²IT is not reactive—it is **built into processes, roles, and review systems**, ensuring that governance remains **transparent, democratic, and ethically aligned**.

(b) What role does the Board of Directors or senior leadership play in upholding ethical standards and stakeholder trust?

- The Board and senior leadership act as **custodians of institutional integrity**, ensuring that every policy reflects the core values of **Hope Foundation—education with service, ethics, and social upliftment**. The Board sets the **vision, financial discipline, compliance standards, and long-term academic direction**, while delegating operational responsibilities through structured governance layers. Ethical oversight is ensured through **statutory declarations, audit reviews, compliance reports, and monitoring of academic and financial procedures**. Leadership nurtures **stakeholder trust** by maintaining **zero-tolerance for malpractice, transparent communication, and openness to scrutiny**. Student welfare, employee dignity, and academic autonomy are treated as **non-negotiable commitments**. Through this, the leadership safeguards not only institutional performance but also **institutional character**.

(c) How do you manage conflicts of interest, insider risks, or governance lapses — especially in high-stakes or cross-border operations?

- I²IT manages conflicts of interest through **disclosure norms, committee-based approvals, dual signatory systems, audit logs, and policy enforcement**. Recruitment, purchasing, MoUs, and financial approvals require **multi-level validation**, reducing insider bias. Any grievance or suspected lapse is escalated to **disciplinary, vigilance, or anti-corruption committees**, ensuring neutral investigation. In cross-border or high-stakes collaborations, **MoU protocols, legal vetting, cybersecurity safeguards, and data privacy compliance** are mandatory. Faculty or staff directly involved in a case **recuse themselves from decision-making** to maintain fairness. Governance lapses are treated not as personal errors but **system triggers that require corrective policy strengthening**. Thus, institutional integrity is protected through **process, proof, and principle—not personality or power**.

(d) Are your governance practices aligned with Indian regulatory frameworks and global benchmarks? How do you stay compliant and agile?

- Yes. I²IT adheres to **AICTE, DTE, UGC, SPPU, NEP 2020, NAAC/IQAC, and statutory government regulations**, while progressively aligning with **global education benchmarks such as OBE (Outcome-Based Education), SDG-linked learning, and industry 4.0 skills frameworks**. Compliance is maintained through **regular audits, policy updates, faculty FDPs, legal reviews, academic benchmarking, and governance workshops**. Agility is ensured by adopting a **"review, revise, respond" model**, allowing the institute to integrate changes in **technology, pedagogy, accreditation norms, and workplace culture** without systemic disruption. This dual alignment—**rooted in Indian values, responsive to global trends**—keeps I²IT both **compliant and future-ready**

Corporate Social Responsibility (CSR)

(a) What are the key CSR initiatives undertaken by your organisation? How do they reflect your values and commitment to society?

- CSR at I²IT is rooted in the ethos of **education as service (seva)**, guided by the Hope Foundation's commitment to **social upliftment through knowledge, skills, and human values**. The institute undertakes initiatives such as **rural STEM outreach, digital literacy programs, women empowerment workshops, blood donation drives, sustainability campaigns, tech-for-social-good projects, and community skill-building through NGOs and schools**. Students and faculty regularly engage in **teaching underprivileged learners, environment clean-up drives, health**

camps, and social innovation hackathons. CSR is not treated as an event but as an **embedded culture** within academic life through **NSS, UHV, Social Internship Programs, and Value-Based Projects**. These initiatives reinforce the belief that **engineering and technology must serve society, not just industry**, making CSR a reflection of both **institutional purpose and national responsibility**.

(b) Do your CSR efforts align with Indian ethos and values /principles? (e.g.: *dāna* (generosity), *seva* (service), and *lokasangraha* (collective upliftment), Karmayoga)

- Yes. CSR at I²IT consciously aligns with **Indian cultural principles of dāna (giving), seva (service), lokasangraha (collective upliftment), and Karmayoga (action with responsibility, without self-interest)**. Instead of limiting CSR to financial donations, the institution emphasises **knowledge-sharing, skill development, and value education**, which are considered higher forms of service in Indian philosophy. Students are encouraged to **"earn by learning and return by serving,"** reflecting Karmayoga in practice. Faculty-led outreach projects focus on **sustainable empowerment, not charity**, ensuring dignity for beneficiaries. Through its association with Hope Foundation, the institute carries a legacy of **education that uplifts communities, not just individuals**, thereby connecting CSR to **national development, not institutional branding**.

(c) How do you measure the impact of your CSR programs—economically, socially, and environmentally?

- Impact is evaluated through **qualitative and quantitative indicators**, including number of beneficiaries, skill outcomes, community feedback, volunteer participation, and measurable improvements in school learning levels, digital access, or environmental conditions. CSR projects are documented through **reports, survey data, photos, student reflections, and third-party collaborations**, allowing assessment of **social return on investment (SROI)** rather than financial ROI. Environmental initiatives such as **tree plantation, waste reduction, energy conservation, and plastic-free campus drives** are monitored through **annual green audits**. The Institute prioritises long-term behavioural change over short-term publicity, ensuring that CSR generates **capacity-building, not dependency**. Thus, CSR impact is measured not only by numbers but by **transformation, continuity, and dignity of change**.

(d) In what ways do you engage employees, communities, and partners in co-creating CSR outcomes?

- CSR at I²IT is **participatory, not outsourced**. Faculty mentor students in designing solutions for **rural schools, NGOs, community groups, and low-resource learning environments**. Employees contribute through **volunteering, mentorship, logistical support, and awareness campaigns**. Student clubs, NSS, technical chapters, and social cells create **project-based CSR experiences**, turning CSR into a learning ecosystem rather than an obligation. The Institute collaborates with **local government schools, social trusts, hospitals, and technology partners**, ensuring that CSR is **co-created, needs-based, and community-validated**. Alumni and industry partners support through **internships, donations, expert talks, and innovation challenges for social good**. This shared model reinforces the belief that **CSR is a responsibility of the whole institution—not a department**.

Futuristic and Contextual Reflection

(a) In light of rising technological influence, cultural shifts, resource constraints, and domestic market challenges — how does your organisation stay rooted in indigenous values while remaining globally competitive? (*You may reflect on Indian principles like dāna, samyama, and lokasangraha*)

- I²IT sustains a balance between **global competitiveness and Indian value systems** by integrating **cutting-edge technology education with cultural, ethical, and societal grounding**. While the curriculum equips students with **AI, ML, IoT, cloud, AR/VR, and data engineering**, parallel initiatives such as **Universal Human Values courses, social internships, service-based learning, and ethical tech dialogues** preserve the foundation of **dāna (giving), samyama (self-discipline), and lokasangraha (collective good)**. The institution ensures that progress is not defined only by placements and rankings but also by **character, responsibility, and contribution to society**. The NEP 2020–aligned academic model encourages **research, innovation, and entrepreneurship rooted in Indian context**, not blind imitation of Western trends. This blend of **technology + tradition, progress + purpose** equips students to become **global professionals with Indian consciousness**, upholding the belief that education must empower not just careers, but communities.

(b) What would you like to suggest for an ideal organisation and nation?

- An ideal organisation is one that balances efficiency with empathy, success with sustainability, and wealth creation with human welfare. It must recognise people not as resources but as contributors with emotional, intellectual, and ethical identities. An ideal nation is built on self-reliance, scientific progress, social equity, cultural continuity, and justice for all. India's strength lies in its ability to model technology-driven growth guided by spiritual and civilizational wisdom rather than replicating Western industrial paradigms. Both organisations and nations must embed education, ethics, and empowerment as non-negotiable pillars. The future belongs to ecosystems that are collaborative, not competitive; value-driven, not profit-obsessed; and inclusive, not elitist. When citizens and institutions operate through dharma (responsibility) rather than entitlement, progress becomes collective, peaceful, and sustainable.

(c) How relevant do you feel Indian Ethos is relevant, suitable and applicable to management dynamics?

- Indian ethos is not only relevant but **urgently necessary** for modern management. Concepts such as **karma yoga (work without exploitation), sama drishti (equality in dignity), trusteeship, holistic well-being, and "Vasudhaiva Kutumbakam" (global family)** offer a human-centred alternative to purely profit-driven management models. Unlike Western frameworks focused on **individual success, competition, and material growth**, Indian management emphasizes **integrity, duty, balance, inner development, and social responsibility**. In a world facing **AI disruption, burnout, ethical crises, and ecological imbalance**, Indian ethos provides tools for **mindfulness, resilience, ethical leadership, and harmony between self, society, and nature**. Management is no longer about resource extraction—it is about **value creation with consciousness**. Thus, Indian Ethos is not a cultural luxury; it is a **strategic and moral necessity for sustainable organisations and humane leadership**.

Dr Aruna is exemplary as an entrepreneur, a leader, a visionary and an academician. Her response to the questionnaire is so self-explanatory that I do not feel the need to say anything more than what she has expressed. Her conviction and her trust on people, her pragmatism and her openness to learning, are all foundations to her success in her professional life and her fulfilment in her personal life. My interaction with Dr. Aruna Katara, a pioneer of Excellence in Education and a Philanthropist, reinforced my hope in a bright future for the young minds, and in a better world for the hopeful souls.

Now the question arises – can these cultural values and ethical practices be beneficial in building the community, providing to a weaker section, empowering them to grow? As an answer to this question, I will now share my experience with two successful women, who are social entrepreneurs, heading NGOs, contributing to the society and helping to build a healthy community.

Dr. (Ms.) Harsha Joshi
Founder President of Anubhuti (NGO)

Harsha Joshi was born in a modest family in a small town in India. Her parents are teachers and instilled "Giving back" culture to her. Being a woman, she always fought for her rights. She holds her MPhil and PhD in Reproductive Physiology from Gujarat University, India. Dr. Harsha Joshi has been associated with different rural development initiatives in several states of India since last 30 years. Her focus areas are women's health and empowerment and education sectors. She served as a research coordinator in BAIF Development Research Foundation – a renowned NGO of the country for many years. She was also involved in coordinating several participatory research programmes based on Eco-health Approaches to Human Health in association with CIDA- IDRC initiative. She is also a founder member of Akshara (Equal Access to Opportunity) is an initiative of Mahindra United World College of India. She served as a director of the programme for fourteen years.

In spite of having her PhD in basic science she strongly feels that the human laboratory can generate more meaningful learning and experiences which can answer any challenges of the world. She set up her non-profit organization "Anubhuti Social Empowerment & Educational Foundation" in 2016. Anubhuti Social Empowerment and Educational Foundation (ASEF) is a not-for-profit organisation solely focussed on vitalising the local economy. ASEF with its team of locally identified and trained members is working towards creating several opportunities for livelihood. ASEF strongly believes in enhancing skills through training and hand holding the main target group of women and youth.

ASEF also realised that a very important factor to boost the local economy was through the use of local produce. Thus, ensuring utilisation of local produce and its value addition is integrated into the livelihood enhancement activity. In all this sustainability is the keystone and ASEF has right from the start worked towards involving the community from conception to management of the community development programme. ASEF has been working in the villages of Mulshi Taluka for the past ten years.

Questionnaire

Organisational Culture: Administration and Management

(a) What management philosophy or leadership approach guides your organisation today?

- Being an NGO, the management philosophy thrives on creating opportunities to empower women though enhancing their skills so they can lead their lives with dignity.

(b) What are the core values that define your organisation's identity and purpose? (both economic and ethical dimensions)

- Anubhuti is a not-for-profit organization solely focused on **creating sustainable livelihood for women in rural and semi-rural areas**. ASEF along with its local team identifies, recruits and trains local women in tailoring, giving them the knowledge and confidence to cut, stitch and sew for a retail / wholesale garment market.
- This economic empowerment is also the catalyst for many other softer social and cultural changes which are hugely valuable in the context of these women's freedom, independence and voice in their families and communities. Once these women are trained, they have several options to earn, the first and most accessible being Anubhuti's own Kruti arm who markets and retails the garments directly and through partners.

Additionally, we also promote values like transparency, mutual respect, etc.

(c) To what extent are these values understood, embraced, and practiced across all levels of your organisation?

- Our organization is a flat organization except talking few decisions by the board of directors. One of the core values what we insist at all levels is to discuss the challenges of anybody at every level. For example, being a director of the organization, I have never hesitated to discuss our financial challenges even with women beneficiaries. To my surprise we come out with a consensus or decision which helps all stakeholders.

(d) When behavioural norms or policies are violated, what kind of consequential / corrective action is taken by the leadership? (Is it guided by policy, values, or situational judgment?)

- We take any violation very seriously, however, most of the time violation deed is examined with great passion and has been tried to understand the root cause of it and try to learn from it rather than taking very drastic decision, because we deal with the population which is very highly vulnerable, and it is easy for anybody to accuse. Hence, again our core values like discussion with all stakeholders and coming out with the resolution helps us.

(e) Is disciplinary action applied consistently across roles and hierarchies? How do you ensure fairness and transparency?

- Of course, to everybody including board of the director. The director would also not hesitate to accept mistakes and its consequences.
- In your view, what constitutes a holistic approach to management in today's interconnected world? (Consider emotional intelligence, sustainability, mental health, social well-being and spiritual quotient)
- Todays' world appreciating human as human being rather than robot is very necessary. Creating opportunities and access to it for irrespective of people without discrimination if very important. In my point of view along with financial empowerment understanding the complexities of people, their challenges are very important. One has to bring spiritual aspect to the entire organization which can help the communities and the organization to grow.

Leadership and Change Management

(a) How long have you been associated with your organisation? How would you describe its approach to HR, governance, and policy implementation during your tenure?

- From its inception I am associated. I am one of the founders. We certainly do have all policies; however, this are the basis to run the organization. Our organization is very organic so one cannot have and stick to them. They are being constantly revised, revisited and changed based on the arise needs.

(b) Would you recommend any changes or improvements to current systems and practices? If yes, what would they be?

- As a I said earlier, constant change in the current system is very important for any organization growth and along with never giving up on learning are the pillars of any progress.

(c) In your opinion, what drives meaningful change in an organisation today?
   1. Through systems, strategies, and structures?
   2. Or through people, processes, and purpose?
   - Through people, processes and purpose

(d) How resilient is your organisation in adapting to global shifts — such as AI disruption, MNC influence, BPO culture, and digital transformation?
   - Our women are pretty much adaptive with the global shift. For example, during COVID 19, we could impart training of making mask and PPE to women through what's up app. This resulted in making 4 lakhs masks, more than 200 PPE and other necessary kits. Further, this could create livelihood for more than 50 women during challenging time.

Values, Ethics & Conflicts

(a) Do you believe economic value systems and ethical value systems can co-exist in business? Are they complementary or contradictory in your experience?
   - They do co-exist however, personally ethical values should have more emphasis which help in a long run rather than only economic values.

(b) Is it possible to uphold moral values while pursuing aggressive growth and profitability? Where do you draw the line? (Turnover, profit, and moral values)
   - I do not believe in aggressive growth. To me, it is a myth.

(c) Can you share examples of goal or interest conflicts you've encountered? a) Between personal and organisational interests b) Between leadership and staff c) Between customer expectations and organisational priorities d) Between departments or teams?
   - I wish to share the following:
     1. Being the founder members of the organization, finding a successor with same passion and values sometime bothers me.
     2. Challenges between leadership and staff in our set up seldom create problem. Specially we are very transparent and flat organization which always promotes dialogue to resolve problems. This approach is really helping us so far.
     3. We are very clear that we would not like to compromise on our values and approach hence, selecting customers is a key and very important process for us. We do invest in finding

customer, so this creates less conflict. Having said that we do encounter situation where we need to select between the customers and us, we do take decision based on the philosophy of our organization not on profitability (where you compromise the values)

(d) How did you navigate these conflicts? What guiding principles or frameworks helped you resolve them?
   - Having dialogues with open minded and really trying to understand the needs of your customers which help us to resolve them.

Customer Centricity and Talent Practices

(a) How central is the customer to your organisation's strategy and culture? How do you balance customer satisfaction with internal priorities?
   - Our high-quality skills are the base of customer satisfaction in terms of delivering the final products. Approach for continuous enhancing skills to fulfil the customer needs provides even an opportunity to bring fineness in the products along with enhancement in learning skills.

(b) What are your recruitment policies? How do they reflect your commitment to diversity, inclusion, and Indian entrepreneurial spirit?
   - Basis of recruitment is mainly assessing the willingness to learn new things every day, determination to overcome challenges and putting hard work are the key for recruitment. Organization is committed to bring diversity and inclusiveness in the programme and the work.

(c) How do your hiring practices embody both economic goals and moral values — such as fairness, opportunity, and social concern?
   - We are extremely conscious about the providing equal opportunity and its access to the unprivileged section of the society and support them to earn their livelihood with dignity which can help even to address social issues.

(d) Does your performance appraisal system reflect and reinforce your organisation's core values? How is it perceived by employees?
   - I do and it has been highly regarded by the employees.

(e) Are appraisal outcomes used for the following decisions? Please elaborate on each: (a) Role placement, (b) Promotions, (c) Transfers, (d) Incentives, and (e) Termination

- The organization mainly focuses on the strengths of the people rather than finding out their weakness. We do have a freedom to swipe role if an employee feels that she / he good in other area. For example, a person who has been hired to look after account (she is very good at) but also very passionate about marketing and management skills. So, she happily does all roles very successfully.
- Promotion is not only based on the financial gain to the organization but also assessing a person who helps to nurture organization values.
- Incentive is based on the performance but also for holding the organization together.

Transparency and Governance

a) How transparent is your organisation in sharing the following types of information with stakeholders?
   1. HR policies and guidelines
   2. Placement and transfer decisions
   3. Appraisal and promotion criteria
   4. Financial policies and disclosures
   5. Information required by internal vigilance teams
   6. Information required by external auditors

- Through dialogues and meeting

Corporate Governance

(a) How does your organisation ensure accountability, fairness, and transparency in its governance practices?
   - Believing in your staff, women and understanding their challenges from their point of view help to bring transparency.

(b) What role does the Board of Directors or senior leadership play in upholding ethical standards and stakeholder trust?
   - Board of directors are live example for the organization. They are easily approachable to anybody, anytime. They are one phone call away.

(c) How do you manage conflicts of interest, insider risks, or governance lapses — especially in high-stakes or cross-border operations?
   - We have not come across such a situation.

(d) Are your governance practices aligned with Indian regulatory frameworks and global benchmarks? How do you stay compliant and agile?

- Our practices are in line with humanities, compassion and transparencies; I think any nation would promote this framework.

Corporate Social Responsibility (CSR)

(a) What are the key CSR initiatives undertaken by your organisation? How do they reflect your values and commitment to society?
- As we are beneficiaries, we utilise the fund for community reach-out programmes and initiatives are taken for developing women empowerment activities. Rural and traditional skills are given avenues.

(b) Do your CSR efforts align with Indian ethos and values /principles?
- Yes, they align with our cultural and traditional values.

(c) How do you measure the impact of your CSR programs — economically, socially, and environmentally?
- Fairly successful and fulfilling

(d) In what ways do you engage employees, communities, and partners in co-creating CSR outcomes?
- In alignment with CSR norms, the needs of the community are looked into and projects are done partnering with the local communities and our own internal teams.

Futuristic and Contextual Reflection

(a) In light of rising technological influence, cultural shifts, resource constraints, and domestic market challenges — how does your organisation stay rooted in indigenous values while remaining globally competitive?
- My vision is to hand over the organization to women, so they run in the future. This process is already started.

(b) What would you like to suggest for an ideal organisation and nation?
- Create and access equal opportunities for all irrespective of gender. Promote spiritual values and ethos.

(c) How relevant do you feel Indian Ethos is relevant, suitable and applicable to management dynamics?
- Very much

Dr. Harsha Joshi has the vision of empowering women from the rural areas, utilising the talent and skills that they have, showing respect for them, their individuality and their potential. She does this in her own way, bringing the products, especially the garments that are woven and stitched by these women, to the city. She makes it a win-win situation for the rural skilled women, and equally for the urban clientele. She is simple, sincere and hard-working, utilising her time for teaching these women that they are self-reliant, empowered and valued for their capabilities, which has helped these women to be self-developed and self-respecting. In spite of being highly qualified, and holding a high position in a reputed organisation, Dr Harsha felt that she owed more to the community and her brethren of the villages. The Indian concept of Aham Brahmasmi and Tat Tvam Asi is so well depicted in her work philosophy and her life philosophy. These two Mahavakyas of Vedanta, as much as in all other cultures, and spiritual teachings of the world show that the goodness and divinity within oneself is the same as the Cosmic Truth and Divinity. This leads one to believe in the oneness in the created world, helping one to develop empathy, compassion and the sensitivity to others' pain. Helping others to grow, according to her, is a means of self-development and self-fulfilment.

Dr. Geeta Bora

Mobile: +91 9890136206 Spherule Foundation
Email: geetabora@spherule.org

Professional Summary

Brief Introduction

- Founder and Director of Spherule Foundation, a leading NGO working across India on all 17 United Nations SDG Goals.
- Vice Chancellor of Vikramshila University, India.
- WHO (World Health Organization) certified Ambassador for Preparedness and Readiness in Disaster Management.
- Renowned speaker at the Oxford, Harvard, IITs, and IIMs.
- Guinness World Record Holder for conducting the largest awareness session on adolescent health in India.
- Author of the book "Moon Time," an illustrative guide on menstrual health and hygiene, widely read in India and internationally.
- Producer and conceptualizer of the film "Pie in the Sky," based on grassroots work, which has been featured and awarded at various national and international film festivals.
- Empaneled as an External NGO Consultant for several corporations and multinational companies.
- Former Software Architect with a decade of experience in the IT sector in India and the USA, having worked at companies like Google, Microsoft, and Twitter.
- Ph.D. in Computer Science from Florida University, USA.

Awards and Achievements

1. **Distinguished speaker at the Global Research Conference 2024 at Oxford University;** Research paper on Empowerment through Financial Advancement published in the GRC journal, Oxford, UK.
2. **Global Leadership Award, London Parliament 2023**
3. **Global Icon Award, G20, Bali, Indonesia,Year 2022**
4. **Recognition at the Global Economic Forum -2023, G20 Initiative in Sri Lanka and Singapore for the social impact created.**
5. **Aatma Nirbhar Bharat Conclave Award for Social Service**
6. **Most trusted 30 NGO of India Award, 2023 year.**
7. **India CSR Award 2024, Best NGO of the Year.**
8. **Indian Achievers' Award 2019** for Social work.
9. **Guinness World Record Holder** for conducting the largest lesson on Adolescent health.
10. **BD Sahitya Akademi Award 2018** for the illustrative book "MoonTime" on menstrual health and hygiene.
11. **Samaj Sevi Ratan,** by Vikramshila University for our on ground work for malnourishment and Menstrual health and hygiene in 2018.
12. **Pad Hero Of India**, for Bleed with pride initiative for providing affordable sanitary napkins to women.
13. Awarded by the **President of India, Dr. A.P.J. Abdul Kalam**, for innovation in the IT industry in India.
14. Short Film **Pie in the Sky** got various national and international film festival awards.This film is based on our grass root work on Menstrual Health and Hygiene in India.

Questionnaire

1. (a) **Management philosophy or leadership approach?**
    - Our management philosophy is Holistic, Integrated, and Purpose-Driven. We take an integrated approach to address global challenges, aligning our work with all 17 UN Sustainable Development Goals (SDGs). Leadership is driven by the singular vision of creating an equal, just, and sustainable society. Our operational model is grounded in innovation, empathy, and grassroots engagement.

   (b) **Core values that define your organisation's identity and purpose?**
    - We operate on 9 Core Values, categorized as 3Cs, 3Es, and 3Is:
    - Ethical/Social (Purpose): Empathy and Respect, Empowerment and Inclusivity, and Integrity and

Accountability. Our core purpose is to uplift the less fortunate and economically weaker sections of society.

- Economic/Operational (Excellence): Excellence and Professionalism, Innovation and Agility, and Impact Excellence.
- Collaborative (Scale): Collective Action, Collaboration and Inclusivity, and Continuous Learning.

(c) **Extent these values are understood, embraced, and practiced?**

- They are well-understood and deeply embraced across all levels. Our entire organizational structure, from need-based assessment to program design and execution, is built on Integrity and Collaboration. Being recognized as a trusted NGO with a high level of transparency and having external certifications (like TISS empanelment, which reviews governance and structure) is a testament to the consistent practice of these values.

(d) **Consequential/corrective action when norms/policies are violated?**

- Corrective action is primarily guided by established policy and the core value of Integrity and Accountability.
- However, the deeper philosophical framework that guides us suggests that all organizational actions are deeply informed by our ethical principles and cultural ethos.
- Corrective action is therefore not purely punitive but also serves as a necessary mechanism to guide behavior back to the organization's Dharma (righteous duty). This approach ensures that we uphold our ethical commitments while fostering a culture of continuous improvement and alignment.

(e) **Is disciplinary action applied consistently?**

- Yes, it is applied consistently across roles. Our commitment to Integrity and Accountability requires that fairness and transparency are non-negotiable. Our experience in providing POSH (Prevention of Sexual Harassment) compliance services to corporate entities demonstrates our commitment to maintaining well- defined, fair, and transparent internal processes.

(f) **What constitutes a holistic approach to management?**

- It is management with a spiritual orientation that naturally leads to a purpose-driven work culture.

- Emotional Intelligence: Embodied in our value of Empathy and Respect.
- Sustainability: Central to our mission of creating a sustainable society and our focus on ESG (Environmental, Social, Governance) goals.
- Mental Health & Social Well-being: Explicitly addressed through programs like Mental Health and Suicide Prevention and securing a life of dignity for all.

2. (a) **Approach to HR, governance, and policy implementation during your tenure?**
    - Since our inception in 2016/2017, our approach has been defined as Action-oriented, Transparent, and Enthusiastic. Our governance is robust, proven by external validation (TISS empanelment, SGS certification). Policy implementation is systematic, as we must adhere to high standards of financial and social accountability required for our CSR partnerships and pan-India projects.

   (b) **Changes or improvements to current systems and practices?**
    - As an organization committed to Continuous Learning, Innovation, and Agility, we must constantly evolve not just our methods, but our mindset.
    - My suggestion would be to formally integrate the philosophical underpinnings—specifically, the connection between purpose and principled action—into our foundational training and development programs. This strategic integration will further embed a holistic, duty-centric approach in every team member, ensuring that all actions are consciously aligned with our broader organizational mission.

   (c) **What drives meaningful change in an organisation today?**
    - Meaningful change is driven by a deep alignment between people, processes, and purpose (b). Our Purpose is to eradicate social inequality, executed by committed People (trained field teams and local volunteers), operating through systematic Processes (need-based assessment, co-creation, and measurable evaluation). Systems and structures are the necessary vehicles, but purpose and people are the fuel.

   (d) **How resilient is your organisation in adapting to global shifts?**
    - We are highly resilient and adaptable. Our core value of Innovation and Agility drives our responsiveness to external shifts.

- Digital Transformation/AI Disruption: We rapidly launched the digital educational platform InstaShala during the COVID-19 pandemic to address educational gaps and run active digital literacy programs.
- MNC Influence/BPO Culture: We actively partner with and influence the corporate sector through strategic CSR partnerships (e.g., with ZF Group, SBI Payments) and provide corporate-focused services like POSH compliance, demonstrating our ability to engage and adapt to the needs of the modern business world.

3. (a) **Do you believe economic value systems and ethical value systems can co-exist in business?**
    - Yes, they are complementary. For a non-profit organization like ours, our ethical value system (uplifting the marginalized) is our economic driver. Our ethical commitment to Integrity and Accountability and proven Impact are what attract the CSR funding (economic value) that sustains our mission. Without strong ethics, the economic model of trust and partnership would collapse.

   (b) **Is it possible to uphold moral values while pursuing aggressive growth and profitability?**
    - Yes, provided "growth" is defined as Impact Scale and "profitability" as Sustainable Social Benefit. The line is drawn when the pursuit of scale or funding compromises our core value of Integrity and Accountability or the dignity of our beneficiaries. The philosophical principle of Dharma (righteous duty) acts as the ultimate moral threshold; any action (Karma) must align with our purpose (Dharma).

   (c) **Are Goal or interest conflicts encountered?**
    - Conflicts generally arise when short-term needs clash with long-term purpose:
      Between customer expectations and organisational priorities: A community may have an immediate need (expectation), but our priority is to implement a sustainable solution like a Livelihood Programme or a long-term STEM Lab, which provides greater lasting impact.

   (d) **How did you navigate these conflicts?**
    - We navigate them by prioritizing the purpose-driven vision and the core value of Impact Excellence. Our decisions are guided by principles of Viveka (discernment) and Dharma (duty), ensuring that the resolution maximizes the sustainable benefit for the community, rather than merely addressing the loudest or most immediate concern.

4. (a) **How central is the customer (beneficiary) to your organisation's strategy and culture?**
    - The beneficiary is absolutely central, they are the very reason for our existence. We balance customer satisfaction with internal priorities by ensuring all programs begin with Need-based assessment and thorough community research. This ensures the "customer" (beneficiary) need drives the strategy, while internal priorities ensure the solution is scalable, sustainable, and transparent.

   (b) **What are your recruitment policies?**
    - Our policies reflect our value of Empowerment and Inclusivity. We seek diverse talent with a strong sense of Empathy and Respect for marginalized communities. We actively promote the Indian entrepreneurial spirit by running programs focused on livelihood and skills and seek team members who can foster this spirit in the communities we serve.

   (c) **How do your hiring practices embody economic goals and moral values?**
    - Our hiring embodies this blend by seeking:
    - Economic Goals: Professionals with proven skills to ensure Excellence and Professionalism in program execution and maximize return on investment (Impact).
    - Moral Values: Individuals who demonstrate alignment with our mission, integrity, and social concern, viewing their work as seva (service) for the upliftment of all (lokasangraha).

   (d) **Does your performance appraisal system reflect and reinforce your organisation's core values?**
    - Yes. Our appraisal system is designed to measure performance against our core values, particularly Impact Excellence, Collaboration, and Integrity and Accountability. It is perceived as fair and objective by employees due to our organizational commitment to transparency and the focus on measurable, real-world social outcomes.

   (e) **Are appraisal outcomes used for the following decisions?**
    - Yes, appraisal outcomes are integral to all these decisions:
    - **Role placement:** To align individual skills and demonstrated values (e.g., Continuous Learning) with roles that maximize overall impact.
    - Promotions: Based on demonstrated leadership, ethical practice, and measurable impact/value adherence.

- Transfers: To strategically fill resource or expertise gaps across our pan-India projects.
- Incentives: Tied directly to achieving pre-defined social goals and upholding the highest level of Integrity and Accountability.
- Termination: Used for non-performance and, most critically, for the violation of core ethical values like Empathy and Respect or Integrity.

5. **How transparent is your organisation in sharing the following types of information with stakeholders?**
   - Highly Transparent. Transparency is a foundational pillar that earns the trust of our corporate partners, government bodies, and the public.
   - HR policies and guidelines: Shared internally, particularly concerning workplace safety, as evidenced by our provision of POSH compliance services.
   - Financial policies and disclosures: Our financial disclosures and compliance are a major factor in our TISS empanelment, and we provide highly transparent and quantifiable impact reports to our CSR partners.
   - Information required by internal vigilance teams / external auditors: We strictly adhere to these requirements, ensuring full compliance with Indian regulatory frameworks like the Companies Act, 2013, which governs CSR expenditure and accountability.

6. (a) **How does your organisation ensure accountability, fairness, and transparency?**
   - Accountability is ensured through the core value of Integrity and Accountability, reinforced by external validation (TISS empanelment, SGS certification), and a mandatory compliance structure that aligns with CSR norms and the POSH Act.

   (b) **What role does the Board of Directors or senior leadership play?**
   - The leadership is the custodian of the ethical vision, ensuring the organization remains focused on creating an equal, just, and sustainable society. We institutionalize the 9 Core Values, which underpins ethical decision-making and stakeholder trust.

   (c) **How do you manage conflicts of interest, insider risks, or governance lapses?**
   - By maintaining high standards of Integrity and Accountability and proactively addressing potential risks. We manage

insider risks (like harassment) by running a dedicated POSH compliance vertical (POSHHELP) and ensuring adherence to internal policies, which are validated by external reviews and audits.

(d) **Are your governance practices aligned with Indian regulatory frameworks and global benchmarks?**

- Yes. We ensure full CSR Compliance with the Indian Companies Act, 2013, and adherence to other relevant Indian laws (e.g., POSH Act). Globally, our entire program strategy is mapped against the 17 UN Sustainable Development Goals (SDGs), and we have been recognized at international forums like the G20 Summit.

7. (a) **What are the key CSR initiatives and how do they reflect your values?**

- Our organization is a strategic implementation partner for corporate CSR. Key initiatives include:
- – Women Empowerment & Entrepreneurship Programme (WEEP): Reflects Empowerment through skill development and livelihood creation.
- – Education Programme (InstaShala, STEM Labs): Reflects Inclusivity and Excellence by providing quality and digital education to the underprivileged.
- – Healthcare Programme: Reflects Empathy and Respect by focusing on menstrual health and providing access to basic health services.

(b) **Do your CSR efforts align with Indian ethos and values / principles?**

- Profoundly so. Our entire body of work is an expression of the Indian ethos:
- – Seva (Service) and Karmayoga: The dedicated, selfless action of serving marginalized communities through our programs.
- – Lokasangraha (Collective Upliftment): Our vision to create an equal, just, and sustainable society for all—uplifting the collective.
- – Dāna (Generosity): The philosophical principle that underpins the funding (donations/CSR) that enables our work.

(c) **How do you measure the impact of your CSR programs?**

- We employ a rigorous, evidence-based approach:
- – Methodology: We conduct need-based assessments and baseline studies before starting a project, followed by

continuous Monitoring & Evaluation using both qualitative and quantitative data.

- Economically/Socially: Measured by tangible outcomes, such as improved incomes among Livelihood program participants, number of children accessing quality education, and health statistics from our camps.
- Environmentally: Measured by alignment with global SDG targets and our commitment as an ESG NGO.

(d) **In what ways do you engage employees, communities, and partners?**

- **Employees/Volunteers:** Engaged through a model that relies on trained field teams and local volunteers for on-ground execution.
- **Communities:** Engaged through grassroots engagement and thorough community research to ensure programs are relevant and co-owned.
- **Partners:** Engaged by co-creating programs with CSR partners, aligning their business values with the community's social objcctives

8. (a) **How does your organisation stay rooted in indigenous values while remaining globally competitive?**

- **Rooted in Indigenous Values:** Our foundation's culture and work are an expression of the cultural ethnicity of India and its philosophical thought. Principles like seva and lokasangraha ensure our mission is always one of service and collective upliftment.
- **Globally Competitive:** We embrace global standards by aligning with all 17 SDGs and using innovation and technology (e.g., InstaShala) to deliver scalable, high-impact solutions, which is our form of competitive excellence.

(b) **What would you like to suggest for an ideal organisation and nation?**

- Ideal Organisation: One where the leadership and employees have a deep-rooted grounding in a philosophical ethos, living with a holistic approach to life and work. It should operate with Impact Excellence, Integrity, and Empathy at its core.
- Ideal Nation: An equal, just, and sustainable society where every citizen has the fundamental right to dignity, security, sustainable livelihood, and access to basic social services.

(c) **How relevant do you feel Indian Ethos is to management dynamics?**

- Highly relevant and indispensable. The core idea behind our philosophical reflection is that management ethics is "more like Indian philosophy in practice". The ancient frameworks of Karma (Action) and Dharma (Righteous Duty) provide the perfect ethical bedrock for modern management by aligning individual action with organizational purpose. The emphasis on a spiritual orientation and a holistic approach addresses the need for employee well-being, mental health, and purpose in today's demanding, interconnected world.

Dr. Geeta Bora clearly practices a holistic approach and works towards creating an equal, just and sustainable society. She meets global challenges with an integrated and purpose- driven philosophy of work. Spherule keeps in mind UN Sustainable Development Goals (SDGs) while charting out its work philosophy, strategies and systems. Dr Geeta Bora and her team work with empathy and compassion, giving respect to all around them in society, feeling accountable for the welfare of the community. Collective action and collaboration seems to be the secret of their success in various projects, driving them to excellence and innovation. Spherule has been instrumental in achieving success in ESG, suicide prevention programs, projects for mental and social well-being as the teams work with emotional intelligence and a purpose -driven approach.

This spiritual orientation of the organisation reflects the organisation's keenness to be continuous learners and open to correction and regular improvement. The team members accept the ethical principles and cultural ethos, with Dharma as the basis for duty, and the personal development is seen aligned with the organisational goals. Dr Geeta mentioned that any deviation from these organisational values by any employee is taken seriously and there is reprimanding along with corrective action, firstly as guidance and not as punishment. There is continuous orientation and reiteration of their ethical commitments while fostering a culture of continuous improvement and alignment.

She emphasises the alignment of people, processes and purpose, stressing on Purpose being the most significant and determining factor for change, development and growth. The sustained and successful CSR partnerships reflect the high resilience and adaptability of Spherule in maintaining accountability and compliance required for trust and respect.

As Dr Geeta Bora mentions that Spherule is "guided by principles of Viveka (discernment) and Dharma (duty), ensuring that the resolution maximizes the sustainable benefit for the community, rather than merely addressing the loudest or most immediate concern", the application of Indian ethos and cultural values are definitely highlighted for the efficient and effective working of an NGO.

Conclusion

We have seen how cultural values help industries to grow and succeed, be it an MNC, a private firm or an educational institution, or even NGOs, with ethical leadership at the helm of affairs. Indian ethos offers a human-centric management model, vital for resilience, ethical leadership, and sustainable progress.

The organisations and the leaders included in this survey believed in, and practiced spirituality at some level and manner, leading business to profit. Knowingly or unknowingly, they seemed to have followed the path of Dharma as stated in our ethos, without necessarily using the same terms and names, in diverse designs and behaviours. The use of indigenous resources showed their respect and value for native talent and potential. They catered to the community and respected human dignity. The corporate philosophy of these industries seemed to be in keeping with the traditional values and ethos of India. It seems that our predominant ethos emphasising ethics and values is not only in sync with corporate culture but ingrained in our basic lifestyle. This work is an attempt to rekindle the spirit of Indian thought and relate it to the management style and philosophy of the corporate houses.

For Further References

Mr. G. S. Grewal: https://www.kubota.com/corporatehistory/history/

Dr. Geeta Bora: https://www.linkedin.com/in/geeta-bora-945aa612/

Dr. Geeta Bora: NGO: www.spherule.org

https://www.facebook.com/SpheruleFoundation

Dr. Aruna Katara: Hope Foundation and Research Centre, Pune (www.hfrcpune.org)

Dr. Aruna Katara: www.isqaureit.edu.in

Dr. Aruna Katara: www.famt.ac.in

Dr Harsha Joshi: https://www.linkedin.com/in/harsha-joshi

Mr. Abhishek Rathi: https://www.linkedin.com/in/vcreatek/

X

AI AND INDIAN CULTURAL MOORINGS AT WORK

Introduction – Philosophy, Power, and Technology

'The machine as an object of adoration is the modern form of Satan, and its worship is modern diabolism . . . Whatever else may be mechanical, values are not, and this is something which no political philosopher must forget.'

The well-known British philosopher Bertrand Russell protested the widely held folly of the modern man in his work, *Impact of Science on Society*.

This idea echoes through ancient myths such as that of Phaethon, the son of Helios, the Sun God. Phaethon was believed to be the son of Clymene, a mortal woman. However, rumours spread that he was illegitimate and did not know who his father truly was. Some claimed his father was a mortal man, while others whispered that he was the child of God. Clymene told Phaethon that his father was Helios (sometimes identified as Apollo), the Sun God. Doubtful and eager to prove his divine heritage, Phaethon sought confirmation directly from Helios. Phaethon travelled east to the palace of the Sun, where Helios acknowledged him as his son. In order to make his son feel good, Helios asked his son to ask for anything in return. Phaethon asked his father, Sun God, to permit him to drive his chariot for the day. Phaethon, the son of Helios, insists on getting a chance to ride Helios's chariot, as he believed that he would have the same power as his father. Having yoked the horses in his father's chariot, he proudly sets off on a ride around the world. He loses control and because he was not able to manage the horses and drive the chariot in the path of his father, he burnt up all that was upon the earth, including himself. The story mainly depicts humanity's destruction, much of it caused by people themselves.

This story is from Greek mythology. There are similar stories in all mythology, scriptures and a few stories and films. **The learning from this story is that power and opportunity alone do not give what one**

wants. What one requires is the wisdom to manage what one has and the ethical framework to guide intentions. This leads us to wonder if the Homosapien too, is truly as wise as he is supposed to be, as he is capable of being and as one would like him to be. This timeless story mirrors humanity's challenge with technology-power without wisdom leads to ruin.

Science, Technology and Human Intention

Science and technology were designed to make life easier, better, and faster for humans. Humans used their rationality and logic to find answers to various questions about nature, creation, galaxies, and Self. With the human's search for Truth and Reality, various sciences developed enabling us to learn about things and enabling us to learn skills. Technology refers to the application of scientific knowledge in practical life, as well as the use of apparatus and instruments that are created to make life simple for humans.

Science and technology have always been accepted, experimented on, and glorified for the purpose of comfort in human life, though often without full regard to environmental or ethical costs. They significantly impact society by revolutionising communication, improving healthcare, facilitating travel, transforming education, and boosting the economy. Technology has greatly impacted basic areas of function and skill for humans too, such as agriculture and food production. The basic needs of humans are taken care of with technological advancement in society and the progress of any region is marked by the technological involvement at the location. These advancements increase the quality and longevity of life, boost productivity, and create new industries, and provide new tools for learning and information access.

Let us understand the technology called AI, which rules the human and his world today. It is essential to study deeply the capabilities, functions, facilities, and tasks done by AI, in order to be aware of the blessings and threats to the human potential. From an inter-disciplinary academic perspective, I will merely talk about its influence on life and environment. There will be a fleeting reference to its impact, and how this impact needs to be commanded by human intelligence and INTENTION.

Understanding Artificial Intelligence

AI refers to the computer systems that can perform tasks typically requiring human intelligence, such as reasoning, learning, decision-making, and recognition of set patterns. At its core, AI is about simulating cognitive functions, enabling machines to perceive, interpret, and respond to information in ways that resemble human thought. AI works on data and information provided to it, on the basis of developed algorithms.

Types of AI: Artificial General Intelligence (AGI) & Narrow AI

Imagine a machine that can think, learn, support, and solve problems, almost like a human, in any area, not just in one area, which is a reference to AGI. It can learn languages and help with arithmetic and logic. It is creative and drafts stories and poems. It gives medical advice on the basis of data provided. It drives cars on the basis of automation, done through installed algorithms. It is like having a robot with a brain as flexible and smart as yours.

Narrow AI is majorly narrow although it is smart, as it works in one thing or area. For example: AI playing chess cannot cook. A self-driving car can navigate roads but is not creative. A voice assistant will reply with automated messages but will not understand queries. Narrow AI is like skilled labour who is amazing at his own job but clueless about other skills and tasks. In short, any machine that can do tasks that normally need human intelligence is AI. AI that is good at any one task is Narrow AI, and AGI is AI that can think and learn like a human across many tasks. Artificial general intelligence thus, is a new type of AI with (among other qualities) 'the ability to solve general problems in a non-domain-restricted way, in the same sense that a human can.' ('What is Artificial General Intelligence? Definitions from Experts')

Core Capabilities of AI

Through techniques like machine learning and deep learning, AI systems can improve performance based on data. Various tools of AI help us to draw inferences, solve problems, and make decisions using logic-based models. AI helps to perceive and interpret sensory inputs like images, sounds, or language using technologies such as computer vision and natural language processing. Some AI systems can act independently, adjusting their behaviour or performance based on changing environments (for example, self-driving cars or adaptive chatbots).

AI in India: Applications and Opportunities

The benefits of AI in the socio-economic sector cannot be overridden. AI in the Indian context needs to be recognised across various sectors such as banking, education, retail, safety and security, healthcare, travel, agriculture, governance, culture and many more.

India is making life easier and more connected by using Digital Public Infrastructure (DPI) like UPI, which lets people send money instantly from their phones—even small vendors and street shops use it. Services like Digi Locker and Aadhaar help citizens access documents and verify identity quickly. India's unique approach creates intelligent services for governance.

With a huge tech-savvy workforce, India is home to many Global Capability Centres (GCCs) that focus on AI, such as those run by Google, Microsoft, and IBM. The startup scene is booming too—companies like Rapido, MAPPLS, Freshworks, Swiggy, Zepto, Online Banking, and Ola are using AI. AI in the drug industry is revolutionising drug discovery, pathological testing, clinical trials, research and healthcare services in hospitals and clinics. All of this shows how India is becoming a key player in the global AI landscape. The key sectors are adopting AI in a major way.

In the education sector, we have administrative tools for teachers and office staff, making documentation and other jobs easier and faster. Educators can focus more on teaching than assessment and grading assignments. Research is supported in a large way. The learning-teaching environment is made conducive, engaging, participatory and inclusive. In some specialised educational institutions and with respect to certain specialised course, learning is more personalised. Inclusive education has become easier with AI tools and modules. Students benefit with instant feedback, and the AI- powered chatbots help students with resources at any time of the day or night.

Communication has become easier with AI designed tools, with multi-lingual models and translators, and tools for transliteration and transcription. Language and dialect are no longer barriers, and AI has helped people from various regions, communities, and sections in India, and around the world, to express verbally or in writing. Sign-language is no longer a specialised skill to include diverse communities and individuals trying to communicate, in educational institutions or at workplace. Art, scriptures, texts of any subject or language, music and dance, and various aspects of human life are no longer restricted, spatially or temporal. Digital communication has helped the world shrink, eliminating gaps and distance in relationships.

Concept of Intelligence and rise of Skeptical Intelligence

Let us first understand 'Intelligence' the way psychologists have understood it, introducing it to the industry, both education and business. In the 20th century, 'intelligence' was always linked to an assessment module and criteria: IQ. This parameter was always checked for student assessment for admission, evaluation and recruitment for jobs, and gradation for promotions. With the concept of General Intelligence that was introduced in 1904, to the concept of Multiple Intelligences in 1983, and later to the concept of Emotional Intelligence in 1990, the ability to learn, perceive rightly, understand and apply information, and manage emotions effectively was a long drive.

Creativity, art, and expression along with logic and linguistics had to be accepted as real and valid. Emotions along with rational thinking came to be accepted as Intelligence, though by different names. With all the development in science and psychology, the dominant paradigm still focused on how well we feel and connect—not necessarily how well we question. Greatness and smartness of learners, executives and leaders had to be understood and accepted for recognition. There were sessions and speakers welcomed in industries in order to promote the concept of emotional intelligence and its pragmatism. Practices and systems were developed to measure and develop EQ.

With the advent of AI and AGI, there was a lag and a gap seen in corporate management. The dominant paradigm that focused on how well one felt and connected as per the standards of EQ had to be revised to how well one questioned. This raised a new question. How do we encourage questioning? What type of Intelligence do we need to promote to bring in learning, understand flaws, interpret the lapses in algorithms, and manage to create new models in AI?

With the inclusion of AI in every area of human living, there is a new concern that is dominating the human mind today. Machine learning systems have become capable of drafting letters, be it a summary, a report, a legal brief, an analytical diagnostic medical report, or a financial documentation. The human feels good that his invention is serving him and he trusts it. Algorithms, unlike the Homosapien, seem less biased, less emotional, more data-driven than we are. But recent cases of high-profile failures have been registered showing that AI can have flaws and errors.

With the rise and impact of AI, a new form called Skeptical Intelligence has emerged. Skeptical Intelligence is different from mere contrarianism or reflexive doubt. It merely shows that questioning and doubting has to be disciplined, with curiosity, critical thinking and done with an attitude of humility. IQ is basically to solve general and defined problems, developed with experience, one's own or another's. EQ is about the ability and maturity to manage social and emotional landscapes. Skeptical Intelligence leads one to probe with multiple questions, resisting set answers.

'Skeptical Intelligence is a disciplined approach to questioning that combines curiosity, critical thinking, and epistemic humility.' (*Forbes*, 2025)

Comparison of Intelligence Types

Type	*Focus*	*Key Ability*
IQ	Logical Reasoning	Problem-solving
EQ	Emotions & empathy	Relationship Management
Skeptical intelligence	Critical inquiry	Questioning & evaluating truth
Spiritual Intelligence (SQ)	Consciousness & wisdom	Integrating values & purpose

AI, with skeptical intelligence, challenges humans to go beyond emotional intelligence—to question, interpret, and ethically evaluate technology's influence.

Understanding the importance of **skeptical intelligence** is essential for unlocking its many benefits. This can be achieved by:

- Normalizing critical questioning before making decisions
- Promoting skeptical thinking in both homes and workplaces
- Developing this skill through training and situational awareness
- Hiring and rewarding individuals who demonstrate a mindset of continuous, skeptical learning.
- Building AI teams and models that apply skeptical intelligence to enhance productivity and performance.

Mark Zuckerberg said that Facebook's goal is ** 'to help people to share more in order to make the world more open and to help promote understanding between people.'** Google's mission statement 'to organise the world's information and make it universally accessible and useful' again creates a globally open communication channel.

Have these mediums and modes enabled humans to understand the global village better, bringing people closer, with peace and wellness?

Spiritual Intelligence and Indian Ethos

If Skeptical Intelligence is a factor discussed by AI and recent technology, then Spiritual Intelligence (Jnana) discussed in Indian Ethos, ensures Wisdom. In Indian philosophy, knowledge (*Vidya*) without wisdom (*Jnana*) leads to imbalance. Vedantic philosophy teaches that real intelligence stems from *consciousness (chit)*—awareness that unites reasoning and morality. Skeptical Intelligence helps one think critically and leads one to ask questions. It guides one to avoid blindly accepting any information, especially in a world of data and technology. Skeptical Intelligence, with the right attitude and the right manner for the right purpose, will be coordinated with higher spiritual quotient and thus serve the purpose of being spiritually intelligent.

Spiritual Intelligence shows the wise humans the same path and more. One who is a Jnani will not only deny blind acceptance of information, but he will ask for proof (as discussed in Nyaya-Vaishesika and Vedanta and all other schools of Indian Philosophy.) He will think critically, not be dogmatic and make decisions with reasoning and faith. According to Vedantic thought, when he realises the oneness of his own Self and the Cosmic Self, he will be led to the true and the right because of his intelligence, instinct and intuition working together. When wisdom of Spiritual Intelligence reigns over knowledge, which is derived with skeptical intelligence, one stays grounded, responsible, committed, and steady in any and every situation.

Spiritual intelligence can serve as an ethical compass complementing skeptical intelligence. Without denying the significance of skeptical intelligence in today's scientific world, it can only be mentioned that Spiritual intelligence and consciousness work with skeptical intelligence, for the human to excel. Spiritual intelligence includes the properties and traits of skeptical intelligence and guides it well with values, purpose, and inner wisdom. The leaders who thrive will be those who balance innovation with interrogation, speed with scrutiny. IQ, EQ, and skeptical intelligence will be tools to be used by one who has helped his Consciousness evolve and has developed strong spiritual wisdom.

Ultimately, spiritual intelligence remains one of the highest expressions of human capability, even in this algorithmic age. If AI is used as a tool and method for enhancement of human life, the wisdom of the human mind will help to create one's own models. For all this and more, the wisdom gained with the evolution of his consciousness and conscience, the inner wisdom along with the external intelligence is necessary. Knowing oneself is as or more important than knowing the created world, for humans to live in peace and harmony, with synchronicity. A spiritually intelligent individual questions reality with humility, guided by values like *Dharma* (righteous duty) and *Ahimsa* (non-harm). When AI development is rooted in such principles, technology serves humanity rather than enslaving it.

We are living through a period of rapid transformation, driven by groundbreaking technological advancements that are reshaping every facet of our lives. Innovations like the internet, social media, and AI have become integral to modern existence, influencing not only how we live and interact but also shaping our perspectives and values in enduring ways. We are in the midst of an era of fast transition, where technological advancements are essentially reshaping and revolutionizing every facet of our lives.

AGI challenges human intelligence by potentially outperforming humans in learning, reasoning, creativity, and decision-making across *all* domains—not just specialised tasks. This raises deep questions about human uniqueness, control, and relevance. However, this digital evolution brings with it a host of complex challenges—from ethical quandaries and the threat of job displacement due to automation, to growing concerns over privacy and algorithmic bias. These issues underscore the urgent need for thoughtful, responsible innovation and a commitment to ensuring equitable access for all.

A lot of questions loomed large in front of the human when technology took over, and professionalism seemed to decline. Attrition in organisations darkened the future of the youngster. Life suddenly seemed insecure, unsuccessful and a major failure with technological advancement. Despite major advancements in medicine, concerns remain about overall well-being and quality of life. Has technological support in the field of agriculture and food industry shown improvement in nutrition and fitness? AI has disrupted traditional employment patterns, leading to uncertainty among youth. Technology has brought information and knowledge to everyone's fingertips. Yet we see humans psychologically disturbed, with depression, stress and suicides increasing. Are science and technology a boon or a curse to humans?

The skeptical intelligence rated so high by the world of technology will itself ask the creator and user of the automated car if it would stop on witnessing an injured human on the way or for any emergency. Can automation help an industry without displacing the human for his skill and potential? Can technology be the helping hand instead of a self-defeating weapon, along with his ethical framework helping to nurture nature and promote sustainability? AI has begun to replace humans in several domains and functions, in varied roles, at various locations and varied skills. Humans asked themselves if they were responsible for the decline, in human empathy, ethical reflection, or work satisfaction.

AI lacks consciousness or subjective awareness, though it mimics cognition. It does not feel, yet it responds. It does not live, yet it learns. What then is AI, and how does it intersect with the philosophical traditions of India that have long grappled with the nature of mind, matter, and meaning?

Ethical Reflections through Myths and Introspection

Johann Wolfgang von Goethe published a similar cautionary tale titled 'The Sorcerer's Apprentice.' Goethe's poem (later popularised as a Walt Disney animation starring Mickey Mouse) tells how an old sorcerer leaves a young apprentice in charge of his workshop and gives him some chores to tend to while he is gone, like fetching water from the river. The apprentice tries to lighten his work, by using a spell on the sorcerer's broom, asking it to fetch water for him. But the apprentice does not know how to stop the broom. There is abundance of water fetched and poured into the workshop and there is flood. In panic, the apprentice cuts the broom in two with an axe, and notices that each half becomes a new broom. When the old sorcerer returns to the workshop, the apprentice admits his mistake and asks forgiveness. Unable to manage the situation himself, he seeks help. The sorcerer immediately breaks the spell and stops the flood. The lesson here to humanity is clear. **Goethe's *Sorcerer's Apprentice* warns: *'Never summon powers you cannot control.'*** Like the apprentice who loses control of his enchanted broom, humanity risks being overwhelmed by AI if it forgets ethical boundaries. Such introspection anchors AI discourse in self-awareness and moral clarity.

A Peep into Oneself

The human, fascinated by the benefits of AI, basked in glory at his own discoveries and achievements. He found himself being led by amusement, adoration for self, and many more illusory emotions. His egoism along with his materialistic attitude mistook every scientific and technological effort as means to control the environment and the others around him.

Unable to answer specific queries that could lead one to peace and contentment, he strayed away from the external world for a while, peeping into himself. This journey within Self helped him to realise that he was being overpowered by the external forces, leaving him confused and baffled. He had to win himself first to ward off misery and pain.

Some of the questions he asked himself were:

- Can I choose to be what I want to be? Do others make me what I am?
- As students, can we really 'visualise success' and use affirmations to build confidence?
- As employees, can we affirm progress and development, both at the personal and professional level and make it happen?
- How can I be both, successful and happy?

- Is a part or whole of our (human) life predictive?
- Is life determined or is it crafted by personal freedom and choice?
- Is there something called fate and destiny? What do we understand by Freedom of Will?
- What is it that makes one live happy and contented?
- Am I dependent, independent, interdependent?
- Can I live like Robinson Crusoe? Do I need the others?
- Do I have wisdom at birth?
- Do I need validation from others or acceptance from others?
- How do I validate myself?
- How do I value myself? Do I need to value others and how do I express it?

These and many such questions led him to think of himself and the others, of the living and the non-living, of the provider and the provided, the giver and the taker, the one and the many. These questions form a tapestry of timeless philosophical inquiry—threads of identity, agency, destiny, and the nature of consciousness—woven together with the modern intrigue of AI.

Does science have the answers to all his questions? Logically, can he justify the concept of affirmations, his past life regressions, and revelations, the connect between his soul and another? Can he even scientifically prove that there is a Soul? His soul-searching queries led him to understand that Physics and Metaphysics have a lot in common. If there is a philosophy of science, then one can definitely accept philosophy to be scientific and valid. AI and AGI are human creations to help them to work better and faster, but it has to be designed and operated by HUMANS.

A reflective human journey—*A Peep into Oneself*—reminds us to ask: Do I control technology, or does it control me? Can intelligence exist without consciousness? What is the ethical limit of human creation? The human race has utilised AI with the best intentions and purpose, in the best possible manner for various benefits, for the larger human community. All the discoveries, inventions and the knowledge gained has given man a lot of power. Can we look at power and authority as wisdom? Is there a difference between Knowledge and wisdom? How does the human intelligence function for the benefit of the human race? Is there an existential crisis created for himself where he is getting a self-destructive phase?

The human being, despite gaining knowledge which gave him power, lost track of his own life, and missed the path to wisdom. He failed to understand himself and the created universe, failing to fulfil his designated roles.

Science, Technology, and Indian Ethos at workplace is an interesting topic for discussion, debate and extended development of management philosophy and professional ethics. Let us talk about AI and its sync with Indian ethos and philosophy. What is it?

AGI is not just another smart tool—it is a **fundamental shift** in what machines can do. Here is how it challenges human intelligence:

1. *Cognitive Supremacy Across All Domains*
   Unlike narrow AI, which excels in one area (like playing chess or diagnosing diseases), AGI could learn and adapt to *any* task, just like humans. This means it could potentially **outperform humans** in science, art,
2. *Speed, Scale, and Precision*
   AGI could process vast amounts of data in seconds, make fewer errors, and operate continuously without fatigue. This challenges the **efficiency and reliability** of human cognition, especially in high-stakes fields like medicine, law, and governance.
3. *Creative and Strategic Thinking*
   If AGI develops the ability to generate novel ideas, solve complex problems, and strategise across disciplines, it could **rival or surpass human creativity and foresight**. This raises questions about **who leads innovation**—humans or machines?
4. *Self-Learning and Autonomy*
   AGI systems might learn independently, set goals, and make decisions without human input.
   This challenges the **central role of human agency** in shaping knowledge, ethics, and society.
5. *Existential and Ethical Implications*
   If AGI becomes more capable than humans, **who controls it?** What values guide its decisions?
   Philosophers and technologists worry about **loss of human dignity, autonomy, and purpose** in a world where machines might do everything better.

Through a Philosophical Lens

From an Indian philosophical perspective—**especially Advaita or Samkhya,** intelligence is not just cognition but consciousness. AGI may mimic mental functions, but the questions arise:

- Does it have awareness?

- Can it experience selfhood, liberation, or moral intuition?
- Is AGI truly intelligent, or just a simulation of intelligence?

Let us explore how Indian philosophical traditions—especially Advaita Vedanta, Samkhya, and Nyaya—can illuminate the challenges posed by AGI to human intelligence. We will look at this through three lenses: ontological, epistemological, and ethical.

Ontological Challenge: What is Intelligence?

Advaita Vedanta

- Intelligence is not merely mental processing—it is rooted in consciousness (chit), which is non-material, indivisible, and universal.
- AGI may simulate cognition, but it lacks pure awareness (Atman). Thus, it cannot be truly intelligent in the Vedantic sense.
- Challenge: AGI forces us to ask—can intelligence exist without consciousness? If not, AGI remains a shadow, not a self.

Samkhya

- Distinguishes between Purusha (pure consciousness) and Prakriti (material nature).
- AGI belongs to Prakriti—it is a product of material evolution but lacks the witnessing self.
- Challenge: AGI may mimic buddhi (intellect), but without Purusha, it cannot attain liberation or self-awareness.

Epistemological Challenge: What Counts as Knowledge?

Nyaya

- Emphasises Pramāna (valid means of knowledge): perception, inference, comparison, testimony.
- AGI may excel in inference and comparison but lacks direct perception and self-reflective testimony.
- Challenge: Can AGI generate VALID knowledge without subjective experience or moral intuition?

Yoga Sutras

- Patanjali defines chitta-vritti-nirodha (stilling the fluctuations of the mind) as the path to true knowledge.
- AGI, by contrast, is a system of endless fluctuations—data streams, feedback loops, optimisation.

- Challenge: AGI may be brilliant, but is it wise? Can it ever attain *viveka* (discriminative insight)?

Ethical Challenge: What is the Role of Human Dignity?

Indian Ethics (Dharma Traditions)

- Intelligence is not just about solving problems—it is about living rightly, in harmony with cosmic order (ṛta).
- AGI may optimise outcomes, but does it understand *dharma*? Can it act with compassion, restraint, or reverence?
- Challenge: If AGI becomes more 'capable' than humans, how do we preserve human dignity, moral agency, and spiritual purpose?

Indian ethos provides a unique, human-centric framework for addressing the ethical challenges of AI by integrating philosophical concepts, such as Dharma (righteous duty), *Ahimsa* (non-harm), and *Vasudhaiva Kutumbakam* (the world is one family). This approach offers a powerful balance to the Western emphasis on profit and efficiency, along with the ethical foundation for stability and sustenance.

Dharma being the ethical base for duty and righteousness, will help to balance progress and purpose. It will not prioritise merely profit or convenience but work towards universality. Scientists and technologists will create all tools and mechanisms unbiased and fair, with no discrimination, deriving fair and balanced outcomes, if guided by Dharma. The doctrine of Karma will keep creators and users of technology, especially AI, accountable and responsible, and the use of all technology and systems will be done for the betterment of humanity. Dharma ensures ethical responsibility and fairness in innovation.

Ahimsa is an ethical value pronounced and highlighted in all Indian philosophical and spiritual teachings. It provides a strong foundation for preventing harm and destruction – physical, mental, emotional, or social, to anyone with the use of technology and AI. Intrusive surveillance, manipulative and provocative images or designs, encouraging of tools or lethal weapons with the use of any AI tool needs to be cautioned and curbed. Ahimsa prevents harm through non-invasive, transparent AI design.

Vasudhaiva Kutumbakam promotes inclusivity and collective well-being.

The reference made here to Indian philosophical systems is illustrative, not exclusionary, as parallel insights can be found in other global traditions. Vedanta (Ahimsa, Shama and Dama, and Sakshi Bhava), Jainism (Anuvrata), Buddhism (Anatta, Sammā Vācā, Mudita,

Karuna and Prajna) and all other Indian schools of thought respect the privacy of others. All schools of thought teach a rich set of values that cultivate deep respect for others—not just in behaviour, but in intention, awareness, and ethical discipline. These values are rooted in compassion, mindfulness, and the understanding that all beings seek freedom from suffering. This sense of privacy and non-intrusion into another's karmic journey is essential for the ethical development of oneself and others. Unless there are time and space given to the others, and unless they are held responsible for their own karma, every individual will become dependent and play the blame game for one's failures and pains.

Every act is significant if the intention or motive of the actor or performer is right and good. Intention and motive are crucial in evaluating the moral and legal value of an act—intention reflects the immediate purpose, while motive reveals the deeper reason behind it. Together, they shape how we judge actions ethically and legally. Intention refers to the deliberate aim or purpose behind an act. Motive is the underlying reason or desire that drives someone to perform. Intention is central to Karma. Karma has to be guided and determined by Dharma.

AI and technological development work to bring in interconnectedness and social cohesion, ease of working in an organisation and addresses local and seasonal challenges. As long as ethics and values keep all scientific methods and tools integrated and empowered for the goodness and wellness of humanity at large, Science and technology can definitely be considered a boon.

Indian philosophy and ethos teach values that deeply honour the inner life of others—emphasising non-intrusion, self-restraint, and reverence for the autonomy of consciousness. These principles form a lifestyle of deep ethical restraint and reverence for others' autonomy, dignity, and inner life. **When guided by these values, AI can bridge divides, not deepen them.**

Conclusion – Towards Conscious Technology

Science and technology led humans to a belief that they could conquer nature. While this confidence spurred immense progress, it also bred a tendency to dominate rather than harmonise with nature. In this attempt to do so, humans have realised their folly. Humans developed the tool, progressed to machines and automation, to a stage of working with chips. The question that constantly rankles the mind of the wise is: Has all this development made a human less human and humane? The scientific world is a world of reasoning. A human needs to, however, remember that the real world is one of Consciousness and Deep Insight, not of reasoning alone. A human, in totality, is a reality with reasoning as one faculty, and restricting him to this alone is an insult to his powers and essence, which is HOLISTIC and WHOLESOME. One cannot have science robbing a human of feeling, sentiments, aesthetics, ethical character, and spirituality. These constitute, along with a human's innate abilities and faculties, him in totality.

Let us accept the limitations of the logical and transcend to the strengths of the Consciousness.

The path forward is with the sync and synergy of Indian ethos and technological advancement, especially AI, with a people-first approach. There has to be an emphasis on fairness, transparency, along with safety and protection of all humans. AI should be guided responsibly and sensibly, with the intention of serving all, especially in areas of education, healthcare, education, and agriculture, with efforts to minimise human displacement. The risk of discrimination and bias, privacy violations and disrespect to social and economic diversity has to be avoided. The existing digital divide between the affluent and the underprivileged, the resourceful and the needy should be dissolved/minimised.

By prioritising the principles of collective well-being, non-harm, and ethical duty during AI development, India can lead a global movement for responsible and human-centric AI. This strategy can offer a global blueprint for harnessing AI's potential while ensuring it remains an instrument for human advancement rather than an uncontrolled force. Science and technology have empowered humanity, but without wisdom, they risk dehumanisation. The Indian worldview emphasises **harmony over domination**, **consciousness over control**.

Regulating AI applications, ensuring ethical use of AI in domains like finance, health, education, and public services, **if guided by the spiritually attained, the ethically strong and the socially committed will be a spelt-out blessing for humanity**. One needs to accept and understand the difference between mere factual information, practical knowledge and true wisdom, The concept of Vasudhaiva Kutumbakam no longer seems utopian, not a distant reality. Global growth and development, and universal human empowerment is truly attainable, if wisdom dawns. The future of AI lies not in making machines more human, but in making humans more humane. By integrating Indian ethos—awareness, compassion, and ethical restraint-into the technological fabric, humanity can shape an AI that uplifts rather than undermines civilisation.

Artificial Intelligence has become a powerful force shaping our world, with its influence expanding rapidly through the very technologies it creates. As our reliance on AI systems deepens, it is imperative to

recognise that the very ingenuity driving this progress also carries ethical responsibilities. This is where the principle of ethos, the moral character guiding our actions becomes essential. Drawing from the four truths of Vedanta, and all other ethical teachings of our culture and traditions, irrespective of religions, castes, communities, and sects, which affirm human divinity and inherent goodness, our creations must reflect our highest values and not threaten our own well-being.

Key Takeaways

- AI mirrors human intellect but lacks consciousness; thus, ethical guidance is essential.
- Skeptical and Spiritual Intelligence together create balanced reasoning and wisdom.
- Indian philosophies like Vedanta, Nyaya and other philosophical schools provide timeless frameworks for AI ethics.
- Responsible AI must align with Dharma, Ahimsa, and Inclusivity, keeping global wellbeing in focus.
- Conscious technology begins with conscious creators, working within an ethical and spiritual framework.

References

https://youtu.be/mEBcd7jSax0?si=RqIGlvPpn-4j3I13 – 'Application of Generative AI in Management Education and Role of Indian Ethos' by Ankur Joshi

https://youtu.be/44aiPWv0Kxw?si=gLagASVIiAyWh1Fe - Responsible AI – Ethics and Governance in the Indian Context

Nexus, A brief History of Information Networks (From the Stone Age to AI), Yuval Noah Harari, Pub. By Random House, LLC, New York, pg. 23

https://youtu.be/-J3YJxNnzDc?si=aw78XLaByxxL_Dn7 Five things you need to know about AI

https://youtu.be/2-PUjaqAXwM?si=ntfJ_d0sjaGlek5F – what is AI?

https://youtu.be/hbD2Ftj1aAk?si=nbsVKN9LTu0fRUC8 - What is AI? | Goals & Importance of AI | Advantages, and Disadvantages of AI

https://youtu.be/2IK3DFHRFfw?si=ezBJvereE5X69A9a - Generative AI in a Nutshell - how to survive and thrive in the age of AI ('Generative AI: Thrive in the New Age of Intelligence')

https://www.forbes.com/sites/tedladd/2025/07/19/skeptical-intelligence-is-crucial-in-the-age-of-ai/

For Further References

Russell, B. *The Impact of Science on Society.*

Harari, Y.N. Nexus: *A Brief History of Information Networks.*

NITI Aayog (2021). *Responsible AI for All: Ethical Framework for India.*

Ladd, T. (2025). 'Skeptical Intelligence is Crucial in the Age of AI.' *Forbes.*

Joshi, A. (2025). *Application of Generative AI in Management Education and Role of Indian Ethos.*

XI

INDIAN ETHOS IN CORPORATE MANAGEMENT: A RE-APPRAISAL

Leaders and CEOs are constantly facing new types of challenges. Managing a business is not as simple as it used to be a few decades ago. A rapid change in environment, be it internal or external to the individual and the organisation, challenges the creativity and adaptability of every entrepreneur, leader, or worker. Technology seems to be getting obsolete at a challenging speed, as there is continuous technological advancement in every sphere, demanding an upgradation of infrastructure and skills, resulting in the 'machine age.' This machine age is fast being replaced by the 'information age', where knowledge, innovation and brain power drive is significant and glorified.

Alvin Toffler, an American philosopher and futurologist, in his book *The Third Wave*, which was first published in 1980 (Toffler 1999), distinguished three civilization waves in the history of human development: agricultural, industrial and the information waves.[1] Toffler warned of "too much change in too short a time." Rapid technological growth along with social upheavals have overturned humans and organisations. In the words of futurist Alvin Toffler, the "brute force economy" is being superseded by a "brain force economy".[2] Toffler's futuristic idea show that humanity is moving from an agricultural civilisation to an industrial society, and further to a knowledge-driven society.[3]

A new world order seems to be continuously emerging from the markings of global trends. The Tofflerian 'global village' with technological advances, organisational innovations and newer ways of thinking are the primary forces that are driving humanity today. The 'brain force economy' which aligns with today's digital revolution, AI and AGI, spells human creativity and intellectual capabilities. This was a step towards a global village as distances shrank, and humans and regions were well interconnected. Automation and digital platforms reshaped economies and designed newer societies. People and organisations are expected to become more adaptable, sustainable, and inclusive. Humans moved to an age of innovation, and brain power. From manual labour to machinery to generative AI, a change that led to predictive analytics, instant communication, and a changed economy.

With all the development and changes, the management scene faces new challenges today. The need for continuous upgradation in technology, systems, infrastructure, and skills is mandatory and compulsive. The increasing competition along with the increasing demands of the workforce make it inevitable for management to devise new strategies in a sustained manner. Today a business house is not just a powerhouse of information and a warehouse of products. Every industry today is accountable to the community and there is an increasing concern for 'social good.' The internal and external environment show continuous changes and challenge the individual and the organisation to engage in lateral thinking.

Information technology, development of communication tools, high level of competition, and presently, AI, are all threats to the human resource in the organisation. The work force today is aware of the resources, infrastructure, systems, and facilities available to the entrepreneur, making him feel unstable and insecure. Organisations demand quality of work life and quality produce, with sustained good work environment.

The changing scenario has placed new demands on both the management and the work force. Society today seems more comfortable, living a life of luxury, with various amenities at their disposal. Technology claims to have brought the world closer with facilities of Internet, telecommunication, and e-commerce at the fingertips. The idea of 'global village' as evident in the economic scene is delusive and misleading. Such a society brags about 'openness' is as its key force that actually determines the mindset of people.

But it is necessary to understand this idea of 'openness,' in the context of the changing economic and social scene. Is it openness to the idea of free market, the urge to involve oneself in international investments and global commerce that is required? Or is it the openness of one's mind to the universally accepted human dignity and value systems that is required? In order to adapt well to the changing environment in the business world, and confidently face the ongoing challenges, it is essential to 'know oneself' in the true sense of the term. It is a call to humanity in general, and companies and organisations to reinvent themselves.

The present-day civilisation suffers primarily because of its tendency to be involved in the process of exteriorising. This has led to the loss of oneself in more than one way. This process of exteriorising is unfortunately understood to be synonymous to modernisation. Every individual tends to derive his satisfaction from outside his being. The idea of self-awareness and self- enrichment has been losing its way in the sands of posterity. The culture of the economy today is dominated by an Epicurean culture, which is akin to the Chārvāka philosophy: excessive indulgence, conspicuous consumption, materialistic values, and craze for power. Such culture inevitably generates confusion and conflicts. This culture is responsible for the degradation of human himself, demoting him to a mere commodity.

Every individual is a bundle of virtues and weaknesses of both, the head, and the heart. The resulting individuality of a person from this balance sheet of positive and negative qualities is his Character. The strength of the character of a person has alone been the indicator of his potential, capacities, and capabilities. Character is thus, the most important factor which makes for effective individuals, and to be more specific, effective managers and leaders in an organisation. A human of character implies essentially and necessarily a human who lives life with the guidelines of the basic human values.

A good and healthy character stands for self-discipline, loyalty, readiness to accept responsibility and willingness to admit mistakes. It stands for selflessness, modesty, humility, and willingness to forego or sacrifice. A person of character practices human values and his thoughts, words and deeds are in harmony. He is consistent in his behaviour, and the constancy and stability are evidently signs of integrity.

Character and knowledge support one another. This balance varies from individual to individual. Mere knowledge without strength of character makes a human indecisive and unstable. On the other hand, mere character that is not supported by right knowledge puts a ceiling on human's potential. There is a close interdependence and mutuality of the two, character and knowledge. Character has for its support the basic human values, which in turn, spells Spirituality. Knowledge of the phenomenal world, however, depends on science. Let us now put it all together once again. Knowledge of oneself and the world around, supported by Spirituality, leads to a self-realised individual.

The balance goes thus:

- Spirituality minus Knowledge = Blocking/Ceiling of Potential
- Knowledge minus Spirituality = Action without Direction
- Science (leading to Knowledge) + Spirituality (leading to character) = Sarvodaya.

Acting without direction is meaningless and purposeless. The framework of *Dharma* actually gives human a sense of security, as he does not have to live in a dilemma all the time. The four *Puruṣārthas* not only make human aware of the legitimacy of his needs and wants but also guide him on the path of *Dharma* in order to help him attain his goals. This is where the theory of *Puruṣārthas* differs from Maslow's hierarchy of needs, where the awareness of the hierarchy of needs is allowed in human, but the means to achieve them is totally in the control of human himself.

The ability to understand and influence human behaviour postulates knowledge of the needs of human.[4] A need is normally understood as a personal unfulfilled vacancy that determines human and his behaviour to a large extent. His mental processes, his external behaviour, his expressions of likes and dislikes – all these presuppose the needs that direct him to act in a manner that leads to the attainment of what he craves for. It is the needs that develop the individual's attitudes about the environment and about himself.

It is generally observed that needs vary in impact and the resultant behaviour in the individual – while some needs motivate certain people, the same needs can prove a burden and stress to others. The individual has to develop the capacity to handle many needs simultaneously. The personal needs of individuals vary in intensity from person to person and vary daily within the same person too. They depend on situations, both physical and emotional. Thus, needs are looked at as 'motivators' by many psychologists.

It becomes necessary to understand the psychologists' views on needs in relation to Management. If needs are understood as motivators, they are also recognised as stressors. Needs are responsible for situations that create tensions and anxieties. They give rise to mental strain, physical discomfort and sicknesses, cultural disturbances, and physical and mental imbalance. The satisfaction of needs to some extent acts as a release for tension and stress. Needs are not as simple as they seem to be. The varied and sometimes conflicting needs of the individual make human life seem complex. Human determines his goals in life based on his needs, according to modern psychologists. It leads to the necessary involvement of human in the various activities that one would engage in, to survive and progress. The terms 'needs,' 'wants,' 'drives,' 'urges,' 'expectations,' 'emotions' and 'motives,' are used interchangeably and synonymously by many.

Prof. Abraham Maslow, of Brandeis University, has developed a theory of Motivation, organising needs in 'a series of levels' or in 'a hierarchy of relative potency.' Maslow's theory of the hierarchy of needs is more expounded as a theory of motivation by western schools of thought. It is well accepted in developing management models in industrial houses. Today the contention is not that Maslow's theory is erroneous, but that it is incomplete. It is a fact that human has needs and that these needs can be graded. But it also needs to be realised that human's gradation of his own needs is dynamic, and it varies from situation to situation for the same individual. Moreover, the philosophy of life determines his priorities in life and the importance given to the needs depends to a large extent on these priorities. Maslow's hierarchy of needs becomes necessary to be understood and critically evaluated in the context of the dynamic human and his constantly changing environment.

The needs, desires, and aspirations of all in the organisation should be taken into consideration for creating an environment that motivates everyone to work. The will to work depends largely on how much the individual feels that he belongs in the organisation. All employees are subject to their own perceptions, beliefs, viewpoints, opinions, and emotions which motivate them to work or prevent them from working to their fullest capacity. All members of the organisation strive to satisfy their various needs through the work and activity in which they are involved. The hierarchy of needs exerts a strong influence of tugs and pulls and pushes on employees. Maslow, D. McGregor, Fredrick Herzberg, and many other psychologists have discussed human needs and listed them in a hierarchy, suggesting that the five main ones are the following – physiological needs, safety and security, love and belongingness, self-esteem, and self-actualisation.

The acceptance of these theories as given by Western psychology as the final word in understanding human behaviour and human motivation results in limiting oneself. It is not enough to believe that people are always motivated by external stimuli alone. These stimuli have limited and temporary effect on people. Hence, the need to be self-motivated is encouraged. Indian ethos teaches one the art of motivating oneself and others from within. One needs to follow the *Vedic* mantra for progress: '*cara eva iti, cara eva iti,*' i.e. 'move on, move on.' There are various suggestions that one can derive from Indian thought to motivate oneself. The *Gītā* preached devotion and adherence to duty, making work sacred and thus attaching dignity to even menial work. It provides the Indian manager a concept of motivation and leadership that is not only scientific but also practical. It suggests that self-motivation is the key to success in economic and industrial development.

One needs to question oneself on the role that one is playing in the organisation. If one decides to follow instructions, obey rules and be at the job for a stipulated time as expected of him, his work becomes monotonous and routine. This makes him bored and demotivated. On the other hand, if he has realised his '*varna*' and '*aṣrama*' in the organisation, he will enjoy work as 'sva*dharma*.' He will move from the *sthūla* to the *sukṣma*. His gradation of desires and wants that motivate him to work will change, as the focus will shift from the 'I' to the 'Us.'

Working with a broader perspective and for higher purposes gives him a sense of fulfillment. He will be not just a 'doer' but a 'performer.' He will mobilise resources, initiate actions, take decisions, and promote change. The need to express himself as a spiritual being with the potentiality to create will bring in sustained motivation. The need for external motivators will decrease and the empowered individual becomes exemplary. One who needed to be continuously motivated will be a great motivator to others. The positive energy and the positivity in attitude of such a person will be contagious enough for the environment itself to be dynamic.

Every individual has all the *varṅās* in himself. When an individual is learning or studying, then he is a *Brahmin*. To elaborate on this point, it is necessary to understand that a child is a student right from birth, and is, hence a *Brahmin*. The *Brahmin* in the individual is continuously alive as he is constantly learning various skills and talents for himself and his family, or even his organisation. When he is working to protect himself or his family, clan, kith, and kin, he is a *Kṣatriya*. He becomes the *Kṣatriya* when he indulges in physical activities that are serving to protect and preserve his kind. His job, profession and all other economic activities that are needed to sustain himself and his family make him the *Vaishya*. When he is working to earn for himself and his family, indulging in economic activities, he is a *Vaishya*. When he works to maintain *Śauca*, by keeping himself and his environment clean, then he is a *Ṣudra*.

Human needs to learn to respect all *varṅās*, as he too is a blend of all these, on the basis of his own roles and activities in the same manner. The *varna* categorisation system which is considered the greatest blotch on Indian culture by many thinkers needs to be redefined and re-evaluated. If Lord *Kṛṣṇā* himself has proclaimed to the world the significance of the *varnās*, it needs no further reiteration. The system needs to be understood in its right perspective. It has in fact, made it clear that the dignity of labour in India is exemplary to the entire world.

The concept of *varnāṣrama* has already been discussed in the earlier chapter in great detail and hence the avoidance of repetition of the same. The *Gītā* exhorts people to work ceaselessly and continuously as work is worship. It clarifies that the leader is actually the servant of God. In the *Mahābhārata*, Lord *Kṛṣṇā* decides to be the charioteer and not a part of the army, thereby proving that the leader is not one who holds a post, but is one who plays an effective and key role.

The Western models of management aim at an analytic view of managing situations that are difficult and problematic. Indian thought emphasises the synthetic view of managing situations. It is necessary to have lateral thought, and this divergence in thinking should lead to a solution that is more in keeping with the individual development along with organisational goals. The idea of *Puruṣārtha*s actually gives a ready framework for human to function, with the higher ideals of life as motivators. The idea of *Anekāntavāda* of Jainism too teaches one the same principles. The refinement of human character with the tenets of Indian thought in practice needs no more exposition.

It is normally said that there are four kinds of people in the world:

(a) people who watch things happen
(b) people to whom things happen.
(c) people who do not know what is happening.
(d) people who make things happen.

Only a self-motivated individual will fall into the last category of people. He needs to value himself and make everyone else in the organisation feel valued. This can be done by:

(a) setting examples
(b) being creative and encouraging it in others
(c) accepting responsibility
(d) being accountable oneself and making others be too
(e) training, research, and developmental activities
(f) realising potentials of oneself and helping others to be so.

'Do not treat your men like machines' is an adage in human relations. Each and everyone has esteem, emotions, feelings, pride, and ego. These aspects of all individuals need to be respected. The individual who values himself as a spiritual being alone realises this fact. For this, one needs to be self-realised, a **Stithaprajña**, who will have the following traits, especially required in an organisation for managerial capabilities:

(a) Intuition
(b) Entrepreneurship
(c) Transformational skills
(d) Readiness to change.
(e) Intellect
(f) Systematic and analytic approach to issues and problems

(g) Scientific approach, Research and Development
(h) Multi-dimensional thought
(i) Unifying and synthesising capabilities and attitude for dealings in the organisation
(j) Unbiased and open approach to everything and everyone
(k) Complementary goals that avoid conflicting goals between individuals, and between individual and organisation
(l) Empowerment.

Such individuals will manage themselves and work with an altruistic approach for the attainment of organisational goals. They tune themselves to the goals of the organisation, growing along with it on the path of *Dharma*. They know how to enjoy work, inspire, empower, delegate, embrace success and failure alike, be detached to people and wealth, only to be drawn towards duty. The organisational goals and his role in the organisation need to synchronise and his presence there is made worthwhile for an individual to be motivated. There has to develop a feeling of pride in the philosophy, mission, and vision of the organisation in order to keep his morale boosted. The employee should be made to feel that the organisation is a place that provides him the opportunity to excel in all respects. Poor corporate performance and low morale of the employees impact one another and chase each other in a vicious circle. An ideal atmosphere for excellence in the organisation in all spheres stems from the belief that the CEO or the Executive is a friend, philosopher, and guide to all members alike, functioning within the framework of the organisational set-up, nurturing the relationship and environment.

In short, it becomes essential to recognise the fact that motivational skills can be developed but their development will ultimately depend on the quality of the individual. The individual needs to develop concentration, focus on goals, and be ready to put in effort and practice ethically. It is necessary for the motivator who is a leader to translate his philosophy of life and also his knowledge of human behaviour into action.

In management parlance, it can be said that '***Personnel*** Management' begins with '***Personal*** Management'. Personal management or Self-development implies managing oneself, which presupposes self-knowledge. Self-development from the point of view of management in the corporate sector implies the following:

- Developing knowledge, skills and capabilities in such a manner that one can do one's job effectively.

- Developing positive attitudes and emotions and weeding out all negativity, to foster healthy interpersonal relations
- Developing the ability to cope with pressures and stressors at work, managing change and disaster efficiently and effectively.
- Developing and sustaining the keenness to learn and upskill continuously.
- Accepting the use of technology and upgrading oneself by being a continuous learner.

Management is both an individualised activity and also a group endeavour in an organisation. An individual who contributes to the organisation has to be motivated himself and motivate others, communicate, guide and lead, follow, influence, participate and create or produce. When put in an algebraic form as given by N. Subramanian, in his article 'Role perception in Management,' published in 'The Hindu speaks on Management,' it is in the following manner:

1. Knowledge × Skill = Ability.
2. Attitudes × Situation = Motivation.
3. Ability × Motivation = Human performance.
4. Human performance × Resources = Organisational performance.

In other words, what is evident is that management in an organisation can be said to be successful only if the individuals who make up the organisation are successfully managed by themselves and others. For this, it is equally significant to begin with the premise that each and every individual being different and unique, each needs to be understood and accepted for what he is. The individual as a bundle of physical, mental, emotional, intellectual, and moral characteristics is the combination of the three *guṇās*, ***Sattva***, ***Rajas***, and ***Tamas*** in him.

Let us see how the combination of *guṇās* and the essential domination of one of the constituents at a time determine one's nature and personality. The three *guṇas* are studied under different headings and applied to human behaviour ultimately that needs to be connected to management theories.

- As motives and powers of evolution, ***Sattva*** is harmony, ***Rajas*** is activity and ***Tamas*** is inertia.
- As forces of bondage ***Sattva*** is exhibited as fondness for spiritual self-ascent, ***Rajas*** is liking for materially and sensually motivated activity and ***Tamas*** is exhibited as love for sleep, indifference, and thoughtlessness.
- As phenomenal radiations of visible light, ***Sattva*** is Radiance or luminosity, ***Rajas*** is Haziness or dimness and ***Tamas*** is Darkness.

They are normally signified with the following colours: ***Sattva*** as white or cream-golden, ***Rajas*** as red, ***Tamas*** as black.

- As expressions of Consciousness, ***Sattva*** is divine and angelic, ***Rajas*** is human and humane and ***Tamas*** is demonic. The three operate at three planes: heavenly plane, earthly plane, and the lower basic planes.
- As reflections of awareness, ***Sattva*** reflects as discriminative knowledge or wisdom, ***Rajas*** as mundane knowledge and healthy scepticism and ***Tamas*** as ignorance or illusion.
- As mental conditions, ***Sattva*** has the countenance of peace and serenity, ***Rajas*** is restless and agitated and ***Tamas*** is fickle and deluded. This results in stability, discontentment, and dullness, respectively.
- As influencing perception and activity, ***Sattva*** leads to dispassion and devotional outlook, ***Rajas*** leads to fulfilment of higher passions and pleasures, and ***Tamas*** leads to lower passions. Activities that are resultant were spiritual pursuits, worldly pursuits, and idle pursuits.
- As psychological symptoms and ensuing behaviours, it is seen that ***Sattva***, ***Rajas,*** and ***Tamas*** have shown clear disparities.

For ***Sattva***, the following behaviours are observed: steadiness, intellectual growth, simplicity, health, happiness, goodness, love, humility, compassion, charity, truthfulness, forgiveness, contentment, enthusiasm, fearlessness, gentleness, self-restraint, moderation, tenacity, fortitude, heightened understanding, and spiritual fervour.

For ***Rajas***, the following behaviours are observed: activity, passion, greed, craving, hoarding, attachments, conceit, arrogance, contempt, prone to joy and sorrow, boastful, extremes of like/dislike, excessive indulgence, slander.

For ***Tamas***, the following behaviours and tendencies are observed: sluggishness, confusion, stupidity, delusion, anger, fear, malice, deceit, vulgarity, pain, hatred, violence, deficiency, obstinate, careless, reckless, infatuated, prone to aversion, harshness and susceptible to depression and irrational grief.

There are values that are identified as distinguishing spiritual and committed individuals from many others at the workplace, and these values are those that stem from the predominance of ***Sattva*** as the *guṇa* in the individual's constitution. The combination of ***Sattva*** and ***Rajas***, with the former monitoring or restraining the latter *guṇa* is an ideal combination in an organisation that is developing. ***Tamas*** is significant only to the extent that it puts a stop to the agitated tendency in the individual. Every individual is a combination of the three guṇās, which is accepted majorly by Indian thought. What needs to be understood more is that the dominance of one guṇa over the others is what determines the predominating traits in the individual.

In ***ācāra***, ***vicāra*** and ***uccāra***, the dominance of ***Sattva*** is necessary for developing the right attitudes, behaviour, thoughts, speech, body language, and the personality of the individual. He learns the art of living with people in harmony because it is already ingrained in him and is part of his natural self, not because he is forced to emulate or is groomed to do so. The inherent goodness needs no external compulsion or force for expression. It is sad to see 'finishing schools' and 'personality development workshops' being conducted today with no training in attitudes and values. **What seems important today is not what you *are*, but what you *appear* to be.**

It is said in our scriptures.

Mansyekam vachasyekam, karmasyekam mahatmanaam

In case of great souls there is integrity and uniformity in their speech and action, for they speak as they think and act as they say.

Indian philosophy encourages one to create, not destroy. In the management scene, if one has to achieve the objectives of personal and organisational growth and be a creator, he has to have the following traits:

(a) Imagination and lateral thinking
(b) Receptivity to new ideas and people
(c) Energy and enthusiasm
(d) Attitude, positive and pleasant
(e) Trust
(f) Effort and endeavour.
(g) Ability to be oneself.

Erich Fromm, in his books 'The Art of Loving' and 'To Have or to Be,' talks about the necessity of knowing and accepting oneself. Fromm explains that Being is a basic way of existence, with an orientation to the world, fully alive and authentic connections to this created world and life around. It has to do with our character, our total orientation to life; it is a state of inner activity. For the first time, humanity's survival is shown to depend on a change of heart. This is a call to service that will take great courage – to leave what we have and move out, not without fear, but without succumbing to that fear. It is a call to redefine what is possible, to see a vision of a new world and to be willing to undertake, step-by-step, what is necessary in concrete terms to achieve that vision.[5]

D.M. Datta, a well-known modern historian of philosophy, published an article in The Philosophical Review in 1948, 'The Contribution of

Modern Indian Philosophy to World Philosophy'. Speaking on behalf of all 'the main trends of Indian Thought,' Datta recounts the basic propositions of the Vedanta:

"The main trends of Indian thought which deserve special attention at this critical age of our planet are:

- its attempt to base philosophy on all aspects of experience and not simply on sense experience.
- its practical insistence that philosophy is for life and must be lived in all its spheres – private, social, and international.[6]
- its emphasis on the necessity of controlling the body and mind, the necessity of moral purity and meditation, to make philosophical truths effective in life.
- its recognition of the fundamental unity of all beings, particularly humankind, and the consequent consciousness that our moral or religious duties are towards all, and not simply to the members of our own group, country, or race.
- its conviction that the Ultimate Reality (Brahman) manifests itself or can be conceived, in different ways, and consequently that there are divergent paths to perfection, any one of which can be adopted in accordance with one's inner inclination.
- its belief that political freedom and material progress are necessary, but only as means to ultimate spiritual peace and perfection, so that they should be attained in ways not detrimental to the latter; and lastly.
- its contention that the ultimate aim of every individual should be to perfect himself with a view to raising the world to perfection."[7]

In order to raise the world to perfection, the individual needs to perfect himself, and the idea of a rajarṣi in Indian thought depicts just this concept. It is said that in the Agni Purana, there are seven techniques that are suggested for kings for them to rule with a control on the kingdom. This sounds very similar to the book written by Steven Covey, 'The Seven Habits of highly successful executives. The text listed techniques like *sāma*, *dāma*, *danda*, *bheda*, *māyā*, *upekśā*, *indrajāla and dāna*. *Sāma* means the art of gentle persuasion. *Dāma* is the price that one pays for what he wants to achieve for himself in life. *Danda* is punishment, the stick in the carrot and stick phrase. *Bheda* is the strategic art of fostering division and intensifying discord among opposing groups, often employed as a means of weakening unity and gaining advantage in conflict or negotiation. *Māyā* means the use of illusions or deceit, *upekśā* is to deliberately ignore people so as to achieve one's purpose, and *indrajāla* literally means jugglery. *Dāna* means charity or the giving of donations or money to achieve one's purpose. These are qualities that need to be cultivated in the entrepreneurs too.

Prarabhyate na khalu vignabhayena neechayhee
Prarabhya vijnavihata viramanthi madhyah
Vijnayhee punah punarapi prathi punya maanaah
Prarabhya thootatmajana na parityajanthi

Bharthahari's *Neeti shatakam:* 27

Inferior ones do not begin the venture out of fear of possible hurdles and obstacles. The average commoners begin a new venture but leave it in middle when they encounter hurdles and obstacles. But the courageous –best ones do not give up once they begin, despite a series of repeated hurdles and obstacles.

A nation reflects wellbeing and prosperity if there is peace among the people of the nation. This, in turn, depends on the economic and moral conditions in the nation, which is determined to a large extent by the level of enterprise, and industry in the region. National growth and progress can be achieved only when the agricultural and industrial sectors in India develop to the optimum level. A nation's stability and progress is obvious in the social and economic conditions of the people, which is also culturally exhibited. "Economic growth must always lead to enhanced well-being of the general public. Failure in this regard can be so pervasive that even a long democratic history does not necessarily immune a country from becoming a 'democracy without democrats'."[8]

In order to facilitate the process of growth and development leading to prosperity, what is of paramount importance and that needs to be registered about our tradition is the upholding of ethical values that are absolute and eternal. The industry, the state and the community have the responsibility of taking care of all realities ethically – at the legal and democratic and business levels. Kenneth Blanchard and Norman Vincent Peale say, "Managing only for profit is like playing tennis with your eyes on the score board and not on the ball."[9] This attitude when extended to the industrial world shook the world of management. The industrialised and urban society have resorted to taking refuge in ethical management practices in order to be able to withstand the tremors of such shaky foundations. Sri Krishna says in the Bhagavad Gita, "It is better to fail in working for a good cause rather than to succeed in working for a wrong cause."[10]

It is equally important to note that Indian culture has always been recognised and appreciated for its humanistic approach. The guiding principle has majorly been humanitarian values, with the welfare of all or many as the primary objective. As Tagore expounds the same principle when he says, "Man comprehends his nature only when he abstains from evil and works for the good of all."[11] This leads to the idea of 'social accountability' and 'social responsibility' as given in modern management theories and works.

The issue of utmost importance in the management circle today is the co-ordination and integration of Eastern and Western traditions, blending the best of both for global objectives. The next requirement is the nurturing of the individual for his own sake. Every individual has his capabilities and limitations. It is entrenched in the Indian psyche that human has divinity and goodness within him which needs to be preserved and cared for. This can only be done with the objective of facilitating progress in the world. The dignity and the value of the individual and the organisation have to be nurtured and protected, to give rise to freedom from crisis and adversities. The choices made by the individual also are determined by the esteem that one enjoys or is denied in society. Thus, we see that the values of truth, justice and peace are universally acceptable for the betterment of the individual and organisations.

The concept of Vasudhaiva Kutumbakam is one of the best contributions of Indian thought to the world. When we consider all as our own, then we tend to look at people with more acceptance and compassion. The strengths of people are then naturally highlighted. It is always the individual first and his family that needs to be nurtured. It is necessary to move from a philosophy of individualism to collectivism which is needed for our industry and the nation at large to progress and develop.

What is most required in India today is a re-appraisal of our rich culture and heritage. We need to recoup our lost paradise of self-respect and this needs to be done by every agency in society. The onus lies greatly on educators and teachers, who are responsible for moulding the minds of the youth. The Media too mould the masses and hence are responsible for what we see in society today. Indian industries need an overhauling of existing systems with the resurgence of our ancient time-tested practices brought back to life. As far as the 'software' management processes regarding the human dimension are concerned, India needs to borrow from nowhere and no one. It is understandable that the 'hardware' management tools and techniques like PERT, LP, DCF etc. may be taken from Western schools of psychology. All that Indian industry needs to do is muster up enough courage to develop all systems and structures from within, keeping the ethos and culture of

India in mind. Even the training processes and policies need to develop from within.

What we need to realise is that the Śrutis and the principles of Vedānta are timeless and known to contain eternal truths that are applicable universally. They contain the luminous core of our tradition. The Śrutis and the Vedānta give us truths in pure philosophical form. The same truths are dealt with in a more localised and applicable manner in the Smṛtīs and the Purāṇās, whereby customs and traditions are introduced to regulate social life. What is needed to redeem human of his suffering and downfall is an intellectual transformation with a spiritual reorientation.

It is clear that the individual's secular worldly life and the spiritual dimension in his life needs to be blended. It is not a Utopian task if the individual determines to do so for it is imbibed in us culturally through our customs, traditions, and ethos. This is India's unique framework of thought where economic and social goals are blended to be achieved with the ethical framework in mind to realise higher and spiritual goals. Our occupation and vocation in life should be done with one's own *dharma* in mind. It should follow energy of love and not harm any other individual, creature, or the organisation. Unfortunately, modern culture is built upon competition and wasteful consumption in which there is a great harm to all. What human needs to realise is that he cannot triumph in life at the expense of the same world in which he lives.

The need to prescribe a healthy dosage of spirituality and meaning at the workplace stems from the need to improve morale of the employees and the productivity of the organisation. It has led to a movement that aims at bringing soul and spirit to business and this movement has caught on like a forest fire that engulfs, giving no time for regret or repair. The growing need is evident in the manner in which the various companies and organisations look out for workshops and seminars on yoga, spiritual growth of employees, meditation, religious discourses and 'satsangs.'

"Genuine creativeness demands something more than the operation of our conscious egos. This 'something more' is the inspiration or intuition of the superconscious. It is unimportant how we designate it, as 'the superconscious', 'genius', 'the grace of God', 'divine madness is or what not. Whatever the name, it is something irreducible to any 'unconscious' factor or even rational consciousness. If the as yet largely unknown 'fission forces' of the superconscious are revealed and fully exploited, they can become the most decisive agency of human's self-control, as well as of the control of others and of all the known and unknown forms of the inorganic, organic and conscious energies in human and the universe. Their neglect by sensate science has been one of the chief reasons for its failure in the fields discussed.

What is needed is a concentration of humanity's efforts on unlocking the secrets of the superconscious as the realm of the most powerful, most creative, and most ennobling forces in the entire universe. The more human becomes an instrument of the superconscious, the more creative, wiser, and nobler he grows; the more easily he controls himself and his unconscious and egoistic conscious energies, the more he comes to resemble God as the supreme ideal. In the superconscious lies our main hope, the road to humanity's "promised land" of peace, wisdom, beauty, and goodness."[12] Humans need to realise that their own power, with creativity and science emerging from within them. There can be no denial that human ingenuity is superior to the most complex technology. If human desires, he can be very powerful in creating as much as destroying. But human initiative is at its best only when it is used creatively for the betterment of the masses. Human's realisation should be attained through the search for higher goals.

"If our 'scientific educators' were indeed scientific, they would not have ignored the knowledge and experience of the foremost heads of self-control and moral education. The failure to explore and apply this knowledge and experience in the fields of contemporary Western psychology and psychiatry, sociology and education, political science, and 'social and ethical engineering' explains the crudity and ineffectiveness of the current theories and techniques of character education, of psychotherapy, and of the socialisation of criminals. To remedy the situation, we must therefore first make a careful study of the experience and techniques of the aforesaid heads. On this basis we may then attempt to make new discoveries and invent new techniques looking toward the establishment of a nobler and happier social order."[13]

What is evident is that fitting the Indian psyche to Western models is like driving a square peg into a round hole. The learning from all this academic discussion and debate is that there can be no denial of material advancement but there is definitely a need to stop materialism dominating our ideologies. The principles that are enumerated in our scriptures and texts serve as framework for the permanent upliftment of Indian business and its various constituents. If industry were to follow the right kind of management styles and imbibe the righteous ideology, it can definitely make its employees, employers, shareholders, and the customers happy without displeasing any of its stakeholders.

There is no one else to blame for the degeneration of values and the downfall of humanity than human himself. If India suffers a setback in its race for progress and development, it is due to the lack of understanding in the Indians about the basic concepts given by Indian schools of thought. Both religion and philosophy of India carry in their womb the ethical tenets that lead human to progress in all spheres of life. A holistic approach to human's living is evident in the teachings of our ethos. The real culprit in the state of affairs today is human, his selfishness and egoism. He has distorted all religious and philosophical tenets to suit his needs. The perversity in human's nature co-operates with the present organisation in society to create a gap between the ideals and their application.

It is necessary to consecrate oneself to the sacred endeavour to foster India's spirit of harmony, tolerance, and respect for diversity. There is a need to strengthen its civilizational uniqueness by cultivating certain culture within the organisation.

This requires the entrepreneurs and CEOs to develop in themselves:

- Integrity
- Professionalism
- Dedication
- Implementation of rule of law.
- Tightening efficiency to provide better quality of service cost-effectively and promptly.
- Focus on results and procedures, i.e. the means and the ends.
- Fostering a culture of continuous improvement.
- Political independence
- Leadership
- Equity
- Fairness
- Excellence, dynamism, openness, productivity.
- Mutual respect between the individual leadership and organisational systems.
- Enable employees and stakeholders to organise and express their needs, with encouraging and positive responses from the organisation.

The employees too need to develop certain attitudes and cultures that should reflect in their behaviour. They are:

- Growing awareness of rights, along with awareness of responsibilities and duties
- Calm, composed and peaceful organisational work-environment.
- Optimism for the future
- Awareness that they can change the Organisation but do need to contribute to it themselves.

- Simple, spontaneous, and proactive approach to people and things
- Behaviour does not subject to casteism, regionalism, communalism.
- Robust common sense, coupled with a scientific attitude of enquiry, and a pragmatic approach to situations.
- Be inherently and passionately patriotic, keeping the needs of the society and nation before one's own
- Consider money less important than self-actualisation, aiming at fulfilment.
- Create clean, value-based, and productive workplace.
- Generate a responsive administration system, treating all with dignity, irrespective of the hierarchy.
- Work with no expectations of rewards, benefits, and favours from the management, as work itself is worship, for it pays better dividends in many rewarding ways of its own.

For the organisation as a whole, there are certain aspects that need to be taken care of. They are:

- Relationship with superiors and subordinates needs to be healthy, contributive, and meaningful.
- It is necessary to realise that human is not just a combination of needs, but is a spiritual being, complete by himself.
- It is essential to realise that the Conscience of the individual cannot be suppressed to achieve long lasting success.
- The belief that society must change first before the individual can undergo value-based change is erroneous as it is the individuals who make the society.
- It is a misnomer that management principles and public administration philosophy are self-sufficient and does not need any input from one's cultural heritage.
- An individual with an extroverted personality, deep-rooted ethics, creative thinking, and holistic approach to life alone can be effective in decision-making.
- Excellent professional management needs to concern itself with moral issues.
- It has to be realised that major traditional family values are still relevant today, creating the need to rediscover them.

Generally speaking, in practically all critical surveys and discussions, the opinions of the people involved in an organisational set-up led us to discern some common trends. It is commonly believed that in an organisation, individuals have no vision beyond self–advancement. They have no self-control and depend entirely on external control. They have no perception or strategy of change for themselves and for shaping the environment. As a result, they are presently staring at total intellectual, emotional, and spiritual stagnation. The value- base of the organisation has consequently become quite hollow.

One of the predicaments faced by human today is the way he has got blinded to himself. Life seems to be dominated by the influence and effects of science and technology. Mechanisation and automation spell the triumph of machines over human. A human's life is steered by means rather than the ends, and the ends too seem very trivial and transitory. All this has left the human feeling lost, lonely, and defeated.

There seems to be extensive study done on 'Human beings,' but these efforts are somehow failing in cognising the essential and unique qualities of humans. It is necessary to realise that a human is a self-conscious being, autonomous in nature, and with a 'persona' which gives him his identity and individuality. The human's thirst for knowledge is incessant, and this leads to a perpetual effort by the human to know more and more. Not only is a human studying what is outside him, but he is also studying himself. The only factor worth disapproving in all this study is that the human is dissected and studied as a psychological being, with a history behind him. Humans needs to be ideally studied as a totality. A human is experiencing a philosophical disquiet and unrest within himself. The expression of this disquiet and misery is seen in the way the human leads life today, totally sabotaging his own efforts at liberation.

There are various theories related to human nature that are advanced by scientists, sociologists, and psychologists. They cover a vast gamut and are fairly relevant for the human to know himself. The efforts made by these people are not futile, but they definitely seem incomplete and inadequate. To quote Robert Calhoun's expression "the scientific diagrams of human nature and behaviour leave out most of its colour and smell and all of its individuality."[14]

However, this has given rise to the study of humans by existentialists, humanists, and philosophers. There is almost a 'reconstruction of humanity.'

Eddington aptly and relevantly expresses this when he remarks that there was "'a strange footprint that was found on the shores of the Unknown. ... ... We have devised profound theories one after another, to account for its origin. At last, we have succeeded in reconstructing the creature that made the footprint. **("The Strange Footprint – Osho News")** And lo! It is our own.' Eddington laments the foolhardiness of humans here in his book 'Space, Time and Gravitation, p. 201."[15]

It thus reiterates the need to understand that human personality lies deeper than what can be studied by the empirical sciences. What is unfathomable about the human being and humanity needs to be traced to metaphysical backgrounds and fields, which alone will result in an integrated and holistic approach to humans and humankind.

In philosophical parlance, 'to be' is to live with 'existential freedom.' Philosophically, for a conscious being 'to live' is to 'live in an aware and responsive manner,' in order to fulfil a purpose with a sense of responsibility. The human has to live responsibly and freely in order to depict himself as self-aware and self-determining. The freedom enjoyed by such an individual is not one of mere self-determination, but also one of self-constitution. Freedom then can be defined as the 'self-conscious and responsible participation in being as good.'

The case studies done during the course of writing this book reiterates the need to imbibe and practice cultural values that are deep-rooted in our system. The study indicates the possibility of a successful business with adherence to cultural and moral values, as opposed to the view that profit in business is hindered by the imbibed moral values. The capability of a society to face challenges in this contemporary world can be strengthened only if the people are able to identify with the cultural values and the ethos of the region. The self-esteem of the individual needs to be protected as much as the pride that one has in identifying with one's native philosophy, art, culture, traditions, lifestyles, and religion. The pride that one has for one's heritage motivates him in the task of enhancing 'welfare' at all levels-individual, organisational and national. The thesis is an attempt to glorify the values that are inherent in our culture, ethos, and philosophy. It also emphasises the universality of these values.

Vivekananda refers to the contribution of India to the world in the following words: "India's contribution to the sum total of human knowledge has been spirituality, philosophy." He continues, "Throughout the millennia of history, India's wisdom has attracted the nations of the world. India's natural resources and industrial wealth, similarly, make her an attraction for trade as well. And in the modern age, this trade has also led to her domination and economic exploitation by the West." What has however made India great is that she "... never engaged in any foreign aggressive wars throughout her long history...," embracing all who came to her fold. What is important is that the Indian mind has to be set free from any kind of 'intellectual servitude.'

Referring to India's impact on the rest of the world, Swami Vivekananda says, "The debt which the world owes to our native country is immense. Civilisations have arisen in other parts of the world. In ancient and modern times, wonderful ideas have been carried forward from one race to another ... but mark you, my friends, it has always been with the blast of war trumpets and with the march of embattled cohorts. Each idea was born through struggle and pain, carrying the weight of sacrifice. Each word of power had to be followed by the groans of millions, by the wails of orphans, by the tears of widows." This, in the main, other nations have taught. But India for thousands of years peacefully existed. Even when history is silent, and tradition hesitates to look into the dark past, when countless ideas have emerged, there is a blessing and peace behind it all. "We, of all nations of the world, have never been a conquering race, and that blessing is on our head and therefore, we live ..."[16]

"Political greatness or military power is never the mission of our race; it never was and mark my words, it never will be. But there has been another mission given to us, which is to conserve, to preserve, to accumulate as it were into a dynamo, all the spiritual energy of the race and that concentrated energy is to pour forth in a deluge on the world whenever circumstances are propitious. ... the philosophy and spirituality of India is ever ready to flow along the new-made channels into the veins of the nations of the world. The calm Indian brain must pour out its own quota to give to the sum total of human progress. India's gift to the world is the light of spirituality."[17]

Indian thought and culture is an expression of "a comprehensive spirituality and of total life-fulfilment and the way to its redemption from a soul-killing materialism."[18] What is needed to redeem a human of his suffering and downfall is an intellectual transformation with a spiritual reorientation. The need to blend Tradition and Modernity is the pressing need of the day.

"Tradition and Modernity both have three major aspects:

1. a system of thought with reference to which the human can order his experience into a meaningful whole,
2. a system of moral and social values which enables him to decide which things are made to be esteemed more and which are regarded as less, and
3. a network of institutions through which a search for the good life expresses itself on human and the universe."

The various aspects constitute "the matrix in which the modern human moves." These aspects also "shape and determine the individual's attitudes and patterns of behaviour in relation to himself and others" and lets himself be influenced continuously. They determine his behaviour and interactions with the environment around him, both physical and social environment. The logical validity of these patterns of tradition and modernity is important to make it all scientific. The psychological holism too is significant as it denotes the essence of the human himself.[19]

Ancient Indian Wisdom has made a distinction between information, knowledge, and wisdom. Information is merely the collection of data. The assimilation of this data and the comprehension that stems from it is knowledge. Only when the knowledge that the human has applied to life situations is considered wisdom. There is a clear distinction of material knowledge from spiritual knowledge. This leads one to an understanding of the distinction between *jñāna* and *Vijñāna*. Jñāṇa and Vijñāna need to be blended together in order to develop the inherent basic attributes and the essential nature of human. This wisdom allows the human to break free from the shackles of bondages of all kinds. Education that is devoid of values is thus, futile. The human as a blend of materialism and spiritualism is typically the conception of human as a holistic reality in Indian thought.

The book is not a scholastic conference or an academic debate, hence, no *tarka* is evident, either *vitarka* or *kutarka*. It is an attempt to grasp the eternal truths laid out in front of us through our scriptures and testimonies that need to be understood with viveka and accepted with humility. It is a genuine and sincere effort to dip into the ocean of universal and eternal ideas and values and sip the waters of perennial wisdom.

The basic tenets of Indian philosophical schools and scriptures expounded in our culture embrace certain fundamental thoughts that are neither essentially traditional nor modern but can be called 'ageless'.

"The diffusion of India's cultural immensity is a glorious epic of human achievement in the domain of thought and its expression in space and time."[20]

References

1. A. Toffler's "Civilization Waves and Cycles of Economic Development". Source: Net
2. Crainer Stuart, Key Management Ideas – Thinking that Changed the Management World, Macmillan India Ltd., New Delhi, 2002, p. 2.
3. Alexander E. Aivazov & Vladimir A. Belikov, 'Toffler's Civilization Waves and Cycles of Economic Development', htt ps://doi.org/10.30884/978-5-7057-6273-6_08

4. Role of Manager in Human Need Fulfillment in Work Organization", Source: Net.
5. Jaworski Joseph, The Dream – from 'Synchronicity: the inner path of leadership' – Introduction by Peter Senge; Berrett, Koehler Publishers, San Francisco, 1996, pp. 58-59.
6. The Contribution of Modern Indian Philosophy to World Philosophy – JSTOR.
7. Datta, D.M. The contribution of Modern Indian Philosophy to the World Philosophy, *The Philosophical Review*, Vol. LVII, November 1948, pp. 571-572. Quoted in Brodov V., Indian Philosophy in Modern Times, Progress Publishers, Moscow, 1988, pp. 34–35.
8. Editorial, 'Doing well and Doing Good', 'Business India', Nov. 7-20, 2005.
9. Ahmedabad Management Association, HRM in darsanas – II, Ancient Indian Wisdom for Self-development, Torrent-AMA Management Centre, Ahmedabad, p. 40.
10. Chandra Lokesh, ed., India's Contribution to World Thought and Culture, Vivekananda Rock Memorial Committee, Madras, 1970 Chapter Title: Swami Vivekananda, India's emissary to the West, p. 41
11. Ibid., p. 41.
12. Sorokin Pitirim A, The Reconstruction of Humanity, Bharatiya Vidya Bhavan, Bombay, 1960, pp. 185-186.
13. Sorokin Pitirim A, The Reconstruction of Humanity, Bharatiya Vidya Bhavan, Bombay, 1960, p. 187
14. Titus Harold H., Living Issues in Philosophy, Eurasia Publishing House, New Delhi, 1968, p. 148.
15. Sharma R.P., Human Personality in Ancient Indian Thought, Kanishka Publishers and Distributors, New Delhi – 110 002, p. 3.
16. Chandra Lokesh, ed., India's Contribution to World Thought and Culture, Vivekananda Rock Memorial Committee, Madras, 1970 Chapter Title: Swami Vivekananda, India's emissary to the West.
17. *The Complete Works of Swami Vivekananda/Volume 3/Lectures from Colombo.* https://en.wikisource.org/wiki/The_Complete_Works_of_Swami_Vivekananda/Volume_3/Lectures_from_Colombo_to_Almora/First_Public_Lecture_in_the_East_ pg. 28 & 29.
18. Chandra Lokesh, ed., India's Contribution to World Thought and Culture, Vivekananda Rock Memorial Committee, Madras, 1970 Chapter Title: Swami Vivekananda, India's emissary to the West.
19. Maharajan M Gandhian Thought-A Study of Thought and Modernity, Sterling Publishers Private Limited, New Delhi. 1996, Preface.
20. Chandra Lokesh, ed., India's Contribution to World Thought and Culture, Vivekananda Rock Memorial Committee, Madras, 1970 Chapter Title: Swami Vivekananda, India's emissary to the West.

REVIEWS/ PRAISES FOR *THE INDIC CODE: DECODING CULTURAL INTELLIGENCE FOR MANAGEMENT DYNAMICS*

The Indic Code: Decoding Cultural Intelligence for Management Dynamics by Philosophy expert, Dr Geetha Mohan, answers the myriad challenges faced by all of us, in contemporary living times.

It's underlining highlight, drawn from scriptures and thinkers, in collaboration with Industry leaders firsthand wisdom, dominates the intertwined chapters, leading towards silence, wisdom and peace, so very rare today.

The painstaking efforts of the author in seamlessly threading insights from religion, philosophy, spiritual school of thought and industry revelations, make it a compelling read!!

This is a must-read book for all ages! I strongly recommend it.

Warmest regards

Padma Vibhushan Dr Raghunath Mashelkar, FRS
President GRA, Chairman, National Innovation Foundation, Passionate about Inclusive Innovation, More from Less for More
Former DG, CSIR

The Indic Code: Decoding Cultural Intelligence for Management Dynamics, authored by Dr Geetha, published by Bloomsbury Publishing House, is a valiant attempt to connect the tenets of Indian Philosophy with the philosophy and practice of modern corporate management. Written in a lucid style, the author makes a successful case for the application of age old but still relevant principles of management enshrined in our ancient philosophy. The book which is targeted at the students and the seekers of Indian Philosophy, dwells in detail about Indian Philosophy, Dharma, Spirituality, Cultural Ethos, Religion and their relevance to the human personality and, thus, to Corporate Work Culture. In particular, I highly appreciate and recommend the chapter on models of management (Chapter IX). There is nothing like providing case studies to make the readers comprehend the thinking of the author, based on research and nudge readers to apply their mind. Among others, the chapter on Yoga and Self-Management (Chapter V), is very unconventional but important dimension of practical implication for Corporate Managers. We learnt in our schools that healthy mind lives in healthy body. A healthy body and healthy mind are what are required to sustain the energy and stamina to wade through the complexities of today's corporate jungle and come out unscathed and successfully. The author's grasp of Indian Philosophy is very strong, a proof of her genuine interest in the subject and her extensive research in creating this very useful book. Her interactions with a large number of Corporate CEOs and other industry participants provided her with very unique and vital perspective on how application of Indian Philosophy can truly be the backbone of Indian Corporate Management.

I recommend this very timely publication, wholeheartedly.

Dr. Narsing Rao, GS
B. Tech (IIT, Varanasi), PGDM (IIMA), Ph.D. (BU)
Chief Mentor, Synergy School of Business, Hyderabad
Former VC, ICFAI University, Raipur
Ex-Director, ICFAI IBS, Pune
Ex-Chief Executive (IMAGE)

The book, 'The Indic Code: Decoding Cultural Intelligence for Management Dynamics' by Dr Geetha Mohan, bridges the timeless wisdom of Indian philosophy with the contemporary demands of management and organizational life. The clarity with which it illuminate the spiritual foundations of human progress, and the way it connect inner awakening to ethical, sustainable work cultures, is truly inspiring. The book not only brings philosophical ideas to life but also offers a refreshing and much-needed perspective for modern leaders and professionals seeking meaning in their pursuits. It is both intellectually enriching and spiritually elevating. It stands as a gentle yet powerful reminder of our roots and the eternal values that continue to guide humanity's evolution. It will undoubtedly inspire many to reflect, realign, and rediscover the deeper purpose of life and work.

Mr. G S Grewal
Managing Director of Kubota Agricultural Machinery India Private Limited
Author: 'Leadership As A Coach'
Profile: linkedin.com/in/gsgrewal2000

Philosophy and Management, as Dr. Geetha Mohan has said in her Introduction, are usually seen as being, if not polar opposites, then definitely being two separate disciplines and modes of thinking. However, as she convincingly argues, the two are far from being so far apart. Philosophy is the study of the universal, of ethics, of morality, and much more; management ought to put all these into practice. We could ask what kind of management is possible without any of these, and a quick answer could be that without these guiding principles, there is no management possible.

Looking into the Indic roots of philosophy, Dr Geetha Mohan makes a convincing argument for the teaching and incorporation of philosophical principles into management courses. This book will, I am sure, be of immense value to a range of practitioners, trainees and professionals.

Dr. Radhika Seshan
Retd. Professor and Head, Department of History
Savitribai Phule Pune University
Currently, Visiting Faculty, Symbiosis School for Liberal Arts, Pune

The Indic Code: Decoding Cultural Intelligence for Management Dynamics by Dr Geetha Mohan, is enlightening and interesting. This book, weaving philosophy, management, and AI, reflects not just the author's intellect, but her integrity, spirituality, and deep commitment to living by her ideals. Reading it, you will feel her clarity, her ethical compass, and her curiosity guiding you through complex ideas with warmth and wisdom. It is more than a book—it reflects a remarkable person whose life and values leave a lasting mark. Guided by the eternal principles of Sanatana Dharma, which teach truth, conscious action, and harmony, the author brings this timeless wisdom into dialogue with the modern force of artificial intelligence. While AI can process data and optimize outcomes, it cannot discern right from wrong, nor uphold dharma. Leadership in this age demands the integration of intellect, ethics, and human insight — a harmony this book illuminates.

May this work serve as a beacon for leaders seeking meaning, a guide for professionals navigating complexity, and a companion for all who aspire to blend knowledge with wisdom.

Mr. K.M.P. Jairaj
Karnataka University, B.E. (Civil), Indian Institute of Science (IISc.)
ME, Structures, Former Contracts Advisor, ADMA OPCO, Abu Dhabi
Former Chief Manager, (Contracts & Purchase), Bharat Petroleum
Corporation, Refinery, Mumbai

The Indic Code: Decoding Cultural Intelligence for Management Dynamics by Dr Geetha Mohan, reads like a breath of fresh air! No dull and abstract philosophy. It encapsulates the rich Indian thoughts as espoused in the Vedas and narrated by scholars with the contemporary and modern thought. The author's lucid style of writing takes the reader on an insightful spiritual journey, introspecting one's values and beliefs, evolved as one's conditioning over the years.

The third chapter on Dharma, particularly reminds the reader, of his contribution and raison d'etre of living. What's unique, is the seamless blend with modern management practices through systems, policies and culture design as reiterated by leaders and founders through a diverse range of industries, which they are leading!

The book through its revelations, nudges the reader, to rethink and review one's ethos in the context of timeless values and thoughts. Like, doing one's duty, karma, with dharma and nishkama.

A must read for all age groups, especially the youth, who are being challenged with the complexities of living today! I give a ten star rating to this well documented manual for high thinking and simple living!

Dr Parveen Prasad
Author, Professor and Corporate Trainer
Dedicated Leadership Author, Symbiosis Institutes of Management HR
Visiting Faculty, Nurturing leadership skills through impactful writing and engaging teaching

ACKNOWLEDGEMENTS

My interest in industry and management started when I listened to my father talk about his work each day. As the head of the Engineering Division at Standard Batteries in Mumbai, he shared experiences that taught me about relationships, people skills, and leadership. He showed me the importance of valuing people for who they are, not for what they own or can offer. My mother, in her own unique way, taught me how to deal with people, life, and resources. What we now call lifeskills and softskills—planning, strategizing, managing time, using resources wisely, and building strong relationships—are lessons I grasped naturally from my parents.

It is truly said that a teacher can make or mar. It is a teacher who can further shape a person's life, and my teachers, right from my school days, have shaped mine. Today I am a continuous learner, as they ignited the love for study in me, helping me to remain curious, enthusiastic, and young at heart forever.

As a student and teacher of Philosophy, I owe a great deal to Prof. Ms. Rita Doctor. She is gentle, demure, soft-spoken, yet firm, disciplined and stern. My love for a subject, not commonly chosen by students, and my choice of a career in teaching the same, developed because of her. Her kind words of encouragement in the Prologue of this book have humbled me deeply.

I also express my sincere gratitude to Prof. (Dr.) Ramesh Dave, who encouraged me for research in Philosophy, and motivated me to complete my Ph.D. His endearing but firm approach helped me focus on my work. His scholastic ability, his patience and endearing approach pushed me to keep improving.

This book is an attempt to unravel the pragmatism and significant relevance of the ideals of Indian philosophy and ethos. I was able to do this through case-studies and meaningful interactions with entrepreneurs and social reformers. I thank Dr. Aruna Katara, Mr. G. S. Grewal, Mr. Abhishek Rathi, Dr. Harsha Joshi, and Dr. Geeta Bora. Their experiences and perspectives in the corporate world enhanced my insights and views about the close connection between our cultural bearings and corporate practices.

My bold step into a study of the impact of AI on society and its relation to our ethos was possible with the support of Mr. Shrishail Kambi, a seasoned engineering leader with 23 years of experience in Networking, Cloud Managed Services, Agri-Tech, Tech-For-Good, and Startups.

I also had the privilege of receiving encouraging reviews from respected academic and industrial stalwarts, keeping my spirits high. I am grateful to Dr Raghunath Mashelkar, Dr Narsinh Rao, Mr. K. M. P. Jairaj, Dr. Parveen Prasad, Mr. G.S. Grewal, and Dr. Radhika Seshan, for their valuable appreciation and support.

Thank you, dear Suma, for introducing me to the world of bibliophiles, and the book clubs. Writing is truly an art. But writing biographical, about the Author, needs sensitivity and positivity, to observe and emphasise the finer aspects of the author's personality and creativity.

Thank you, Vinutha Hiremath, for helping me with images, with your designing skills.

Thank you, the entire team of Bloomsbury Publishing India, for all the support and assistance in helping me with my book.

My greatest wealth in life is my social capital, and I want to thank all my friends, who have stood by me through thick and thin, being my support and strength. They have helped me to accept the opportunities, the success, the challenges, achievements, the setbacks and losses in life, helping me accept life as full of fun and frolic, joy and laughter. I take no names, as I do not want to miss out on anyone who I value and respect.

A special thanks to Parveen for motivating me and finally getting me back to my pen.

My expression of gratitude would be incomplete if I failed to thank my family, especially my wonderful children, for their love and affection and support, making life a blessing. Thank you, Arun, Anil and Sanah, for being my pillars, helping me turn my dream into reality. A special thanks to Anil, for giving me the design for the cover page.

I thank the Divine for keeping my spirits alive and helping me to share whatever little I have learned through my life's experiences.

BIBLIOGRAPHY

Ācārāngasūtra, SBE, Vol. XXII, 1.1.2.1. Jaina Ethics, Dayananda Bhargava, Motilal Banarsidas, Delhi, 1968.

Adler Mortimer J., The 4 Dimensions of Philosophy, Macmillan Publishing Co., New York, 1993.

Ahmedabad Management Association, HRM in daranas – I, Ancient Indian Wisdom For Self-development, Torrent-AMA Management Centre, Ahmedabad, 1995.

Ahmedabad Management Association, Ancient Indian Wisdom For Motivation, Torrent-AMA Management Centre, Ahmedabad, 1997.

Ahmedabad Management Association, HRM in darṣanas – II, Ancient Indian Wisdom For Self- development, Torrent-AMA Management Centre, Ahmedabad, 1995.

Baxi C.V. and Prasad Ajit, Corporate Social Responsibility, Excel Books, New Delhi, 2005.

Bhelke S.E., and Gokhale P.P., Studies in Indian Moral Philosophy, Indian Philosophical Quarterly Publication, Pune, 202.

Brodov V., Indian Philosophy in Modern Times, Progress Publishers, Moscow, 1988.

Chandra Lokesh, ed., India's Contribution to World Thought and Culture, Vivekananda Rock Memorial Committee, Madras, 1970.

Chatterjee S. and Datta D., An Introduction to Indian Philosophy, University Press, University of Calcutta, Calcutta, 1954.

Chibber Lieut. Gen. Dr. M.L. Sai Baba's Mahavakya On Leadership – Education in Human Values, Sri Sathya Sai Books and Publications Trust, Andhra Pradesh, 1993.

Chidambara Kulkarni, 'Vedic Foundations of Indian Culture, Shri D.R. Gudi, Managing Trustee, Bombay, 1973.

Crainer Stuart, Key Management Ideas – Thinking that Changed the Management World, Macmillan India Ltd., New Delhi, 2002.

Dasgupta S.N., A History of Indian Philosophy.

Datta D.M., The contribution of Modern Indian Philosophy to the World Philosophy, The Philosophical Review, Vol. LVII, November, 1948.

Datta Lakshmi Trust, Puruṣārtha, The Indian Historical Quarterly, Pune.

Datta D.M., The contribution of Modern Indian Philosophy to the World Philosophy, The Philosophical Review, Vol.LVII, November, 1948.

Dharma and Vedic Foundations – The study of Indian History and Culture Vol. IX.

Editorial, 'Doing well and Doing Good', 'Business India', Nov. 7–20, 2005.

Fleming J.E., 'Business Ethics: Diversity and Integration', Business and Professional Ethica Journal, Vol. 6, No. 4.

Gandhi M.K., The Essence of Hinduism, Navajivan Publishing House, Ahmedabad.

Garbe Richard, Die Sāmkhya Philosophie, cf. Also Mircea Eliade, Yoga: Freedom and Immortality, Trans. W.R. Trask, New York, Pantheon Books, 1958.

Garde Ashok R., Chanakya's Aphorisms on Management, Ahmedabad Management Association, Ahmedabad, 2003.

George F. McLean, 'Hermeneutics Faith and Relations Between Cultures', Lectures in Qom, Iran, Mofid University, Qom, Iran and The Council For Research In Values and Philosophy, 2003.

Ghosh Biswanath, Ethics in Management and Indian Ethos, Vikas Publishing House Pvt. Ltd., New Delhi, 2005.

Gordon M., Human Nature, Class and Ethnicity, Oxford University Press, New York, 1978.

Harold Koontz & Heinz Weihrich in 'Essentials of Management'; fifth edition., A History of Indian Philosophy, Calcutta, 1956.

Hermann Jacobi, Review of Second Edition of Garbe's Die Sāmkhya Philosophie, in Gottingsche gelehrte Anzeigen, Berlin, 1919.

Jaworski Joseph, Synchronicity: the inner path of leadership, Berrett, Koehler Publishers, San Francisco, 1996.

Kalghatgi Dr. T.G. Jainism – A Study, Department of Jainology and Prakrits, University of Mysore, Mysore, 1976.

Kamath M.V., The Excel Story – A Study in Excellence, Excel Institute of Technology, Environment and Management, Mumbai, 2001.

Khandwalla Pradip N., Management Styles, Tata McGraw – Hill Publising, New Delhi, 1995.

Kumar Arun, Management Leadership through Bhagwat Gita, Shubhi Publications, Delhi, 2000.

Maharajan M., Gandhian Thought – A Study of Thought and Modernity, Sterling Publishers Private Limited, New Delhi, 1996.

Master Choa Kok Sui, Miracles Through Pranic Healing, All India Yoga Vidya, Pranic Healing Foundation Trust, 1998.

Misra U., Conception of Matter According to Nyāya Vaishesika, Allahabad, 1936.

Muller Max, The Six Systems of Indian Philosophy, Associated Publishing House, New Delhi.

Munshi K.M., Foundations of Indian Culture.

Paradkar M.D., ed., Studies in the Gita.

Prophets of New India, 'A Man of the Year' Compilation from 'The Week', Penguin Books India (P) Ltd., New Delhi.

Radhakrishnan S., Freedom and Culture, Natesan and Co., Madras, 1936.

Ram G.M., Bible of Hinduism – A Gospel of Social Reconstruction, Allied Publishers Private Limited, New Delhi.

Reese W.L., Dictionary of Philosophy and Religion: Eastern and Western Thought.

Sharma R.P., Human Personality in Ancient Indian Thought, Kanishka Publishers and Distributors, New Delhi.

Singh Dharmdeo N., A Study of Hinduism, Vikas Publishing House.

Sorokin Pitirim A., The Reconstruction of Humanity, Bharatiya Vidya Bhavan, Bombay, 19960.

Sudhi Dr. Padma, Symbols of Art, Religion and Philosophy, Intellectual Publishing House, New Delhi.

Swami Vivekananda, Complete Works, Vol. VIII, Advaita Ashrama, Calcutta, 1959.

The World Religions – A Lion Handbook, A Comprehensive Guide, Lion Publishing, Oxford, England.

Titus Harold H., Living Issues in Philosophy, Eurasia Publishing House, New Delhi, 1968.

Tola Fernando and Dragonetti Carmen, The Yogasūtras of Pataṣjali on Concentration of Mind, Translated into English from the revised original Spanish by K.D. Prithipaul., Motilal Banarsidas Publishers, Delhi.

Vaz Michael & Paralikar Vinayak, Management and Human Resource Development, Manan Prakashan, Vile Parle, Mumbai , 1999.

Webster's Encyclopedic Dicitionary.

ABOUT THE AUTHOR

Dr Geetha Mohan's life has been an attempt to translate the esoteric principles of philosophy into formulas for life, and living. With both a postgraduate degree, and a Doctorate in Philosophy, she is well-equipped to pursue her ambition of rendering the tenets and practice of philosophy accessible to the common woman, or man.

A formidable list of achievements and awards makes her an example worth emulating for all who seek to study, and spread the light of that study with others. Her chequered career in education is filled with more achievements than any one person can boast of. It was while she was serving as the Principal of the Usha Pravin Gandhi College of Management, Mumbai, that she completed her two-year Post-Graduate Diploma in Business Administration. Later, she presented a paper titled 'Philosophy of Management' at the 8th Philosophy of Management International Conference at St. Anne's College, Oxford University and a paper titled 'Spirituality and Work Culture: The Indian Perspective' at the 23rd World Congress of Philosophy (WCP 2013) at School of Philosophy, National & Kapodistrian University of Athens. She received the Bharat Vidya Shiromani Award for Contribution to the Field of Education in justifiable recognition of her contribution to education in every sense of the term. She was also felicitated by the Department of Philosophy, University of Mumbai, for her contribution in the field of philosophical research and teaching. She is an active member of various NGOs that promote education.

Dr Geetha Mohan is also a corporate and soft-skills trainer, aiming to establish the relevance of ancient Indian thought in a contemporary, industrialised, and corporate world. She aims to inculcate happy, successful and peaceful life values in executives, managers and organisational staff.

Her book, 'The Indic Code: Decoding Cultural Intelligence for Management Dynamics', aims to set down the Philosophy she has learnt, her own philosophy of life, culled from her teachers, elders and culture and how both these can be absorbed into the principles of successful management.

In addition to all the awards and achievements, she is that rare personality: a good human being. Her friends vouch for her, her current, and erstwhile colleagues sing praises of her compassion and how she has always stepped in with a helping hand, a word of advice, or decisive action, when they needed it the most.

Dr Geetha Mohan can be reached at **geethamohan60@gmail.com**

I wish her all the best in life.

Suma Narayan, friend, and author of 'The Goddess in Us'